KT-115-516

Start and Run Your Own
Coffee Shop
and Lunch Bar

Second edition

Heather Lyon

A How To Book

ROBINSON

ROBINSON

First published in Great Britain in 2008 by How To Books Ltd
This revised edition published in 2010

Reprinted in 2015 by Robinson

Copyright © Heather Lyon 2008, 2010

3 5 7 9 10 8 6 4

The moral right of the author has been asserted.

All rights reserved.
No part of this publication may be reproduced, stored in a retrieval system, or transmitted, in any form, or by any means, without the prior permission in writing of the publisher, nor be otherwise circulated in any form of binding or cover other than that in which it is published and without a similar condition including this condition being imposed on the subsequent purchaser.

A CIP catalogue record for this book is available from the British Library.

ISBN: 978-1-84528-424-4

Produced for How To Books by Deer Park Productions, Tavistock
Designed and typeset by Mousemat Design Ltd
Printed and bound in Great Britain by Bell & Bain Ltd, Glasgow

Robinson
An imprint of
Little, Brown Book Group
Carmelite House
50 Victoria Embankment
London EC4Y 0DZ

An Hachette UK Company
www.hachette.co.uk

www.littlebrown.co.uk

NOTE: The material contained in this book is set out in good faith for general guidance and no liability can be accepted for loss or expense incurred as a result of relying in particular circumstances on statements made in the book. Laws and regulations are complex and liable to change, and readers should check the current position with relevant authorities before making personal arrangements.

How To Books are published by Robinson, an imprint of Little, Brown Book Group. We welcome proposals from authors who have first-hand experience of their subjects. Please set out the aims of your book, its target market and its suggested contents in an email to Nikki.Read@howtobooks.co.uk

Start and Run Your Own

Coffee Shop
and Lunch Bar

This book is dedicated to Robert Pirrie, my late partner, who initially encouraged me to write this book.

CONTENTS

Acknowledgements   xi
Preface   xiii

Chapter 1   **Getting started**   **1**
Planning your business   1
Thinking about your business agreement   3
Choosing a location   3
Offering a delivery service   8
Doing your research   9

Chapter 2   **Choosing your shop unit**   **11**
Are you going to purchase or lease your premises?   11
Purchasing your premises   11
Leasing your premises   12

Chapter 3   **Getting advice**   **15**
Working with professional advisers   15
Understanding insurance   19
Finding help in your area   20
When do you need a licence?   21
Drawing up a business plan   21

Chapter 4   **Creating your own coffee shop**   **25**
Choosing a name   25
Building an image   26
Making the most of your menu   30
Should you opt for self-service or table service?   33
Deciding your opening hours   34

Chapter 5   **Devising your menu**   **35**
Catering to suit your customer   35
Serving cold-filled snacks and sandwiches   35
Serving hot-filled snacks and sandwiches   38

Making your own soup   38
Serving breakfasts   40
Serving home-cooked meals   40
Catering for children   41
Baking your own cakes   41
Offering a choice of hot and cold drinks   44

Chapter 6   Purchasing and leasing catering equipment   46
Buying new equipment   46
Buying second-hand equipment   47
Buying or leasing kitchen equipment   47
Buying furniture and fittings   59

Chapter 7   Choosing your suppliers   61
Finding your food suppliers   61
Buying from supermarkets   65
Using a cash and carry   65
Handling food safely   66

Chapter 8   Employing staff   67
Deciding how many staff you need   67
Employing immigrants   67
Recruiting your staff   68
Interviewing prospective employees   73
Dismissing staff   75

Chapter 9   Training your staff   81
Training staff on the job   81
Compiling a staff manual   82
Following up training   83
Teaching staff how to generate good customer relations   83
Dealing with difficult customers   84
Organizing regular staff meetings   86
Tackling absenteeism   87
Hanging on to good staff   88

Chapter 10   Complying with health, safety and hygiene laws 91
Be committed to cleanliness   91
Drawing up a cleaning schedule   91

Tips for effective cleaning 93
Working with your local Environmental Health Department 95
Complying with the rules and regulations 96
Inspections by the Environmental Health Officer 98
Preparing and storing food safely 99
Eradicating food hazards 102
Getting advice about health and safety issues 104
Carrying out a risk assessment 105

Chapter 11 How to increase your business 108
Developing your marketing strategy 108
Using vouchers and flyers 109
Some more ideas for attracting customers 111
Handing out customer questionnaires 113
Using local radio and newspapers 114
Using your local tourist board 115
Using an outside agency 115

Chapter 12 Popular coffee shop recipes 116
Soups 119
Savoury recipes 135
Fillings or toppings for baked potatoes 143
Fillings for sandwiches 148
Popular cake recipes 150
Tray bakes 169

Chapter 13 The 12 skills you need to run a successful coffee shop
184

Appendix 1 Employment contract – full-time staff 185
Appendix 2 Employment contract – part-time staff 191
Appendix 3 Employment contract – weekend staff 197
Appendix 4 Job description pro forma 203
Appendix 5 Employee handbook 205
Appendix 6 Customer questionnaire 218
Appendix 7 Useful contact numbers and addresses 220

Index 223

ACKNOWLEDGEMENTS

I would like to thank Nikki Read at How to Books for her expertise, encouragement and all her editorial contributions during the initial stages of the book.

My heartfelt thanks to Gordon and Dorothy Swan for all their time, support, encouragement and knowledgeable help over the last few months.

My special thanks to Adrian and Julie Hodge for their time, support and outstanding contributions to this book.

My sincere thanks to Paul Wigley and Mark Gregory for their time and useful contributions.

Finally, I would like to thank my local Environmental Health Department for their expertise and very helpful contribution.

PREFACE

So you want to open and run your own coffee shop!

Many people dream about starting their own business and once you have done it you won't want to go back to working for anyone else. You can get started in business with a relatively small investment and realize a good profit if you make a success of your enterprise.

Starting and running your own coffee shop is an exciting and satisfying challenge and can give you a good income, providing you are prepared to invest a lot of time and energy into making it successful.

However, to have a good idea is one thing; being able to turn your idea into a business is quite another. Before you decide to go into business it is essential that you consider very carefully the advantages and disadvantages of owning your own business.

Advantages

☐ Pride in owning and running your own coffee shop.

☐ Potential to earn more than you would if you were employed.

☐ Flexible working hours.

☐ You make all the decisions regarding your business.

Disadvantages

☐ You will have a high level of responsibility.

☐ You won't have a regular fixed income.

☐ You will probably have to work long hours.

☐ You have the responsibility of making difficult decisions.

Now ask yourself a few questions before you make any decisions.

☐ Do you like being in charge?

☐ Can you delegate?

☐ Can you cope with stress?

☐ Are you customer friendly?

☐ Can you be positive through the bad times as well as the good times?

☐ Are your family supportive about you starting your own coffee shop?

☐ Does the prospect of financial insecurity motivate rather than scare you?

☐ Are you prepared for hard work and long hours?

☐ Are you prepared to work weekends and public holidays?

☐ Are you able to sacrifice some things, such as holidays, and to cut back financially until you get your coffee shop established?

☐ Are you prepared to learn new skills?

☐ Do you have self-motivation, determination and stamina?

☐ Are you in good health?

☐ Do you believe in yourself?

These questions are not meant to put you off opening your coffee shop but to make you think about the skills you require. If you are able to answer yes to all the questions, and you are still passionate about opening your own coffee shop, you should learn as much as you can about this business; do your research and get to know your market.

There are many reasons why businesses fail within a few years: perhaps because there has not been enough effort put into understanding the importance of getting the best location possible; perhaps not enough research has been done, or not enough capital raised to get started; perhaps the business plan was not a good one; maybe failure is down to lack of organisation and management skills, or not employing the right staff, or simply being unable to be that bit better than your competition.

The most important thing you should do when starting your business is to make sure you are well prepared. This comprehensive book will give you all the information and advice you will ever need to help you set up and run your own coffee shop. In it I have given you my advice and experience, along with expert tips, popular recipes and crucial data to help you make the most of your coffee shop. The practical information contained in this book, together with the commitment and passion you have for your coffee shop, will ensure that your chances of success are high.

1
GETTING STARTED

Planning Your Business

One of the first decisions you have to make, and possibly one of the most difficult, is: Are you going into business alone or with a partner or partners?

GOING INTO BUSINESS WITH FRIENDS OR FAMILY

A partnership is defined as an association of two or more people to carry on a business with a view to making a profit.

You have probably thought of going into business with a friend or your spouse. However, no matter how well you get on with your friend or spouse, there will always be disagreements when starting and running a business. Unless you can agree on most things, in my view, you should keep your friendship separate from your business. Spouses on the other hand are used to making joint decisions and working through financial problems, so going into business together could work out.

If, however, you do want to go into business with a friend I would suggest that you consult a solicitor who is experienced in commercial law and ask him or her to draw up a partnership agreement. It will seem a nuisance at the start but it could save a lot of unforeseeable problems in the future. If business partnerships are formed without any forethought they are more than likely to be doomed to failure.

Informal agreements can fall apart whereas a partnership agreement outlines the contribution that each partner will put into the business and it defines the roles of the partners.

> ❝ *I know of a business that collapsed because when two friends decided to start a business together they thought that their friendship was strong enough to stand up to any difficulties which they would encounter in their partnership. One of the partners continually took time off to attend to family commitments and left the other partner to cope with running the business. They had not entered into a partnership agreement and unfortunately when their business collapsed so did their friendship. I feel that it is essential to get good legal advice if you are considering entering into any type of partnership.* ❞

If you do decide to go into partnership with someone, give it a lot of thought and choose the person very carefully. If you don't trust that person, don't even consider starting a business with him or her.

SOME OF THE ADVANTAGES OF HAVING A PARTNER

☐ You will be working with someone you can trust and who you know will not let you down.

☐ You will be able to cover each other's holidays or time off for family events etc.

☐ You share the risk of starting a new business.

☐ At the outset you will both be able to contribute an equal share of money to start up the business. This should enable you to spend more money on your premises and on fitting out your coffee shop.

☐ You have a combination of ideas and the experience of two or more people to help set up and run your coffee shop. Everyone has different skills and talents which they bring to a business and this is beneficial.

☐ You share the responsibility for business debts.

☐ Shared decision-making can be a good thing as it increases your confidence in making the right choices.

SOME OF THE DISADVANTAGES OF HAVING A PARTNER

☐ One partner may not be able to work such long hours as the other due to family commitments and this may cause ill feeling and lead to arguments.

☐ The profits will have to be shared and you will have to agree with your partner when they can be taken out of the business and what they are going to be used for. What percentage of the profit is going to be put back into the business to improve it, for example, redecorating or buying new equipment, or will the profit just be shared equally for the partners to spend as they wish?

☐ Decision-making has to be shared as you will have to obtain the approval of your partner. You can't just decide to sell the business or close it for two or three weeks while you go on holiday without your partner's agreement.

☐ If the business fails it is very likely that it will put a tremendous strain on the relationship with your friend and you will have to be prepared to lose that friendship.

☐ If one partner dies, or wants to terminate the partnership, the other partner will have to find the capital to take over the business as sole owner or proprietor.

If you are absolutely certain that you want to go into business with your partner or spouse and you both have the same goals and aspirations, then discuss it fully. I would recommend that you put an informal partnership agreement together which will define issues like your areas of responsibility and share of profits before you go into business.

Thinking about your business agreement

You may wish to consider the following issues when making a business agreement with your spouse or civil partner:

☐ What will happen if one of you has to take maternity leave or has to take a long period off work due to illness?

☐ How do you want the business and property to be shared?

☐ Are you agreed on what each partner will be able to draw as a salary, and how the profits will be distributed?

☐ Are you agreed on what hours each partner will work?

☐ Are you agreed on how you will divide your responsibilities? For instance, one of you may have management skills and the other may have customer skills, so stick to what you do best.

> ❝ *When I was young and inexperienced I helped my husband in his retail business but sometimes he would go off to play golf and I was left to work in the shop and watch the children at the same time. This caused a great deal of ill feeling and if we had initially discussed and agreed on the terms of working in the business, these problems might not have arisen.* ❞

In conclusion, whatever type of partnership you enter into, make sure it is an equal partnership and that the work is divided equally. However, you should be flexible and be prepared to give and take in certain circumstances if one of you requires extra time off for something special.

 You can form a limited liability partnership which is similar to a normal partnership but also reduces personal responsibility for debt. For more information on this go into the website www.companieshouse.gov.uk

Choosing a location

The location of your coffee shop can be a major contribution to its success or failure. Choosing the most suitable location may therefore be your single most important decision. It requires a great deal of thought and planning. Don't just decide to rent or buy a shop because it is inexpensive; if you choose the wrong location you could be setting yourself up to fail. A poor location is one of the major causes of failure for a business whereas a good location is sometimes all it takes to make your business thrive. I know of a coffee shop/lunch bar which is situated in a very good location and with very little competition. In my opinion the food is not good value for money as they serve small portions, do not garnish their food, charge extra for garlic bread, salad or chips and they serve yesterday's bread with the soup however they appear to always be busy and make a good profit therefore the location of their business is their best asset.

The best way to choose a location for your coffee shop is by doing research. This allows you to build up a picture of potential areas and also allows you to look at the pros and cons of each area so that you can choose a location that gives your business the most advantage.

You should consider the following points before making your decision on a location.

☐ What competition is there in the area?

☐ Is there adequate parking?

☐ How close is it to your customer base?

☐ Is there a steady flow of foot traffic which will guarantee walk-in customers?

☐ What image do you want your coffee shop to project?

It cannot be stressed enough that the location of your enterprise is of paramount importance. What follows are a few comments on the principal categories of coffee shop location.

A SHOP ON THE MAIN STREET

The most desirable location for a coffee shop, in my opinion, would be situated on a main shopping street which has a steady flow of foot traffic as most of your business will come from people walking past. However, this is not absolutely necessary and if you can rent space in a large retail outlet you can make it just as successful.

You could choose a shop in a popular busy area of town which may be a student area or consist of other shops, businesses and offices. You would then benefit from a stable customer base and would have constant passing foot traffic.

Good visibility and easy access are beneficial because the more people who know that your coffee shop exists, the better. There is no use in having the most fantastic coffee shop up a lane or above another shop or business because that is putting you at an immediate disadvantage.

The benefit of opening a coffee shop on a prime site in a busy town is, if you can afford it, huge. You just have to concentrate on making your coffee shop better than the competition and somewhere that people will want to return to again and again.

The downside of opening a coffee shop in a prime area is the high price you will have to pay for rent and rates. You will have to make enough money to cover these expenses before you make any profit.

Buying or renting an established business

You may decide to purchase or rent an already established coffee shop situated in a prime position. The benefit of this is that you will be able to see what the turnover of the business is from their prepared accounts and whether you think you can improve on that turnover. You will also have the benefit of an existing customer base that you can build on so that you do not have to start from scratch.

In addition, it may be easier to get finance by producing a business plan, together with the prepared accounts, to show the bank what profit the previous owner made and how you intend to improve it.

An already established coffee shop should include all fittings and fixtures and it should already have a kitchen fitted out. If the fittings and fixtures are in quite good condition and you think that you can make do until you can afford to change them, it is worthwhile having them included in the sale or lease agreement. This will save a lot of expense initially if you are working on a tight budget and you should not need to replace any large items until you make enough profit to do so. However, you may want to invest in a few up-to-date items such as a good commercial microwave, a toasted sandwich machine, a contact grill for making paninis and a good commercial dishwasher (a godsend) if a dishwasher is not already installed. On the other hand, if the equipment is in poor condition it would be worth asking the landlord or owner to have them removed. You will then have a blank canvas to design your own kitchen.

You will probably want to redecorate the coffee shop to your taste and perhaps add a few items such as bright, pretty tablecloths, blinds or fashionable curtains. If the flooring is shabby you could put down a hard-wearing, easy-to-clean type of flooring or carpet tiles which you can replace if someone stains the tile and the stain can't be removed. Carpet tiles can be vacuumed at night and shampooed if required. Whatever you choose, try to make your coffee shop warm and inviting.

A SHOP WITHIN A RETAIL STORE

Another option is to open your coffee shop in a retail unit like B&Q, Homebase, a garden centre, a bookshop or somewhere similar. Anywhere that you think there is a need for a coffee shop and there is a good customer base already.

The benefit is that there is an established customer base coming into the shop who will potentially visit your coffee shop if you make it attractive to them. Many of the retail shop's customers would probably be happy to be able to sit down and enjoy a hot drink and something to eat while shopping. If you offer a good service with good food and beverages at a reasonable price they will return and also tell their friends about it. Your business will soon be booming and it will also help to increase the business of the retailer.

Our coffee shop is situated in a large retail unit in a small town. It is very busy, especially at weekends and during the school holidays.

The only downside that I can think of is that if the retail store is open seven days a week you will probably have to open your coffee shop every day.

Look around your area and if there are any large, busy retail units that you think would be suitable, approach the owners.

> *I was in Cambridge recently and visited a retail park just outside the town. Although there were some large retail units situated there, not one had a coffee shop where we could get something to eat and drink. We were so desperate for a drink and a snack that we went to a supermarket on the site and bought a sandwich and a cold drink and returned to sit in the car to eat and drink them. Here was an ideal opportunity for someone to open a really good business within one of these large retail units. A healthy profit could be made if you served good food at a reasonable price. Alternatively, you could set up a coffee and sandwich stall in a retail site.*

 If you decide on renting space in an already established retail unit make sure you get a lease and agree a reasonable rent for the area you are intending to use.

How to negotiate space in a retail shop

Prepare a well-thought-out, well-written and nicely presented business proposal. Make sure your proposal sounds attractive to the retailer and is open-ended enough to allow you room to negotiate. Make a list with details of ways in which you think your coffee shop would benefit their business. Below is an example of what your list could include.

☐ Your coffee shop will increase customer volume and potential profit for the retail store. There is potential for your customers to look around the retail store and purchase something before or after visiting your shop.

☐ You could offer a discount to the staff in the retail store. This would be a benefit to the retailer as they would be able to offer this perk when employing staff, especially if there is no place to purchase food in the vicinity of the store.

☐ Produce a sample menu which will let the retailer know what type of food and drinks you are intending to serve.

☐ Draw a plan (or get your architect to sketch one for you) of what you intend the coffee shop to look like so that the retailer will have some idea of what type of shop it will be.

☐ Your shop will enhance the retail store.

☐ If you advertise your coffee shop in the newspaper or on the local radio station, potentially it could bring new customers to the retail store. You could ask the local newspaper to write a feature, with photographs, on the opening of your coffee shop, to let the public know where you are and what you intend to offer them.

If it is agreed that you can rent a portion of the retail store, enquire if the store would be prepared to set up the coffee shop and lease it to you. If they only want to rent you the space, you would have to purchase all the equipment and set up the coffee shop yourself. However, if you are purchasing all the equipment yourself, then you may be able to negotiate the first few months rent free to allow you to get started.

 **If your coffee shop is situated in a retail store it is a good idea to place a blackboard at the entrance of the store to advertise your business and make it obvious to customers that you exist.**

A COFFEE STALL

Another option is to find a site to set up a coffee stall.

The benefit is that, if you find the right site, you can often make a lot of money from your business as you do not have the same overheads as the owner of a shop.

The downside is that it can be cold and if the weather is very bad it could affect your takings.

You can see coffee stalls situated in railway stations, shopping centres and markets all over the country.

Some coffee stalls in railway stations have tables and chairs situated around the stall. They serve coffees and teas and perhaps hot soup, rolls filled with bacon, sausage or egg and ready-made sandwiches for customers to take away or eat at one of the tables. They also tend to sell chocolate biscuits, muffins and sweets. Initially you would be able to run this type of business single-handed and if you build up a good business, you could then employ another member of staff.

Before embarking on setting up a coffee stall or kiosk you should check with your local Environmental Health Department to see what is legally required for this type of business.

A FRANCHISE

Some coffee shops and coffee stalls are franchised. The franchise company takes on much of the responsibility for decision-making. It grants you the right to sell its products.

The benefits are that the company may offer you a good site and give you start-up offers and good background information on running your shop, stall or kiosk. You benefit from the goodwill that the name and reputation of the franchise has already generated, and also from the support of the company in the selection of a location. Usually you will get free advertising and support during your initial set-up period.

The downside is that the company will want a reasonable share of your profit so you should weigh up the pros and cons of this type of set-up. The amount you will have to pay the franchisor for the benefits provided could be more than 10%. You will more than likely be restricted in what you are allowed to sell and you must adhere to the franchisor's standards. If you are considering taking out a franchise you should:

☐ learn as much as you can about the whole franchise process;

☐ find out what questions to ask the company with which you are thinking of taking out the franchise;

☐ if possible, take advice from other people who already have that franchise in order to determine the pros and cons.

If you do decide to take out a franchise make sure you get the promises made by the company written into the agreement.

Think very carefully about taking out a franchise because it is not easy to recover from choosing the wrong franchise company.

 Check out the internet for more information about which companies will franchise on www.franchisedirect.co.uk

No matter where your coffee shop is situated, as long as you have done your homework and know that the chosen location has the potential to be busy, you are halfway there.

Offering a delivery service

Wherever you open your coffee shop you could offer a delivery service to staff in surrounding businesses. Staff working in local authority offices – for example, social services, housing departments, the police station and also local banks – are always pleased to try new places that offer good food at a reasonable price. Most of these office workers are too busy to spend time in their lunch break waiting for service in a coffee shop and would be delighted to have their order delivered to them.

If you do offer a delivery service, you will either have to deliver the orders yourself or employ someone to do this for you. You could do it yourself until you have an order service established and then if you think it will be profitable you could employ someone for a specific time, e.g. first orders 12.00 noon and last orders 2 p.m. If you employed someone you would also have to be prepared to allow them to use your car or to pay them mileage for the use of their own car.

Doing your research

You have some great ideas and you are eager to get started but first of all you have to test your market and this involves serious research.

Market research is essential; the success of your business may depend on it. You need to know who your competition is and you need to assess the customers who will support your business.

CHECKING OUT THE COMPETITION

Once you have identified the town, village or retail shop where you want to open your coffee shop, check out the surrounding area to see what competition, if any, you will have.

Study your potential competitors and think how you could make your coffee shop more appealing. What could you do to ensure that it stands out from the others?

Look at your competitors in terms of:
- location;
- quality;
- presentation;
- price;
- service;
- reputation;
- surroundings.

When you have done this, consider what they don't serve that you could.

Your competitors will be just as interested in you as you are in them and they won't wait around for you to get established. They will use various tactics to hang on to their business: for example, reducing their prices; introducing new items to their menu; aggressive marketing; refurbishing their shop.

Visit as many coffee shops as you can and take note of what they have to offer in terms of price, quality and presentation of coffee and cakes as well as décor and atmosphere. If you find a coffee shop that you would like to model your own on and it is not in the same location as where you are going to open your shop, ask the owner for some advice and tips.

> *I asked someone in another town for some advice and information and the coffee shop owner was only too pleased to help. He also gave me names and addresses of local suppliers which he had found had good products and were reliable. This information helped me enormously and saved me precious time going through the Yellow Pages.*

If you find that there is competition, do make sure that particular area can support more than one coffee shop. Some competition is good for business as it makes you work harder to build up your enterprise and prevents you from becoming complacent. However, there is no point in going to all the expense of fitting out a new shop if there is not going to be enough business in the area to support an additional coffee shop. You will be setting yourself up to fail before you even get started.

Ask friends and family what they would expect from a coffee shop. Do they go to a specific place because they enjoy the coffee, the cakes or the atmosphere?   Your friends will be quite happy to give you their thoughts on what makes a good coffee shop.

Ultimately, you will have to judge whether or not another coffee shop will succeed on the basis of your experience, information gathering and intuition.

> *I knew some people who did not research the market before opening a coffee shop and opened their shop in a small village. Although they were situated on the main street, there was no parking available.*
>
> *The owners refurbished their premises to a really high standard with good lighting and décor and the general atmosphere was appealing. However, their food was expensive and not particularly good and their customers did not return.*
>
> *The owners of the coffee shop thought that if they made a very good profit on everything they would be successful. They forgot that they had to work hard at getting customers through the door because of their location. They missed the opportunity of impressing their customers with good value for money. The quieter the business got the more depressed they became and if they had a particularly quiet day they would just close early. Their customers voted with their feet and didn't return.*
>
> *This particular coffee shop closed after being in business for a short time. The owners didn't do their research, they were in the wrong location, they didn't offer good food and coffee at a reasonable price and they didn't keep to their stated opening hours.*

Word of mouth is a great advert; if people are pleased with the food and coffee they are given they will tell their friends. However, this also works in reverse and if they don't like what they get, they will also tell their friends.

2
CHOOSING YOUR SHOP UNIT

Whether you choose to purchase or lease your own premises, it is a huge commitment so do make sure you consider all the pros and cons before making a decision.

Are you going to purchase or lease your premises?

It is difficult to say whether it is better to purchase a property or lease it. It depends on several factors, for example:

☐ whether you can afford to purchase the property you have chosen;

☐ whether the property you have chosen is available for purchase, or only for lease.

The reason that some properties are only available for lease is that many landlords prefer to retain their property because of the income it provides.

When you have completed your research and identified the property which you think is best for your coffee shop, discuss with your bank or building society exactly how much your monthly repayments will be. Add to this the costs of new equipment and setting up your business in order to get an accurate picture of the outlay ahead.

However, if purchase is not an option for you and you still think that this is the shop you really want then you should approach the owner to see if you can rent it for a period of time with the option to purchase it at a later date.

The most desirable agreement for you as you are starting a new business would be a two-year lease with the option to renew the lease at the end of the period and a guaranteed rent to be increased at a five-year period.

Alternatively, if the shop owner would agree to lease it to you for a period of one or two years with an option to purchase the property at the end of this period, this would allow you to see how much profit you can make before making a commitment to purchase the premises. Also you will be able to purchase it at market value without having to compete with other interested parties.

Purchasing your premises
ADVANTAGES OF PURCHASING

☐ Purchasing a property will give you an investment which, if it is in a good area, will increase in value. In the future, if you decide to retire you can sell the property and make a profit, or lease it out to someone else. This will give you a good income.

☐ Your mortgage repayments could be less than the rental payments.

☐ You can claim interest payments against your tax.

☐ You won't have large rent increases.

DISADVANTAGES OF PURCHASING

☐ You may have to put down a large deposit as you won't get a 100% mortgage.

☐ You will be responsible for maintenance, fixtures and fittings and decoration.

Do not purchase a property in a poor site because it is less expensive. You will always struggle to attract customers and if you decide to sell or lease the property you may find it difficult. You could be left with an empty shop and no income.

Leasing your premises

A lease is a legally binding contract between the landlord and the tenant and it sets out the terms, conditions and obligations of both parties in relation to the tenancy.

ADVANTAGES OF LEASING

☐ Leasing a property allows you to set up your coffee shop with the smallest outlay.

☐ Leasing allows you to spend more money on equipment and décor for your coffee shop.

DISADVANTAGES OF LEASING

☐ You many be exposed to a large rent increase.

☐ You will always have to get permission from your landlord to change anything in the shop.

Should you decide that you are going to lease, it is essential that you ask your solicitor to examine all the papers for you and discuss with you the implications of each clause before you sign. A lease is a very complex document.

NEGOTIATING THE TERMS OF YOUR LEASE

It is always worth negotiating the terms of the lease with the landlord because if it is unfavourable to you it could leave you with burdensome costs and liabilities. You may want to consider asking a solicitor who is familiar with leasing and purchasing commercial premises to negotiate for you. He or she will be able to draft your offer and may be able to negotiate a few months rent free or a few months at a reduced rent to allow you to set up and equip your coffee shop. Also, if there are any repairs to be carried out or any redecoration to be done, you could ask for a rent-free period or discount until these things are completed. If a rent-free period is agreed, ask your solicitor to insert a clause in the agreement stating what period of time you are allowed rent free.

If there are any items you want your landlord to leave in the premises, for example, fixtures and fittings, including kitchen equipment, or if you want your landlord to do any repairs before you take over the lease, your solicitor will insert a list of conditions in your offer to lease the premises. It is better to get these things agreed in writing before you take over the lease.

If you negotiate your lease you may be able to save yourself quite a lot of money. The rental price is not always the most important consideration for landlords. They may be more concerned with acquiring a good, reliable tenant than leasing the premises at a higher rent to a 'fly by night' tenant.

Your solicitor will be able to guide you in all aspects of the lease and will also be able to decipher the fine print on the lease that you may overlook.

You should always check with your local council on planning permission for change of use and for putting up a sign. Your solicitor should be able to do this for you.

☐ When taking out a lease on a shop, unless you are sure that you want a long lease, you may want to consider taking a short lease on the property with the option to renew it after a period of time.

☐ If possible, negotiate a cancellation clause which would safeguard you if you had to terminate your lease. You could agree a fee which would be payable to the landlords to allow you to terminate the lease.

> *I know someone who took out a long lease on the property they were interested in; unfortunately, when their circumstances changed, they were unable to sublet it. This was because the landlord had the right to vet each person interested in the property and if they didn't consider them suitable tenants, the sublet would fall through. If the landlord does not approve of the potential new tenant you will probably have to continue to pay rent until the lease is finished unless you have included a cancellation clause in the lease.*

You never know when your circumstances could change or you find that your business is not doing as well as you expected, so it is better to be cautious and if possible opt for a shorter lease. If, after being in business for a while, you know that you want to continue to trade in your premises, you could approach your landlord and enquire if you could increase the term of the lease.

Finally, before making a decision on whether to purchase or lease premises for your coffee shop, decide what is the best available site that will give you the greatest opportunity to make the most of your business. Once you have done this, look at all the financial aspects of your chosen property and if you think you can afford it and make money, then go for it whether it is for lease or purchase.

3
GETTING ADVICE

Working with professional advisers

Professional advisers are experts in business matters and will be able to offer you guidance on many aspects of your business.

It is important to build up a good and trusting relationship with your professional advisers because you will probably be working with the same ones for many years. If you get on well with them, don't consider changing simply in order to save a few pounds — you might not get such good service with someone else.

SOLICITORS

No matter how well you get on with your solicitor, make sure you ask them for a written quote for the work they are going to do for you. Never allow your solicitor to start work before they have given you a written quote for their fees and outlays (registration fees, searches etc.). This applies not only to solicitors but also to any professionals you are planning to employ, for example, a surveyor, architect or accountant. You would never dream of having your house painted or a new kitchen or bathroom installed without knowing exactly how much it is going to cost you so always get a quotation from the professional firms you are going to employ before instructing them.

 I was employed as a secretary with a firm of solicitors for approximately 10 years and I know that clients who asked for a written quote for fees before going ahead were charged less than those clients who did not request a written quote prior to commencing the work.

Finding the right solicitor

It is very important to find a good solicitor who has experience in dealing with small businesses and who specialises in the leasing and purchasing of commercial property.

If you already have a solicitor that you know and trust, you should make an appointment with them to discuss your ideas about purchasing or leasing premises to use as a coffee shop. If you have decided to go into business with a partner, ask your solicitor to draw up a partnership agreement for you.

If the solicitor you consult is experienced in litigation then they probably won't have any experience in commercial law and you could ask them to refer you to another partner in the firm who does have this experience or to another practice. Although solicitors do not like to turn away business, I have always found that they would rather refer you to someone with more experience in this particular field in the hope that you will come back to them in the future for another legal transaction. However, if you don't have a solicitor, you could ask friends to recommend someone who they think is good, or you can contact the Law Society who keep a register of solicitors in your area who are experienced in this type of work.

Before meeting your solicitor, take time to write down all the questions you want them to answer because it is easy to forget something important, especially if you are excited or nervous.

Your solicitor should be able to recommend other professionals, for example, a good accountant, architect and surveyor, and if you require finance they should also be able to help you with your loan proposal and business plan.

ACCOUNTANTS

A good accountant is essential when starting a business, especially if you have no previous experience in setting up your own business. Your accountant is employed by you to make sure that you pay as little tax as possible. He or she will be able to advise you exactly what expenses you can claim back against your tax and also give you advice on other business matters.

☐ Your accountant's firm may be able to deal with PAYE and National Insurance contributions for your staff if you do not want to do this yourself. Or, alternatively, they should be able to advise you on how to do it yourself.

☐ They will be able to tell you how to keep records and what expenses receipts they require in order to claim back against your tax return.

☐ They know what allowances you will be entitled to against your tax return.

☐ They will be able to register you for VAT and show you how to complete your VAT return.

Finding an accountant

Your solicitor may be able to refer you to an accountant that they know will deal with small businesses. Alternatively, you may be recommended one by friends or family. However, if you are still unable to find an accountant you can contact the Institute of Chartered Accountants and they should be able to give you details of local accountants.

Get into the habit of maintaining good records and keeping all your receipts because if your accountant has all the information required then they will be able to complete your tax return in a shorter time than if they have to keep contacting you for further information. Paperwork is an important part of your business and if your accountant can complete your return quickly it should cost you less.

Remember, you will have to use an accountant every year to complete your annual tax return unless you are able to do this yourself. Your accountant will be able to guide you on how to pay the least tax using all the allowances to which you are legitimately entitled. They will also be able to advise you about VAT registration, PAYE and National Insurance.

Again, do ask your accountant for a quote for the work to be carried out for you as this may also save you money in the long run. They may not be able to give you the exact cost of the work to be done but I don't see any reason why you cannot get a close estimate.

SURVEYORS

Surveyors offer impartial specialist advice on property issues.

Finding a surveyor

Your solicitor will instruct a surveyor to conduct a survey on any property you are planning to purchase. If by any chance you don't want to use the firm of surveyors recommended by your solicitor, you can contact the Royal Institute of Chartered Surveyors; their website is www.rics.org. You can search on that site for a suitable surveyor in your area. The RICS is the regulating body for chartered surveyors.

Don't be tempted to ask for a walk-through valuation because it is cheaper. It is probably a false economy as it is a valuation only and does not go into detail about any essential repairs which have to be carried out. You want to know, for example, if there is any damp, woodworm, dry rot, wet rot, if the property requires rewiring or the building is subsiding. Always get an in-depth survey and not just a walk-through valuation.

If you are buying a property

The surveyor will give you the market value of the property and let you know what repairs are necessary. If they think the property is in need of a number of repairs and in poor condition, they may ask your lender to retain an amount of your loan equal to the cost of carrying out the repairs until they are completed, or if the property is in really bad condition, they could advise the lender not to lend any money on the property until all the work has been completed.

If you are borrowing money on the property you will be required to have a survey carried out by a surveyor who is approved by the bank or lending institution which is providing your loan. They will receive a copy of the survey, as will your solicitor. It is important to sit down with your solicitor and go through the survey report thoroughly because a bad survey report could be the deciding factor on whether or not you go ahead with the purchase.

If you are leasing a property

If you are leasing the property a surveyor could check out the building to see if it requires any major repairs. If so, you should ask the owner to carry out these before you take occupancy of the shop. The surveyor will also be able to give you an idea of the market rent for the premises you have decided to lease.

ARCHITECTS

An architect is best involved at the earliest planning stages and can manage your project until it is completed. They can advise and help you if you are planning to change the use of the property – for example, from a dress shop to a coffee shop – or if you want to carry out any alterations to the property. Remember, you will need permission from your local authority to carry out any major alterations to the premises and in these circumstances a good architect is worth their weight in gold.

Finding an architect

Personal recommendation is a good way to find an architect. However, if you don't know anyone who can recommend one, you can contact the Royal Institute of British Architects at www.architecture.com to help you choose the right architect for your project, whether it is large or small.

BANKS AND BUILDING SOCIETIES

Finance does not always need to be raised through a bank or building society. There are other ways; for example, you may be able to borrow money from friends and family or, as a last resort, you could remortgage your house. However, for many people, the bank or building society is the first port of call.

Getting the best deal

Shop around to find the best bank or building society to suit your needs. There is a lot of competition between them to attract new business. Find out whether you will be tied to the institution that is going to lend you money to start your business. If you do not need to get a loan for your business, or if you are not tied into a specific institution, you should check out interest rates and charges with a few banks and building societies and negotiate the rate of interest you will pay. Charges vary for such things as overdrafts, dishonoured cheques and supplying change, so get the best deal you can.

If the name of your business does not include your own name you must open an account under the business name. Cheques made payable to your company can then be paid into this account.

If you are borrowing from a bank you may find they have a pro forma business plan already set out. All you have to do then is to supply the information required. Do speak to the business manager to enquire if they have a pro forma business plan before going to the trouble of completing one yourself. (See pages 21 – 24 for details on drawing up a business plan.)

INSURANCE BROKERS

You should always plan for potential problems when opening your coffee shop and if possible insure against them.

Insurance brokers claim to be independent of any specific company, and state that they will try to find you the best insurance cover for the lowest premium. They are knowledgeable about different types of insurance policies and can advise you on the best one to suit your needs. Enquire if the broker has experience in insuring coffee shops, cafés and restaurants; if not, go to someone else who has this experience.

In any case, it is important that you obtain quotes from another two insurance brokers before making a decision about who you are going to take out your insurance policy with.

Again, personal recommendation is invaluable. If you have friends who run coffee shops or restaurants, ask them to recommend insurance companies, then approach these companies for quotes.

Understanding insurance

There are several types of insurance cover you must consider; basically, you need insurance to cover the building, contents and your liabilities. The main types are listed below.

GENERAL LIABILITY

□ This covers you for negligence that results in injury to your customers and employees.

PRODUCT LIABILITY

□ This covers you for problems that arise caused by any food or drink you serve on your premises. For example, you would be liable if a customer found a foreign object in anything you serve in your coffee shop. Customers will sue you for anything they can, so insure against this.

FIRE, THEFT, STORM, TEMPEST, MALICIOUS DAMAGE AND GLASS COVER INSURANCE
BUSINESS INTERRUPTION INSURANCE

□ This covers lost income in the event that your business has to be interrupted. This could be because of flooding or damage to your property. The amount covered is based on your previous year's income for the same time of year, not on your figures for the busiest period of trade. The cover is to replace the lost income for the time you are unable to continue your business.

> ❛We had to wait several months before we received payment from the insurance company for a claim for flood damage and loss of earnings.❜

Insurance companies often send a loss adjuster to your premises to negotiate the amount of money that the company will agree to pay your business. This process can take quite a long time so, when you take out the policy, ask if you can get a policy that will give you payment weekly to cover your costs.

BUILDING AND CONTENTS INSURANCE

☐ This should cover the cost of replacing and repairing your buildings and contents so you must be sure to get a realistic quote and include extras for the cleaning up of the premises, removal of debris and any professional fees which might be incurred.

☐ Make a list of all the items you want covered and then get your quotes.

Finding help in your area

Government-supported agencies located throughout Britain offer information for people who are starting their own business. It is worth looking at the website which covers your own area to find out if you could benefit from the type of help they are offering. Information and support are available in the form of:

☐ start-up seminars;

☐ training courses;

☐ advice on financial management;

☐ sales and marketing advice;

☐ advice on helping existing businesses to grow;

☐ help and guidance in applying for a grant;

☐ access to database which contains information about grant and support schemes from central and local government;

☐ updates on relevant regulations.

Listed below are the contact details for the agencies.

ENGLAND

Business Link, tel.: 0845 600 9 006; website: www.businesslink.gov.uk

WALES

Business Eye, tel.: 08457 96 97 98; website: www.businesseye.org.uk

SCOTLAND

Small Business Gateway, tel.: 0845 609 6611; website: www.bgateway.com

HIGHLANDS AND ISLANDS ENTERPRISE

The Highlands and Islands have their own government-supported agency to assist and support new and existing businesses. The agency offers:

- □ business support services;
- □ training and learning programmes;
- □ information on business finance.

Tel.: 01463 234171; website: www.hie.co.uk

NORTHERN IRELAND

Invest North Ireland, tel.: 028 9023 9090; website: www.nibusinessinfo.co.uk

When do you need a licence?

You will have to obtain a licence to:

- □ sell alcohol;
- □ provide entertainment such as live music;
- □ play recorded music (contact the Performing Rights Society);
- □ sell food from a stall or van on the street.

To find out more information on licences you should contact your local authority.

Drawing up a business plan

Many people new to business often miss out the vital step of preparing a business plan when they are thinking about starting a business. It takes time and discipline to write an effective business plan but it is vital to think about your costs and how you will sustain the business.

When your bank manager or lender reads your business plan, they will know the name of your prospective business, what type of business it will be, the amount of loan you require and what the funds are to be used for.

Preparing a business plan has many benefits for you, too. It will help you to:

- □ think carefully about why you want to start your coffee shop;
- □ set your goals for the business;
- □ work out how much money you will need, from initially setting up and equipping the business to running it smoothly and profitably;
- □ look at the risks involved when starting a business;
- □ address the strengths and weaknesses of your proposed business;
- □ plan where you want to go in business and the best way to get there.

Your bank manager or finance manager will want to see that you have done your homework before lending you any money. Therefore, you will need a thorough, detailed business plan which should be specific about the use of the funds. You should support your request with estimates for work to be carried out and for purchasing equipment. Include a marketing strategy indicating who your prospective customers will be and how you will reach them. Your business plan should contain as much information as possible yet at the same time it must be concise.

YOUR BUSINESS PLAN SHOULD INCLUDE THE FOLLOWING:

A cover page which should include:

☐ the name of your business;

☐ business address;

☐ telephone number;

☐ date of preparation of the business plan;

☐ your own name.

A concise statement of the purpose and objectives of the business

☐ This part of the plan should give details of your proposed business.

☐ Outline the type of coffee shop you plan to open and stress the uniqueness of your shop and service; explain how you propose to attract your customers.

☐ State what you expect to accomplish in the future.

Full details of the management of your business

☐ If you are the sole owner of the business give your details, including any previous experience you have and any qualifications you may have.

☐ If you are going into business with a partner give their details, experience and qualifications also, and what skills they can bring to the business. Include a copy of the partnership agreement.

The location of your business

☐ If you have chosen a good location for your coffee shop, give your reason for choosing this location and emphasize its potential for attracting passing trade.

☐ If your coffee shop is situated beside well-known high street shops and businesses, state this fact.

☐ If there is good parking in the area you should include a diagram of the parking facilities.

☐ Include any drawings, plans and photographs you have of the proposed coffee shop and location. This will help the bank manager or lender to envisage what trade will be like.

What competition (if any) you will face

If you have competition, don't hide the fact but instead detail what you are proposing to offer your customers to make your coffee shop better and busier than any other coffee shops in the area. Compile an information sheet on your competitors, including:

- □ the names of other coffee shops;
- □ their location;
- □ their décor and atmosphere;
- □ the price and quality of their beverages and food;
- □ the service and staff attitude;

Then explain in detail how you plan to be better than the competition.

Your projected start-up costs

List what you think all your general expenses will be. These should include rates, rent (if you lease), electricity, gas, telephone bills, equipment, staff wages, together with loan repayments and advertising and any other expenses you can think of.

Some of these costs you will know, such as the rent, and if you don't know how much the rates will be you can contact your local council who will provide this information for you. You will be able to calculate staff wages by multiplying the total amount of hours worked by whatever hourly rate you are going to pay them. There is a minimum hourly rate set which you are legally bound to pay your employees.

The minimum wage applicable at the time of going to press is:

- □ age 16 – 17, £3.57 per hour;
- □ age 18 – 19, £4.83 per hour;
- □ age 22 and over, £5.80 per hour.

You will have to keep adequate pay records so that you can prove that you are paying your staff the minimum wage. If any member of your staff suspect that they are being underpaid they can request to inspect and copy any records that you have that will establish whether this is true or not. If there is a dispute you will have to prove that you have paid the minimum wage. Therefore it is important to keep good records.

If you do not keep adequate records or keep false records you will be committing a criminal offence and you could be fined up to £5,000 and in addition, if it is discovered that you are not paying the minimum wage, you will have to pay arrears within 14 days and a penalty of a quarter of the amount owed in arrears. If you do not pay within 14 days the penalty will double and if you still fail to pay you will risk prosecution and an additional fine.

You can contact the National Minimum Wage Information Service for information on how much the current minimum wage is, or you can request their booklet, 'A Detailed Guide to the National Minimum Wage', by telephoning 0845 8450 360.

Electricity, gas and telephone expenses will be more difficult to calculate. If you already know someone who has a similar shop it would be worth asking them for an estimate of their utility costs.

If you are going to employ staff it is advisable to state at the beginning that no one should use the coffee shop telephone for personal calls. Instruct your staff that it should only be used for calls related to the business; for example, ordering supplies for the shop.

How much capital you require

This is again difficult to calculate but if you add together all your outgoings each week and allow some extra for unexpected expenditure you will have a rough idea. It will take a number of months before you are established and taking in enough money to make a profit. I recommend that you put aside a minimum of six months – if possible, one year's – expenses to help with the capital required to run the business.

Your projected turnover and profit/loss

Again this will be difficult to calculate but if you work out an average spend per customer and the number of customers you think will be in your shop per week you will be able to guess what turnover you will have.

If you have competition close by, you could sit in your car and count the number of customers that go in for coffee and multiply that by an average spend per head. This will give you an approximate figure for your projected turnover.

How you will deal with difficulties that may affect your business

You may unexpectedly have to take time off work – for example because of an accident or ill health. You should have plans in place to cover any such incidents. You could, for instance, train a good manager to run the coffee shop for you.

When you are preparing your business plan to present to the bank for the purpose of securing a loan, include a sketch of the layout of your proposed coffee shop, along with a sample menu with prices. It looks more professional if you laminate each page of your business plan and put them into a ring binder. This will keep all the pages in sequence and neatly together.

4
CREATING YOUR OWN COFFEE SHOP

You are aiming to create a coffee shop which is an attractive, congenial meeting place where friends and families can enjoy a warm welcome, excellent tea or coffee and pleasant company. Coffee shops are popular places to socialise over a drink and something to eat. Age is no barrier when it comes to visiting a good coffee shop. Senior citizens visit them, mothers with young children meet their friends there, professionals dash in and out for a quick cappuccino and students sometimes study there while enjoying a coffee and a snack.

It is time to get your dream off the paper and turn it into reality.

Choosing a name

First impressions count, so it's important to choose the right name for your coffee shop. You should choose a name that reflects the type of image you want to project because that is what will draw in your customers and that is what they will initially remember about your coffee shop. You want your coffee shop to be one of the most important places in the community and it should be not only somewhere for people to gather and relax but also a place that they remember.

 When you are choosing a name, bear in mind that it will be easier for people to remember, pronounce and spell if it is made up of two syllables.

Your coffee shop's name will be on your external sign, your business cards, menus and perhaps on the napkins too, so make sure you choose a name that you really like because it will be expensive if you want to change it a few months later.

Listed below are a few things you should consider when choosing a name for your coffee shop.

☐ It should appeal to and attract potential customers;

☐ It should be easily remembered;

☐ It should be catchy;

☐ It should be unique and stand out from your competitors.

Ask friends and family to suggest ideas for names. Then write them all on a list and brainstorm them.

INVOLVING THE LOCAL COMMUNITY

One way of solving the problem – as well as generating useful publicity – is to approach your local newspaper and ask them to run a competition to choose the name for your coffee shop. You could announce the competition one week in a feature about you and your coffee shop, and the following week give the result, in another feature with photographs of you and the winner taken outside your coffee shop.

You would have to offer a prize to the winner; perhaps a free cup of coffee and a cake or scone for two, to be taken during a certain period of time, or a cash prize.

If you prefer, you could use your local radio station in the same way. Again this would give you free advertising (apart from the cost of the prize) for two weeks prior to opening. Whichever medium you decide to use, make sure you let people know where your coffee shop is situated, what you intend to offer your customers and when you intend to open.

If you do decide to have a competition to name your coffee shop, wait until you are just about to open so that the effect of advertising is not wasted.

Building an image
DESIGNING YOUR LOGO

Now that you have decided on the name of your coffee shop it is time to design a logo. A logo is a visual symbol which will serve as the signature piece for your business. Your coffee shop name and logo will help to establish a strong business identity. They can be put onto your letterheads, menus, napkins and business cards. Your logo will also be used when you advertise in your local newspaper and on any promotional material you give out, including flyers.

Give out as many business cards as you can to friends, customers and people you meet. You could also leave some in waiting rooms, for example, at train or bus stations and in doctors' and dentists' surgeries. This is an inexpensive way of advertising.

Creating the right atmosphere

You will have to take into consideration the kind of area your coffee shop is based in when you are thinking about the atmosphere you want to project. Are you in an area where your customers will predominately be shoppers or business people?

If you have competitors based in the same area you will also have to offer something quite different. The general atmosphere of your coffee shop should be appealing to your customers and to you. If you don't feel comfortable in the shop, your customers certainly won't.

The following are all important aspects to consider when you are creating a unique and appealing atmosphere for your coffee shop:

Lighting

Good lighting is essential but avoid harsh fluorescent lights which can cause headaches. Instead choose soft lighting which is bright enough to read by but gives a warm, cosy feel. Also good natural light from windows is great.

Music

Pleasant background music can enhance the atmosphere of a coffee shop. Invest in a good music system but don't play the music too loudly as customers will complain if they are unable to carry on a conversation. Ask your customers whether they prefer light music or no music at all. (Remember, if you decide to play recorded music you will have to obtain a licence from the Performing Rights Society.)

Furnishings

Whichever kind of atmosphere you are aiming for, your coffee shop must be a warm and inviting haven where people can relax in comfort. If it is in the style of an 'olde worlde' teashop, pretty tablecloths and matching curtains would help to create a traditional look, but make sure they also complement your colour scheme.

If your coffee shop has a more contemporary feel you might prefer modern blinds and either wooden or glass-topped tables and some stainless steel. No matter what type of tables you choose, whether they are glass tops, wooden or laminate, make sure that they are easy to clean and fit in with the rest of your décor.

Comfortable chairs are a must. I always think high bar stools are really uncomfortable and I would always avoid them when possible.

Some attractive pictures on the walls and a few large plants will add the finishing touches to your coffee shop.

Flooring

Think carefully when you are buying flooring for the sitting area in your coffee shop; there are many types on the market now. You should choose something that is hard-wearing and easy to keep clean because you are bound to have some spillage.

There are some excellent designs available and some of the more expensive makes come with a 20-year guarantee. However, if you have a large area to cover, you might want to consider something cheaper. Laminate or hardwood flooring are popular but if they get wet they can warp over time.

Floor tiles appear to be the best option as they are hard-wearing and easy to clean. They are permanent and if they are of good quality they shouldn't chip easily. You can choose self-coloured or speckled tiles. The speckled ones don't show the dirt as quickly.

Carpet tiles are warm, can be vacuumed and the tiles can be replaced one by one. If you are going to use carpet tiles make sure you purchase extra tiles to replace any that become stained. I wouldn't recommend a carpet because it is difficult to clean well and there is no doubt that it will quickly become stained with coffee and food.

Cleanliness

No matter what the style of your coffee shop, cleanliness is of paramount importance. Always make sure your staff wipe the tables when they clear them of dirty dishes. If they are busy they may find it easier simply to remove the used crockery. This gives a dreadful impression and is a practice which must be discouraged.

Many customers judge a coffee shop or restaurant by the toilets. Pleasant washrooms with nice soap and paper towels create a good impression. Have a rota for staff to check the toilets during opening hours to ensure that they are clean and that there is always a ready supply of toilet tissue and paper towels.

It is advisable to fix your soap dispensers to the wall as, unfortunately, soap tends to disappear. And sometimes children who are allowed to go to the washroom on their own will make a game of scooting the soap all over the walls and floor. (Yes, it does happen – on more than one occasion in our coffee shop toilets.)

Do place a large enough waste bin in the wash-basin area because overflowing bins look unsightly.

DEVISING A STAFF UNIFORM

The image projected by your staff is very important in helping to ensure the success of your coffee shop. Customers prefer to be served food and drink by someone who looks neat, clean and smartly dressed. A uniform conveys professionalism and helps to reinforce your coffee shop's identity.

The benefits for staff are that they are saved the expense of buying clothing for work and they also don't have to think about what they are going to wear each day. However, it's important that staff know that you are sensitive to their needs so you must provide them with uniforms that, as well as looking good, are also comfortable, practical and easy to wear.

Your basic uniform could consist of the following:

☐ an apron;

☐ a shirt, polo shirt or smart T-shirt;

☐ black trousers.

If you like, you could include a neck tie/scarf or a cap.

Aprons

You will need a good supply of these. They are essential for waiting staff who will undoubtedly spill tea or coffee on them during the day. Dark colours are best as they will disguise stains more effectively. Black is a favourite colour and is easy to find in any workwear shop.

Aprons with bibs are more practical as they provide protection against splashes from coffee and tea. However, younger staff and male staff tend to prefer a bib-less, knee length or below the knee length apron. Aprons should also be made of a heavy material, be machine washable and non iron.

You can have the name of your coffee shop and your logo, if you have one, printed on the aprons. This can be done either by having the items embroidered or by using an iron-on transfer. There are companies who will do this for you but try to negotiate a good price. Uniform suppliers may be able to put your logo on a wide variety of clothing in your chosen colour.

It is a good idea to wash the aprons belonging to your staff yourself as they tend to lose them by leaving them on the train or the bus. It is a bit of a nuisance but saves you money in the long run. If you have a washing machine/dryer on the premises, all the better but, if not, either take them home with you to wash, or send them to the laundry.

Remember, you will also use a few dozen tea towels and dish cloths in the kitchen each day that will also have to be washed or sent to the laundry. You will save a lot of money by doing them yourself but you may be able to negotiate with your local laundry service and agree a reduced price for guaranteeing them the business for a certain period of time.

Shirts

You could opt for either an easy to iron shirt, a polo shirt or a T-shirt. Short-sleeved shirts work best because long sleeves tend to get dirty quite quickly when wiping and clearing tables.

A white shirt, when new, always looks crisp and clean and looks good with black trousers and a black apron. Remember though that when it has been washed a number of times it could appear grey and dingy so it may be better to choose a colour instead. A check or striped shirt also looks smart and does not show stains as much as a self colour does.

You could also try to link the uniform to your logo by picking out a colour from your logo and matching all the shirts to that particular colour. Alternatively, you could have your logo embroidered on the pockets of the shirts, or have a transfer of your logo ironed onto the shirts.

Trousers

Black trousers or a black skirt always look smart, will go with any colour of shirt and are easy to keep clean.

Even if you decide not to supply your staff with uniforms you must stipulate what they should wear. Inappropriate dress such as bare midriffs or low-cut necklines on female staff will be off-putting to most customers.

 It is well worth supplying at least a T-shirt so that all your staff are dressed in similar fashion.

Insist on your staff coming to work wearing clean, pressed clothes and shoes that are polished and in good repair.

Ask both female and male staff to tie long hair back. This is more hygienic and looks neat and tidy.

Making the most of your menu

Your printed menu is extremely important; it shows your customers exactly what you have to offer. You can have the menu printed with your name and logo on the front and everything you are selling inside.

 **Don't have too many menus printed initially as you will need to have them reprinted when you change your prices. You may also want to add new items to your menu or delete certain ones which you recognize are not selling well.**

Care must be taken when planning your menu. It should reflect what you can cope with so don't get too ambitious. Keep it simple; it is better to offer less to start with and build up a more comprehensive menu after being in business for a while.

You should have a daily specials board, either one mounted on the wall or a sandwich board. As well as listing specials on this board, you should look ahead and if a dish or a filling is not selling as fast as you would like, add it to the specials board and reduce the price. It is better to get some profit from it while it is still fresh rather than having to throw it away when it is past its sell by date.

Most coffee shops offer soup, light bites and home baking. You could simply offer soup of the day on your menu and specify what soup it will be for that day on your specials board. Soup always sells well, even in the summer, and you can make a good profit from it.

List paninis, toasted sandwiches, sandwiches and filled rolls, together with the fillings available. On your menu print the most common fillings but put one or two more unusual fillings on your daily specials board. You will then be able to see what your customers like without committing yourself to offering these fillings every day. Try to give as much detail as possible for your fillings. Don't just list cheese and ham, for instance; find out where the cheese comes from and what type of ham it is and describe your filling as, for example, Orkney Cheddar Cheese with Honey Roast Ham. Your ingredients will sound much more appealing and suggestive of quality if you say 'Scottish Smoked Salmon and Philadelphia Cream Cheese', or 'Egg Mayonnaise made from Organic Eggs and the best Creamy Mayonnaise'. (See Chapter 5 for more details on menus.)

Print out a suggestion sheet for your customers to propose fillings or other food they would like you to offer. You could also ask them to make general comments and recommendations. This feedback is invaluable as it will help you improve your business. See Appendix 6 for an example of a customer questionnaire.

Next you should list all your speciality coffees, teas including fruit and herbal teas, hot chocolate and cold drinks. Remember to list children's beverages, including sugar-free drinks.

Be aware of what is popular and keep up with trends by reading food magazines and visiting other good coffee shops when time permits.

Don't ever sell anything that is past its sell by date. If you do you could jeopardise your business.

Don't use chalk to write on your specials board because you will find that children will rub off your menu as soon as you turn your back. Use a dry marker pen instead. You can purchase them in various bright colours and children won't be able to rub the writing off the board.

PRICING YOUR MENU

One of the most difficult tasks is establishing prices that will cover your overheads and give you a profit.

In order to work out your prices you will need to calculate the cost of each item by adding up the cost of all the ingredients in the recipe and taking into account the time it took to make the item. Some items will be less expensive and less time consuming to make than others. For example, a carrot cake takes longer and is more expensive to make than a plain sponge. I would recommend you lower your profit on the carrot cake and increase your profit on the plain sponge and sell them both at the same price.

In general you should work on achieving a 60% profit although you may be guided by what your competitors are charging. If your prices are higher than those of your competitors, you may find that customers will be prepared to pay a bit more if you are offering something special; for example, good service, a friendly atmosphere or great coffee and home baking.

In our coffee shop we work on a 50% gross profit because we opt for a large volume at lower prices. However, some small exclusive coffee shops work on low volume with high prices.

Always aim to give your customers value for money. People expect to pay a fair price for good coffee and good food.

Size matters! I know of a most successful coffee/teashop in the Highlands of Scotland, close to a railway station and also on the main road into one of the few large(ish) towns for many miles around. The customer profile is a mixture of passing tourists, local ladies who meet for coffee or tea and those from a wider area who from time to time drive past the shop on their way into the town for provisions. The teashop is famous for its scones. Few who visit fail to return, as the scones are just magnificent. The coffee shop offers three varieties – plain, fruit and cheese. They are all so good that customers sometimes struggle to select which one they want. Then one day the owners had a mental aberration and decided to offer two sizes of scone. They dithered over whether to call them 'large' and 'small' or 'standard' and 'large'. Finally they settled on 'scones' and 'large scones' and had their menus printed. Within a week the table staff were on the point of industrial action. They were being driven demented as customers who already couldn't decide what type of scone to have now wanted to know just how large a 'large scone' was. Some customers decided to share a large scone and some argued that the large scone on one plate wasn't all that much bigger than the standard scone on another plate. It took twice as long for the staff to take a simple order. The following week the menus were reprinted once again and – lo- only one size of scone appeared!

The moral of this story is that it is better to try out new ideas for a while before changing your menu, because if it doesn't work, you won't have incurred the expense of having to get your menu reprinted.

Should you opt for self-service or table service?

This is a personal choice though I believe it depends on the location and size of your coffee shop. If you have a large seating area I think, on balance, it is better to have self-service because:

☐ you will save money on the cost of waiting staff;

☐ you can make sure that everyone has paid for their order before receiving it. Customers then shouldn't be able to walk out without paying.

Even though we have self-service in our coffee shop, on one occasion a customer took a cake and slid it around the corner so that the person taking her money didn't see it and therefore didn't charge her for it. When it was discovered that she had done this, it was too late and she had eaten the evidence!

If you have a small coffee shop, table service is best because:

☐ your customers receive better customer care;

☐ customers enjoy the attention they get from their waiter/waitress;

☐ customers will probably order more from the waiting staff;

☐ waiting staff can boost your profits by promoting your food and drink. They can suggest to your customers that they try a particular sandwich, cake or coffee that they think tastes great;

☐ your staff receive more tips when they give table service.

Americans mostly favour self-service but the British are more formal and prefer table service. Urban likes self-service – rural likes table service.

Deciding your opening hours

You will have to decide what are the optimum opening hours for your premises. This depends not only on the area in which you are situated but also on your customer profile.

Our coffee shop is situated within a retail shop, therefore we open the coffee shop at the same time as the retail shop, which is 10 a.m. We close the coffee shop at 5 p.m. to allow the staff time to clean the sitting area, toilets and kitchen before the retail shop closes at 6 p.m.

If you are in an area where the other shops open at 9 a.m. you may want to open at 8.30 a.m. to catch people going to work; and if you are going to sell hot bacon or egg rolls for breakfast you may also want to open early. Most people are going home at around 5 p.m. so you would probably want to close at that time to allow your staff to clean up ready for the next day.

No matter what hours you decide to open your shop, you will have to be there yourself early in the morning to take in deliveries of milk, bread and rolls, fresh vegetables and other orders. Also if you are going to bake your own scones and cakes you will probably have to start around 7 a.m. so that you are prepared for opening.

> *When we first started our coffee shop I honestly thought that I would only have to arrive at work about half an hour before opening time. How wrong I was. I start at 6 a.m. to take in all the deliveries, set up the coffee machine and start baking!*

You have to be able to prepare yourself for an early start unless you have a good manager who will do all these jobs for you. However, most people can't afford to take on a manager when they first start their business. As long as you are in good health, are physically fit and you are passionate about what you do, it won't feel like work.

5
DEVISING YOUR MENU

Creating the menu for your coffee shop is one of your most important tasks. You will need to consider carefully what type of food and which hot and cold beverages you are going to serve.

Catering to suit your customer

You will need to cater for the particular type of customer base in your area. For example, if your coffee shop is located in a less affluent area, you should create your menu to suit your customers' pockets, but perhaps include a daily special which is more unusual. Conversely, if your location is in a more affluent district, you may be able to include more up-market ingredients.

You will probably have tried many varieties of sandwich, panini and baked potato while you were doing your research, but try to be objective as your customers won't necessarily enjoy the same food as you do. If you concentrate on a range of basic or core fillings and introduce one or two special dishes or fillings of the day for your sandwiches and baked potatoes, you will soon get to know what your customers like.

 TIP Don't make too large a quantity of a new item until you see how your customers like it or you will risk throwing away more than you sell. It is always better to run out of something rather than have to throw it away!

Serving cold-filled snacks and sandwiches
COLD FILLINGS

It is a good idea to offer several cold fillings for paninis, toasted sandwiches, sandwiches and baked potatoes. Some of those that I have found to be popular are:

- ☐ tuna mayonnaise;

- ☐ chicken mayonnaise or chicken and sweetcorn;

- ☐ coronation chicken or chicken tikka;

- ☐ cheese, ham and tomato;

- ☐ cheese and pickle;

☐ egg mayonnaise;

☐ prawns, naked or with a Marie Rose sauce;

☐ BLT (bacon, lettuce and tomato).

More unusual fillings for your daily special

If you want to experiment with more unusual fillings to try out on your customers as daily specials, check out other coffee shops and recipe books to give you some ideas. In Chapter 12 I have included some suggestions for fillings which have proved popular with my customers. In addition, I have listed below a few fillings which I have tried and found to be successful:

☐ smoked salmon and cream cheese;

☐ corned beef with mayonnaise, spring onion and tomato;

☐ chicken and cranberry sauce and mayonnaise;

☐ peanut butter and banana (might appeal to vegetarians);

☐ lobster meat with mayonnaise and cayenne pepper;

☐ avocado and Brie or another cheese (again might appeal to vegetarians);

☐ roast beef and horseradish;

☐ cream cheese or cottage cheese with crisp bacon or ham.

Do try to make up your fillings fresh in the morning and keep them in the fridge to use as required. Also prepare fresh tubs of salad every morning for garnishing and using in sandwiches. You could also offer a variety of salads that can be made up to order based around your sandwich ingredients – and you could also include a special salad on your menu.

MAKING SANDWICHES AND ROLLS TO ORDER

It really is better to make your sandwiches to order as customers prefer to see their sandwich freshly made to their own specification. Also, you will have less waste at the end of the day. Simply offer a choice of bread available and a selection of fillings which can be priced by having an extra key especially for fillings on your till.

Garnishes

Whichever sandwich or baked potato you are serving, a salad garnish makes it look much more appetizing and professional. We always serve our sandwiches with a salad garnish and crisps but you can decide yourself what garnish looks best. Again, when doing your research of other coffee shops, take note of what garnish they use and what looks more appealing to you.

Mayonnaise is used in most sandwiches because it tastes good and makes the sandwich moist. However not everyone wants mayonnaise – especially if they are watching the calories – so do keep some cooked chicken and prawns aside so that you can offer mayonnaise-free sandwiches.

MAKING YOUR SANDWICHES IN ADVANCE

Filled sandwiches can, of course, be made in advance and wrapped in cling film to keep them fresh. If you want to do this, make a small selection to begin with to see how well they sell. The downside of this is that the filled sandwiches/rolls have not only to be wrapped separately but also to be individually labelled. This takes up a lot of time. Also, the filled sandwiches/rolls take up precious room, unless you have chilled counters with a lot of space.

You could, of course, buy in ready-made sandwiches but I personally do not think this would entice people into your coffee shop as they can buy this type of sandwich in super-markets or other outlets.

OFFERING A VARIETY OF BREADS

There are so many different types of bread and rolls on the market now, such as:

☐ mixed grain;

☐ poppy seed;

☐ ciabatta;

☐ focaccia;

☐ bagels;

to name but a few.

In my experience, a large number of customers still like ordinary sliced white and brown bread or rolls. So do offer a basic white and brown pan loaf and experiment with a few of the more unusual types until you discover what your customers like. Then you can add these to your menu. It is really trial and error to begin with and again I would recommend only buying a small quantity of different breads otherwise you could end up throwing away your profit as well as the bread at the end of the day!

Fresh is best

One of the important skills you will learn, occasionally the hard way, is to purchase only the perishable food that you actually require. You can, of course, freeze surplus bread at the end of the day and use it at a later date; it is always advisable to freeze a small amount of bread just in case you are extremely busy and run out of fresh bread. To retain freshness, bread must be frozen and never refrigerated. Generally, of course, I prefer to use fresh bread and rolls daily, but a good way to use up your defrosted bread is to use it for toast and toasted sandwiches.

Getting your daily bread

Suppliers are keen to give you free samples of their bread so take advantage of this as it will allow you to discover what type of bread and rolls your customers prefer. Try to get a supplier who will deliver your rolls and bread daily. Alternatively, you could buy them from the supermarket in the morning before opening your shop. It may be less expensive to do this at first and you can decide each morning what quantity you will need. The downside to this is that it will take up your time in the morning before you go to work. Remember, you will have to start early – 6 a.m. – 7 a.m. – to get all your deliveries in and do all your preparations, baking, etc. prior to opening time.

Serving hot-filled snacks and sandwiches

Baked potatoes and paninis are very popular and can be made with hot or cold fillings. For baked potatoes you can use some of the cold fillings listed above and also a variety of hot fillings listed below. See also Chapter 12 for more ideas for fillings. Popular hot fillings include:

- chilli con carne;
- curry;
- haggis;
- cheese and coleslaw;
- baked beans and cheese;
- creamed mushrooms;
- macaroni and cheese.

QUICHE

I find that, in the summer, home-made quiche is a great favourite with customers. I serve it hot or cold, with salad or salad garnish and chips. Quiche is easy to make and is a profitable meal to serve. You can choose a variety of fillings but always include at least one that is suitable for vegetarians.

Making your own soup

Home-made soup is also very popular and in fact is one of the best selling items on our menu. When we first opened our coffee shop we made one large 8-pint pot of traditional soup which sold well but now that we are established we sell approximately 5 gallons of traditional soup and 8 pints of cream soup per day. We give a good-sized bowl of soup (two ladlesful) along with a slice of fresh crusty bread and butter or a fresh roll and butter. Don't be tempted to use up yesterday's bread as your customers will notice and will think you are not giving value for money. Nor should you use packet or tinned soup – there is no comparison to good home-made soup.

 Remember, you will have some customers who are vegetarian, so advertise your vegetable soups as being suitable for vegetarians, and make sure no meat stock has been used in them.

Here are some of the most popular soups that I serve in our coffee shop:

- lentil;
- chicken and rice;
- leek and potato;
- broth;
- chicken noodle;
- minestrone.

You can also offer a cream soup daily (make a smaller pot as not everyone likes cream soups). The following are popular with my customers:

- cream of mushroom;
- cream of chicken;
- cream of carrot and coriander;
- cream of parsnip and curry;
- cream of cauliflower or broccoli and stilton;
- cream of sweet potato and chilli;
- cullen skink (a Scottish soup made from smoked haddock and cream).

 Offer a combination of a bowl of soup plus a filled sandwich at a specially reduced price. And for children you could offer half a bowl of soup plus a small sandwich.

You could also offer cartons of soup to carry out as this suits people in a hurry at lunchtime, who don't have time to sit in and eat.

You will find some of my soup recipes in Chapter 12.

Serving breakfasts

If you decide to serve breakfasts it is advisable to give a cut-off time – say, 11.30 a.m. – or you will get caught up in trying to cook breakfasts and serve lunches at the same time, which is not ideal. However, if you do have space and time, you could offer an all-day breakfast.

Rolls filled with sausage, bacon or egg sell well throughout the day, or you could offer a roll with a double filling of bacon and egg or sausage and egg.

Scrambled eggs on toast and beans on toast are easy and quick to make and there is a good profit margin on these simple dishes.

A recipe I picked up from a friend in the USA is a Breakfast Casserole which is a bit different from the traditional English Breakfast and tastes delicious. It can be prepared the day before and put into the fridge and cooked the next morning. Portions can be served with toast or crusty bread. See Chapter 12 for the recipe.

Serving home-cooked meals

Should you decide to increase your menu to include home-cooked meals you could try some of the following, but remember not to make too much at first until you see what you can sell in a day. You could make one or two interesting meals as special items on your menu until your business is established and you know what type of food your customers are looking for.

WELL KNOWN FAVOURITES

Home-made lasagne is still very popular and if you make a large tray of it you can freeze some of the portions for use at a later date.

Unless you have an upmarket coffee shop, fish and chips, scampi, mince and potatoes, braised sausage, and steak pie are still old favourites with customers. Chilli con carne or curry served with rice or chips, and pasta bolognaise also sell well. However, it is important to make all these recipes on the premises and not to buy in frozen substitutes. If you make the food yourself, your coffee shop will get a reputation for serving good home-made food at a reasonable price. Customers want value for money.

MORE ADVENTUROUS FARE

If you do have an upmarket coffee shop and you decide to include cooked meals, the sky is the limit and you can make a variety of unusual and interesting meals from your own recipes or from recipes you have collected when doing your research. You can also include a few of the old favourites.

Catering for children

Young couples will probably frequent your coffee shop and it is advisable to offer meals for their children. You can do this by buying in such things as fish fingers, chicken burgers and small pizzas. You can also offer children's portions of the food you are making for adults.

PORTION SIZES

However, be aware that offering children's portions can cause problems. Some adults may be tempted to order a child's meal because it is cheaper and the portion can be almost as large as the adult portion! This can lead to a delicate situation – and you must avoid disputes with your customers. You must have a clear policy. You could ensure that your kitchen staff serve a half-sized portion for half the price, unless you do not mind adults purchasing a child's meal even though it cuts down on your profit.

Beef, chicken and vegetable burgers are favourites with children and teenagers, and can be topped with cheese, fried onions or egg, and served with a salad garnish or chips. They are easy to make as you can cook them from frozen, or indeed you can make your own fresh burgers.

ICE CREAM AND ICE LOLLIES

If you have room for a freezer, you may want to consider selling ice creams and ice lollies. Ice cream companies will sometimes provide you with a freezer on loan, or free, if you agree to sell their products. If this is what you want to do then contact a few companies to find out what deals they can offer you. They may also discount your first order or they may give you a longer period of credit before you have to pay for the stock. Do bear in mind though that freezers take up a lot of space, and while you probably won't sell many ice creams in the winter, you will have money tied up in keeping your freezer well stocked. Think carefully before making a decision about offering ices on your menu.

Baking your own cakes

If you want to attract customers to your coffee shop home baking is a must. Always try to bake your own cakes and tray bakes on the premises as your customers will be able to tell the difference. Alternatively, you could purchase cakes from someone who bakes them at home, providing the baker is registered with the Environmental Health Department of your local council. In our coffee shop we sell over 150 cakes and tray bakes a day, and on a Saturday we sell about 200 cakes and tray bakes, all of which are home-baked on the premises.

Last year we had a problem with our oven and couldn't use it for four days. We bought in bakes but our customers complained about the size of the portions and the lack of variety. Our cakes and tray bakes are always a generous portion and our customers are used to that. It is important always to be consistent in portion size and quality. People do really appreciate home-made cakes and tray bakes and not all coffee shops provide these, so it really is worth making it a priority. But always find out where you can purchase bakery just in case you have to do so in an emergency.

FAVOURITE CAKES

I have listed below some of our customers' favourite cakes. Some I put out every day as they are consistently good sellers and others I offer occasionally as specials. I usually offer a choice of 12 to 14 cakes including tray bakes each day but it is better to offer a smaller selection until you get established.

Remember to give your customers a good portion, a good choice and value for money, and you can't go wrong.

Everyday favourites
- ☐ Apple Pie
- ☐ Doughnuts
- ☐ Fruit Loaf
- ☐ Fudge Slice
- ☐ Mars Bar Crispy Cake
- ☐ Millionaire Shortbread
- ☐ Plain Sponge
- ☐ Rhubarb Pie
- ☐ Scones with Butter
- ☐ Scones with Cream and Jam
- ☐ Scottish Butter Shortbread

Occasional 'specials'

- ☐ Apple, Cinnamon and Chocolate Chip Cake
- ☐ Banana, Cranberry and Nut Loaf
- ☐ Banoffee Pie
- ☐ Carrot Cake
- ☐ Chocolate Cake
- ☐ Coconut Slice
- ☐ Crispy Surprise
- ☐ Cup Cakes
- ☐ Empire Biscuits
- ☐ Gingerbread
- ☐ Lemon Cheesecake
- ☐ Lemon Slice
- ☐ Malteser Slice
- ☐ Meringues
- ☐ Mint Slice
- ☐ Muffins
- ☐ Key Lime Pie
- ☐ Scottish Tablet
- ☐ Sticky Toffee Buns
- ☐ Strawberry Tarts

I always make scones and doughnuts first thing in the morning so that they are fresh and ready to serve when we open. Home-made meringues are a fantastic seller and I could sell them all every day but as they take a long time to cook at a low temperature it is not always possible to monopolise the oven for that length of time.

Some coffee shops also offer a range of desserts, for example, sticky toffee pudding, bread and butter pudding, apple crumble. However, this requires time and the use of your microwave oven, possibly at the busiest time of the day, which is not always possible. Again, it is a case of trial and error, and you could do well with old favourite desserts and also a few new, exciting ones.

Once again, I have included some of my recipes in Chapter 12.

Offering a choice of hot and cold drinks
COFFEE

We serve the following coffees in our coffee shop:

☐ cappuccino;

☐ filter coffee;

☐ espresso;

☐ latte coffee (plain or flavoured with vanilla or caramel);

☐ mocha;

☐ Nescafé decaf.

Before deciding on which ground coffee and coffee beans you are going to use in your shop, visit other coffee shops, sample theirs and, if you like it, ask the name of their supplier. Usually suppliers will give you samples of coffee to try before you decide which one you think would appeal to your customers. We like Matthew Algie coffee and I have given the contact details in the Chapter 6.

If you don't want the expense of purchasing an espresso coffee machine it is possible to lease one from your coffee supplier.

Don't install a coffee machine that does everything at the press of a button as these automatic machines usually use powdered coffee and powdered milk. In my opinion there is no comparison to the flavour of coffee made in an authentic espresso coffee machine, which uses freshly ground coffee beans and fresh milk. Don't let anyone persuade you otherwise. You can make cappuccino, mocha, white coffee and black coffee. Hot chocolate can also be made using powdered chocolate and fresh steamed milk.

TEA

Using a good-quality tea is a must although, if you want to make a larger profit, you can purchase a less expensive tea. However, your customers may not enjoy it as much.

Offer Earl Grey tea and a choice of flavoured and herbal teas as these are very popular with some customers.

COLD DRINKS

Offer a good choice of diet, non-diet drinks and sugar-free drinks. Find out what drinks are popular and include them in your selection. Also keep a good range of drinks suitable for children. The following is a good selection to offer:

☐ Pepsi or Coca-Cola;

☐ Fanta Lemon and Fanta Orange;

☐ Iron Bru (a Scottish favourite);

☐ Sprite;

☐ carbonated flavoured water;

☐ still flavoured water;

☐ still natural water;

☐ a selection of children's drinks and juices.

Try offering milk shakes made with flavoured syrups plus ice cream, or simply flavoured milk. You can buy flavoured milk in cartons or you can make it up yourself with syrup in a blender. It only takes seconds and there is more profit to be made in the one you make up yourself.

Smoothies are very popular with health-conscious customers and also children, but unless you have time to juice fruit yourself I would advise buying in ready-made cartons or bottles.

 **Make sure your staff know that when they fill the drinks chiller they must always bring the older drinks to the front in order that you are not left with out-of-date cans and bottles. Staff sometimes overlook this when the coffee shop is busy, but you must impress upon them how important it is.**

Remember to keep a stock of drinking straws as some customers prefer to have a straw with the bottle instead of a glass, and most children love to have a straw in their drink.

You will be surprised how many customers are on diets and request sweeteners for their coffee and tea as an alternative to sugar, so it is a good idea to have a supply available.

A university student who worked for us at weekends and in the holidays came to me one day to ask if a serviette was a sweetener! A customer had asked her for a serviette and she thought it was another name for Sweetex.

6
PURCHASING AND LEASING CATERING EQUIPMENT

You can choose either to purchase or lease most equipment, but in some cases it is better to lease.

Buying new equipment

We started our coffee shop from scratch and had to buy everything. Having no experience in this type of business, it was trial and error.

If you can afford it, you should always try to purchase new equipment. When you buy new you usually get one year's guarantee, so you will have peace of mind for that year. Keep all your guarantees and manuals in a file for easy access because you never know when you might have to have a piece of equipment repaired.

Before investing money on new or second-hand equipment, you should do your homework thoroughly. Talk to other coffee shop or restaurant owners to see what equipment they prefer to have, and why. Also check the internet to see if there is any information on the item of equipment you are considering purchasing.

> *We have had to have our food mixer repaired three times since we bought it. The first time it was still under the guarantee, but on the other two occasions we had to pay for the repair and the postage.*

If you are taking over an already established business you should have all the fittings and fixtures included in the sale or lease and the kitchen should already be fitted out. This will save you purchasing a lot of expensive items initially and, hopefully, you should not need to replace any large items until you have made enough profit to do so.

 It is said that catering equipment only lasts approximately five to six years, especially if you are going to open your coffee shop six or seven days a week. It is advisable therefore to plan to renew an item every five years.

Buying second-hand equipment

If you are working to a tight budget you can often purchase second-hand and reconditioned equipment at a good price from auction sales, dealers or from shops that are closing down.

Sometimes it is worth buying second-hand as it can save you a lot of money. Remember, you may have to transport the equipment that you have purchased. You might have to hire a van or pay a delivery charge, so take the cost of that into account.

> *I know a coffee shop owner, working on a limited budget, who purchased all his tables and chairs second-hand for £60 at an auction. He was delighted with his purchases and simply covered the tables with pretty oilcloth tablecloths. I'm sure you will agree that this purchase saved him quite a lot of money. He also bought most of his kitchen equipment and fitments second-hand and so far he hasn't had any problems with them.*

Buyer, beware: if you decide to buy any equipment through classified advertisements, at an auction, or from a dealer who is not reputable, then take great care as you will not have any guarantee with these items. If your budget is tight, you will have to be ready to take a chance, but do your homework first. Go to see the item before you buy, if that is possible. Ask how old it is and if you can test it to see if it is working. Also, ask if there have been any repairs done to the item and, if so, what they were, and how much they cost. Better still, if you know someone who has some knowledge about the equipment you are considering purchasing, take that person with you to check it out.

Buying or leasing kitchen equipment

There are companies who will design and install your kitchen for you and, if you are going to go down this road, do get several quotations before you make a final decision. You will be able to search for these companies on the internet and also look in the Yellow Pages.

Before you buy or lease any equipment do try to visit other commercial kitchens to see their layouts. Ask the owners or managers what equipment they think is essential. I have listed the kitchen equipment which I think is essential and I have included some items which I think are desirable.

Upgrading or fitting a commercial kitchen can be expensive, so you could consider leasing instead of purchasing your equipment.

ESPRESSO COFFEE MACHINE

Purchasing or leasing the right coffee machine is very important because if you don't serve good coffee your customers won't return.

A good authentic coffee machine is very expensive to purchase and you will have to sell an awful lot of coffees to cover the cost. We did our research and decided to lease our coffee machine. We also entered into a maintenance agreement. At the time you will think that a maintenance agreement seems to be an expensive outlay but in the event that your coffee machine breaks down during a busy period you will be thankful that you made the investment. We found that it was advantageous because the company we lease from guarantee to send an engineer to the customer's premises as soon as possible after they report a breakdown.

The company you lease your machine from will come to your shop and give your staff training on making different types of coffee, and instructions on how to keep the machine clean.

We lease an Elektra Maxi Espresso Coffee Machine from Matthew Algie. It costs approximately £100 per month to lease but you can lease a smaller one for about £80 per month. This amount also includes a precision coffee grinder and the cost of the maintenance. Matthew Algie offer staff training in their Coffee School and on your premises.

We also purchase our coffee beans, ground coffee and flavoured syrups from Matthew Algie as they offer a next-day delivery service. You can look at their website which is www.matthewalgie.co.uk and can telephone them on 0141 429 2817.

It is essential that you clean the hot milk wand after each use or the milk will harden onto the wand and it will be difficult to clean at the end of the day. You should also ensure that you clean your machine on a daily basis to the manufacturer's instructions because failure to do so causes a build-up of oily residue in the pipes which gives the coffee a bitter taste.

FILTER COFFEE MACHINE

I would also advise you to get a filter coffee machine, firstly, because some people prefer filter coffee; and, secondly, because if your espresso machine breaks down you can offer filter coffee to your customers until your other machine is repaired. If you don't want to go to the expense of purchasing a filter coffee machine (which could cost you around £100), companies that lease machines will usually be able to supply you with one free on loan as long as you agree to purchase their ground coffee.

COFFEE GRINDER

A coffee grinder is essential. You will need to grind the coffee beans to use in your coffee machine. You can get a grinder from the company you are leasing your coffee machine from. If you were to purchase a coffee grinder it would cost you approximately £380 so, if you can include this in your lease agreement, it is worthwhile.

WATER BOILER

You will require constant boiling water to make pots of tea so a water boiler is essential. It saves you time because the water is always at the correct temperature and you don't have to wait for a kettle to boil. A manual-fill water boiler will cost around £110. You can purchase a boiler which is plumbed in, but they are more expensive, costing from around £270. They are much more convenient but you will have to get a plumber to connect it to the mains water supply. You can get water boilers in different sizes from 5 litres to 20 litres.

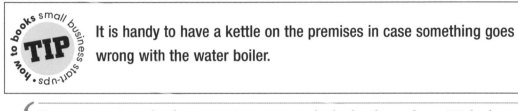

TIP It is handy to have a kettle on the premises in case something goes wrong with the water boiler.

‘ On two occasions the thermostat in our water boiler has burned out. We had to use a kettle and the espresso machine until the engineer replaced the thermostat. ’

Most coffee machines will give you instant boiling water. I have found that this is all right in an emergency, but if you use them continually for making tea, you will have to wait for the steam to build up again before you can make another cappuccino or café latte.

It is necessary to have the espresso machine and your water boiler plumbed in because they fill automatically and the excess water has to be drained.

DISHWASHER

Dishwashers are preferable to manual washing and are said to be more economical and very efficient at disinfecting dishes, cutlery, pots and pans and small items of equipment.

A good commercial dishwasher is both a must and a godsend. The washing cycle takes a fraction of the time a domestic dishwasher takes; it can be set to take one, two or three minutes to wash the dishes. We set our dishwasher for the three-minute cycle. You fill the basket neatly so that items do not overlap and then place it in the dishwasher, close the lid and three minutes later the dishes are washed. You will be surprised at the amount of dishes you can wash at one time.

You can purchase a commercial pass-through dishwasher from around £2,118.00 including VAT, or you can lease one from about £12 per week.

We did invest in a spray which is situated over the sink to rinse off the excess food before washing the dishes in the machine. This piece of equipment is not essential but I would recommend purchasing one if you can afford it.

Follow the manufacturer's recommendations for loading and using your dishwasher. Rinse any large particles of food off the dishes before you put them in the machine. You will find that you also have to scrub your pots before putting them in the dishwasher.

You will have to use a good commercial dishwasher liquid, and a rinse aid which is fed into the machine automatically and which is approved by the Environmental Health Agency.

WASTE DISPOSAL SYSTEM

A waste disposal in the sink is not essential but it is excellent for getting rid of left-over food. Alternatively you could place a small bin with a plastic liner inserted in it beside the sink to scrape the left-over food off the dishes before putting them into the dishwasher.

We have found that a large majority of people won't eat salad and it comes back untouched and has to be thrown away. This is certainly wasteful but food looks so much better presented with a garnish.

FREEZER

You will find that commercial freezers are expensive to purchase but they are built to withstand the hash and bash of the kitchen staff. We store frozen paninis, bread, chips, fish, meat and chicken, as well as ice cream and some bakery.

Do remember to place thermometers in your freezers so that you can maintain the correct temperature to keep food fresh.

REFRIGERATOR

Commercial fridges are also expensive but are built to withstand the number of times the door has to be opened and closed during a busy working day. A fridge which displays its temperature on the outside is beneficial because you can make sure that it is at the correct temperature at all times (1°C to 4°C). You will have to record these readings on your temperature chart twice a day, in the morning and in the afternoon. If your fridges don't have a visible temperature display, make sure that you place thermometers inside them.

You will probably want to have an upright fridge cooler for your cold drinks. If you don't want to purchase a drinks cooler, some drinks companies will supply them free of charge as long as you purchase their brand of drinks.

FOOD DISPLAY UNIT

You will require a chilled food display unit if you are going to display cream cakes or ready-made sandwiches. You can also purchase a display unit which is not chilled to display cakes and confectionery at an ambient temperature.

 If you are not going to sell ready-made sandwiches or cream cakes you should choose the ordinary display unit because the chilled version will make the edges of your sponges and cakes hard.

 Do purchase a display case that is not self-service because you will find that some customers will lift the cakes and in some instances feel them with their fingers before making a final choice.

COOKER

You should invest in a good commercial oven because a domestic oven will not withstand the abuse it will have to take.

I personally think a gas oven and burners are better than an electric oven and burners because the heat is instant and you can control it. A double oven is a must if you are going to do your own baking on the premises. You can choose either four or six burners but, if you have space, I would opt for six burners.

You can purchase a four-burner range cooker for about £1,200 or lease one for around £9 per week. A six-burner range cooker will cost you around £1,500 to buy, or you can lease one for around £11.50 per week.

BAIN-MARIE

If you are going to serve hot food a bain-marie is a convenient way of holding hot vegetables, beans, soup, macaroni cheese and other foods. It has thermostatic control which allows you to keep the food at the required temperature.

GRILL

A high-level grill is a must because you can keep an eye on what is grilling without having to bend down all the time.

PANINI GRILL

This is a heavy-duty contact grill to use for making paninis but you can also make toasted sandwiches on it. It takes a little while to heat up so turn it on in the morning and leave it on until after your lunchtime rush.

'Paninis are one of our best sellers so the panini grill has been a really worthwhile piece of equipment in our kitchen; it has paid for itself many times over.'

Think very carefully before you enter into the type of contract that ties you into buying a company's products. You can, for instance, get a free oven which cooks part-baked paninis and various pastries from a well-known company but you have to agree to take a certain amount of their produce every week. When you have just started in business, you do not know how many paninis and pastries you will be able to sell per week.

GRIDDLE

A griddle is excellent if you are going to be serving quite a lot of bacon, eggs, sausage and burgers and also if you have space to install it. It saves time messing around with frying pans. If you have a griddle you should turn it on first thing in the morning as it takes a considerable time to heat up.

'I know a coffee shop owner who serves rolls filled with sausage, bacon, egg and burgers, and they get into such a mess because they have to use a frying pan each time they get an order. Unfortunately, they don't have room to install a griddle.'

MICROWAVE

A good commercial microwave is essential; you will be amazed at how useful you will find it. Initially, we started off with two microwaves but have recently bought another one.

If you are going to offer scrambled egg on your menu, always cook it in the microwave as it saves cleaning dirty scrambled egg pots.

TOASTED SANDWICH MAKER

Do purchase a toasted sandwich maker that toasts four to six sandwiches at a time because it takes quite a few minutes for each one to toast. You may, for example, have four customers at the same table who all order toasted sandwiches. If your machine only toasts two at a time, you will have to try to keep the first two hot while you make the remaining two, in order to serve everyone at the same time.

If you lack space, or you cannot afford to buy a toasted sandwich maker, you can use your panini contact grill to toast sandwiches.

TOASTER

An ordinary toaster is necessary for serving dishes such as scrambled egg or beans on toast. Again I would recommend one that toasts at least four slices at one time. Remember, if you purchase a domestic toaster you will not be given a warranty. A four- slice commercial toaster can cost from approximately £100 up to £250 and you can purchase a six-slice commercial toaster from about £150.

We use a domestic toaster and just replace it when anything goes wrong, but you must consider how much yours is going to be used and then decide what type you think would suit your business..

SOUP KETTLE

A soup kettle is not expensive but in my opinion it is invaluable if you are going to serve home-made soup. It will hold approximately 10 litres of soup, it is thermostatically controlled and it has an inner removable pot for easy cleaning. A soup kettle costs from approximately £49.99 plus VAT.

Soup has to be served at a high temperature of 63°C or above. A soup kettle will keep it at the correct temperature and at the same time prevent your soup sticking to the bottom of the pot. If you leave soup simmering on top of the cooker during lunchtime, more than likely it will stick to the bottom of the pot and in some cases burn. Once this happens there is no way you can serve it and it will have to be thrown away.

FOOD MIXER

Don't be tempted to purchase a small domestic food mixer if you are going to be doing all your own baking as it will not last. A good food mixer like a Kenwood Chef or a Kitchen Aid is essential but if you intend to do a lot of baking and you want to splash out you can purchase a Buffalo mixer which will cost you over £1,000.

The cost of a Kitchen Aid mixer is from approximately £234 and a commercial Kenwood Chef from approximately £349.99 and £239.99 (no commercial warrenty) plus VAT.

I do a large amount of baking and I have a Kenwood Chef which cost £352. It has an extra strong gearbox, an 800-watt motor and a 6.7-litre mixing bowl.

LIQUIDIZER OR HAND BLENDER

A liquidizer is handy but I tend to use a hand blender more because I find it is quicker and less expensive than a conventional blender. You could probably buy a good-quality domestic blender or liquidizer as they are relatively inexpensive and you should be able to afford to replace them when they break down.

Commercial liquidizers can cost anything from £100 upwards, as opposed to £20 upwards for a domestic one. You can purchase a domestic hand blender for a few pounds but you can pay from £75 to £200 for a heavy-duty commercial one.

ROBOT COUPE

This is a professional food processor which will grate, slice and chop all your vegetables and also grate your cheese, liquidize soup and make fresh breadcrumbs. It comes with 2 mm and 3 mm slicing and grating discs. The Robot Coupe is expensive but, if you are going to make your own soup, coleslaw and grate your own cheese, this machine is invaluable. You can, however, purchase a domestic food processor but you will not get a commercial warranty with this.

The price of a Robot Coupe is in excess of £500 but you can lease one from £4.55 per week. The website is www.nisbets.com and the telephone number is 0845 1405555.

TIP Should you decide to purchase any domestic items of equipment to use in your coffee shop kitchen, the retailer will not give you any guarantee. Therefore, unless the piece of equipment is inexpensive, and you don't mind replacing it when it stops working, you should always purchase commercial equipment.

FOOD THERMOMETER WITH PROBE

This is another essential piece of equipment because you will have to take the core temperature of any hot food, whether it is freshly cooked or reheated, to make sure that it has reached the correct temperature, 82°C for reheated food and 63°C for holding food hot (see page 103), before you serve it to your customers. You will also have to record the temperature of hot and reheated food twice a day on a temperature control chart.

You can purchase a basic food thermometer for as little as £9.99 and an Ecco Temp thermometer for £22.99 plus VAT.

COLOUR-CODED CHOPPING BOARDS

You will need to purchase chopping boards which are colour-coded so that bacteria are not transferred from one type of food to another. A good chopping board should not split or warp and you should be able to put it through the dishwasher.

☐ White is used for bakery and dairy food;

☐ Brown is used for vegetables;

☐ Green is used for salads and fruit;

☐ Blue is used for raw fish;

☐ Yellow is used for cooked meat;

☐ Red is used for raw meat.

The most economical way to purchase these boards is in a pack which contains one of each colour and a free stand which is approximately £30 including VAT. You can also purchase antibacterial high-density chopping boards which come in the same colours but are a bit more expensive, costing approximately £11.74 each including VAT. Extra boards can be purchased singly if required.

 It is a good idea to put up a wall chart to remind your staff what each board is to be used for.

SINK

You are required by the Environmental Health Department to have a large double sink installed.

WASH HAND BASIN

You have to have at least one wash hand basin installed because you are not allowed to use the sinks to wash your hands. The Environmental Health Officer will require you to supply antibacterial soap in a dispenser and paper towels for each hand sink. Paper towels are more hygienic than cloth towels which can spread bacteria from user to user.

RUBBISH BIN

A rubbish bin with a swing-top lid, conveniently placed in your kitchen, is a good idea as it is a nuisance having to take the lid off the bin every time you put rubbish in it. According to the Environmental Health Officer, you are not allowed to use a rubbish bin without a lid.

Do also put a smaller bin in the coffee shop for customers to put their rubbish in otherwise they will leave it on the table or drop it on the floor for your staff to pick up.

 Use a black bin liner as it keeps the bin cleaner and ask your staff to wash out the bin with disinfectant every night.

We have a Biffa Bin, which is a bin for commercial waste, placed outside at the back of the coffee shop and it is emptied every week. It would surprise you just how much is thrown away, especially empty drinks cans. If you find you have a lot of waste it would be worthwhile making enquiries from your local council about a Biffa Bin. There is a charge for emptying it.

MAGNETIC STRIP FOR KNIVES

You can put all your knives onto this strong magnetic strip, which makes it easier and quicker to choose the knife you want to use and also prevents blade damage. These are relatively cheap to buy, costing approximately £11 each including VAT.

ORDER STRIP

This is a strip which is fixed to the wall in the kitchen so that orders taken can be put directly onto it in the sequence in which the order is taken. This lets you see at a glance what orders have come into the kitchen, and if more than one person is preparing food, everyone knows which has to be prepared first.

FLY-KILLER

These are necessary for your kitchen and for the sitting area in your coffee shop. They are electrical units which are fixed to the wall or ceiling. They have a drawer beneath them which traps flies and insects. The drawer should be emptied of dead insects on a regular basis. They are supplied either wall- or ceiling-mounted and are available in various sizes. They cost from around £35.

OTHER KITCHEN EQUIPMENT YOU WILL NEED

Good heavy pots and a frying pan (you require a heavy base so that you don't burn soup when you are making it);

☐ A colander;

☐ Sieves;

☐ A good set of knives, including vegetable knife, bread knife, carving knife, chopping knife, palette knife;

☐ Whisks;

☐ Potato peelers;

☐ Wooden spoons;

☐ Slotted spoons;

☐ Large serving spoons;

☐ Tongs;

☐ Measuring spoons;

☐ Spatulas;

☐ Ladles;

☐ Kitchen scissors;

☐ Food scales (digital are better because they are more accurate for measuring small quantities);

☐ Baking trays (a few different sizes);

☐ Pastry brushes;

☐ Lemon zester;

☐ Mixing bowls (a few different sizes);

☐ Measuring jug;

☐ Plastic food storage containers.

TABLEWARE

White, rather than patterned, tableware is best. Food looks better on it and it's easier to replace. Try to get hardwearing tableware which is oven, microwave, dishwasher and freezer proof. You would be surprised how much crockery gets chipped and broken

You will need the following:

☐ Soup bowls;

☐ Tea plates;

☐ Medium-sized dinner plates;

☐ Large dinner plates (if you decide to increase your menu to include light meals);

☐ Salt and pepper pots (try to get containers that don't need to be filled every five minutes and that have good-fitting tops);

 Do get your staff to check the salt and pepper pots each night to ensure that the tops are tightly closed because some children loosen them for a joke.

We have had to replace a few meals because a child has loosened the top of one of the salt or pepper pots. Of course, when the next customer has used it, the whole pot has emptied over their meal.

☐ Small stainless steel milk jugs (this works out cheaper than supplying individual portions of milk);

☐ Large sugar dispensers for each table. They can be glass or plastic so that your staff can see when they need to be refilled. Free pour dispensers are best;

☐ Tumblers (for cold drinks) that can be chilled without breaking;

☐ Teapots for one and two people;

☐ Teacups and saucers;

☐ Tall café latte glasses for speciality coffees;

☐ Espresso cups and saucers;

☐ Cappuccino cups and saucers.

If you are going to offer two or three sizes of coffee you will have to purchase different-sized coffee cups and mugs.

Do make sure you get heavy-duty coffee mugs and cappuccino cups and saucers that won't break or chip easily. However, they must be inexpensive enough for you to be able to replace them when they get broken by your staff or customers.

 **A few coffee suppliers will supply you with mugs, espresso cups and saucers and cappuccino cups and saucers if you agree to purchase all your coffee from them. Ask the representative of your coffee supplier what perks they can offer you.**

CUTLERY

Good-quality plain stainless steel cutlery is best because it won't date, it will last longer and you can replace it easily.

☐ Knives;

☐ Forks;

☐ Soup spoons;

☐ Teaspoons.

It is surprising how many customers will just take your teaspoons home with them, and also how many will be thrown out by accident by your staff. If you find you are losing a lot of teaspoons you can buy plastic stirrers. My view is that plastic stirrers look tatty and although we lose about 100 teaspoons every year we still prefer them to the plastic disposable alternatives.

 Purchase the least expensive teaspoons you can find.

NAPKIN DISPENSERS

Despite the cost, it is advisable to purchase a napkin dispenser because it cuts down the number of napkins a customer will take at one time.

 You might want to place a sign beside the napkin dispenser asking your customers to take only the number of napkins they need.

CASH REGISTER

There are many different styles of cash register on the market and your choice depends on what you need it to do for you. We recently replaced our basic cash register with a sophisticated one which can tell you at the push of a button:

☐ how much money you take in a day, in any number of weeks, or in a year;

☐ the average spend per customer;

☐ how many of a particular item were sold in a day, in any number of weeks, or in a year.

This allows us to know which items are our best sellers and which are poor sellers, and other important sales information.

It is not necessary to have such a sophisticated cash register so do your homework and find one that will do everything you want it to do and will last you for a long time because they are not cheap. You can buy a simple cash register for about £100 but you could probably purchase a second-hand one for a fraction of the price.

 If you want to purchase, lease or just find out the price of items of equipment for your kitchen, look at the website for Nisbets who offer a quick delivery service for most items. They also offer a leasing service for some equipment. The website is www.nisbets.com and the telephone number is 0845 1405555. Also check your Yellow Pages and the internet for other suppliers as it is always better to shop around for the best price.

Buying furniture and fittings
TABLES

Do purchase tables that are easy to clean, whether they are made of wood, glass or Formica. If you decide to have tablecloths, remember that you will either have to wash them yourself each night or you will have to send them to the laundry, unless they are made from oilcloth and then you can just wipe them clean.

A coffee shop owner once informed me that if you send tablecloths to the laundry and submit this account against your income tax return, then the Inland Revenue can calculate how many tables you serve in the year. I'm not sure whether to believe this tale or not!

I knew someone who thought that marble tables would look great in his restaurant. Unfortunately though they stained easily and some of the stains were impossible to remove.

Consider having tables that seat two or four people; if you have a larger party you can always put two tables together. You will find that your customers are usually made up of two people or a family of four. Please don't put the tables too close together as people like some space and don't want to think that their neighbours are listening to everything they say.

CHAIRS

A comfortable chair is essential so choose the chairs for your coffee shop with care. Avoid straight, high-back chairs, bar stools and chairs that are very low and difficult to get out of. These are all very uncomfortable. Basket chairs and benches with padded cushions are relatively comfortable.

Before you make a purchase try out several chairs to see what you think is the most comfortable one. If you wouldn't like to sit on a chair for a period of time, neither will your customers.

Choose chairs that are well made and strong because you will find that customers will rock backwards and forwards on their chairs and you don't want to be sued if one collapses when someone is seated.

If you have sufficient space, it is prudent to keep a few extra chairs so that you can immediately replace any that become damaged or broken. Customers are not always careful with your furniture and they often allow their children to climb and stand on the chairs. In the current litigious culture customers could well try to sue you for damages if they are injured because of a broken or damaged chair.

HIGH CHAIRS

Do buy at least two high chairs because they are essential if you are going to be a child-friendly coffee shop and want to encourage parents and grandparents to come into your shop with their youngsters.

7
CHOOSING YOUR SUPPLIERS

Once you have decided what products you require, your next step is to choose suppliers for these products. If you can do this before you open, you will save valuable time that would be spent later, searching through the Yellow Pages and the internet. Ask other coffee shop or restaurant owners for advice in choosing suppliers because they will know, through experience, which ones to use and which ones to avoid.

Finding your food suppliers

Do make a list of what products you are going to require and then choose suppliers for these products. You will find out very quickly that you won't be able to obtain everything you need from one supplier.

Here are some of the suppliers you will require:

☐ **Baker** for fresh bread, rolls, croissants and cakes

☐ **Greengrocer** for fresh fruit and vegetables
You will require fresh vegetables for making soup and fresh salad ingredients for salad garnish and salads.

☐ **Milkman** for milk and cream
Full cream milk is necessary for making cappuccinos and you will require cream for cake fillings, making cheesecakes and to serve with apple pies etc.

☐ **Butcher** for ham, bacon, sausages, burgers and cold meats

☐ **Coffee beans and flavoured syrups** can be supplied by the company from which you lease or purchase your coffee machine.

☐ **Baking ingredients** can be purchased from a specialist company, e.g. Bako, or from the supermarket. However, you could check with your general supplier who may be able to supply you with these products.

☐ **General supplier** for frozen foods, including paninis, and run of the mill things like cheese, bacon, mayonnaise, sugar, salt, jam and butter portions and much more.

☐ You can also get a special oven on loan as long as you agree to purchase paninis and pastries from a well-known company but I think it is a very expensive way of providing this type of food.

☐ **Newsagent** – have a newsagent deliver daily papers and a few magazines for your customers to read while they are enjoying a coffee and cake in your shop.

 I find that frozen paninis are much better for our coffee shop because they can be taken out of the freezer in the morning and defrosted ready to use from mid morning. If you run out of defrosted paninis you can put them in the microwave and they will defrost in a few minutes.

As I mentioned previously, you can find suppliers' names from asking other coffee shop or restaurant owners or by looking through your local Yellow Pages. Don't be afraid to ask other coffee shop owners where they buy their fruit and vegetables, bread, cakes, etc. If they don't want to give you this information they can always say no.

I asked a coffee shop owner from another town who he bought his produce from and he was good enough to give me a list of his suppliers. This was a great help to me and it does show that some people are only too willing to help someone new to the business.

Take into account the suppliers' reputation, the quality and price of their products, their delivery times and reliability. You don't want to be still waiting for your fresh milk, morning rolls and bread to be delivered after opening time.

ESTABLISHING A RAPPORT WITH YOUR SUPPLIERS

It is important to establish a good relationship with your suppliers because they can be very helpful. For example, if you forget to order a product and they have a few extra on their delivery van they will usually give them to you to help you out. They will also know what products sell well and can recommend that you try them out, or they may even give you a few free samples to try.

Ask a sales representative to meet you to discuss their company's terms and conditions. You may also want to ask some of the following:

☐ Can they give you a printout of the products they can supply and the prices they are going to charge you for them? You can compare price lists with those of other companies.

☐ Do they give discount for larger orders?

☐ How often do they deliver to your area?

☐ What time of day will they deliver to your shop?

☐ What time does the order have to be telephoned in to them for next-day delivery?

☐ Do they have an answering machine for taking orders out of business hours?

> *Occasionally I have remembered an item I had forgotten to order during the day and I have left a message on the answering machine after midnight for the order to be delivered the following day.*

Will they give you the names and contact numbers of a few of their other customers so that you can get a reference from them? Suppliers are usually keen to do business with you and if they have nothing to hide they will be only too glad to give you this information.

Always be polite to the sales reps on the phone, and when they visit your coffee shop you could offer them a cup of coffee while you discuss business with them. This will help build up a good relationship with the supplier.

If you can obtain a product from another supplier at a cheaper price, inform the representative of your normal supplier and they will usually agree to reduce their price or match the other supplier's price.

ASKING FOR CREDIT

Initially you won't get credit from suppliers until you make an application for credit and you are able to supply them with trade references. If you are starting a new business, more than likely you won't have any credit references and in that case the suppliers usually like you to pay cash on delivery for a certain period of time. Once you have done this for the time specified you should then be able to apply for credit. Having credit accounts will give you time to pay your bills but make sure you pay your suppliers on time as they also need to pay their bills.

If you don't have any trade references, ask your suppliers if you can use personal credit references including a reference from your bank. If they won't allow this then you should respect their decision because they are only protecting themselves against bad debts.

Do type out a list of products so that you can use this list each time you place an order. For example, you can put a number or a tick beside each item you require and, when you telephone your order, you just have to read it off the list. Some suppliers have ordering forms you can use and if this is the case ask them for a good supply or photocopy a good amount for yourself.

Make sure that you state clearly when you telephone your order whether you require one case or one box as a case consists of a number of boxes.

Some orders you will have to get daily, and probably before you open in the morning, for example, milk, bread, rolls and fresh vegetables. If you are buying in cakes, scones and tray bakes, you will also have to have these delivered before you open for business.

We don't have a lot of freezer space so we usually get our frozen products delivered as we need them. The benefit of this is that our frozen products are down to the last few before we replace them.

We are very lucky in that our main supplier delivers six days a week.

Ask the baker who is supplying your rolls and bread to give you samples of other special breads and rolls. This way you can try various different types before you decide to place an order for any of them. The baker should also give you samples of cakes if you are not going to bake your own.

Try to get other orders delivered at a time when the coffee shop is quieter so as not to disrupt business. You will also want to put away the food immediately, especially if you have some frozen and refrigerated items in your delivery.

CHECKING YOUR ORDER

When your order arrives, always check it carefully, no matter how busy you are, to verify that everything you ordered has arrived. Tick items off the delivery note before you sign it because if the delivery person is in a hurry, they could leave something on the van in error.

Do always check the use by dates on each item and if anything is unacceptable in terms of quality, out of date, has a short lifespan, or is partially defrosted, then send it back at the time of delivery. Mark clearly on the delivery note why it is being returned and ask for a replacement. Once you have signed the delivery note you have accepted the order and it would be very difficult then to go back and complain to the supplier.

Never be tempted to use inferior produce because you think it is too much trouble to send it back, or because you don't want to upset your supplier.

If you are not satisfied with the freshness of the produce you receive, you can always change suppliers. However, most suppliers are keen to keep your business and they are very careful about what they deliver.

Buying from supermarkets

Sometimes it is cheaper and more convenient to purchase some of your stock from a supermarket.

☐ You don't have to buy in large amounts or large packages or jars;

☐ You can place your order online in the evening to save time at work;

☐ You can have it delivered for a small charge, or free if you place a large order;

☐ You can purchase more unusual items;

☐ The produce is usually fresh.

> *When we first opened our coffee shop we bought almost everything from a local supermarket because we did not know the quantities we would use, and for us this was the best way. I would go to the supermarket in the morning before opening the coffee shop and get what I thought we required for the day. This, however, was time-consuming and expensive so, over time, I gradually ordered most of the goods from suppliers and settled for a single order delivered from the supermarket once a week.*

Using a cash and carry

If you have a 'cash and carry' outlet in your area do go and look around and compare prices and products. They are handy if your supplier has run out of a product you require immediately. Sometimes too they have more unusual products which you may like to try out.

The downside of using a cash and carry is the time it takes out of your day or evening. Remember, you will have to walk around the various aisles choosing products and then, after you have paid for them, you have to load up your car. You are not finished even then because you have to unload the goods at the coffee shop and put everything away in its place.

You will probably have to buy in bulk; for example, a case of baked beans or a case of mayonnaise. If you don't have the storage space, or if you are not going to be able to use the whole case before the use by date, don't be tempted to buy this way.

The benefit of most cash and carry units is that they are usually open from early in the morning until late at night. Despite this, I would recommend that, if you are going to use the cash and carry, you try to use it only once a week.

Handling food safely

FROZEN FOOD

Put frozen products away first, placing them beneath older items in your freezer, because you need to rotate your stock and use the food in date order. Stock rotation is important, not only to maintain quality and freshness, but also because of waste. You don't want to have to throw away products that have been buried for months under newer stock and then you find they are out of date.

If you are getting a delivery from the butcher, ask them to put labels with the date onto each item before it is delivered to you.

REFRIGERATED FOOD

Next, put your refrigerated products away and again move the older items to the front of the fridge with use by dates visible so that they are easily seen by the staff.

BREAD

If you are going to store bread, to retain freshness it must always be frozen immediately and not kept in the fridge.

Try to have your bread and rolls delivered daily, especially when you are using them for sandwiches. If you have to use bread that has been frozen it is best used for toasted sandwiches and toast.

CANS AND DRIED FOODS

Store these in dry cupboards, and remember to rotate your stock with the earliest sell by date at the front of the shelves. Put your drink cans into the chiller cabinet and again remember to rotate your stock.

Once a can of food has been opened, never put the contents into the fridge still in the can; always empty the contents into a clean container, cover, and then put into the fridge.

8
EMPLOYING STAFF

It is very important to choose your staff with care. Ideally, you want to employ someone who is going to be an asset to your business. You want staff who will smile and be friendly towards customers, and who are honest and reliable. If you find someone good you can train them to be great.

Once you have found your ideal recruit you are obliged to provide them with an employment contract. It is likely that your staff will be employed on a full-time or part-time basis – I have included in Appendices 1-3 examples of employment contracts for:

☐ full-time staff;

☐ part-time staff;

☐ part-time (weekend) staff.

These contract documents reflect what I use in my coffee shop. You will of course have to tailor them to meet your own unique requirements.

Deciding how many staff you need

You will simply not be able to do everything yourself and you will have to consider employing someone to help you. You can begin by getting one full-time person and one or two part-time workers. The part-time workers may be interested in working full time when the need arises but in the meantime you will know how many workers you will require to work certain hours during the day, e.g. during lunchtime between 12 noon and 2 p.m.

Do not employ too many staff to begin with because it will be very difficult to terminate someone's employment if you find that business is slow. Only when your coffee shop gets busier should you think about employing other workers.

 If you employ a worker part-time and their wage is under £100 per week they will not have to pay income tax or national insurance contributions.

Employing immigrants

More people are coming from Europe to seek work in the UK. If you are considering employing one of these people, you need to ensure that he or she has the right to work here.

All citizens of the European Union have the right to come to the UK but not all of them necessarily have the right to work in the UK! You should check the applicant's documents before the person starts work. If the person has the right to work in the UK, they will be able to produce the following documents:

☐ a passport confirming that the applicant is a British citizen;

☐ a document giving the applicant's National Insurance number, plus their full UK birth certificate;

☐ a passport or identity card of an EEA (European Economic Area) national.

If the applicant is from Romania or Bulgaria they will require more evidence of their right to work.

Since January 2007, when Romania and Bulgaria joined the EU, people from these two countries have been allowed to come into the UK without visas but they are not permitted to work in the UK without a Work Authorization Document. Similar restrictions apply to non-EU immigrants.

It is a criminal offence to employ anyone who is not entitled to work in the UK. Therefore, it is essential that you ensure that the person you are considering employing has the right to work in this country.

There is a penalty of £10,000 for each person you employ who is an unregistered worker from any of the following countries:

Latvia, Slovakia, Poland, Czech Republic, Lithuania, Slovenia, Estonia and Hungary.

If you employ a worker from any of these countries you must make sure they have the right to work in this country by checking their EEA (European Economic Area) passport or identity card. You must then advise the worker to complete an application form and send it, along with evidence of their employment, to the Home Office to register immediately they start work.

If you are considering employing someone from Europe, do contact the Home Office to get up-to-date information on recruitment and immigration. A list of acceptable documents to confirm the right to work in the UK is available from the Home Office website, www.homeoffice.gov.uk or, for more information, you can ring the Home Office Employers' Helpline on 0845 010 6677.

Recruiting your staff

Finding the right staff is very important because they represent your business. Good staff can help you to create a warm, welcoming atmosphere in your coffee shop. Poor staff on the other hand can scare away your customers. So give yourself plenty of time to find staff before you open your coffee shop.

ADVERTISING IN YOUR LOCAL NEWSPAPER

Placing an advert in your local newspaper is a good way of finding staff because all jobseekers read the vacancy pages in their newspaper. Also you tend to attract local people who don't have to travel far to their employment. This is an advantage if you require staff to work at short notice – for instance, if another member of staff has telephoned in sick.

The wording of your advertisement is crucial in attracting the right person for the job, so make sure you get it right.

Some things to consider when writing a job advertisement

☐ Keep it short and simple (you will be charged by the line);

☐ Give the name and address of your coffee shop and include your logo if you have one;

☐ State the job title and the type of person you are looking for, e.g. experienced, friendly, outgoing;

☐ State the hours required and if you want the employee to cover holidays, sickness, etc.;

☐ Give the starting date;

☐ Include details on how to reply and to whom and the closing date for applications.

 Although you are trying to keep your advertisement short, try to make it interesting enough so that if you were to read it yourself, you would be tempted to apply for the job.

ADVERTISING IN YOUR OWN SHOP

This is an inexpensive way of finding staff. You could display a notice inside the shop and another on the window asking people to apply for the position. You will be able to customize your own application form and ask all people who are interested in the job to complete one. You will want them to answer specific questions which should include the names and contact numbers of referees.

 Always check the references of anyone you are considering for a job because you would be surprised how many people lie about their previous employment.

> *I interviewed a potential member of staff who informed me that he had baked all the cakes, tray bakes and gateaux in his previous employment. However, when I checked with the owner of that particular coffee shop, I was informed that he had never heard of the person and he had certainly not been employed there.*

USING THE JOB CENTRE

This is a free national service and it is underused by companies. Sometimes you can be lucky and get a really good, experienced candidate through this service. However, I have discovered that the majority of applications you get are from candidates who don't fit your profile. Do ask the person taking details of the vacancy from you not to give application forms to anyone who does not fulfil the criteria you have set. Quite often the Job Centre will give application forms to people who are not really interested in your job but they must make applications or attend interviews in order to continue to qualify for benefits. Often they don't turn up for an interview if you do contact them.

CONTACTING YOU LOCAL COLLEGE

You could contact your local college and ask the catering department if they know anyone suitable who might be interested in a job in your shop. If they don't know anyone at that time, type out an interesting advert, send it to the college and ask if they would display it on the college notice board.

USING AN AGENCY

Don't contact an agency unless you are really desperate as this can be a very costly way of finding staff.

> *We nearly employed a young man who was recommended by an agency. Before we did so, we checked his references from his previous employer and discovered that he had been given the sack because he allegedly put cannabis into the lasagne he was making. I was surprised that the agency hadn't checked his references before taking him on as a client.*

WORD OF MOUTH

Once your coffee shop has opened you can often attract good staff by word of mouth via friends and customers. However, it is not always a good thing to employ a friend of a friend because if things don't work out it can be awkward.

THE NEW DEAL SCHEME

New Deal is a key part of the Government's Welfare to Work strategy. It aims to give unemployed people new opportunities to train and gain work experience, and to help businesses that have staff shortages.

Everyone taking part in New Deal has a personal adviser who provides support and arranges training, if required, before the person is ready to be employed. By the time the candidate is presented to you they should be employable because they have been through a skills assessment and, where necessary, given training to update their skills to prepare them for work. Support is provided to the employer after the person has started work.

Financial help is also given to the employer through an employment subsidy.

The Government New Deal Schemes are constantly changing and you should go to the Directgov website for up-to-date information at www.direct.gov.co.uk

For age 18 –24 the New Deal Scheme is still in existence unless you live in an area where the Flexible New Deal applies. There is also a New Deal Scheme for people aged 25 – 60 which is called New Deal 25 Plus. However, again if you live in an area where Flexible New Deal applies, you will have to take part in this scheme.

Under the New Deal Scheme, if someone is out of work for a set period, an employer will be subsidised for taking that person on. This subsidy lasts for 6 months but you may be able to employ this person after if you think they are suitable for the job.

You will be asked to sign an agreement confirming that you will:

☐ keep the person for as long as they show the ability and commitment you need;

☐ give them the same training as anyone else doing the job;

☐ monitor and record their progress and identify the areas for action, in the same way you would for any other employee, to help them settle in and make progress;

☐ employ them for at least 26 weeks;

☐ fill in a health and safety questionnaire to ensure that your business meets certain standards.

For more information or to place a vacancy you can contact the Job Centre Plus on www.jobcentreplus.gov.uk/employers or telephone 0845 601 2001.

WORK TRIALS

Fill in the gaps in your business and utilise cost-effective staffing and government support. You can offer volunteer places while providing work experience and apprenticeships by taking on a young person for a work trial.

Work trials allow you to find out if a person is suited to the job you are offering and it also lets the person see if it is the right job for them.

A person has to have been out of work for at least six months. They will continue to receive benefit, travel expenses and a meal allowance while they are on trial.

Again you will have to sign an agreement and fill in a health and safety questionnaire.

You will have to employ the person for 16 or more hours per week.

For more information or to place a vacancy you can contact the Job Centre Plus on www.jobcentreplus.gov.uk/employers or telephone 0845 601 2001.

BACK TO WORK

There is a Government-funded scheme to help support people back into work who have been out of work for a set period of time. The programme gives them an opportunity to gain work experience and training.

You are required to offer the worker an opportunity to gain experience in the workplace and they are paid by the government so they have an incentive to work. They are technically supposed to be surplus to the core workforce and they will be paid by the government for 20 hours a week for six months.

You can assess the worker over the six-month period with a view to employing them yourself on a permanent basis, or you can apply for another worker through the scheme. During the six-month period you can part company with the worker if you think they are not suitable for your business. Before you take part in this scheme your business will have to be assessed against a health and safety checklist and you will have to agree to some basic requirements.

To enquire about obtaining staff through a Government-funded scheme, contact your local Job Centre Plus or Employer Direct. They will get a labour market adviser to contact you with the information available for the type of person you wish to employ. You can get in touch with Employer Direct from Monday to Friday, 8 a.m. until 8 p.m. and Saturday, 10 a.m. until 4 p.m. The telephone number is 0845 601 2001.

SKILLSEEKERS

Skillseekers is only available in Scotland and the training is funded by the government.

The employer has to pay the Skillseeker an allowance of a minimum of £55 per week (it is up to the employer if they want to pay more) and the Government funds the training. The Skillseeker usually works four days a week and spends one day a week at a college or approved training supplier who will provide and manage the training.

To talk through options and find out more, contact the Careers Scotland Centre on 0845 8502502; your local Enterprise Agency; or Skills Development Scotland, 150 Broomielaw, Atlantic Quay, Glasgow, G2 8LU. Their website is www.skillsdevelopmentscotland.co.uk and their email address is info@skillsdevelopment.co.uk

In England the Modern Apprenticeship is a similar scheme. It is up to the employer what they pay the employee and there is no minimum allowance. Again the training is Government-funded and the employee is expected to work four days a week and attend college for training one day a week.

For further information and advice telephone 08000 150 400 or check out the website, www.employersforapprenticeships.gov.uk

The Learning and Skills Council find and manage apprenticeships in England. Their website is www.apprenticeships.org.uk

STUDENTS

Students are usually interested in earning extra pocket money but they are only available at weekends or during school, college or university holidays. They are generally good workers and you can find them by contacting local schools, colleges and universities and asking them to display an advertisement on their notice board.

The downside of employing a student is that they are often out late on a Friday night with their friends and there is a chance that they will phone in sick on a Saturday morning. This of course is the time you need them most.

Interviewing prospective employees

The interview is your opportunity to assess each candidate carefully and make sure you pick the right person for the job. It can be a daunting task so it essential to prepare well in advance.

DEFINING THE JOB

Before the interview you should prepare a job description form and show this to the candidate. It should be succinct and cover the key features of the job. (I have included a one-page pro forma in Appendix 4.)

When you have made a job offer, and the candidate has accepted this, they should sign the form to say that they have read it and agree to carry out the duties detailed on it. You should then give them a copy and keep a copy on file. You can refer to this if, in the future, the member of staff complains that 'That's not my job'.

PREPARING YOUR QUESTIONS

It is essential to prepare a list of questions that you want to ask candidates at interview so that you keep the discussions on track. Don't be tempted to make up the questions as you go along as you won't find out the details you really want to know. Print out your list of questions and leave enough room on the paper to make concise notes during the interview. Don't try to write down everything that is said; you won't be able to concentrate on the interview. Wait until after the interview, then write down your impressions while they are still fresh in your mind. Leave at least 15 minutes between interviews to allow you to complete your notes for each candidate.

At the end of each interview staple the interview questionnaire to the job application or Curriculum Vitae so that you have all the information to hand about each candidate when you come to make your decision.

CONDUCTING THE INTERVIEW

Ask the applicants to come for an interview at a specific time, and allow half an hour for each appointment. Set aside a period of time, say 4 p.m. to 6 p.m. on a quiet day, so that you are not rushed. Set up the interview in a comfortable place and try to create a relaxed atmosphere to allow the candidates to feel at ease. Do your best to ensure that you are not interrupted during the interviews, either by the telephone ringing or by other members of staff.

You should begin the interview by telling the applicant a bit about your business and describing the duties involved in the job, the working hours and the wages. Point out any perks that go with the job – for example, how the tips are divided, any discount on food and drink in the coffee shop, or a free lunch during working hours.

The questions you ask should be designed to find out if candidates have the skills and qualities required for the job, so use open questions – those that begin with the words how, why, where, when, what, etc. – to encourage candidates to talk.

As well as asking the right questions, you need to have good listening skills so that you are able to interpret what is being said and, if necessary, tease out anything you feel is being withheld.

Summarize from time to time during the interview, to clarify what information you have obtained, and then move on to another topic.

Questions you should ask

☐ Do they have any relevant work experience and what do they think they can bring to the job?

☐ What do they think their strengths and weaknesses are?

☐ What did they enjoy most about their previous job?

☐ How do they react to criticism?

☐ How did they get on with their previous employer?

☐ What was their reason for leaving their previous job? (If aspects of their previous job that they didn't like are present in the job you are offering, this will cause problems – for example, if someone didn't like being told what to do, or they didn't like having to work at weekends, you are certainly going to have problems.)

Something which I found useful was to ask the candidate what they would do in a particular scenario, for example, if a customer complained that his coffee wasn't served hot enough, or he was given the wrong filling in his sandwich.

How many days have they had off work for sickness in the last two years? (You don't want to employ someone who is in the habit of taking days off on a regular basis.)

What do they expect from the job?

At the end of the interview ask the candidate if there are any questions they would like to ask you about the job. Remember to enquire if they have any holidays booked, when they can start working for you and, if they are presently working, what notice they have to give their employers.

You should ask if they have any doubts about this position and if they still wish to be considered for it now that they have heard what is expected of them.

> *Someone I know always drops a piece of paper on the floor when he is showing a candidate into the room for their interview, to see if they pick it up. He maintains that it says a lot about whether a person is tidy or not.*

Questions you are not allowed to ask
It is illegal to discriminate on grounds of:

Race
- You cannot ask questions on ethnic background or country of origin.

Sex
- You cannot ask someone if they are planning to start a family and then use an affirmative answer as a reason for not employing them.

Disability
- You cannot use a person's disability as a reason not to employ them unless you can justify this.

Dismissing staff

This can be one of your most difficult tasks. It is somewhat unfair, and an oversimplification, to suggest that you can avoid the necessity of dismissing an employee if you take care in selecting your staff in the first place, and in training, cajoling and guiding them thereafter. Occasionally you may have a member of staff who is either just not capable of discharging their tasks or through stubbornness believes that your rules are for others and not for themselves.

Running a coffee shop with a very small staff may not be in the same league as running a large manufacturing organization with thousands of employees but the relationship between you and your staff is essentially the same.

Should the situation arise when you feel that staff behaviour has crossed the line such that you have no alternative but to dismiss the employee, then it is essential that you follow the statutory disciplinary and dismissal procedure (DDPs) in precisely the same way as the manager of the large manufacturing organization would.

You and your staff will deal directly with the public and you have a duty of care for the public's safety and health. So the responsibilities of your staff must not be trivialized and should they fall short then you must take appropriate action.

You must know what to do before the situation arises – you will not have time to read the literature once you are faced with a volatile situation that could lead to a dismissal.

The Employment Act (Dispute Resolution) is updated from time to time so it is useful to familiarize yourself with the up-to-date advice on resolving disputes from the Department of Trade and Industry: see www.dti.gov.uk/er/resolvingdisputes.htm

There is plenty of literature to help you. The text which follows is a fairly loose extraction from some of this freely available literature and as such forms a summary of the main rules which you must follow. There is also an excellent and fairly succinct fact sheet by Cobweb Information Ltd which is available from www.scavenger.net for a small fee.

WHEN YOU MAY DISMISS AN EMPLOYEE

You may dismiss an employee for:

☐ misconduct;

☐ inability to perform;

☐ redundancy;

☐ other substantial reasons.

Misconduct

Dismissing an employee for misconduct is usually the most straightforward of all dismissal situations – but only if you have prepared the way by having the necessary rules in place for your business.

Write down clear, reasonable rules and procedures. They should include:

☐ an explanation of which are disciplinary offences;

☐ what procedures will be followed if an employee commits a disciplinary offence, (these procedures must now be at least as good as the statutory minimum);

☐ which offences provide grounds for summary dismissal;

☐ what rights of representation and appeal the employees have.

Make employees aware of the rules.

☐ Give each employee a copy of the rules and explain them. It is difficult to discipline employees for breaking rules they are not aware of.

☐ You are legally required either to include the rules and procedures in your written terms of employment or to make it plain where a copy is available.

Most offences will lead to a series of oral and written warnings before any dismissal.

☐ Investigate the circumstances of the offence before taking any formal action.

☐ Typically, you might give an employee one spoken warning and two written warnings before dismissal. Spoken warnings will often be removed from an employee's disciplinary record after six months, and written warnings after 12 months (if there are no further disciplinary offences).

☐ A formal warning should include a time limit within which you expect improvement, and an explanation of the consequences otherwise.

☐ Apply the rules fairly and consistently. An employee who can show that you applied the rules inconsistently may be able to claim unfair dismissal.

☐ Keep written records of all disciplinary action you take. Include a record of any steps you have taken to investigate and address the cause of the problem.

☐ All employees have the right to be accompanied by a colleague or trade union official at any disciplinary hearing.

☐ Remind employees of their right to explain their conduct or suggest counter-proposals.

'Gross misconduct' can provide grounds for summary dismissal, but the statutory procedure must still be followed.

☐ Gross misconduct typically includes theft, fighting or physical assault, drunkenness or drug-taking, wilful damage to company property, and intentional or reckless disregard for safety rules.

☐ In most cases the standard procedure involves three steps which must be followed: a written explanation of the problem, a face-to-face meeting, and an opportunity for the employee to appeal.

☐ In exceptional circumstances, you might be justified in using a 'modified', two-step procedure – a written explanation of the problem, with details of why you think the employee is the guilty party, and an opportunity for them to appeal.

Employees have the right to appeal against all disciplinary decisions, including dismissal. Give employees the appropriate notice, unless they have been summarily dismissed.

You must provide written reasons for the dismissal. You are legally required to do this:

☐ within 14 days of a written request from an employee who has completed at least one year's continuous employment;

☐ whenever you dismiss an employee who is pregnant or on maternity leave, and regardless of how long she has worked for you.

Inability to perform

It is most unlikely that you should need to dismiss someone in your coffee shop for this reason. If you fail to identify such a problem with a candidate at interview, then normally anyone who is incompetent will be discovered fairly soon thereafter. They can then be dismissed without running such a high risk of a claim for unfair dismissal.

There are four 'permitted' reasons for dismissing employees who are unable to perform their jobs, though presumably only the first two will apply to your coffee shop worker:

☐ Incompetence (lacking the skills or aptitude to carry out duties effectively):

☐ Sickness or injury (usually associated with frequent or prolonged absenteeism, although a long-term sickness or injury may qualify as a disability);

☐ Lack of relevant academic, technical or professional qualifications;

☐ Because it would be illegal for the employee to carry on working in the job (for example, if the employee loses the required driving licence).

You must be able to demonstrate that you acted fairly and reasonably, both in deciding to dismiss and in the way you did it.

☐ Was the employee really unable to perform or was this an excuse for dismissal? For example, has the employee worked satisfactorily in the past?

☐ Did you (where needed) provide appropriate support or training?

☐ Did you investigate the circumstances fully?

☐ Did you consider alternative options?

☐ Did you set out your concerns in writing, give the employee time to consider them, then discuss them with the employee?

☐ Did you ensure that the employee knew about his or her right to appeal?

Redundancy

You may dismiss an employee because their job has become redundant; if, for example, you downsize your shop.

Other reasons

You may dismiss a member of staff for 'some other substantial reason'; for example, a refusal to co-operate with a generally accepted change in working practices. You may also dismiss a temporary replacement once the permanent employee returns to work (e.g. after maternity leave).

WHEN IT IS UNFAIR OR UNLAWFUL TO DISMISS AN EMPLOYEE

There are a number of reasons for which it will be deemed unfair or indeed unlawful to dismiss an employee.

It is an inadmissible reason to dismiss any employee for:

☐ being pregnant, giving birth or taking advantage of statutory maternity rights;

☐ pointing out or reacting to imminent risks to health and safety;

☐ membership (or non-membership) of a trade union;

☐ questioning or challenging your apparent disregard for statutory employment rights;

☐ reporting superiors or colleagues for illegal or dangerous activities ('whistleblowing');

☐ jury service;

☐ to facilitate the sale of your business.

It is unlawful to dismiss any employee on the grounds of:

☐ sex or marital status;

☐ race, nationality or national or ethnic origins;

☐ sexual orientation, actual or perceived;

☐ disability;

☐ religion or philosophical belief.

Some employers assume that if their employees have not been employed by them for 12 months, they can terminate their employment without being sued for unfair dismissal. That assumption is only partly right and it is risky to rely on it.

Some dismissals are classed as 'automatically unfair', even if the employer acted reasonably at the time of the dismissal and there is no length of service issue. If the employer dismisses an employee for one of these reasons that employee has the right to bring a claim against the employer. There are quite a number of reasons deemed as 'automatically unfair' and I have listed only a few of them below. It is always wise to check out the most up-to-date law. The reasons include:

☐ pregnancy or any reason connected with maternity;

☐ taking, or seeking to take, parental leave, paternity leave, adoption leave or time off for dependants;

☐ failure to return from maternity leave or adoption leave because the employer did not give any, or gave inadequate, notice of when the leave period should end;

☐ refusing or proposing to refuse to do shop work on a Sunday;

☐ grounds relating to the national minimum wage;

☐ grounds relating to Working Tax Credit;

☐ grounds relating to jury service.

If an employee can show that their dismissal was discriminatory under any of the relevant discrimination acts then they can sue their employer for unfair dismissal even though they have not been in continuous employment for 12 months. In this case the compensation claim can be increased as a result of the employer's failure to follow the statutory dismissal procedure.

The best advice I was given before I started my coffee shop was never to attempt to dismiss anyone while 'my blood was hot'.

Even in circumstances where the employee's behaviour is clearly gross misconduct and lays them open to immediate dismissal, this should still not be done without following the formal procedure and without carrying out an investigation into the incident in question. It would be best to suspend the employee (on full pay) while an investigation takes place and invite them in writing to attend a formal hearing, prior to making a decision. Don't forget that all employees have the right to appeal.

Don't make hasty decisions

Even at this meeting you should not inform the employee of your intent to dismiss them. This is because a very quick decision may make it look as if you had made up your mind before hearing their side of the story. It is always best to take 24 hours after the final meeting to go over the information that you have, and any additional information that has been supplied by the employee in the meeting, before you make a decision.

The other advice I was given was to seek the help of a specialist consultant if the grounds for dismissal might appear a touch shaky!

9
TRAINING YOUR STAFF

Proper staff training is the key to your success.

It is essential, for the success and the safe running of your business, that your staff all know why and how a job has to be done. Good training helps them to give quality service, and to reduce the number of accidents in the workplace.

It is also necessary for your staff's well-being that you help them develop their potential and improve their skills. If they can do their jobs well they will have greater job satisfaction.

Training staff on the job

When you find someone you think is a suitable employee you should arrange to train them on the job. This can be done by yourself or, if you have a particularly competent employee, he or she can do it for you. In-house training ensures that your standards are instilled from the beginning and you can judge how well your new employee works.

Do consider the following when training your staff:

☐ Put the employee at ease so that they feel comfortable with you.

☐ Ask what they already know about the job.

☐ Give them an explanation, a demonstration, and practise with each task.

Sometimes, if you are training staff to take orders and wait on tables, role-playing is helpful. First the member of staff plays the part of the customer and you take their order. You then reverse the roles and you become the customer and ask the trainee to take the order.

☐ Before you move on to the next step, make sure that what you have shown the trainee has been understood – if not, show them again.

☐ Ask your employee to try to do the task themselves. Again, if they are having problems with it, repeat your demonstration slowly.

☐ Encourage them to ask questions if they are not sure about anything.

☐ Be prepared to answer questions accurately and, if you don't know all the answers, admit it and promise to find out. Try to anticipate the sort of questions you may be asked, so that you will have your answers ready.

☐ Never ask an employee to do something that you wouldn't do yourself.

☐ Treat each employee as an individual.

☐ It is a good idea to send members of staff to a local college for basic environmental health training. This will give them useful knowledge about hygiene and safe handling of food. They will also be awarded a certificate, which will instil in them a sense of pride and achievement.

USING AN OUTSIDE AGENCY

You don't have to offer in-house training as there are agencies that undertake training on a day-release basis. Contact your local authority or local college for information.

Compiling a staff manual

An idea is to write a staff manual which you can print out and then give a copy to each new member of staff before they start work. Make sure they do read it. If you have two members of staff starting at the same time, one way of reinforcing the contents of the manual is to ask them a few questions on it or have a quiz. This might be daunting for one member of staff alone, so instead you could ask them if they have any questions on the manual or if they need anything clarified.

An advantage of using a staff manual is that it ensures that all your staff have the same basic level of understanding. This is very important if you want to give high-quality service to your customers.

A copy of the staff handbook which I used in my coffee shop can be found in Appendix 5. My staff manual was fairly formal and included procedures and consequences in relation to:

☐ sexual harassment;

☐ bullying;

☐ drug and alcohol abuse;

☐ bad timekeeping;

☐ failure to show up for work;

☐ procedures for disciplining a member of staff;

☐ all regulations and guidelines employees should know.

You may wish to consider some of these when compiling your own manual or handbook.

Your manual should include the following:

Timekeeping: This is very important; if one member of staff comes in late on a regular basis it causes discontent with other employees. Staff should be ready to start work with their aprons on at 9 a.m. and not just arriving at 9 a.m.

Cleanliness and appearance: Everything you need to know about cleanliness is detailed in the Environmental Health Office manual. This is available from your local authority (see page 96). Include the form of dress required and the importance of tying back long hair.

Professional behaviour: Impress upon staff the importance of constant awareness of one's responsibilities when dealing with both the public and colleagues.

General care: After clearing dirty dishes from a table, the table should always be wiped with a spray cleaner and covered with a clean cloth ready for the next customer. If staff are clearing a table where a customer is still sitting, they should ask them first of all if they are finished and then if they would like the member of staff to get them anything else.

Staff should wipe down the chairs and make sure that they clean all rubbish from the floor.

They should examine sugar dispensers and salt and pepper pots to make sure they are not empty and the lids are securely screwed on.

Following up training

Remember that staff require ongoing training as they sometimes pick up bad habits and these should be corrected before they are passed on to new members of staff.

Review your staff performance every three or four months. This will help them to stay motivated and to continue to give your customers excellent service.

Teaching staff how to generate good customer relations

Your staff must learn the art of greeting a customer in a way that makes the customer feel valued and special. Staff should acknowledge their customer no matter how busy they are. As well as giving a verbal greeting, they should smile and make eye contact. A warm, genuine smile that reaches their eyes as well as their mouth will show the customer that he or she is important to the staff.

HOW YOUR STAFF CAN HELP YOUR BUSINESS

You want your staff to increase the amount of money the customer spends in your coffee shop by making a suggestion or a recommendation. For example, when taking an order for coffee, your staff could try to promote an item by asking the customer if he or she would like to try today's special sandwich or one of the newly baked scones which are just out of the oven and still hot. This is important to the success of your business and you will lose money if your staff don't take these opportunities.

The attitude of your staff plays an important part in building and maintaining your business. If they appear happy and enthusiastic and give great service the customer will be won over and will return to your coffee shop. Respect your staff and praise them when they work well and they will become one of your most effective forms of public relations.

Dealing with difficult customers

Sometimes, despite the best efforts of the staff, a customer may complain about something he or she is not happy with. You will have to be diplomatic in this type of situation and although you may often think that the problem is not your fault, you will on most occasions have to let the customer win. An unhappy customer will tell an average of 10 people about his or her experience. You want to ensure that your customers leave with a positive impression of your coffee shop.

TURNING THE SITUATION TO YOUR ADVANTAGE

Customers are looking for quality service and if you do not provide this you will risk losing them and may eventually lose your business. However, in some cases you can turn a complaint into something positive by listening to the complaint and learning from it. You will also feel a sense of satisfaction if you can solve your customer's complaint satisfactorily.

Some difficult customers you may encounter are:

- the angry customer who is upset and emotional about the incident;

- the demanding customer who is insisting that something be done immediately;

- the intimidating customer who is showing hostility by talking loudly, making sarcastic remarks and perhaps pointing a finger at a member of staff.

Different as they are, all these customers feel that they have been wronged and they are upset and emotional about it.

DEFUSING THE SITUATION

First of all ask your customer to move to a quiet place in the coffee shop and instruct your staff not to interrupt you. Then try to defuse the situation by:

- staying calm and not losing your temper;

- letting your customer talk;

- listening to what they have to say;

- gathering information;

- not taking the complaints personally.

Stay calm and listen

Listen carefully to what your customer has to say without interrupting and at the same time try to read their body language. Allow them to air their feelings and get rid of some of their anger. Don't say anything in return; instead just nod occasionally and make eye contact to show that you are listening and paying attention to them. Remember that your body language will also convey to the customer how you are feeling so don't stand with your hands on your hips in a confrontational manner. Watch the tone of your voice, too.

Put yourself in your customer's shoes

Put yourself in your customer's shoes and say that you understand how they feel about the incident, although you don't have to agree with them. Summarize in your own words what you understand the problem to be, and be sincere because you don't want your customer to feel as if you are patronizing them. This lets your customer know that you have been listening to what they have said. When the customer sees that you care about the problem they will probably begin to calm down.

Don't blame anyone for the incident or mistake.

RESOLVING THE PROBLEM

Learn as much as possible about the situation before you attempt to find a solution. When you have gathered all the information you need you can begin to resolve the problem. Your customer will appreciate your dealing with their complaint quickly and in a professional manner.

Thank the customer for bringing the incident to your attention and assure them that you will make sure that it doesn't happen again. At this stage you could offer your customer a refund and a complimentary coffee the next time they visit your coffee shop. Or you could ask them what you could do to compensate them for any inconvenience they have been caused. Personally, I would rather use the first solution because if you ask someone what you can do to compensate them they usually say that they are not looking for anything.

If you stay calm and reasonable, there is a good chance that you will placate your customer. If you offer a complimentary coffee, they may return.

DON'T TAKE IT PERSONALLY

Sometimes a complaint can be the fault of a member of your staff; however, it may just be that the customer is a constant complainer, or is in a bad mood about something else, or even simply trying to get a free coffee or meal. Don't take the complaint personally, act in a professional manner and remember that 'the customer is always right'.

It is a good idea to keep a note of customers' complaints. Include:

□ the date and time of the complaint;

□ the customer's name and address;

□ the nature of the complaint.

This will enable you to see if the same complaint comes up more than once, and who was working on the dates concerned. You can then talk to staff and try to prevent the situation happening again. If you have the customer's name and address, send them a voucher for a free coffee when you are doing your next promotion.

> *We had a customer who ordered a baked potato with a chilli con carne filling (we always give a generous portion). She ate most of the filling and then sent the meal back to the kitchen, complaining that there was too little filling in the potato. It was easier just to give her an extra portion of the filling, even though I felt that she did not have a reason to complain.*

If a customer is abusive don't react as they will use this to justify their behaviour and become even more abusive. Keep calm and ask them to tell you what the problem is. If they continue to use abusive language, tell them that you will have to ask them to leave.

> *I was in a restaurant recently and a customer started shouting loudly that he wasn't happy about his bill. The young girl who was serving him spoke quietly and when he continued being abusive she walked away and asked the manager to take over. He politely asked the customer to leave the restaurant and then left the table. The man sat for another five minutes before getting up and putting his coat on. Before leaving the restaurant, he turned and looked at the member of staff in a threatening manner. For a moment it looked as if he was going to go back and say something else but he decided against it and left. In my opinion the staff handled the situation well, remaining calm and polite.*

Organizing regular staff meetings

Staff meetings are important to staff development and morale. They give everyone a chance to raise matters which concern them. It is better to get any problems out into the open and try to find a solution for them.

You will probably have to hold meetings after the shop has closed to allow all members of staff to attend and ensure there are no interruptions from customers.

☐ Set a date and time limit for the meeting;

☐ Before the meeting circulate a sheet of paper among your staff for them to write on it what they would like to discuss;

☐ Compile an agenda from the staff suggestions, including items you would like to discuss, and stick to it (this is a good opportunity to discuss such problems as bad timekeeping).

Tackling absenteeism

One of the worst problems I have encountered is absenteeism in the workplace. Staff, including weekend workers, telephone in the morning to inform you that they will not be coming to work because they are 'sick'. Sometimes they just don't turn up at all. (I often wonder how they always manage to be sick on working days after they have been out late the night before!)

Some absences will be a result of genuine sickness but recent research has found that the average sick leave for an employee is 8.7 days per year. There are certain professions that have a greater problem than others, and the catering business appears to be one of them.

I feel strongly about absenteeism by workers and I am convinced that since self-certification of sickness came into force absenteeism in the workplace has significantly increased. Workers can simply phone in 'sick' if they feel like a day or two off work.

It is reported that 20 million sick notes are written by GPs each year and as many as 5 million of these are believed to be bogus. This has given rise to the belief in the 'sick note' culture of Britain.

Do not pay anyone who is off work sick. If they are genuinely unwell they will be able to claim sickness benefit. Their contract of employment should state clearly that they are not entitled to payment when they are off work because of illness. To pay them could well send a confusing message to staff and may set an unfortunate precedent.

There are steps you can take to tackle absenteeism.

☐ Keep a record of sick leave, when and why a member of staff has been off work.

☐ Let your staff know that if someone keeps taking time off from work they are putting other members of staff under pressure, and if they repeatedly take time off without a genuine reason then you will have to take disciplinary procedures.

☐ Return to work interviews can be an effective way of tackling absenteeism. Interview your employee when they return to work to try to discover and address any problems they may have that have caused their absence.

☐ Look at your employee's contract of employment to see what action can be taken for repeated absence. You can request that your employee gives you a sick note obtained from their doctor, and if they are off for a considerable time you may be able to ask them to have a medical carried out by an independent doctor.

It is a good idea to employ a floating member of staff who can be on standby to cover sickness at short notice as well as holidays. You can guarantee that there will always be someone off for sickness or holidays.

Hanging on to good staff

People working in a coffee shop don't tend to stay in the job for very long. Sometimes though, you will get someone who will continue to work for you for a number of years. I have found that the staff who stay longer and who are more committed are women returning to work after bringing up their children. They often prefer to work part-time.

I often think that two good part-time workers are worth more than one full-time person who has no commitment to the job. Also part-time workers can often fill in for each other for holidays or sickness.

INSTILLING A SENSE OF LOYALTY

Once you have trained your employees, how do you keep your staff happy and productive and how do you instil a sense of loyalty in them?

- ☐ Offer competitive salaries;

- ☐ Pay a Christmas bonus;

- ☐ Allow them day-release to train and obtain a qualification;

- ☐ Provide a great-looking uniform;

- ☐ Initiate a worker of the month scheme where the winner gets a gift or bonus;

- ☐ Praise your staff for good work;

- ☐ Offer a chance for promotion within the business.

Don't get too familiar with staff as you might find it difficult to give criticism or discipline them. They do not have the same interest in the business as you have or any particular loyalty unless they have a share in it. Quite often they will move on to another job if the pay or hours are better.

LEARNING TO BE A GOOD BOSS

Employees work better for a good boss – that's a fact. To get the best from your staff you must earn their respect by setting an example that they can aspire to. Always be polite, fair and behave towards them with integrity. Let them know that you care about their welfare and appreciate their efforts.

Communication

Be careful how you express yourself to your staff. Your feelings are conveyed by your body language, attitude, tone of voice and the words you use when talking to them. Try to be patient and remember when you are giving them instructions that not everyone can process information in the same way; some people have to be shown a task several times before they understand how to do it properly.

What you should do:

☐ **Do** be patient with your staff and try to use positive rather than negative words when talking to them.

☐ **Do** try to be good-humoured and create a happy working environment.

☐ **Do** make sure that you can plan, organize and delegate jobs that have to be done in the coffee shop.

☐ **Do** try to build a feeling of teamwork; your staff will work better in a contented team.

☐ **Do** think of yourself as part of the team and contribute significantly.

☐ **Do** make yourself available when one of your employees needs help and guidance.

☐ **Do** inspire confidence.

☐ **Do** listen to your employees and try to see issues from their point of view.

☐ **Do** treat seriously any ideas of your staff to improve your business.

☐ **Do** help your employees to develop their skills.

☐ **Do** recognize good work and achievements and give praise for tasks done well.

☐ **Do** always concentrate on improvements and not on shortfalls.

☐ **Do** thank all your staff at the end of the day for the good work they have done.

What you should not do:

☐ **Don't** try to do everything yourself because you may make your employees feel that they are not good enough to do the task themselves.

☐ **Don't** criticize a member of staff in front of other employees or your customers. If you have something to say to them, ask them to wait behind or take them into another room.

☐ **Don't** demean an employee as a form of punishment.

☐ **Don't** shout at your staff.

☐ **Don't** show favouritism.

Finally, I've said this before but it's worth repeating: never ask a member of your staff to do something you wouldn't do yourself.

10
COMPLYING WITH HEALTH, SAFETY AND HYGIENE LAWS

Now that you have opened your coffee shop and found good staff to help you run it, one of your top priorities is keeping your shop spotlessly clean at all times. This is not just to keep it looking good, it is essential for the health and safety of your customers and your staff, and the success of your business.

Be committed to cleanliness

You have a legal requirement to keep your shop clean and hygienic. Any shop that serves food and drink must maintain very strict standards of cleanliness and hygiene. If you do not, you will not only risk losing customers to your competitors, you could risk making them sick from food poisoning. Your business can be closed down by the Environmental Health Department of your local authority if you do not satisfy legal requirements.

Effective cleaning helps prevent bacteria from spreading from hands, equipment and surfaces. Train your staff to use quiet periods to keep on top of all essential cleaning tasks. They should always be aware of items that constantly need to be cleaned, and when the shop is quiet they can take the initiative on such jobs as wiping trays, cleaning finger-marks off the doors or wiping out the fridge.

It is a good idea to make out a cleaning schedule for equipment and surfaces that have to be cleaned each day and for areas which need to be attended to less frequently. Do have your schedule laminated and fix it to the wall of the kitchen. Make another list to be initialled by the member of staff who carries out each job. If the job has not been done satisfactorily you will know who carried it out. It would surprise you how many times I have heard 'I didn't do that job' or 'That isn't my job'. To avoid disputes you can make certain members of staff responsible for cleaning a specific area each night.

Always use antibacterial, food-safe chemicals; and use colour-coded cloths – a different colour for cleaning different areas or equipment.

Drawing up a cleaning schedule

Here is a sample cleaning schedule you could use. This routine should be carried out each night after you have closed the shop.

COFFEE SHOP AREA

☐ Wipe down seating areas, tables and chairs;

☐ Wipe trays and stack neatly;

☐ Wipe over serving counter;

☐ Empty rubbish bins, wipe out with disinfectant and replace old bin liner with a fresh one;

☐ Check cutlery is clean and has been polished with a clean cloth;

☐ Tidy magazines and remove old newspapers;

☐ Fill all sugar containers, salt and pepper pots, napkin and straw dispensers;

☐ Vacuum carpet or sweep and mop floor.

TOILETS

☐ Clean toilets with toilet brush, put bleach down the pan and leave overnight;

☐ Empty rubbish bins and wash with disinfectant;

☐ Clean sinks and fill soap dispensers;

☐ Restock toilet rolls;

☐ Brush and mop floor;

☐ Switch off lights and extractor fans.

Check that the lights have been turned off in the toilet area. Although I continually remind staff that they must be turned off after all the cleaning has been completed, there have been occasions when I have come to work to find the lights have been left on overnight.

KITCHEN AREA

☐ Thoroughly clean dishwasher as per manufacturer's instructions;

☐ Empty rubbish bin, wash it out and place a fresh bin liner inside it;

☐ Clean microwave;

☐ Clean oven and hob;

☐ Clean sinks with appropriate cleaner;

☐ Sweep and mop floor;

☐ Wipe all surfaces and doors;

☐ Wipe down fridge and freezer doors.

FRONT OF SHOP AND COFFEE AREA

☐ Clean cake cabinet and wipe down counters;

☐ Backflush coffee machine as per manufacturer's instruction and clean all other parts, including the drain tray and the filters;

☐ To keep drainage of coffee refuge unobstructed, pour a jug of boiling water down the drain box;

☐ Scrub the milk steaming jugs with steel wool;

☐ Empty and wash filter coffee pot;

☐ Brush and mop floor.

Ask your staff to carry out other tasks like wiping out the fridge and the drinks chiller, cleaning windows and dusting window ledges when they are not busy serving customers.

If you have a washing machine on the premises, designate a member of staff to collect the dish towels and washing cloths at the end of the day and put them in the washing machine so that they are ready to be dried the following morning.

Tips for effective cleaning

☐ Do not use sponges in the kitchen as they provide one of the friendliest environments for bacteria, allowing them to multiply rapidly.

 **To help your staff to use a separate cloth for different areas to be cleaned, buy different-coloured cloths, e.g. blue for the toilets, yellow for tables and green for the fridge. Never use the same cloth you use for cleaning the microwave to clean the rubbish bin or the floor.**

☐ Microfibre cloths come in five colours in packs of 10, containing two cloths of each colour. You can buy them from www.micro-pro.co.uk at about £5 for a pack of 10. These cloths can be used dry for dusting or wet for cleaning. They are hard-wearing, tough, very absorbent, easily kept clean and will last for a long time.

☐ Always use antibacterial food-safe chemicals for cleaning, and disinfect your cleaning cloths regularly.

□ Milk steaming jugs have to be scrubbed with steel wool each night and then put through the dishwasher to get rid of the hardened milk which has built up during the day.

□ Make sure staff keep all areas of your baking display case immaculately clean, especially those parts seen by customers when they are standing in front of them. Serving tongs and other utensils should be kept clean at all times. All bakery products should be removed from the display case before you clean it in order to protect them from any of the cleaning materials.

□ If you use thermal jugs for keeping filter coffee warm you cannot submerge these in water. Clean them by letting them steep overnight using a solution of baking soda and hot water. For stubborn stains use a long-handled brush to scrub the inside and simply wipe clean the outside. You must always remember to rinse them out thoroughly before you use them again.

□ Do show your staff which cleaning products to use and how they should be diluted and stored.

FLOORS

Ask your staff to sweep the floor throughout the day and to mop up any spills that may occur. Sweep and mop the floor last thing every night so that your customers and staff are not walking over wet floors. Wash with hot water and the appropriate cleaning solution (as approved by the Environmental Health Office). Wash out the mops and leave them to dry overnight.

KITCHEN AREA

The kitchen area should be spotless and this requires continual cleaning by staff. Washing down areas and equipment is common sense but sometimes you have to keep reminding staff to do this.

□ Keep walls and extractor fans clean by washing them down regularly;

□ Empty rubbish bins throughout the day as you don't want them to overflow;

□ Keep the floor free of debris by sweeping regularly throughout the day;

□ Make sure you have antibacterial soap available on each washbasin for staff use. It is essential that staff wash their hands before handling any food items, after emptying the rubbish bin, and especially after going to the toilet or handling money.

WASHING DISHES

A dishwasher is a more hygienic way of washing dishes than washing them in the sink. Follow the manufacturer's instructions and use the recommended cleaning and rinsing solution. First rinse off any food particles left on the dishes before loading them into the machine. Pans usually have to be scrubbed before putting them through the dishwasher as the machine won't remove stubborn stains or baked on food.

If you don't have a dishwasher you will have to use the double sink method. Rinse off the particles of food, wash the dishes in hot soapy water with a detergent approved by the Environmental Health Office, rinse them in clean hot water and then allow them to drip dry.

Believe me when I say that a dishwasher is a godsend.

Inform your staff that when they are handling mugs, cups and glasses they should not touch the rims with their hands. When handling cutlery they should only touch the handles.

TOILETS

☐ Make sure the toilets are checked regularly throughout the day;

☐ Keep toilet paper and paper hand towels (if used) well stocked;

☐ Make sure bins are emptied when they are full;

☐ Keep soap dispensers topped up.

Working with your local Environmental Health Department

When you are planning to start a coffee shop, you should contact the Environmental Health Department of your local authority. An officer will come to your premises and give you advice and information about what you will need to do before opening to comply with the legal requirements. They will also give you information on how to register your premises. Try to build up a good relationship with your local Environmental Health Officers; their advice can be invaluable, especially when you are planning a new business.

If you are considering taking over an already established coffee shop it may be worth your while contacting your local Environmental Health Department to invite them to look over your shop to see if it requires updating or anything renewing. The officer will give you advice and guidance about what you can and cannot do to the premises. This also gives you an idea how much money you will have to spend on the premises before you can open for business.

You can obtain information on preparing and serving food in booklet form from your local Environmental Health Department. You can also obtain up-to-date publications on food hygiene, 'A Guide for Businesses' and 'Starting Up' from the Food standards Agency at www.food.gov.uk or telephone 0845 606 0667. The Food Standards Agency is a UK-wide independent government agency which provides advice to the public and the government on food safety, diet and nutrition.

REGISTERING YOUR BUSINESS

Before opening your coffee shop, you are required by law to register your business with the Environmental Health Department of your local authority. You must register your business at least 28 days before opening. This applies to most types of food businesses, including catering run from home, or temporary premises such as stalls and vans.

If you use two or more premises you will need to register all of them. For example, if you are going to use the kitchen in your own home for baking or making up any fillings for sandwiches to sell in your coffee shop, you must also register these premises.

You must always inform your local authority if you make any significant changes to the way you run your business.

Complying with the rules and regulations

You are required by law to comply with the following rules and regulations.

PREMISES

☐ Your premises must be suitable for the purpose of your business;

☐ The premises must be suitable for preparing food safely;

☐ You must keep your premises clean, in good repair and well maintained at all times;

☐ You must be able to follow good hygiene practices including protection against contamination;

☐ To prevent contamination from the spread of disease, you must carry out integrated pest control.

HAND WASHING FACILITIES AND TOILETS

You must have enough hand wash basins for your staff to wash and dry their hands and they must have hot and cold running water. You must provide an approved antibacterial hand wash for staff to wash their hands, and materials for drying them hygienically.

Paper towels are more hygienic than fabric towels. You can purchase a unit and rolls of paper towels from a company selling janitorial items, or you can simply fit a domestic fitment and ordinary kitchen roll yourself.

☐ There must be sufficient toilets, and these must not communicate directly with the area where food is being prepared.

☐ You must also have adequate ventilation, lighting and drainage.

☐ You must store disinfecting and all cleaning chemicals away from the food handling area.

FLOORS, WALLS AND DOORS

☐ The floor in your kitchen must be well maintained and in good condition and should be easy to clean and disinfect.

☐ The surface of the floor should be made of materials that do not allow fluid to pass through it, washable and non-toxic.

☐ Walls and doors should be easy to clean and should be smooth and hard-wearing and in a good state of repair.

SURFACES

☐ In areas where food is being handled, surfaces (including surfaces of equipment) must be easy to clean, in good condition and, where necessary, be able to be disinfected.

☐ Surfaces should be smooth, washable, corrosion-resistant and non-toxic, e.g. stainless steel.

WASHING EQUIPMENT AND FOOD

☐ Your shop must have adequate facilities and a good supply of hot and cold water for cleaning, disinfecting and storing utensils and equipment.

☐ Your shop must have an adequate supply of hot and/or cold water available for every sink used for washing food.

FOOD WASTE AND RUBBISH

☐ You must remove rubbish and food waste from your kitchen as quickly as possible.

☐ Do not let bins overflow in the kitchen.

☐ You must have adequate facilities for storing and disposing of rubbish and food waste because there are specific rules about how certain foods must be collected and disposed of. Contact your local authority for details of how this should be done.

☐ You must be able to keep the storage area clean and free from animals and pests.

WATER SUPPLY

☐ You must have an adequate supply of 'potable' (drinking quality) water available and it must be used when washing food to ensure that contamination does not occur.

If you are going to use ice in your coffee shop it must be made using potable water.

Inspections by the Environmental Health Officer

An Environmental Health Officer will usually come to check your premises before you open your coffee shop and thereafter may visit every six months, or once a year. The Environmental Health Officer can turn up at any time and they do not tell you when they are coming. If a customer informs them that they have been ill after eating food in your shop, someone from the department will also visit you at that time.

WHAT IS THE INSPECTOR LOOKING FOR?

When the Environmental Health Officer visits your premises they will ask you or, if you are not present, a member of your staff a number of questions and check some of the following facilities:

☐ They will run their hand along the insides of cupboards for dust.

☐ They will check your kitchen, seating area, toilet facilities and cupboards or storage space.

☐ They may check that all the fillings in the fridge are in containers and are labelled and dated.

☐ They will ask to see a record of your food temperatures for reheating and keeping food hot.

☐ They will check that all freezer and fridge temperature charts are kept up to date.

☐ They will ask if you use the correct chopping boards.

☐ They will check that the kitchen is kept clean and in good repair.

☐ They will check that you have pest control measures in use.

☐ They will check that there are adequate hand wash facilities for the number of staff you have and the size of your kitchen.

☐ They will check that you have adequate rubbish bin and waste disposal.

☐ They will check that all food is stored above floor level and where there is no risk of contamination.

WHAT HAPPENS IF THERE ARE PROBLEMS?

You will receive written information about any problems, along with advice and guidance on how to rectify them. You will be given a reasonable time to put things right.

If you fail to comply with regulations relating to hygiene or to the processing or treatment of food, the inspector can serve an improvement notice on you. The notice must state the grounds on which the notice is served (i.e. in what way you are failing to comply), the contraventions and the time allowed to meet the statutory requirements.

If you are convicted of an offence under the regulations and the court is satisfied that the business involves an imminent health risk to your customers, the inspector can issue an emergency prohibition order which forbids the use of your premises or equipment.

You will be able to appeal the decision of the Environmental Health Inspector if you disagree with it and, if you are in this position, you should enquire what the procedures are.

Preparing and storing food safely

Anyone serving food in their coffee shop has a legal, commercial and moral obligation to provide food that is safe; that will not cause illness or food poisoning. Therefore you must ensure that the food you serve is protected from the risk of contamination.

Hygiene is more than mere cleanliness; it encompasses all measures necessary to ensure the safety of food during preparation, processing, manufacture, storage, transportation and handling. It is extremely important to train new staff in food hygiene and ideally this should be done as soon as possible after they start working with you. It would do no harm either to give your other staff a refresher course at the same time.

PERSONAL HYGIENE

☐ Staff working in food handling areas must maintain a high standard of personal cleanliness. They should wear suitable clean clothing and, where appropriate, protective clothing.

☐ Staff should keep their hair tied back (if they have long hair).

☐ Staff should not wear nail varnish, watches or jewellery when preparing food.

☐ Staff should not touch their face or hair, sneeze, eat or chew gum when they are working with food.

Any member of staff known or suspected to be suffering from any of the following should not be allowed to enter a food handling area:

☐ if they have a food-borne disease which could contaminate food with pathogens;

☐ if they have any infected wounds, skin infections or sores;

☐ if they have diarrhoea and/or vomiting.

Staff who are suffering from any of the above should contact the business owner or manager immediately.

 You must purchase blue adhesive plasters and dressings to use on any cuts you or your staff might get when working with food. It is also advisable to have a burn relief spray or gel in the kitchen in case of accidents.

Staff with diarrhoea or vomiting should not return to work until they have been symptom-free for 48 hours. You will have seen from the news how quickly norovirus (the most common cause of gastroenteritis) spreads.

HAND WASHING

Even though you give your staff food hygiene training, you may from time to time have to remind them why it is so important to know the basic rules.

Do make sure that your staff wash their hands thoroughly. This is essential to prevent harmful bacteria being transmitted from people's hands to food, surfaces and equipment. They should be particularly careful in the following circumstances:

☐ after a break or going to the toilet;

☐ before preparing and handling food;

☐ after blowing their nose;

☐ after scratching their head or touching their hair;

☐ after emptying the rubbish bin;

☐ after touching raw food;

☐ after sweeping the floor or cleaning.

THE COST OF POOR HYGIENE

☐ Poor hygiene and cleanliness in your coffee shop can result in the closure of your business by the local authority and the loss of your reputation.

☐ If you are found to be selling unfit food you can be fined and will have to pay legal fees because of contraventions of hygiene legislation.

☐ You could be sued by customers suffering from food poisoning.

☐ Staff will lose their jobs if your premises are closed down.

Do complete a formal course in Food Hygiene even if it is just a basic course to begin with. It is so important to have this knowledge.

COURSES IN FOOD HYGIENE

Some Environmental Health Departments offer formal courses at a reduced price for catering businesses. If you employ a large staff they will run a basic course on your premises.

You can also approach your local college to enquire about Food Hygiene courses. If you cannot afford to take time off work there is a basic course being offered through distance learning which you can do at home.

You can deduct the cost of training against your income tax.

All staff working in the food industry should be trained in the basic level of food hygiene within three months of starting work. The basic/elementary course is a one-day course lasting six hours with an exam at the end of it.

❝I had no informed knowledge about food and hygiene when I was planning to open a coffee shop so I signed up for a basic course in Food Hygiene and then an intermediate course which was going to take place two weeks later. Unfortunately, the first course was cancelled because there were not enough candidates and I had to go ahead with the intermediate course without any background knowledge. The course lasted a week and then there was a three-hour exam on the following Monday morning. It was really difficult for me because I had no food and hygiene background and most of the other people taking the course were either managers or owners of restaurants, work canteens and cafés. Fortunately I did pass first time. This gave me the Intermediate Food Hygiene Certificate of the Royal Environmental Health Institute of Scotland which is a second-level qualification in food hygiene, recognized nationally in all sectors of the food industry.❞

If you follow the rules of hygiene and prevention of cross-contamination:

☐ there will be a reduced risk of food poisoning;

☐ your business will earn a good reputation for cleanliness and serving good safe food;

☐ you will be working within the rules and regulations of the food safety legislation.

Eradicating food hazards

In order to keep your coffee shop clean and the food you serve safe, it is necessary to put food safety management procedures in place. These procedures are crucial to ensure food safety. They are based on HACCP (Hazard Analysis Critical Control Point). A food hazard is any contamination which could cause harm to the consumer.

There are three classifications of food hazard: microbiological, chemical or physical.

☐ Microbiological could be, for example, bacteria present in or on food, or other micro-organisms that cause food poisoning;

☐ Chemical could be, for example, cleaning materials or insecticides;

☐ Physical could be, for example, glass or a hair clip.

Identify the areas where food hazards may occur. You will then need to put in place sufficient controls and to monitor procedures at those critical points in order to minimize risks. You must review your risk assessment and control procedures regularly and also whenever there is any change in the way you handle food. (Full details on identifying hazards and carrying out a risk assessment are on page 105.)

CHECKING AND ROTATING YOUR STOCK

Always check date marks on products when goods are delivered to you and return them immediately if:

☐ they are out of date;

☐ any of the packaging is damaged;

☐ frozen goods have started to defrost.

Make sure that you rotate your stock and check for out of date products on a daily basis. If any are out of date you must throw them away. This is a waste of food; however, if you rotate your stock properly you should not have this problem.

Never be tempted to serve out of date food to your customers.

❛I was in a coffee shop recently and picked up a packet of produce being sold in the shop and checked the date on it before going to pay for it. It was seven days out of date and there were a few other packets on the shelf also out of date. I brought this to the attention of the shop owner who didn't appear to be over concerned. This stock was obviously not checked on a regular basis. I am now wary of purchasing anything else from this particular coffee shop.❜

KEEPING FOOD AT THE RIGHT TEMPERATURE

One of my first tasks in the morning was to test the temperature of the fridges and freezers and record the reading on the appropriate chart. You are required to take a note of these temperatures twice a day.

Temperature controls are very important when you are storing food and also for cooking and reheating food. The Cook Safe Guide, developed by the Food Standards Agency Scotland, contains details of the different types of foods and the temperatures that apply to them. The Cook Safe system is also available in Chinese, Urdu and Punjabi. The equivalent used in England and Wales is 'Safer Food, Better Business' and in Northern Ireland it is called 'Safe Catering'.

These guides will give you all the information you require with regard to temperature control. You can get copies of each of them from your local authority and you can view 'Safer Food, Better Business' online at www.food.gov.uk/sfbb.

It is imperative that you keep foods at the correct temperatures so that you do not cause a risk to the health of your customers.

Cold foods

In England, Wales and Northern Ireland the legal requirement for food being kept cold is for it to be kept at 8°C or below. In Scotland the requirement is 5°C or below.

You will need to keep a temperature chart for inspection by the Environmental Health Officer. If you don't have a digital temperature display on the front of your fridge you should keep a fridge thermometer in the fridge at all times.

Keep a temperature chart on the door or side of your fridge to record daily temperatures of your fridge and freezers. If it is placed where staff can see it, it will remind them to check the temperature readings.

Hot food

There is a requirement throughout the UK that food being kept hot, for example soup, must be kept at 63°C or above.

There is a regulation in Scotland (apparently not in England and Wales) covering reheated food. Chilli con carne, for example, reheated in a microwave, has to reach 82°C. The exception is when such a temperature would be detrimental to the type of food; for instance, quiche could not tolerate this temperature.

Hot food which is not going to be served immediately should be cooled rapidly. However, it should not be placed immediately into the fridge as it could raise the fridge temperature and affect the food already stored there. Freshly cooked chilled foods have a maximum shelf life of five days and must be kept between 0°C and 3°C.

> You will find that smaller portions of food put into shallow square containers will cool down more quickly.

Frozen food

Frozen food should be stored at −18°C

Put frozen food into the freezer as quickly as possible and do not allow it to remain at an ambient temperature for more than 15 minutes.

Do not overfill the freezer.

Do implement effective stock rotation and make sure that older food is used first to prevent waste.

> If your freezer breaks down or food becomes thawed you may be able to treat it as fresh and in certain circumstances it may be cooked and refrozen. However, you should contact your local Environmental Health Department for advice on this.

LABELLING PRODUCTS CORRECTLY

If you buy in pre-packed sandwiches from a manufacturer to sell to your customers they must be labelled by the manufacturer with full details of ingredients and a 'use by' date. You will be in breach of regulations if the manufacturer has not labelled them correctly.

It is good practice to label the containers in which you store your fillings, stating what they are and on what date they were made.

Getting advice about health and safety issues

Every business, however small, has legal responsibilities to ensure the health and safety of employees and other people affected by the business, including customers, trades people, cleaners and suppliers.

First of all, as explained earlier in the chapter, you must register with your local authority. An Environmental Health Officer will visit your premises and advise you on what you need to do to comply with legal requirements. If you are just starting up in business and you want some help with health and safety in your workplace you can buy a Health and Safety Purchase Pack which provides a comprehensive, low-cost introduction to health and safety for new businesses.

The pack costs £35 and contains most of the basic health and safety advice you need. It also contains copies of the Health and Safety Law poster which must by law be displayed in your premises, and also the Health and Safety Executive Accident Book. For further information about Health and Safety the infoline telephone number is 08701 545500 and if you need to purchase any publications the website is www.hsebooks.co.uk or telephone 01787 881165. You can also download free leaflets from HSE's website www.hse.gov.uk

WHAT ELSE YOU SHOULD KNOW ABOUT HEALTH AND SAFETY

Insurance

You are legally required to have employers' liability insurance if you employ anyone. This is necessary to cover you in case someone takes legal action against you because they have been injured on your premises, owing to your negligence.

You must display a current certificate of insurance on your premises.

Ask your insurance broker to get you quotes for this type of insurance cover. The insurance company may want to visit your premises to make their own risk assessment.

First aid kit

You must keep a first aid kit on the premises and you must make sure all your staff know where it is kept.

Fire prevention equipment

You are required to have at least one fire extinguisher in good working order placed in the kitchen and, depending on the size of your premises, you might need to have another one in the sitting area of the coffee shop. You are also required to have fire blankets on the premises. You should contact your local fire prevention officer who will inspect your premises and advise you on what you require. You will have to get the fire extinguishers checked annually.

Carrying out a risk assessment

It is a legal requirement to carry out a thorough health and safety risk assessment to identify any potential areas of risk there may be in your coffee shop. This will minimize the risk of anyone having an accident on your premises or becoming unwell as a result of visiting your premises.

There are five main areas to look at when carrying out a risk assessment and these are:

IDENTIFY THE HAZARDS

☐ Check your premises to see if there are any significant hazards. You must check each section of your premises and take a note of anything you think may be a hazard.

WHO MIGHT BE HARMED?

☐ Consider everyone who works in your premises, your customers and people who will occasionally be on your premises, e.g. tradesmen or cleaners.

MINIMIZE THE RISKS

☐ Try to eradicate any hazards you have on your list or at the very least minimize or control the risk.

RECORD YOUR FINDINGS

☐ If you have five or more employees you will have to write down your findings and conclusions. If you have fewer than five employees you don't have to record them in writing. However, for your own information it might be helpful to make a list of significant hazards and what you need to do to get rid of the risk or minimize it.

PRIORITIZE YOUR ACTIONS

☐ You should prioritize the items on your list and carry out improvements on the most significant hazards first, especially those that could cause accidents or ill health. Once you have made all the improvements necessary, make sure that you keep a checklist to ensure that the control measures stay in place.

There are areas relevant to a coffee shop that you should check and I have listed a few below.

☐ Ensure that protective clothing such as aprons, and protective work wear such as oven gloves and rubber gloves, are provided.

☐ Check all electrical equipment is safe and, if it is not, get it repaired.

☐ Do not leave electric cables loose or trailing.

☐ Make sure that all floors are in good condition and that you put up a warning notice if they are wet and slippery.

☐ Ensure that all areas are well lit.

☐ Make sure that there are no objects left lying about where someone could trip over them. (This is one of the most common hazards in a coffee shop.)

☐ Provide adequate training to all your staff.

☐ Make sure that your staff have regular tea breaks.

☐ Ensure that all chemicals and cleaning substances are stored in the designated place.

☐ Look for any other areas where you think there may be hazards, and take steps to improve them.

REGULARLY REVIEW YOUR ASSESSMENT

Do review your assessment from time to time to make sure that your precautions are still effective and there are no new hazards that you need to deal with.

> *A member of staff in our coffee shop left the electric cable for the food mixer trailing on the floor and this was noted by the Health and Safety Inspector.*

It is your responsibility to train your staff to be aware of potential hazards and how to deal with them. Ask them if they know of any risks on the premises that have not been addressed; sometimes staff can be more aware of problems than you are.

Remember, it is not cost effective to ignore hazards that may be present on your premises. Complying with health and safety regulations will mean some expense for you, but it could cost you a lot more if a serious accident or illness occurs because of your negligence.

11
HOW TO INCREASE YOUR BUSINESS

Initially, when you are just starting your business, you will have to advertise quite frequently, and the amount you have to spend will seem quite high in relation to your turnover. Do work out how much you want to spend on marketing your business and stick to your budget.

I cannot emphasize strongly enough how important your staff can be in retaining customers and expanding your business. Train staff to welcome your customers with a smile and a 'Hello, nice to see you again'. People like to be recognized and if you make them feel valued they will return again and again.

Developing your marketing strategy

Your marketing strategy encompasses all your plans for increasing your sales. This entails attracting new people to visit your coffee shop and encouraging your customers to spend more per person and to return more often.

MEASURE RESULTS

You must measure the results of each strategy you use and if something doesn't work, don't try it again. Note in a diary the date and the type of promotion you have used. This will allow you to see if your turnover has increased after the promotion and by how much. If the promotion was successful then do it again at another time in the year. Particular occasions such as Valentines Day, Mother's Day, Easter or Hallowe'en are good times to choose for promotions.

AREAS YOU SHOULD CONCENTRATE ON

When you are developing your marketing strategy, you should concentrate on the areas detailed below:

☐ Identify your market using the information you gathered when you were doing your original research (see Chapter 1).

☐ Find out what your competition is doing to promote their coffee shop and create a strategy to improve on this and make your shop better and different.

☐ Choose advertising methods that will be effective.

☐ Research the costs of different types of advertising then set your advertising budget.

☐ Make sure your advertisements reflect the character and image of your coffee shop effectively. Give thought to the way you word them; they must be enticing enough to tempt new customers to your shop.

☐ To assess the effectiveness of your advertising campaign you could use vouchers which must be handed in to your shop in exchange for a free tea or coffee. You will then be able to see if this particular type of advertising is working for you.

No matter where or in what way you advertise, your headline must be eye-catching and interesting enough to get the attention of your target market. A free gift or a discount is always an incentive to encourage new customers.

Using vouchers and flyers
VOUCHERS

One of the best ways to create new business is to offer a free coffee using vouchers. We have used this method of advertising several times and have found it to be quite effective.

Advertising in the local paper

If you advertise in your local paper people can cut out the voucher and exchange it for a free coffee. Alternatively you could offer a free coffee and 10% off other food ordered at the same time as the drink.

Working with a local business

Try approaching a local business, such as a gym, hairdressing salon, record store or anywhere else with a good customer base and ask them to hand out your vouchers to their customers. You could approach several businesses and use them at different times throughout the year. You may have to promote their business in return. This is a relatively inexpensive way of advertising, as you would only have to pay the cost of having the vouchers printed.

Counting the vouchers

You must remind your staff to collect the vouchers so that you know how successful your promotion has been and if it is worth repeating it. If you don't record the number of vouchers you have taken in during the promotion you won't know whether it has been successful or not, or whether it is the best way to attract new customers.

People love something for nothing and if the customer is getting a free cup of tea or coffee, more than likely they will purchase a sandwich or a cake to go with it. You are creating goodwill among local people and at the same time you are building up your customer base.

If you are only offering a free coffee at a certain time during the day, do state this quite clearly on the voucher. Also state the 'valid from' and 'valid to' dates.

‘*Recently, like every other M&S cardholder, I received a voucher for a complimentary coffee with any purchase at any M&S café. I didn't notice on the voucher that the coffee had to be taken before 12 noon and I arrived at 2 p.m. and ordered a cappuccino and a toasted sandwich. The girl behind the counter pointed out that the voucher could only be used before 12 noon. The time was stated on the voucher but did not stand out and I admit that I had not read the details.*’

I think M&S are quite clever when using marketing strategies, so let's look at the way they promoted their café:

☐ They offered a complimentary coffee or hot drink with *any purchase* in the café, so you had to buy something else from the café to get your free drink.

☐ They advertised on the voucher other items available in the café, for example, 'tempting pastries, fresh sandwiches, cakes and hot and cold drinks, it's the perfect place for breakfast, lunch or a quick snack. . . come and have a look!'

Your voucher should include:

☐ the name of your coffee shop, address and telephone number, and your logo (if you have one);

☐ **'FREE COFFEE'** in bold letters;

☐ details of the offer;

☐ some information on the other food and drink that you sell;

☐ coffee shop opening times;

☐ 'Valid from– to–' dates

If you are going to ask another business to give out vouchers for you, get quotes from a few printers before deciding which one to use. Then have the vouchers printed and deliver them personally to whichever business you are going to use.

If you are going to use the local newspaper for this type of advertising you may be able to come to an agreement whereby you will pay for an advertisement if they will do a story on your coffee shop free of charge.

FLYERS

You could design an attractive flyer that will appeal to the public.

Some of the things to consider include:

1. an attention grabbing headline;

2. making your offer sound irresistible;

3. eye-catching colours;

4. your layout;

5. your method of delivery.

☐ Head the flyer with the offer; this could include a free coffee, or coffee and a scone or cake at a discounted price during the quietest time in your shop. You could also offer a free mug or, at Christmas time, a free diary. Have your logo and the name of your shop printed on the gifts, to remind your customers of your coffee shop.

☐ List the tempting food and drinks you sell.

☐ Make sure the name of your coffee shop, address and telephone number are prominently displayed. Include your logo (if you have one).

☐ Give your coffee shop opening times.

☐ Have your flyer printed in eye-catching colours or colours that match the colour theme or logo of your coffee shop.

Note: You can send out flyers that only contains information about your coffee shop and the food and drink you sell, but if you offer something free you are guaranteed to get more results from the promotion.

Distributing your flyers

Flyers can be distributed in several ways. You can have them inserted into your local newspaper, delivered by hand by someone you employ or by the post office. The price for distributing flyers through the local paper or the post office will vary. Do enquire about prices before you decide to go ahead with flyers. You will have to give the post office a few weeks' notice as they have a waiting list for this service.

Some more ideas for attracting customers

☐ The best method of advertising by far is word of mouth, so offer an exceptional service with a smile, value for money and a comfortable, relaxing immaculately clean environment. Customers like to feel important; train your staff to smile when they greet customers, ask them if they enjoyed their coffee, and say that they look forward to seeing them again. A happy customer will not only return, they will sing the praises of your coffee shop to others and you will soon be busier than you ever expected.

☐ Consider special deals and multibuys, especially good for increasing business during quieter times of the day. For example, offer a cup of coffee or tea and a scone for 99p at a certain time, or a 'buy a cake and get a free coffee' deal.

◻ Create loyalty in your customers. Ask for their feedback on a small form and, if they leave their name and address, you can build up a simple database and either email them or mail them once a month with a preferential special offer. This builds up trust and loyalty in your customers and encourages them to come back. When they receive these offers, they often feel as if they know you personally.

◻ A customer loyalty card is a successful way of encouraging customers to return. Ask customers to have their card stamped each time they purchase a cup of coffee in your shop, and when they have collected six stamps they will get a free cup of coffee. Your customers will more than likely purchase a cake, scone or sandwich to go along with their free coffee, so it is unlikely that you will be losing any money during the promotion. Don't ask customers if they want a card; instead, just present them with one. The cards will remind customers of your coffee shop each time they open their purse or wallet.

Do take the loyalty card from the customer after it has been stamped six times and present them with a new one. You could ask your customers to put a contact name and telephone number on the card. You could then have a monthly prize draw. As a prize, you could give a mug or an item bearing your logo on it, or a cake and a coffee the next time the customer visits your shop.

◻ Send out preferential vouchers or discount cards to staff that work for other companies in your area.

◻ If you can handle it, offer a takeaway service for these companies, or allow them to phone in their order in advance. Staff often have short lunch breaks and no time to wait in a queue.

◻ Give vouchers to your staff, friends and family to give to people they know to help build up your customer base.

◻ If you are in a busy shopping area, you could prepare trays of sample coffees and mini cakes and go out into the area offering the samples to the public, as well as money-off vouchers to attract them into your coffee shop.

◻ You could try offering cut-price drinks, such as 10p for a regular coffee (not cappuccino or speciality coffees) or tea. This would probably just cover the cost of your coffee, tea and milk. You will probably find that most people will purchase something else anyway. Often this will work better than a 'free' promotion.

◻ Offering free refills on all regular coffees and tea usually works well.

❛*We once had five customers at one table who ordered two pots of tea and five cups and then asked for a free refill. They certainly got value for their money!* ❜

☐ If you want to promote speciality drinks to make more profit, try offering a 'special drink of the day' at a reduced price. You could also do the same with items of food.

Handing out customer questionnaires

Always encourage feedback from your customers, good or bad. Just as a happy customer can help build up your business by spreading good words, an unhappy one can do just the opposite. If you have a problem customer, try to sort out their grievance there and then and don't let it escalate. A customer feedback questionnaire can give you valuable insights into the way your business is viewed.

I have given you a sample of a customer questionnaire in Appendix 6, but of course you will know what specific questions you want answered by your customers. Make it multiple-choice questions and leave a space for your customers to tick the appropriate box, and then space for them to leave their comments and ideas.

This is a good opportunity to collect customers' names and addresses for future promotions. The ideal way to do this would be to run a competition with prizes, or to offer those who return the questionnaires a discount if they join your loyalty programme.

Ask your customers to leave their contact details on the questionnaires and to post the forms into a box that you have located in a prominent position in your café. You can determine how often you need to draw a winner – once a week or once a month – from the number of entries in the box. The prize might be a bottle of wine, for instance, or a meal for two.

ENCOURAGING CUSTOMERS TO RETURN

The real beauty of this would be that you could write to all the other entrants, thanking them for their comments, and telling them that you are sorry they did not win the main prize this month, but they have won a 'free coffee' on their next visit, or something along those lines. This would encourage these customers to visit your coffee shop again within a relatively short time. It is always a good idea to give a cut-off date on any such offer; for example, within the next 14 days. Twenty-one days is too long a time and 10 days is not long enough.

DEALING WITH NEGATIVE FEEDBACK

If you get a particularly bad customer comment, it would be worth contacting that customer, if you have their details, to discuss the problem and to assure them that it won't happen again. You could also offer the customer a refund or a free lunch to make up for their bad experience. There could be nothing worse for your new coffee shop than a disgruntled customer telling others about their bad experience.

Urge customers to let you know if there is a problem so that it can be rectified, and encourage satisfied customers to tell their friends about your shop. You will always get one or two awkward customers; it is just a fact of dealing with the public. However, but you can do your best to be prepared for them and know how to appease them should the situation arise. See Chapter 9 on how to handle difficult customers.

 Allow regular customers to try mini free samples of new items you have put on your menu. You could give them a voucher for 10% off their next purchase to encourage them back. However, put a 14-day expiry date on the voucher so that they will return during that time.

I sometimes make small samples of shortbread to give out with a cup of coffee or tea. This allows customers to try the shortbread and at the same time feel that they are getting something free.

Using local radio and newspapers

Advertising in a local newspaper or on a local radio station is much more effective than on a national one because their target audience will more than likely be your potential customers. However, advertising in newspapers and on radio is very expensive so you need to think very carefully about it and only spend what you can afford to lose. Alternatively, try to think up a unique and creative way to get free media coverage for your coffee shop.

FINDING A UNIQUE ANGLE FOR YOUR COFFEE SHOP

Send a press release about your coffee shop to your local newspaper and radio station; this is a great way to get free publicity. However, you may have to think up an unusual, interesting, even unique angle to get people in your community interested: for example, you are using your great-grandmother's 100-year-old recipe for the most delicious caramel apple pie. Or perhaps you have lived all your life in the USA and have just moved to this area to open a speciality coffee shop in an old garage or somewhere unusual. You could coincide the opening of your coffee shop with your silver wedding anniversary, your 30th birthday or another special occasion.

If you can afford the expense, hiring a celebrity or well-known band to open your shop would get you newspaper coverage and you would also attract quite a lot of people to the shop.

The offer of a prize for a competition run by your local radio station or newspaper should get you a free write-up and perhaps a photograph of your coffee shop. All you should have to pay for is the prize. I previously mentioned in Chapter 4 that a competition to name your coffee shop is an excellent idea to get you free publicity in your local newspaper.

FUND-RAISING FOR A CHARITY

One way to get free radio advertising would be to organize a fund-raising morning or afternoon for a local charity and ask one of your well-known suppliers, e.g. Coca-Cola, Pepsi cola, or your supplier of coffee beans, to provide some small prize. You could give cans of Coke, Pepsi or packets of coffee to your first 50 customers or you could make a small charge for them which would go to the charity.

Whatever you do, make your story clear and interesting enough to attract the attention of potential customers.

If you are advertising on the radio, be very specific and clear about the message you want to get across. State who your are, what you are offering and where you are, for example, 'Get down to Mandy's coffee shop for the best breakfast in town. For just £2.99 you get the full works and a bottomless mug of tea or coffee. Mandy's is at 25 High Street, Anytown.'

If you do get free radio or newspaper coverage it is a good idea to write to the journalist or presenter, thanking them for the great story they ran about your coffee shop. You could also include some vouchers for a complimentary coffee or lunch for two people, for them to give to some of their friends.

Using your local tourist board

You could contact your local tourist board to enquire if you can be included in their brochure. This is usually placed in the bedrooms of hotels and B&B establishments. In my experience you have to get your own page designed and printed for inclusion in the guide and then you also have to pay a sum of money to the tourist board. Check out the price of doing this first of all because it may not be the best or the most cost-effective way for you to advertise.

Using an outside agency

Should you or your team run out of ideas but would still like to break out and create something new you can always contact a facilitator to help you consider new ideas for expansion. In the past I have used Paul Wigley who can be contacted on 0777 805 8026 or paul@howmightwe.co.uk or www.howmightwe.co.uk. I have found Paul very helpful and he is prepared to chat on the telephone.

12
POPULAR COFFEE SHOP RECIPES

Soups

☐ Minestroni Soup

☐ Leek and Potato Soup

☐ Chicken and Rice Soup

☐ Split Pea Soup

☐ Lentil Soup

☐ Quick French Onion Soup

☐ Scotch Broth

☐ Cream of Cauliflower and Stilton Soup

☐ Cream of Celery Soup

☐ Parsnip and Chilli Soup

☐ Cream of Carrot and Coriander Soup

☐ Cream of Carrot and Ham Soup

☐ Cream of Mushroom Soup

☐ Cullen Skink

☐ Cream of Tomato and Basil Soup

☐ Tomato and Basil Soup

☐ Italian Sausage Soup

☐ Croutons

Savoury recipes

☐ Breakfast Casserole

☐ Meat Loaf

☐ Quiche

- ☐ Leek and Smoked Haddock Quiche

- ☐ Chicken and Mushroom Casserole

- ☐ Chicken Casserole

- ☐ Mince, Mushroom and Pasta Casserole

- ☐ Cheesy Chilli Pasta

- ☐ Smoked Fish Crumble

Fillings or toppings for baked potatoes

- ☐ Chilli Con Carne

- ☐ Chicken Tikka

- ☐ Chicken Curry

- ☐ Coronation Chicken

Popular cake recipes

- ☐ Sweet Shortcrust Pastry

- ☐ Coconut Slice

- ☐ Oven Scones

- ☐ Savoury Scones

- ☐ American Style Muffins

- ☐ Carrot Cake

- ☐ Cream Cheese Icing

- ☐ Fruit Loaf

- ☐ Cranberry Nut Loaf

- ☐ Apple Spice Loaf

- ☐ Apple Spice Chocolate Chip Cake

- ☐ Sticky Toffee Buns

- ☐ Caramel Butter Icing

- ☐ Toffee Sauce

- ☐ Cupcakes

- ☐ Butter Icing

- ☐ Gingerbread

- ☐ Plain Sponge

- ☐ Chocolate Cake

- ☐ Quick and Easy Shortbread

- ☐ Fine Shortbread

- ☐ Empire Biscuits

- ☐ Aunt Isa's Custard Creams

- ☐ Lemon Meringue Pie

Tray bakes

- ☐ Fudge Slices

- ☐ Rich Chocolate Shortcake

- ☐ Mars Bar Squares

- ☐ Millionaire Shortbread

- ☐ Strawberry Tarts

- ☐ Toffee Tarts

- ☐ Cornflake Crunch

- ☐ Crispy Date Cake

- ☐ Chocolate Coconut Squares

- ☐ Lemon Squares

- ☐ Crispy Surprise

- ☐ Banoffee Pie

- ☐ Strawberry and Vanilla Cheesecake

- ☐ Scottish Tablet

- ☐ Vanilla Fudge

- ☐ Peppermint Slice

- ☐ Truffles

Home baking is something that really brings in customers as there are very few shops nowadays that bake their own cakes and tray bakes. Most coffee shops and tea rooms take the easy option and buy in. This tends to give them an appearance of sameness. If you can manage it, do bake for your coffee shop yourself. If this isn't possible, you should employ a good home baker to do it for you. There is no comparison between the taste of home baking and cakes bought in from a local bakery.

I have included a few recipes which I find popular. It would probably surprise you to discover that customers generally buy more of what I call plain baking, e.g. plain sponge topped with icing and filled with jam and cream, scones, shortbread, fruit loaf and empire biscuits rather than chocolate cake and cheesecake.

The recipe for tablet has been around for many years. My grandmother made it to sell in her shop and then my mother made it for the family. You can sell it either in slices or cut into small squares and give it to your customers to eat with their coffee. I never have any left at the end of the day!

Soups

The soup in our coffee shop is made fresh every day but I do know a coffee shop owner who makes soup in a large batch and freezes half of it to use at a later date.

I was always told that the secret of making tasty soup was to sauté the vegetables in a little butter to begin with. This appears to bring out their flavour.

CREAM SOUPS

I prefer to make cream soup with double cream but if you want to make a cheaper version you can use half the amount of stock and the other half milk, e.g. 600 ml (1pint) stock and 600ml (1pint) full cream milk and then thicken the soup with cornflour.

Knorr makes a range of Bouillon which comes in various flavours including vegetable, chicken, ham, lamb and beef. It is similar to stock cubes but comes in a large tub.

VEGETARIAN SOUPS

If you want to make the soup suitable for vegetarians, substitute the chicken or ham stock with vegetable stock.

> *When we first opened we made stock from either cooked chickens or hams but soon found out that it was time-consuming and we now use Knorr Bouillon for making stock for all our soups.*

The following soups are easy to make and popular with our customers. I usually make a large pot of a run of the mill soup and a small pot of a cream soup every day.

Don't make too large a quantity of soup to begin with until you see how much you are likely to sell in a day. It is better to run out of something rather than to have to throw it away.

You should give your customers a soup portion of 250 ml to 300 ml each. The recipes below should give you approximately 12 – 14 portions of run of the mill soup and approximately 8 portions of cream soup.

Double the quantities of ingredients if you want to increase the quantity of soup you make, and if it is too thick add some more stock. If you don't know how much soup you will sell initially, you could make two large pots of run of the mill soup and if you do not use the second pot, you could freeze it or refrigerate it to use another day.

MINESTRONI SOUP

This is a very chunky soup but it tastes delicious.

---

400 g (14 oz) borlotti beans
4 large leeks, sliced and washed
6 carrots
250 g (9 oz) turnip
4 large potatoes
4 sticks celery
50 g (2 oz) butter, melted
250 g (9oz) uncooked ham, chopped, or bacon (optional)
3.4 litres (6 pints) ham stock (made from Knorr ham bouillon,
or vegetable bouillon if you want to make it suitable for vegetarians)
3 cloves garlic
6 tomatoes or a 400 g tin of chopped tomatoes
2 tsp mixed or Italian herbs
1tsp sugar
2 oz butter
Salt and pepper to taste
Pasta, approx 125 g (4 oz) (spaghetti pasta is best), broken into 2 inch pieces
Parmesan cheese (optional)

---

1 Dice vegetables and sauté them in the melted butter for about 10 minutes or until soft.

2 Add the chopped ham and cook for a further few minutes.

3 Add ham stock, garlic, tomatoes and bring to the boil and then simmer for about 20 minutes.

4 Add the mixed herbs and sugar, then season to taste.

5 Add the pasta and bring back to the boil, stirring all the time.

6 Lower the heat and simmer for 5 minutes or until the pasta is cooked.

Optional Serve with some Parmesan cheese sprinkled on top of the soup, and a portion of garlic bread.

Variations Use tagliatelle or small pasta shapes instead of spaghetti, or haricot or butter beans instead of borlotti beans. I often use French beans as they are quite cheap and give the soup some more colour, and don't really alter the flavour. This soup is also very nice liquidised with a little cream added and a sprinkle of parsley.

LEEK AND POTATO SOUP

8 large leeks, washed and sliced
50 g (2 oz) butter
3.4 litres (6 pints) chicken stock
6 medium potatoes, chopped into large chunks
6 medium carrots, grated
2 bay leaves
Salt and pepper to taste
2 handfuls of parsley, chopped

1 Slice and sauté the leeks in butter for 10 minutes or until soft.

2 Add stock, potatoes, grated carrot and bay leaves.

3 Bring to the boil then turn down the heat and simmer for about 20 to 25 minutes.

4 Season to taste and remove bay leaves.

5 Add chopped parsley.

Variation This soup is also very nice liquidised and with a little cream added and a sprinkle of parsley.

CHICKEN AND RICE SOUP

6 large leeks, washed and sliced
2 sticks celery, finely chopped
50 g (2 oz) butter
4.6 litres (8 pints) chicken stock
4 large carrots, grated
4 chicken breasts (or you can substitute chicken legs), finely diced
250 g (9 oz) American long grain rice
Salt and pepper to taste
2 handfuls parsley, chopped

1 Sauté leeks and celery in butter for 10 minutes or until soft.

2 Add stock, carrots and chicken.

3 Bring to the boil, then turn down the heat and simmer for about 15 minutes.

4 Add rice and simmer for another 10 – 15 minutes until the rice is cooked.

5 Season to taste.

6 Add the chopped parsley.

SPLIT PEA SOUP

1kg (2 lb) split peas
8 leeks
2 sticks of celery
500 g (1 lb 2 oz) potatoes, diced
50 g (2 oz) butter
1 ham bone
4.6 litres (8 pints) water or ham stock
2 handfuls parsley, chopped
Salt and pepper to taste

1 Steep the peas overnight in cold water, then drain.

2 Sauté leeks, celery and potatoes in butter.

3 Place ham bone in the pot with the vegetables and peas.

4 Cover with the water and bring to the boil.

5 Turn down heat and simmer until peas are cooked, approximately 1 hour.

6 Remove the ham bone, cool the mixture slightly and liquidize.

7 Strip the cooked ham off the bone and return it to the soup.

8 Add the parsley.

9 Season to taste and if you have used a ham bone you may also have to add some ham bouillon to increase the flavour of the soup.

Variations If you do not have a ham bone you can use ham stock instead and then add some cooked bacon or ham after liquidizing the soup.
For vegetarian soup, omit the ham and ham stock and use vegetable stock.

LENTIL SOUP

1kg (2 lb) leeks, sliced and washed
4 carrots
50 g (2oz) butter
6.9 litres (12 pints) ham stock
675 g (1 lb 8 oz) red lentils, washed
Salt and pepper

---

1 Slice the leeks, grate the carrots and sauté in butter for about 10 minutes or until soft.

2 Add ham stock and bring to the boil.

3 Add the lentils to the pot, bring gently back to the boil and then simmer gently for about ¾ – 1 hour, stirring occasionally to prevent the lentils from sticking to the bottom of the pan.

4 Season to taste.

5 If the soup is too thick just add some more stock or water.

Variations You can add chopped ham if you like but it makes the soup more expensive to make.

For a change you can add 2 large cans of Heinz tomato soup or some tomato purée to make the lentil soup into Tomato Lentil Soup.

For Garlicky Lentil Soup add 4 large garlic cloves when you add the stock, or add some chopped garlic sausage. You might find, however, that most of your customers don't like garlic and in that case you could make a small amount of it as 'soup of the day'.

QUICK FRENCH ONION SOUP

1kg (2 lbs) onions, sliced
25 g (1 oz) butter
2 tbs vegetable oil
50 g (2 oz) plain flour
4.6 litres (8 pints) chicken or beef stock
2 bay leaves
Salt and pepper to taste

1 Sauté onions in butter and oil until soft.

2 Stir in flour and cook for 1 minute.

3 Stir in stock gradually and add bay leaves.

4 Bring to the boil and then simmer for approximately 15 minutes.

5 Season to taste.

Serve with croutons or garlic bread.

Variation You can sprinkle some grated Gruyère cheese over the soup and put it under the grill to melt. (This makes the soup a bit more expensive but you can charge more for it.)

SCOTCH BROTH

This is quite a filling soup.

---

4 large carrots, grated
1 large turnip, grated
2 large onions
3 large leeks sliced and washed
100 g (4 oz) butter
4.6 litres (8 pints) of lamb stock
500 g (1 lb 2 oz) broth mix (steeped overnight in cold water)
2 handfuls parsley, chopped
Salt and pepper to taste

---

1 Sauté carrots, turnip, onions and leeks in the melted butter.

2 Add the lamb stock and broth mix and bring to the boil.

3 Simmer for about 1 hour, stirring occasionally so that the soup does not stick to the bottom of the pan.

4 Add the parsley and simmer for another few minutes.

5 Season to taste.

6 If the soup is too thick, thin it by adding more stock.

Serve with crusty bread, or a bread roll and butter.

CREAM OF CAULIFLOWER AND STILTON SOUP

If you want to make a less expensive variation of this soup, add milk and use less cream.

1 kg (2 lb) cauliflower, chopped
4 sticks of celery, chopped
2 large onions, sliced
75 g (3 oz) butter
1.2 litres (2 pints) chicken stock
150 g(5 oz) Stilton cheese, chopped
Pinch of nutmeg
240 ml (8 fl oz) double cream or 600 ml (1 pint) milk plus 50 ml (2 fl oz) double cream
Salt and pepper to taste
Parsley to garnish

1 Sauté cauliflower, celery and onions in butter.

2 Add chicken stock and milk (if using) and simmer until the vegetables are almost cooked.

3 Add Stilton cheese and cook for another 5 minutes.

4 Cool slightly and liquidize.

5 Put back into pan and add nutmeg and double cream.

6 Heat slowly and season to taste.

To serve, sprinkle each serving with a teaspoon of parsley.

Variation You can substitute broccoli for the cauliflower and celery to make Broccoli and Stilton Soup.

CREAM OF CELERY SOUP

---

2 heads of celery, finely sliced
1 large onion, sliced
2 leeks, sliced and washed
100 g (4 oz) butter
1.2 litres (2 pints) chicken stock
240 ml (8 fl oz) double cream
Salt and pepper to taste

---

1 Sauté the celery, onion and leeks in the melted butter for about 10 minutes.

2 Add chicken stock and bring to the boil, then turn down to simmer for about 20 minutes. Cool slightly and liquidize, then return to the pan and heat gently.

3 Add cream and season to taste.

PARSNIP AND CHILLI SOUP

---

4 onions, sliced
8 parsnips, peeled, quartered and wood centres removed
100 g (4 oz) butter
2 large cloves of garlic, chopped
1.2 litres (2 pints) of chicken stock
½ tsp hot chilli powder (add more to taste if you like)
Salt and pepper to taste
240 ml (8 fl oz) double cream

---

1 Sauté onions and parsnips in the melted butter for about 8 –10 mins until they begin to soften, then add the chopped garlic and cook for another 2 minutes.

2 Add the chicken stock and chilli powder and cook until the parsnips are tender.

3 Cool slightly and then liquidize.

4 Season to taste and add more chilli powder if required.

5 Return to the pan and mix in the cream and heat through.

Serve with a swirl of cream on top.

Variation For a different flavour, instead of using chilli powder you can use curry powder.

CREAM OF CARROT AND CORIANDER SOUP

6 leeks, sliced and washed
1kg (2 lb) carrots, sliced or grated
100 g (4 oz) butter
2.3 litres (4 pints) chicken stock
A handful of fresh coriander, chopped (you can use ground coriander
but I think fresh tastes better), plus a little coriander or parsley to garnish
240 ml (8fl oz) double cream
Salt and pepper to taste

1 Sauté the leeks and carrots in melted butter for about 10 minutes until they soften.

2 Add chicken stock and bring to the boil.

3 Add chopped coriander and bring back to the boil, cover and simmer for about 20 minutes until the leeks and carrots are cooked.

4 Cool slightly and liquidize.

5 Return to the pan and add the cream, reheat gently and then season to taste.

Serve with a swirl of cream and a little chopped coriander or chopped parsley.

Variation You can omit the coriander and add fresh minced ginger root and a pinch of nutmeg to make Carrot and Ginger Soup.

CREAM OF CARROT AND HAM SOUP

4 onions, finely sliced
225 g (8 oz) bacon or ham, chopped
100g (4 oz) butter
2.3 litres (4 pints) ham stock
900 g (2 lb) carrots, sliced
240 ml (8 fl oz) double cream
Salt and pepper to taste
A little chopped parsley, to garnish

❶ Sauté onions and chopped bacon together in butter until soft.

❷ Add ham stock and carrots and bring to the boil.

❸ Simmer and cook for about 20 minutes. Cool slightly and liquidize.

❹ Return to the pan, add the cream and heat gently.

❺ Season to taste.

Serve with a swirl of cream and a little chopped parsley.

CREAM OF MUSHROOM SOUP

2 onions, finely sliced
550 g (1lb 4 oz) mushrooms, finely sliced
100 g (4 oz) butter
1.2 litres (2 pints) chicken stock
240 ml (8 fl oz) double cream
Salt and pepper to taste

❶ Sauté the onions and the mushrooms in butter for approximately 2 minutes, then cover and sauté for about 8 minutes.

❷ Add stock and bring to the boil, then simmer for about 15 minutes.

❸ Cool slightly and liquidize. Return to the pan and add the cream and heat gently.

❹ Season to taste.

CULLEN SKINK

This is a Scottish smoked fish soup which is delicious.

2 onions, finely chopped
2 leeks, sliced and washed
50 g (2oz) butter
500 g undyed smoked haddock (fresh or frozen but, if frozen, defrost first)
2.3 litres (4 pints) full cream milk
2 bay leaves
4 large potatoes, chopped
150 ml (½ pint) double cream
Salt and pepper to taste
2 handfuls of fresh parsley, chopped

1 Sauté the onions and leeks in melted butter until soft.

2 Place the smoked haddock on top and add enough milk to cover the fish.

3 Add the bay leaves and simmer for 5 minutes.

4 The fish should now be cooked so lift it from the pan and set aside.

5 Add the chopped potato and remaining milk to the pan and simmer for another 20 minutes. While this is simmering remove any skin and bones from the fish.

6 Break the fish into flakes.

7 Remove the bay leaves and liquidize the milk and vegetable mixture.

8 Return mixture to the pan, add the cream and heat through gently.

9 Finally, add the flaked fish and season to taste.

Serve sprinkled with chopped parsley.

CREAM OF TOMATO AND BASIL SOUP

---

4 onions, sliced
100 g (4 oz) butter
4 x 400 g tins of tomatoes plus a little tomato purée
3.4 litres (6 pints) chicken stock
1 tsp sugar
A handful of fresh basil, chopped
240 ml (8 fl oz) double cream
Salt and pepper to taste

---

1 Sauté onions in melted butter until soft and then add tins of tomatoes and chicken stock.

2 Bring to the boil then simmer for about 15 minutes.

3 Add sugar and chopped basil and simmer for another 5 minutes.

4 Cool slightly and liquidize.

5 Return to the pan, add double cream and heat gently.

6 Season to taste and if you think the soup requires more tomato, add some tomato purée and check the taste again until you have added sufficient.

Serve garnished with chopped basil leaves.

TOMATO AND BASIL SOUP

4 tins of chopped tomatoes (400g tins)
4 carrots (diced small or grated)
4 sticks of celery (cut thinly)
2 large onions (slice thinly)
2 cloves of garlic (crush)
Handful of fresh basil
Vegetable stock or chicken stock
25g (1 oz) butter
Seasoning

1 Chop carrots, celery and onions and sauté in butter.

2 Add tins of tomatoes, crushed garlic, stock and a little sugar.

3 Cook until the vegetables are soft then liquidise.

4 Add chopped basil and heat through.

5 Season to taste and if required add a little tomato puree

Variation You can add chilli powder or cayenne pepper and finish with a swirl of sour cream.

If you have tomatoes which need to be used up you can blanche them in boiling water for one minute then plunge them into cold water. Remove the skin and chop the flesh then replace the tins of tomatoes with the freshly shopped ones.

ITALIAN SAUSAGE SOUP

2 garlic sausages (sliced)
2 large onions (sliced)
250g (9 oz) mushrooms (sliced)
3 cloves of garlic
1 tin chopped tomatoes (400g)
2.3 litres (4 pints) chicken stock
½ cup of long grain rice
50g (2 oz) butter
Mixed herbs

1 Sauté onions in butter until soft then add mushrooms and cook for 2 – 3 minutes.

2 Add stock, garlic, tomatoes and cook for about 15 minutes then add rice and garlic sausage.

3 Add mixed herbs, a little sugar and season to taste.

CROUTONS

Croutons add a finishing touch, served with some of the soup recipes.
It is best to bake them in the oven.

Small cubes of white or brown bread
Olive or vegetable oil

1 Line a baking tray with baking paper.

2 Spread oil all over the baking sheet.

3 Arrange cubes of bread on the sheet and cover them with the oil by turning them over until they are evenly coated.

4 Bake in a preheated oven at 180°C (350°F), Gas Mark 4 for about 10 minutes.

Variation If you want garlic-flavoured croutons, mix some garlic powder with the oil before spreading it on the baking sheet. Another variation is to spread the bread thinly with mayonnaise and sprinkle with a pinch or onion powder then grill until golden.

Savoury Recipes

I have included some popular recipes that are easy to make and are highly profitable.

BREAKFAST CASSEROLE
Serves 6 – 8

---

4 slices of bread
450 g (1 lb) sliced sausage, or spicy sausage for a change
2 cups (225 g or 8 oz) strong Cheddar cheese, grated
6 large eggs
2 cups (600 ml or 1 pint) milk
1 tsp salt
Dash of pepper
1 tsp dry mustard

---

1 Tear up bread and place in a greased baking dish, 32.5 x 7.5 x 5 cm (13 x 9 x 2 in).

2 Brown and drain sausage meat. Spoon sausage over bread.

3 Sprinkle with grated cheese.

4 Beat together eggs, milk, salt, pepper and dry mustard.

5 Pour over the mixture in the baking dish.

6 Cover and refrigerate for 30 minutes. (It tastes even better if refrigerated overnight.)

7 Bake at 180°C (350°F), Gas Mark 4 for 35 – 40 minutes. The cheese will rise to the top during baking.

MEAT LOAF

1 kg (2 lb) minced beef
2 large onions
6 rashers of bacon, chopped
250 g (9 oz) mushrooms, chopped
Vegetable or olive oil
4 cups (450 g or 1 lb) fresh breadcrumbs (more if required)
2 handfuls fresh parsley, chopped
2 eggs, beaten
Salt and pepper to taste

1 Brown the mince and set aside.

2 Fry the onions and mushrooms in a little oil until soft.

3 Add the onions, mushrooms and breadcrumbs to the browned mince.

4 Add chopped parsley and bind with the eggs. Mix well.

5 Grease and line 2 x 1 kg (2 lb) loaf tins and fill with mixture. Cover the top with greaseproof paper to stop the top of the loaf forming a crust.

6 Cook in a preheated oven at 180°C (360°F), Gas Mark 4 for 45 mins to1 hour.

Serve sliced, hot with gravy, or cold with salad and crusty bread. (You will be able to get a good profit from this.)

QUICHE
For the pastry

250 g (9 oz) plain flour
142 g (5 oz) hard Stork margarine or butter
1 egg
20 ml (1 fl oz) cold water

For the filling
You can use various fillings but I find that this is the most popular one.
1 onion, chopped
4 slices of bacon, sliced
2 tomatoes
125 g (4 oz) medium Cheddar cheese, grated
1 cup (225 ml or 8 fl oz) double cream
½ cup (110 ml or 4 fl oz) milk
5 eggs
Salt to taste

To make the pastry

1 Sift flour into a mixing bowl.

2 Rub in margarine or butter, or mix in a food processor, until the mixture resembles fine breadcrumbs.

3 Whisk egg and water together and add gradually to the flour mixture until it comes together in a ball.

4 Cover with clingfilm and leave in the fridge for 30 min.

5 Roll out the pastry on a lightly floured surface.

6 Grease a 25 cm (10 in) flan dish and line with the pastry.

7 Prick the base and then bake blind at 200°C (400°F), Gas Mark 6 for approximately 20 minutes or until the pastry is a pale golden colour.

To make the filling

1 Sauté the onion until soft, and add the bacon strips and cook for a further few minutes until cooked.

2 Place onion and bacon on top of the pastry case.

3 Slice the tomatoes and lay them on top of the onion and bacon.

4 Sprinkle the grated cheese over the top.

5 Whisk the cream, milk and eggs together, add salt to taste.

6 Pour the mixture on top of the quiche.

7 Bake in a preheated oven at 180°C (350°F), Gas Mark 4 for 30 – 40 minutes or until the egg mixture has set and is a light golden colour.

Serve hot or cold with salad.

Place the flan dish containing the filling on a baking tray before you pour over the egg mixture. This will save you spilling any if it runs over.

LEEK AND SMOKED HADDOCK QUICHE
Make the pastry base as on page 137 in a 25 cm (10 in) flan dish

For the filling

450 g (1 lb) smoked haddock
300 ml (½ pint) milk
300 ml (½ pint) double cream
1 bay leaf
Pinch of nutmeg
6 black peppercorns
450 g (1 lb) leeks
50 g (2 oz) butter
4 eggs
25 g (1 oz) medium Cheddar or Gruyère cheese, grated

1 Poach the haddock in the milk and half the cream with the bay leaf, nutmeg and peppercorns for 5 mins.

2 Remove the fish, strain the poaching liquid into a jug and set aside to cool.

3 Remove any skin or bones from the fish and flake it.

4 Sauté the leeks in the butter until soft.

5 Place the leeks and the flaked fish on the pastry case.

6 Sprinkle the grated cheese on top.

7 Whisk together the eggs, poaching milk and remaining double cream.

8 Pour egg mixture on top of quiche.

9 Bake in a preheated oven at 180°C (350°F), Gas Mark 4 for 35 – 40 minutes or until the egg mixture has set and is a light golden colour.

CHICKEN AND MUSHROOM CASSEROLE

8 chicken breasts (cut into ¾ inch strips)
1 cup mayonnaise
1 tsp curry powder or chilli powder
1 cup double cream
2 tins of condensed cream of mushroom soup
500g (1 lb 2 oz)mushrooms (sliced)
1 tablespoon lemon juice
Broccoli florettes (enough to cover the bottom of the casserole)
1 layer of partially cooked potatoes (sliced)
Cheddar cheese (grated and enough for covering the top of the casserole)
Seasoning

❶ Lay sliced potatoes on the bottom of the casserole.

❷ Blanche broccoli and cover the bottom of a casserole dish with it and the sliced mushrooms.

❸ In a bowl combine cream, soup, mayonnaise, curry powder or chilli powder and lemon juice, seasoning and mix well.

❹ Spoon the mixture over the chicken and vegetables making sure that it completely covers the casserole.

❺ Cover the casserole then bake in the oven at 180 degrees for 30 minutes.

❻ Take out the casserole and cover with the grated cheese and return to the oven until the cheese has melted.

Serve with crusty bread and butter.

CHICKEN CASSEROLE

---

8 chicken breasts (cut into strips)
4 onions
8 mushrooms (sliced)
4tbs vegetable oil
50 g (2 oz) plain flour
2 chicken stock cubes or equivalent chicken bouillon made up
with 850 ml (1½ pints) boiling water
4 tbs tomato puree
Pinch of sugar
Seasoning
Chopped parsley
1 large green pepper and one red pepper (optional)

---

1 Sauté onions in oil until soft.

2 Remove and brown chicken and add flour.

3 Blend in the stock, tomato puree, salt, pepper and sugar.

4 Place the chicken in the casserole and top with sliced mushrooms and pepper.

5 Cover with the chicken stock and cook in a covered dish 180 degrees for 1 hour.

6 Sprinkle with chopped parsley.

Serve with potatoes or pasta.

MINCE, MUSHROOM AND PASTA CASSEROLE

900g (2 lbs) minced beef
10 mushrooms (sliced)
2 carrots (grated)
2 stalks celery
2 onions (sliced)
2 packets of Passata (sieved tomatoes)
1 tsp sugar
Half a cup of double cream
Cheddar Cheese (grated)
500g (1 lb 2 oz) macaroni pasta or any other pasta (cooked)
Seasoning

❶ Put cooked pasta in the bottom of the casserole dish.

❷ Brown mince, carrot, celery and onion in a little vegetable oil and add to casserole.

❸ Top with sliced mushroom.

❹ Mix stock, tomato puree, cream, salt and pepper and sugar in a bowl and pour onto the casserole.

❺ Cover casserole and cook in oven at 180°C (350°F), Gas Mark 4 for about 30 minutes.

❻ Transfer the cooked casserole into individual Grattan dishes and cover with grated cheese and put under the grill until the cheese has melted.

Serve with garlic bread.

CHEESY CHILLI PASTA

❶ Make chilli from recipe on page 144.

❷ Cook some tagliatelli pasta.

❷ Mix the some of the chilli with the pasta and transfer to individual Grattan dishes.

❹ Cover with grated cheddar cheese and put under the grill to melt the cheese.

Serve with garlic bread.

SMOKED FISH CRUMBLE

---

6 smoked haddock fillets (undyed)
Broccoli spears
600 ml (1 pint) white sauce
180–220g (6 – 8oz) brown bread crumbs (you can use up yesterday's bread)
100g (4 oz) cheddar cheese
50 g (2 oz) parmesan cheese
Seasoning

---

1 Place broccoli spears on the bottom of a buttered casserole dish.

2 Place the haddock fillets over the broccoli and pour over the white sauce.

3 Add grated cheddar cheese to bread crumbs and cover the fish with them.

4 Sprinkle parmesan cheese over the top.

5 Bake for 30–35 minutes in an oven at 200°C (400°F), Gas Mark 6.

Serving suggestion: again you could transfer some of the fish casserole into individual dishes before stage 3 and top them with the bread crumbs and cheese and put under the grill to brown.

Fillings or Toppings for Baked Potatoes

Baked potatoes are very popular because they are easy to prepare and fill. There are many varieties of toppings and I have listed below a few of the most popular, as well as some more unusual ones.

Do use your imagination to create appetizing toppings and gradually add some of them to your menu. If they don't sell well, take them off the menu and introduce different ones.

VEGETARIAN OPTIONS

- ☐ Broccoli in a cheese sauce
- ☐ Broccoli, onions and sour cream
- ☐ Sour cream and chives
- ☐ Baked beans with grated cheese
- ☐ Cheese and leek
- ☐ Creamed garlic mushrooms
- ☐ Mature Cheddar cheese
- ☐ Coleslaw

NON-VEGETARIAN OPTIONS

- ☐ Chilli con carne, grated cheese and sour cream
- ☐ Bacon bits and sour cream
- ☐ Chicken mayonnaise or chicken, sweetcorn and mayonnaise
- ☐ Coronation Chicken
- ☐ Prawns with pineapple, mayonnaise and a sprinkling of paprika
- ☐ Chicken curry
- ☐ Steak strips with onions
- ☐ Smoked salmon and cream cheese
- ☐ Tuna, sweetcorn and mayonnaise
- ☐ Smoked haddock in a cream sauce

□ Haggis

□ Diced ham, onion, red peppers and mayonnaise

□ Diced ham with sour cream and chives

CHILLI CON CARNE

---

2 kg (4 lb) beef mince
8 large onions, finely chopped
6 cloves of garlic, finely chopped
4 Oxo cubes
1 – 1¼ litres (2 – 2½ pints) water
300 g (11 oz) tomato purée
1–2 tsp hot chilli powder (start off with 1 tsp and then add more if required)
2 tsp sugar
2 x 400 g cans red kidney beans
Salt to taste

---

❶ Brown the mince in a large pot.

❷ Add finely chopped onion and garlic and cook for 5 minutes.

❸ Crush Oxo cubes and add to 600 ml (1 pint) of boiling water, then add tomato purée.

❹ Add all the liquid to the mince.

❺ Add chilli powder and sugar.

❻ Bring to the boil then turn down heat and simmer for about 1 hour (alternatively, you can cook it in a casserole in the oven).

❼ Check how hot the chilli tastes and add more chilli powder if required.

❽ Check to see if the mixture requires more water or more tomato purée.

❾ Add the drained kidney beans and simmer for another 10 minutes.

❿ Season to taste.

CHICKEN TIKKA

3 large onions, finely chopped
100 g (4 oz) butter
8 cloves garlic
2 tsp cumin seeds
2 tsp coriander seeds
8 cardamom pods
4 tsp turmeric
4 tsp ginger powder
2 tsp chilli powder
8 chicken breasts, chopped into cubes
600 ml (1 pint) chicken stock made from chicken bouillon
300 ml (½ pint) double cream
Salt to taste

1 Sauté onions in butter until soft.

2 Add garlic and spices and cook for a few minutes.

3 Add chicken and cook for about 5 minutes.

4 Add chicken stock.

5 Cover and simmer for about 20 minutes until chicken is cooked.

6 Remove from heat and add double cream.

7 Season to taste.

CHICKEN CURRY

4 onions, chopped
100 g (4 oz) butter
6 cloves of garlic, crushed (you can substitute garlic powder or lazy garlic)
2 tsp coriander
2 tsp ginger
1 tsp turmeric
8 chicken breasts, chopped into cubes
2 x 400 g tins chopped tomatoes
Pinch of sugar
25 g (1 oz) portion of chicken bouillon made up
in a jug with (225 ml or 8 fl oz) of boiling water
300 ml (½ pint) double cream
Salt to taste

1 Sauté onions in butter until soft.

2 Add garlic and spices and cook for a few minutes.

3 Add diced chicken and cook for about 5 minutes.

4 Add tomatoes, sugar, chicken bouillon and simmer for about 30 minutes.

5 Remove from heat and, just before serving, add cream.

6 Season to taste.

CORONATION CHICKEN

Coronation Chicken is time-consuming to make. I would purchase Coronation-flavoured mayonnaise and mix it with freshly cooked, chopped chicken breast.

This is a quick recipe which you could try if you want to make your own Coronation Chicken.

250 g (9 oz) onion, chopped
A little vegetable oil
1 litre (2 pints) mayonnaise
2 heaped tsp tomato purée
2 heaped tbs curry powder or paste
1 tbs lemon juice
4 tbs mango chutney
225 ml (8 fl oz) double cream
Salt and pepper to taste

❶ Gently fry onions in oil and leave to cool.

❷ Mix together mayonnaise, tomato purée, curry powder and lemon juice

❸ Add mango chutney and mix well.

❹ Add double cream and season to taste.

❺ If required, add more curry powder and a little more mango chutney.

Fillings for sandwiches

There are endless varieties of fillings for sandwiches, wraps and paninis and I have listed below a few suggestions.

> List on your menu several everyday varieties of sandwiches, wraps and paninis and a few of the more unusual ones. Or you could ask your customers to design their own sandwich. You could fix a price for a basic sandwich or wrap and then add an extra amount for each additional item they choose. For example, Cheese, Ham and Tomato would be £1.75 for a plain cheese sandwich or wrap, plus 50p for the ham and 30p for the tomato, making a total of £2.55 for that particular sandwich. You would obviously charge a bit more for a more expensive filling than you would for a salad filling.

- ☐ Chicken mayonnaise

- ☐ Prawn Marie Rose

- ☐ Prawn in sweet chilli and lime sauce

- ☐ Ham, cheese and tomato

- ☐ Hot roast beef with horseradish sauce

- ☐ Corned beef, tomato and spring onion with mayonnaise

- ☐ Barbeque chicken with mayonnaise and caramelized onions

- ☐ Cream cheese or cottage cheese with crispy bacon pieces

VEGETARIAN OPTIONS

- ☐ Cheese and apple coleslaw

- ☐ Brie, tomato and mayonnaise

- ☐ Avocado and Brie

- ☐ Egg mayonnaise

- ☐ Cheese and tomato

- ☐ Cheese and pickle

- ☐ Carrots, green pepper and cream cheese

TOASTED SANDWICHES AND PANINIS

☐ Cheese and ham

☐ Cheese, ham and pineapple

☐ Chicken, cheese and caramelized onion

☐ Chicken, cranberry sauce and mayonnaise

☐ Chicken, sweetcorn and mayonnaise

☐ Bacon, Brie and cranberry sauce with mayonnaise

☐ Bacon, Brie, tomato and mayonnaise

☐ Ham, roast peppers and cream cheese

☐ Smoked salmon and cream cheese

☐ Cheese, caramelized onion and mayonnaise

☐ Cheese and onion

☐ Brie, tomato and onion

☐ Cheese and pickle

☐ Cream cheese, roast peppers and onion

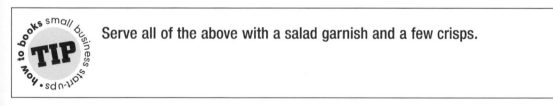

Serve all of the above with a salad garnish and a few crisps.

You can purchase plain or flavoured mayonnaise – for example, Tikka and Coronation mayonnaise – already made up in 5 or 10 litre tubs from most suppliers.

Popular cake and traybake recipes

SWEET SHORTCRUST PASTRY

500 g (1 lb 2 oz) plain flour
275 g (10 oz) Stork margarine
1 egg
50 ml (2 fl oz) cold water
150 g (5 oz) caster sugar

1 Sift flour into a bowl.

2 Cut the margarine into cubes and then rub it into the flour with your fingertips until the mixture resembles coarse breadcrumbs.

3 Mix the egg, water and sugar with a whisk and then gradually add enough of the liquid to bind the dough.

4 Gather into a ball, wrap in clingfilm and put into the fridge for about 20 minutes.

5 On a lightly floured surface, roll out the dough to the shape of the flan dish or baking tray.

 You can use this pastry for pies and other recipes that require a pastry base.

 You can purchase tubs of ready-to-use chilled rhubarb and chilled Bramley apple pie filling from Baco. (See the useful contacts section in Appendix 7.)

COCONUT SLICE
1 recipe sweet shortcrust pastry (see page 150)

For the filling
300 g (11 oz) coconut
150 ml (¼ pint) hot milk
225 g (8 oz) margarine
225 g (8 oz) caster sugar
75 g (3 oz) rice flour
3 whole eggs and 1 egg white
Approx 450 g (1 lb) raspberry jam
A little melted chocolate

---

❶ Soak the coconut in the hot milk.

❷ Cream the margarine and sugar together.

❸ Mix in the rice flour, add the eggs and beat well.

❹ Add the softened coconut and mix well.

❺ Use sweet shortcrust pastry to line the base of a baking tray measuring 34 cm x 23 cm (13½ in x 9 in) and cover with a layer of raspberry jam.*

❻ Top with the coconut mixture and bake at 190°C (375°F), Gas Mark 5 for 45 mins or until golden.

❼ When cool, drizzle with melted chocolate.

Note: I use seedless raspberry jam which is available in large jars from Tesco.

* (You probably won't need to use all the jam.)

OVEN SCONES

---

500 g (1 lb 2 oz) self-raising flour
4 heaped tsp baking powder
125 g (4 oz) caster sugar
2 eggs
130 ml (4 fl oz) milk
100 ml (3½ fl oz) vegetable oil

---

1 Sift together the flour and baking powder and then add the caster sugar.

2 Whisk the eggs, milk and vegetable oil together and pour into the dry ingredients.

3 Mix with a fork to form a soft dough.

4 Roll out on a lightly floured surface and cut into rounds about 2½ – 3 cm (1 – 1¼ in) thick with an 8 cm (3 in) cutter.

5 Bake on a non-stick baking sheet at 200°C (400°F), Gas Mark 6 for 10 – 12 minutes or until golden.

You can increase or decrease the size of the scones if you want to.

Variations For fruit scones just add 150 g (5 oz) sultanas or dried fruit to the mix before adding the liquid to the dry ingredients. You can try crystallized ginger, dates, cranberries or cheese for a change.

For jam and cream scones, cool the scones, split them open and spread strawberry jam on one side and whipped double cream on the other, then sandwich them together. These are delicious and sell very well.

SAVOURY SCONES

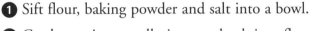

450 g (1lb) self raising flour
2 teasps baking powder
125 g (4 oz) butter
1 tsp salt
225 g (8 oz) cheddar cheese
2 eggs
75 mls (2½ fl oz) milk
75 mls (2½ fl oz) single cream

1 Sift flour, baking powder and salt into a bowl.

2 Cut butter into small pieces and rub into flour mixture until it resembles breadcrumbs.

3 Stir in the cheese.

4 Whisk the milk and eggs together and add to the flour mixture until you have a soft dough.

5 Roll out on a lightly floured board to 2½–3cm (1½ in) thick and cut with a 8cm (3in) cutter.

6 Brush the top of the scones with the remainder of the egg mixture or with some milk.

7 Bake in the oven for 10 – 15 minutes 220°C (425°F), Gas Mark 7 or until risen and golden.

Variations There are many flavours you can add to the scone mixture such as:
Cheese and olive, cheese and ham, cheese and onion, smokey sausage and wholemeal or anything you think will taste good.

AMERICAN STYLE MUFFINS

300g (10 oz) plain flour
2 level tsps baking powder
150g (5 oz) golden caster sugar
125g (4 oz) blueberries
1 medium egg
1 tsp vanilla flavouring
225ml (8 fl oz) milk
50g (2 oz) butter

---

1 Line muffin tin with paper cases.

2 Sift flour and baking powder.

3 Stir in caster sugar.

4 Melt the butter.

5 Mix together the melted butter, egg, milk and vanilla flavouring.

6 Add blueberries and mix.

7 Fill muffin cases to ¾ full.

8 Bake at 200°C (400°F), Gas Mark 6 for 20 – 25 minutes.

Variation Substitute another fruit or jam to make other flavoured muffins such as: cranberry, sultana, chocolate chip, milk and white chocolate chip, ginger and orange, toffee and banana, sweet mincemeat, apple and toffee.

CARROT CAKE

For the cake

450 ml (¾ pint) vegetable oil

8 eggs

450 g (1 lb) caster sugar

2 tsp vanilla flavouring

450 g plain flour

15 g (½ oz) bicarbonate of soda

15 g (½ oz) baking powder

20 g (¾ oz) cinnamon

15 g (½ oz) salt

5 g (⅛ oz) mixed spice

625 g (1 lb 6 oz) carrots, grated

150 g (5 oz) walnut pieces, chopped quite small

To make the cake

❶ Mix oil, eggs, sugar and vanilla flavouring.

❷ Sieve all dry ingredients.

❸ Add dry ingredients to oil, eggs, sugar and vanilla flavouring and mix.

❹ Add grated carrots and chopped walnuts and mix well.

❺ Grease and line a 35 cm x 25 cm (14 in x 10 in) cake tin with non-stick baking paper.

❻ Bake at 180°C (350°F), Gas Mark 4 for 45 mins – 1 hour (for a fan oven, reduce the temperature to 170°C).

If you like a spicier cake you can add more mixed spice and cinnamon.

 I always use Tesco unbleached non-stick Baking paper for lining all the baking trays.

I usually ice half of the cake to sell in the coffee shop and wrap the other half of the cake in tin foil to use the following day. Alternatively, you can freeze the other half if you don't think you will use it within three or four days. This cake keeps for up to four days in a sealed container.

For the cream cheese icing
125 g (4 oz) soft margarine or butter
250 g (9 oz) cream cheese
500 g (1 lb 2 oz) icing sugar
1 tsp vanilla flavouring

To make the icing

❶ Cream the margarine and cream cheese together.

❷ Add the vanilla flavouring and enough icing sugar to make a thick topping for the cake. If the icing is too stiff add a little water and mix until you are happy with the consistency. If the icing is too thin then add more icing sugar.

FRUIT LOAF

1½ cups (225 g or 8 oz) sultanas or mixed dried fruit
1 tsp mixed spice
1 tsp bicarbonate of soda
1 cup (125 g or 4 oz) sugar
225 g (8 oz) margarine
1 cup (300 ml or ½ pint) water
1 cup (125 g or 4 oz) self-raising flour
1 cup (125 g or 4 oz) plain flour
2 eggs

---

❶ Put the sultanas, mixed spice, bicarbonate of soda, sugar, margarine and water into a pot and bring to the boil for one minute.

❷ Cool and add the flour and eggs and mix thoroughly.

❸ Put the mixture into a greased and lined 900 g (2lb) loaf tin.

❹ Bake at 180°C (350°F), Gas Mark 4 for 1 – 1¼ hours.

❺ Test with a cake tester or toothpick and if it comes out clean the cake is ready.

CRANBERRY NUT LOAF

120 ml (4 fl oz) vegetable oil
200 g (7 oz) soft brown or muscovado sugar
2 eggs, beaten
3 very ripe bananas, mashed
290 g (11 oz) self-raising flour
½ tsp baking powder
1 tsp baking soda
½ tsp salt
3 tbs milk
1 tsp vanilla flavouring
115 g (4 ½ oz) chopped walnuts
150 g (5 oz) dried cranberries

1 Beat the oil and sugar together.

2 Add the eggs and mashed bananas and beat well.

3 Add the sifted dry ingredients, milk and vanilla flavouring.

4 Mix well and stir in the nuts and cranberries.

5 Pour mixture into a greased and lined 700 g (1½ lb) loaf tin.

6 Bake for 1 hour to 1 hour and 10 mins at 180°C (350°F), Gas Mark 4 or until a cake tester or toothpick comes out clean.

APPLE SPICE LOAF

This is a very easy recipe as it is all done in a food processor.

---

120 ml (4 fl oz) vegetable oil
2 large eggs
200 g (7 oz) soft brown or muscovado sugar
300 ml (½ pint) partly cooked apples or tinned apples, diced
215 g (7½ oz) self-raising flour
4 tsp cinnamon
2 tsp mixed spice
1 heaped tsp baking soda
½ tsp salt
115 g (4 oz) chopped walnuts

---

❶ Put all the ingredients into a food processor and switch on for about 10 seconds.

❷ Scrape down the bowl and put the machine on to pulse until all the ingredients are mixed thoroughly. Do not over process.

❸ Scrape out the bowl and put the mixture into a lined 700 g (1½ lb) loaf tin and bake at 190°C (375°F), Gas Mark 5 for about 1 hour or until a cake tester or toothpick comes out clean when inserted into the centre of the loaf.

You can purchase a tub of Bramley apples for using in cakes and pies from Baco (see the useful contacts section in Appendix 7). This will save you a lot of time peeling and slicing cooking apples.

APPLE SPICE CHOCOLATE CHIP CAKE

---

240 ml (8½ fl oz) vegetable oil
4 large eggs
400 g (14 oz) soft brown or muscovado sugar
600 ml (1 pint) partly cooked apples or tinned apples, diced
450 g (1 lb) self-raising flour
3 tsp baking soda
1 tsp salt
8 tsp cinnamon
4 tsp mixed spice
200 g (7 oz) milk chocolate chips
100 g (4 oz) milk chocolate chips for decoration

---

1 Mix all the ingredients except the chocolate chips together in a food processor for about 15 seconds.

2 Scrape down the bowl and add 200 g chocolate chips. Put the machine on to pulse until the ingredients are mixed thoroughly. Do not over process.

3 Scrape the mixture into a lined cake tin 35 cm x 25 cm (14 in x 10 in) and bake in a preheated oven at 190°C (375°F), Gas Mark 5 for about 1 hour or until the cake tester or toothpick comes out clean when inserted into the centre of the cake.

4 When the cake is cool, ice with butter icing and sprinkle with chocolate chips.

If you want to make a smaller cake use half of the ingredients and bake in a lined 23 cm x 18 cm (9 in x 7 in) cake tin.

STICKY TOFFEE BUNS

---

85 g (3½ oz) butter
175 g (6 oz) soft brown or muscovado sugar
1 tsp mixed spice
1 tsp cinnamon
2 eggs beaten
175 g (6 oz) self-raising flour
250 ml (9 fl oz) tea
½ tsp bicarbonate of soda
250 g (9 oz) stoned dates, chopped

---

1 Cream the butter and sugar together.

2 Add the mixed spice and cinnamon.

3 Add the beaten egg and flour alternately.

4 Make the tea using one tea bag and 250 ml (9 fl oz) boiling water.

5 Remove the tea bag, pour the tea into a saucepan, add the bicarbonate of soda and dates then simmer for approximately 3 minutes or until the dates are soft.

6 Let the date mixture cool slightly before folding it into the butter, sugar and egg mixture.

7 Put the mixture into large muffin cases in a muffin tray and tray and bake in a pre-heated oven at 180°C (350°F), Gas Mark 4 for about 20 – 25 minutes.

8 To see if the buns are ready, insert a cake tester or toothpick into the middle of one and if it comes out clean the buns are ready.

9 When the buns are cool, ice them with caramel butter icing or, for a sticky topping, spread a little boiled, condensed milk over them.

For the caramel butter icing
100 g (4 oz) dark muscovado sugar
100 g (4 oz) butter
130 ml (4½ oz) double cream
1 tsp vanilla flavouring
300 g (11 oz) icing sugar, sifted

To make the caramel butter icing

1 Bring the sugar, butter and cream slowly to the boil.

2 Add the vanilla flavouring.

3 Remove from the heat and leave to cool.

④ Add the icing sugar and blend until the mixture is smooth.

⑤ Add a little more cream or a little more icing sugar until you reach the desired consistency.

Variation To serve as a dessert, you can top a sticky toffee bun with ice cream and sticky toffee sauce.

For the toffee sauce
100 g (4 oz) dark muscovado sugar
100 g (4 oz) butter
130 ml (4½ fl oz) double cream
1 tsp vanilla flavouring

To make the toffee sauce

❶ Melt the sugar, butter and cream together.

❷ Add the vanilla flavouring.

❸ Simmer until the sauce is a nice toffee colour.

CUPCAKES

125 g (4 oz) butter or soft margarine
375 g (13 oz) caster sugar
1 tsp vanilla flavouring
4 eggs plus 2 yolks
315 g (11½ oz) self-raising flour or McDougall's supreme sponge flour
½ tsp salt
250 ml (9 fl oz) double cream

1 Cream the butter or margarine and sugar together until light and fluffy.

2 Add the vanilla flavouring.

3 Add the eggs and yolks one at a time, beating well after you add each one.

4 Add the sifted flour and the cream alternately, beginning and ending with the flour.

5 Put the mixture into large muffin cases in a muffin tin.

6 Bake in a preheated oven at 180°C (350°F), Gas Mark 4 for 15 to 20 minutes or until the tops are golden and a cake tester inserted into the centre comes out clean.

7 When cool, ice with coloured butter icing, e.g. pink, lemon, blue.

Variations You can decorate the cupcakes with sugar strands, Smarties or miniature chocolate easter eggs. Children love these cakes, especially if they are brightly decorated.

You can also use this recipe to make butterfly cakes.

To make butterfly cakes

1 Slice the top off each cake and cut this slice in half.

2 Pipe a swirl of whipped double cream in the centre of each cake.

3 Place the half slices of cake into the cream at an angle to resemble butterfly wings.

4 Dust the cake with icing sugar.

If you don't want to use double cream you can use butter icing.

To make butter icing
200 g (7 oz) butter or margarine, softened
700 g (1 lb 8 oz) icing sugar, sifted

1 Mix ingredients together until you get a creamy consistency.

GINGERBREAD

*It took me over a year to get a really good gingerbread recipe
and this one is delicious every time.*

---

450 g (1 lb) soft margarine or butter
450 g (1 lb) light soft brown or light muscovado sugar
350 g (12 oz) golden syrup
100 g (4 oz) treacle
700 g (1 lb 8 oz) plain flour
8 level tsp ground ginger
4 level tsp mixed spice
4 eggs, beaten
4 level tsp bicarbonate of soda
600 ml (1pint) milk, warmed

---

1 Melt the margarine or butter, brown sugar, syrup and treacle together in a pot.

2 Sift the flour and spices together then stir into the melted mixture along with the beaten eggs.

3 Add the bicarbonate of soda to the warm milk and stir to mix thoroughly.

4 Slowly add the warm milk and bicarbonate of soda to the mixture in the pot and stir well to make sure all the flour is free of lumps.

5 Pour into a lined cake tin 35 cm x 25 cm (14 in x 10 in) and bake in a preheated oven at 150°C (300°F), Gas Mark 2 for 45 min, then cover the top with a sheet of greaseproof paper for the final 15 min.

6 The gingerbread is ready when a cake tester inserted into the centre comes out clean.

Ice with a thick icing made from icing sugar and a little water.

I usually use half the cake and wrap the other half in tin foil to use in the next couple of days. This cake will keep well in a sealed container for three days. The gingerbread can also be frozen.

PLAIN SPONGE

If you want to make a very light sponge then use McDougall's supreme sponge flour. It works out more expensive but it is really very good.

450 g (1 lb) caster sugar
450 g (1 lb) soft margarine or butter
8 eggs
550 g (1 lb 4 oz) self-raising flour
4 tsp baking powder
7 tablespoons milk
1 tbs vanilla flavouring

1 Cream the sugar and margarine or butter until light and fluffy and then beat the eggs in one at a time.

2 Fold in the sieved flour and baking powder alternately with the milk.

3 Add the vanilla flavouring.

4 Pour into a lined baking tin 35 cm x 25 cm (14 in x 10 in) and bake in a preheated oven at 180°C (350°F), Gas Mark 4 for 45 – 50 minutes.

You can use half the mixture to make a small sponge in a 23 cm x 18 cm (9 in x 7 in) cake tin or you can use the mixture to make cupcakes.

Variations Instead of vanilla flavouring use the juice and rind of 2 lemons and make lemon-flavoured water icing for the top.

Omit the vanilla flavouring and add 200 g (7oz) dark Belgian chocolate, melted, to make a chocolate cake. Top with chocolate butter icing and sprinkle with grated chocolate.

When the sponge has cooled, split it in half and spread raspberry or strawberry jam over one half and whipped double cream over the other half. Then sandwich the two halves together and dust the top with icing sugar.

CHOCOLATE CAKE

340 g (12 oz) McDougall's Supreme Sponge flour
2 tsp baking powder
4 eggs (yolks and whites separate)
222 g (8 oz) soft stork margarine
200 g (7 oz) plain Belgian cooking chocolate
240 mls (8 fl oz) milk

1 Cream together sugar and margarine.

2 Blend in melted chocolate.

3 Sift baking powder and flour.

4 Add egg yolks and then milk and flour alternately.

5 Fold in stiffly beaten egg whites.

6 Pour into a lined baking tin 25cm x 35cm.

7 Bake for approximately 45 minutes in a preheated oven at 180°C (350°F), Gas Mark 4 until the cake tester comes out clean.

8 Ice with chocolate butter icing and sprinkle the top with chocolate chips or grated chocolate.

Variation You can make a chocolate spice cake by adding 1 tsp mixed spice, 1 tsp powdered ginger and 1 tsp cinnamon.

QUICK AND EASY SHORTBREAD

This is a very easy recipe and the shortbread sells well in our coffee shop. Always use butter for shortbread as there is a difference in the taste if you use margarine.

---

340 g (12 oz) butter
170 g (6 oz) castor sugar
500 g (1 lb 2 oz) plain flour

---

1 Cream the butter and sugar together.

2 Add the sieved flour and mix well but do not over mix.

3 Roll out on a lightly floured surface and cut with a large fluted cutter to the size you require. Place on a tray lined with non-stick baking paper.

4 Prick the shortbread all over with a fork and bake at 160°C (325°F), Gas Mark 3 in a preheated oven until shortbread is a pale golden colour.

5 Remove shortbread from the oven and immediately dust them with caster sugar.

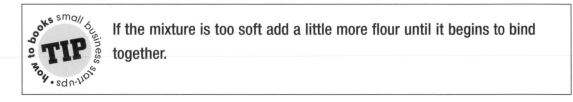

TIP If the mixture is too soft add a little more flour until it begins to bind together.

FINE SHORTBREAD

---

225 g (8 oz) butter
100 g (4 oz) caster sugar
225 g (8 oz) plain flour
100 g (4 oz) cornflour

---

1 Cream the butter and sugar together.

2 Sift the flour and cornflour together then add them to the butter and sugar mixture.

3 Knead the mixture lightly it until it forms a dough.

4 Roll out on a lightly floured surface. Cut out large fluted shapes to the size you require and place on a tray lined with non-stick baking paper.

5 Prick the shortbread all over with a fork and bake in a preheated oven at 160°C (325°F), Gas Mark 3 for about 30 minutes or until they are a light golden colour.

6 Immediately you take them out of the oven, sprinkle caster sugar all over them.

EMPIRE BISCUITS

This is the recipe we use in our coffee shop and these biscuits sell very well.

450 g (1 lb) plain flour
225 g (8 oz) icing sugar
225 g (8 oz) cornflour
450 g (1 lb) soft margarine

1. Sift all the dry ingredients together.

2. Mix in the margarine until the mixture forms a dough.

3. Roll out the dough on a lightly floured surface and cut out shapes with a large cutter the size of the required biscuit. Place on a tray lined with non-stick baking paper.

4. Bake in a preheated oven at 160°C (325°F), Gas Mark 3 for about 35 minutes or until biscuits are a very light golden colour.

5. Cool on a rack then sandwich together with seedless raspberry jam.

6. Ice the tops of the biscuits with icing and decorate with a cherry or coloured sugar strands.

AUNT ISA'S CUSTARD CREAMS

250 g (9 oz) self raising flour
250 g (9 oz) margarine
80 g (3 oz) caster sugar
80 g (3 oz) custard powder
Melted chocolate

For the butter cream icing
250 g (9 oz) butter
250 g (9 oz) icing sugar
2 tsp vanilla essence

1. Beat the margarine and sugar together until soft and fluffy.

2. Sift the dry ingredients.

3. Stir the flour into the margarine and sugar and mix well.

4. Put the mixture into a piping bag and pipe either sausage shapes or rounds onto a baking tray lined with non stick baking paper.

5. Bake at 190°C (375°F), Gas Mark 5 for approx 20 minutes until golden.

6. Allow to cool then sandwich together with butter icing.

7. Dip ends in melted chocolate.

LEMON MERINGUE PIE

This is very popular with customers

Sweet shortcrust pastry (see page 150)
60g (2 oz) cornflour
125g (4 oz) caster sugar
3 large eggs
Juice and finely grated zest of 3 unwaxed lemons
50g (2 oz) butter
300 mls (½ pt) cold water

For the topping
3 large egg whites
120g (4 oz) caster sugar

---

1 Lightly grease a 9in flan tin and line with pastry.

2 Prick the bottom with a fork.

3 Bake in oven for approx 15 minutes at 200°C (400°F), Gas Mark 6.

4 Mix 300 mls cold water into cornflour and sugar.

5 Cook on a moderate heat until boiling, stirring continuously.

6 When the mixture has thickened, remove from the heat and whisk in egg yolks, lemon juice and zest and butter until smooth, about 5 minutes.

7 Pour the filling into the pastry case.

8 Whisk the egg whites until stiff and then slowly add the sugar a little at a time until very stiff and glossy.

9 Spoon the meringue onto the top of the filling.

10 Bake for 45 minutes at 150°C (300°F), Gas Mark 2 or until the pie is crisp and pale golden on the outside.

Use egg whites at room temperature rather than straight from the fridge. Make sure that the bowl you use is free from grease. Only add the sugar when the whites are very stiff.

Tray bakes

FUDGE SLICES

225 g (8 oz) margarine
1 large tin condensed milk
4 tbs golden syrup
500 g (1 lb 2 oz) digestive biscuits, crushed
300 g (11 oz) milk chocolate, melted

❶ Melt margarine, condensed milk and syrup in a pan together and bring to the boil.

❷ Boil for 4 minutes.

❸ Remove from the heat and add the crushed digestive biscuits and mix quickly.

❹ Press into a Swiss roll tin.

❺ Cover with melted chocolate.

Instead of making the caramel in steps 1 and 2 you can melt luxury caramel purchased from Baco (see Appendix 7 for contact details).

RICH CHOCOLATE SHORTCAKE

---

125 g (4 oz) hard margarine
1 small tin condensed milk
275 g (10 oz) crushed shortbread crumbs
300 g (11 oz) Supercook Belgian milk chocolate
300 g (11 oz) Supercook Belgian white chocolate
50 g (2 oz) melted milk or plain chocolate for drizzling over the finished tray bake

---

1 Melt the milk chocolate.

2 Melt the margarine and add the melted chocolate and condensed milk.

3 Add the crushed shortbread crumbs to the mixture.

4 Press shortcake into a tray 20 cm x 30 cm (8 in x 12 in).

5 Leave to cool (not in the fridge).

6 Cover with melted white chocolate and leave to harden.

7 When the chocolate is hard, drizzle milk or plain chocolate over it.

8 Cut the shortcake into approximately 10 -12 slices.

Variation Instead of drizzling chocolate over the shortcake you can sprinkle it with milk chocolate chips immediately after covering the bake with melted white chocolate.

When you are making shortbread, make extra and crush it for use in the above recipe. You can do this in advance and store it in an airtight container.

MARS BAR SQUARES

*Most people know how to make this but I have included the recipe
because it is always popular.*

9 Mars bars
225 g (8 oz) hard margarine
1 tbs golden syrup
8 – 9 mugs of Rice Krispies
600 g (1 lb 5 oz) melted Scotbloc cake cover or Belgian milk chocolate

1. Melt the Mars bars, syrup and margarine together.

2. Remove from heat and immediately mix in the Rice Krispies.

3. Spread the mixture over a large tray approximately 30 cm x 40 cm (12 in x 16 in).

4. Leave to cool then cover with melted chocolate.

5. Leave to set and cut into approximately 20 – 24 squares.

MILLIONAIRE SHORTBREAD

For the shortbread base
225 g (8 oz) caster sugar
450 g (1 lb) butter or margarine
675 g (1 lb 8 oz) plain flour

1 Cream the sugar and butter together.

2 Add the flour and mix until a dough forms.

3 Press into a large tray measuring 34 cm x 24 cm (13½ in x 9½ in).

4 Bake at 180°C (350°F), Gas Mark 4 until the shortbread is a light golden colour.

For the caramel
225 g (8 oz) margarine or butter
225 g (8 oz) golden caster sugar
1 large tin condensed milk
4 tbs golden syrup
300 g (11 oz) milk Scotbloc

1 Melt the margarine, sugar, condensed milk and syrup in a saucepan.

2 Boil slowly for 5 minutes, stirring continuously.

3 Pour the mixture over the cooled shortbread base.

4 When the caramel is cool, cover with melted Scotbloc.

Variation For a change, use white Supercook Scotbloc to cover the caramel shortbread.

If you haven't time to make the caramel filling for Millionaire Shortbread and Crispy Surprise (on page 177) you can purchase a large tub of luxury caramel from Baco (see Appendix 7 for contact details) and melt it slightly to use on the shortbread base. This is more convenient and less time-consuming if you are going to make quite a lot of tray bakes.

I use the Millionaire Shortbread mixture to make tart cases for Strawberry Tart and Toffee Tart.

To make the tart cases

1 Line greased tart tins with the shortbread mixture.

2 Bake in a preheated oven at 180°C (350°F), Gas Mark 4 until golden.

3 Leave to cool.

To make the Strawberry Tarts

1 Fill the tarts with whipped double cream and slices of fresh strawberries.

2 Cover with raspberry or strawberry jelly (tubs are obtainable from your major supplier).

To make the Toffee Tarts

1 Fill the tart cases with ready-boiled condensed milk (available from the supermarket).

2 Drizzle with melted chocolate.

CORNFLAKE CRUNCH

3 cups self raising flour
3 cups coconut
1½ cups caster sugar
3 cups corn flakes, finely crushed
450 g (1lb) margarine

1 Mix dry ingredients together in a large bowl.

2 Melt margarine and pour over mixture.

3 Press into two swiss roll tins.

4 Bake in oven at 180°C (350°F), Gas Mark 4 for 25 – 30 minutes.

5 Allow to cool and ice when cold.

6 Cut into squares or fingers.

CRISPY DATE CAKE

---

225 g (8 oz) butter or hard margarine
340 g (12 oz) dates, chopped
85g (3 oz) rice crispies
225g (8 oz) caster sugar
4 tbs drinking chocolate
Milk chocolate block or Belgian cooking chocolate for covering

---

1 Melt butter.

2 Add sugar and stir until dissolved.

3 Add chopped dates and simmer until dates have softened.

4 Stir in the rice crispies and drinking chocolate.

5 Pour into greased tin and top with melted chocolate.

6 Allow to set and then cut into fingers or squares.

Variation You can substitute sultanas for the dates.

CHOCOLATE COCONUT SQUARES

450 g (1lb) plain chocolate
225 g (8 oz) margarine
450 g (1lb) caster sugar
4 eggs
450 g (1lb) desiccated coconut
225 g (8 oz) chopped glace cherries

1 Melt chocolate.

2 Line tin with tinfoil and pour on chocolate.

3 Put into fridge for 10 minutes until hard.

4 Cream margarine and sugar then add eggs, coconut and cherries.

5 Spread on top of the chocolate.

6 Bake at 180°C (350°F), Gas Mark 4 for 25 – 30 minutes until well risen and golden.

7 Leave in tin until completely cold then turn out and peel off the foil.

8 Cut into squares.

Variation When creaming the margarine and sugar you can add 1tsp almond essence to give it a slightly different flavour.

LEMON SQUARES

This is a recipe I got from a coffee shop in Florida.
It takes a bit of time but tastes delicious.

50 g (2 oz) icing sugar
170 g (6 oz) butter
170 g (6 oz) plain flour
Pinch of salt

For the filling
340 g (12 oz) caster sugar
130 mls (4 fl oz)lemon juice and the grated rind of 1 lemon
4 eggs
200 mls (7 fl oz) double cream (lightly whisked)
Icing sugar for dusting

1 Cut the butter into small pieces.

2 Sift the flour, icing sugar and salt into a bowl.

3 Rub the butter into the dry ingredients until it resembles breadcrumbs.

4 Grease a swiss roll tin 33 cm x 23 cm (13" x 9") tin and press the mixture into it.

5 Bake at 170°C (340°F), Gas Mark 4 until golden.

6 While the base is baking whisk the eggs and sugar together .

7 Add the lemon juice and grated rind and mix well.

8 Fold the whisked cream into the lemon mixture and pour over the warm base.

9 Bake for about 40 minutes until set.

10 Allow to cool and then dust with icing sugar and cut into squares.

CRISPY SURPRISE

Make a base in a lined Swiss roll tin 20 cm x 30 cm (8 in x 12 in) using the shortbread mixture above on page 172.

For the caramel
225 g (8 oz) margarine or butter
225 g (8 oz) golden caster sugar
1 large tin condensed milk
4 tbs golden syrup

1 Melt the margarine or butter, sugar, condensed milk and syrup in a pan.

2 Boil slowly for 5 minutes, stirring continuously

3 Pour the mixture over the cooled shortbread base.

For the topping
200 g (7 oz) dessicated coconut
1 large tin condensed milk
250 g (9 oz) chocolate
125 g (4 oz) Rice Krispies

1 Mix the desiccated coconut with the condensed milk.

2 Spread over the caramel base.

3 Mix the melted chocolate and Rice Krispies and spread on top of the coconut layer.

4 Allow to cool and cut into 12 pieces.

I use Belgian chocolate for a better flavour, but you can use Scotbloc for a less expensive recipe.

 I would have some muffin cases ready and put the remainder of the chocolate crispy mix into them to make individual crispy cakes. This saves any waste.

BANOFFEE PIE

---

100 g (4 oz) butter or margarine
225 g (8 oz) digestive biscuits, crushed
1 can condensed milk, boiled (or a ready-boiled can of condensed milk)
2 bananas
300 ml (½ pint) double cream
2 plain chocolate, grated

---

1 Grease a 25 cm (10 in) flan dish.

2 Melt the butter in the microwave, add the crushed digestive biscuits and mix well.

3 Press the biscuit mixture into the flan dish and put into the fridge for 30 minutes.

4 Open the cooled can of caramel and spread over the biscuit base.

5 Slice the bananas and place on top of the caramel.

6 Whisk the cream and spread it over the bananas.

7 Sprinkle with grated chocolate or vermicelli to finish.

You can make your own caramel filling by covering cans of condensed milk with hot water and boiling for 3 hours. Always keep the cans covered with water and do not allow them to boil dry. You can boil several cans at a time and they will keep for a few weeks unopened.

STRAWBERRY AND VANILLA CHEESECAKE

225 g (8 oz) digestive biscuits, crushed
100 g (4 oz) butter
350 g (12 oz) full fat cream cheese
75 g (3 oz) caster sugar
2 eggs, separated
1 tsp vanilla flavouring
1 tsp gelatine
300 ml (½ pint) whipping cream
A few strawberries to decorate

❶ Grease a 25 cm (10 in) flan dish.

❷ Melt the butter in the microwave, add the crushed digestive biscuits and mix well.

❸ Press the biscuit mixture into the flan dish and put into the fridge for 30 minutes.

❹ Put the cream cheese and sugar in a bowl and mix together until the cheese softens.

❺ Stir in the egg yolks and vanilla flavouring.

❻ Mix the gelatine with 2 tbs hot water in a small bowl and stand the bowl in a pan of hot water until the gelatine is clear.

❼ Whip the cream until it forms soft peaks.

❽ Whisk the egg whites in a clean, dry bowl until they peak softly.

❾ Once the gelatine has cooled slightly beat it into the cheese mixture and fold in ½ of the cream.

❿ Spread the mixture over the biscuit base.

⓫ Chill in the fridge until the mixture has set.

⓬ Pipe the remaining cream onto the top of the cheesecake and decorate with halves of strawberries.

SCOTTISH TABLET

1 large can condensed milk
100 g (4 oz) butter
1 cup (225 ml or 8 fl oz) full cream milk
900 g (2 lb) granulated sugar
1tsp vanilla flavouring

1 Melt the butter in a heavy-based pot, add the milk and condensed milk and heat gently.

2 Add the sugar and when it has dissolved, bring the mixture to the boil and then turn down the heat to a fast simmer for approximately 20 minutes.

3 Stir continuously to prevent the mixture sticking to the bottom of the pan and burning. The colour will turn to light caramel.

4 To test the mixture, drop a teaspoon of it into a cup of ice-cold water and leave it for about 15 seconds. If you can roll it into a soft ball the mixture is ready. If it is not ready, simmer for a few more minutes and test it again.

5 Remove the mixture from the heat and add the vanilla flavouring.

6 Beat the mixture rapidly with a wooden spoon until you feel it getting grainy.

7 Pour mixture into a greased, lined tin 20 cm x 30 cm (8 in x 12 in).

8 Leave to cool and cut into 12 slices or into smaller squares.

Variation You can omit the vanilla flavouring and add Bailey's Irish Cream, almond flavouring or any other flavouring you would like to try.

VANILLA FUDGE

300 ml (½ pint) full cream milk
225 g (8 oz) butter
900 g (2 lb) granulated sugar
2 tbs golden syrup
1 can condensed milk
1 tsp vanilla flavouring

1 Melt the butter, milk and condensed milk together and heat gently.

2 Add the sugar and allow it to dissolve.

3 Add the syrup and bring the mixture slowly to the boil.

4 Turn down the heat and simmer gently, stirring occasionally, for about 35 minutes.

5 To test the mixture, drop a teaspoon of it into a cup of ice-cold water, leave it for about 15 seconds and if you can then roll it into a soft ball it is ready.

6 Remove the mixture from the heat and leave to cool for 5 minutes.

7 Add the vanilla flavouring and beat the mixture vigorously with a wooden spoon until it is thick and grainy.

8 Pour quickly into a greased and lined tin 20 cm x 30 cm (8 in x 12 in).

9 When the fudge is cold cut it into squares.

Baco can supply you with most of the ingredients required for baking but they also supply Muffin Mix which is excellent – all you have to do is add whatever fruit etc. you wish; and Craig Millar Scone Mix – just add sultanas, cheese, dates, ginger, cranberries or whatever else you want in your oven scones. See Appendix 7 for contact details.

PEPPERMINT SLICE

225 g (8 oz) digestive biscuits crushed
50 g (2 oz) icing sugar
1 level teaspoon cocoa
50 g (2 oz) coconut
100 g (4 oz) margarine melted with 3 level teaspoons syrup

For the filling
175 g (6 oz) margarine
340 g (12 oz) icing sugar
Peppermint flavouring
A few drops of green colouring

Melted chocolate to cover

1 Mix together the crushed biscuits, icing sugar, cocoa, coconut and margarine

2 Press into a greased swiss roll baking tin and put into the fridge to harden

3 Mix together the ingredients for the filling and taste the mixture when you add the peppermint flavouring. Keep adding a few drops at a time until you get the correct strength of peppermint

4 Spread the filling onto the base and put it back into the fridge to harden

5 Cover with melted chocolate and cut into slices or squares

 Tip I usually use vanilla and almond flavouring because it is much cheaper than the essence.

TRUFFLES

8 tbs coconut

8 tbs coco powder

450 g (1 lb) crushed digestive biscuits

450 g (1 lb) butter

2 tins condensed milk

1 Melt butter and condensed milk slowly.

2 Mix coco powder, crushed digestive biscuits and coconut into the butter mixture.

3 Leave to cool in fridge (preferably overnight).

4 Roll into the size of balls you want and roll in coconut or chocolate vermicelli.

13
THE 12 SKILLS YOU NEED TO RUN A SUCCESSFUL COFFEE SHOP

Now that you have opened your coffee shop in a great location you will be wondering what it takes to run it successfully. I have listed below 12 essential skills that I think you must have in order to do this.

1. Keep your coffee shop spotlessly clean.

2. Offer good and interesting food at a reasonable price.

3. Give excellent customer service.

4. Have good communication skills.

5. Be friendly and approachable; talk to your customers.

6. Be open to suggestions on how to improve your service.

7. Be a great boss.

8. Set a good example to your staff.

9. Be a skilful manager.

10. Develop problem-solving skills.

11. Try to keep calm under all circumstances.

12. Be able to evaluate your progress and set feasible goals for the future.

I wish you every success in your new venture.

APPENDIX 1
EMPLOYMENT CONTRACT: FULL-TIME STAFF

(This is a copy of the contract document which I used in my coffee shop.)

ANOTHER COFFEE SHOP LTD

STATEMENT OF PARTICULARS OF EMPLOYMENT

COFFEE SHOP: FULL-TIME NEW EMPLOYEES

This Statement dated ....………. sets out the main terms of your employment with **Another Coffee Shop Ltd, 125 Broccoli Street, Glasgow G21 9AB** which the Company is required to provide to you under the Employment Rights Act 1996. This Statement together with your offer letter and the Employee Handbook form your written contract of employment.

Employee: …………………………………..

Employee Handbook:
The Employee Handbook is available for you to consult in the Office.

Commencement of Employment:
Your employment with the Company commenced on…………………

Job Title:
The title of the job which you are employed to do is ………………………….

The Company may amend your duties from time to time and may require you to undertake other duties as necessary to meet the needs of the business.

Probationary Period:
Your employment is subject to satisfactory completion of a three-month probationary period. The Company reserves the right to extend this period at its discretion.

The Company will assess and review your work performance during this time and reserves the right to terminate your employment at any time during the probationary period.

During the first month of your probationary period, either the Company or you may give one day's notice to terminate your employment. After one month's service and up to satisfactory completion of your probationary period, the Company or you may terminate your employment by giving one week's notice.

Place of Work:

Your usual place of work is ……………………………………………………………..

Pay:

Your rate of pay is £……………… per hour, payable weekly on a Friday by credit transfer, in arrears.

Deductions:

The Company reserves the right to deduct any outstanding monies you owe to the Company from your pay or, on termination of employment, from your final pay. This includes any previous error or overpayment, holiday or time off in lieu taken but not yet accrued, the costs of cash shortages from the till, and the cost of personal calls on Company telephones.

Hours of Work:

Your working week will comprise 20 hours between the hours of 10 a.m. and 6 p.m. The hours you are required to work will vary depending on the needs of the business and will be organized according to a rota, which you will be notified of on a weekly basis.

You are entitled to a daily half hour paid meal break.

The Company may require you to perform a reasonable amount of work outside your normal hours of work, depending on the needs of the business. You are entitled to receive payment for this work at your normal rate of pay.

Short-Time Working and Lay-Off:

The Company reserves the right to introduce short-time working or a period of temporary lay-off without pay where this is necessary to avoid redundancies or where there is a shortage of work. The Company will comply with any statutory guaranteed minimum payment obligations.

Statutory Rights in Relation to Sunday Shop Work:

You have become employed as a shop worker and are or can be required under your contract of employment to do the Sunday work your contract provides for.
However, if you wish, you can give a notice, as described in the next paragraph, to your employer and you will then have the right not to work in or about a shop on any Sunday on which the shop is open once three months have passed from the date on which you gave the notice.

Your notice must:

☐ be in writing;

☐ be signed and dated by you;

☐ say that you object to Sunday working.

For three months after you give the notice, your employer can still require you to do all the Sunday work your contract provides for. After the three-month period has ended, you have the right to complain to an employment tribunal if, because of your refusal to work on Sundays on which the shop is open, your employer:

☐ dismisses you; or

☐ does something else detrimental to you, for example, failing to promote you.

Once you have the rights described, you can surrender them only by giving your employer a further notice, signed and dated by you, saying that you wish to work on Sunday or that you do not object to Sunday working and then agreeing with your employer to work on Sundays or on a particular Sunday.

Annual Holidays:

The holiday year runs from 1st January to 31st December.

Your annual holiday entitlement in any holiday year is four weeks excluding all public holidays.

Holiday Entitlement:

Annual holiday entitlement accrues at the rate of one twelfth of the full annual holiday entitlement, on the 1st of each month, in advance during the first year of employment.

You will be paid at the normal rate of pay in respect of periods of annual holiday. Overtime will not normally be included in the calculation of holiday pay, except where the overtime is contractually guaranteed.

In the event of termination of employment, you will be entitled to holiday pay calculated on a pro-rata basis in respect of all annual holiday already accrued but not taken at the date of termination of employment.

If, on termination of employment, you have taken more annual holiday entitlement than you have accrued in that holiday year, an appropriate deduction will be made from your final payment.

Public Holidays:

Full-time employees are entitled to four public holidays each year, and will be advised of the relevant dates as early as possible. The public holidays that are recognized are:

....

Where the coffee shop closes on a public holiday and the employee has exhausted his or her pro rata public holiday entitlement, the employee will not be paid for this day. If the employee wishes to be paid for this day, he or she should take this time from his or her annual holiday entitlement, or arrange to work on an alternative day, at the sole discretion of the Company in accordance with the needs of the business.

Where a recognized public holiday falls on a Saturday or a Sunday, alternative dates will not be substituted for these. Employees will be advised of these as early as possible.

Sick Pay:

If you are absent from work because of sickness or injury you will be entitled to Statutory Sick Pay, provided you meet the qualifying conditions.

Absence Reporting:

You are required to notify the Company as soon as possible of your sickness absence and the reasons for it. You should do this personally at the earliest opportunity to the coffee shop owner, no later than 10 a.m. on the first day of your absence.

Notice:

Following successful completion of your probationary period, you are required to give two weeks' notice in writing to terminate your employment with the Company.

Following successful completion of your probationary period, you are entitled to receive the following written notice of termination of employment from the Company:

End of probationary period but less than
two years' continuous service: One week.

Two years' continuous service or longer: One week for each complete
                                               year of service up to a maximum
                                               of 12 weeks after 12 years' service.

The Company may exclude these notice provisions in the event of dismissal for gross misconduct.

The Company reserves the right to make payment in lieu of notice.

Disciplinary and Dismissal Appeals:

If you are dissatisfied with any disciplinary or dismissal decision taken in respect of you, you have the right of appeal.

Grievance Procedure:

Your employer encourages all employees to settle grievances informally. If, however, you have a grievance relating to any aspect of your employment which you would like to be resolved formally, you must set out the grievance and the basis for it in writing and submit it to the coffee shop owner.

Post-Termination Grievance:

Should you wish to raise a grievance after your employment has ended, you should submit the grievance in writing to the coffee shop owner.

Dress and Appearance:

You are required to dress smartly during working hours and to wear any Company clothing which has been supplied to you. Should you turn up for work dressed inappropriately, the Company reserves the right to send you home.

UNIFORMS:

It is a condition of your employment that you wear a uniform at all times during your working hours.

The Company will supply you with the necessary uniform at the Company's expense. You are expected to take care of this and to maintain it in a reasonable condition.

You are required to return your uniform in reasonable condition upon termination of your employment.

Health and Safety:

You are required to gain an understanding of the Company's health and safety procedures, observe them, and ensure that safety equipment and clothing are always used. The Company's health and safety information is displayed on the Coffee Shop notice board.

Staff Discount:

The Coffee Shop operates a staff discount scheme which you are entitled to take advantage of. Full details of the scheme are available from the coffee shop manager.

Changes to Terms of Employment:

The Company reserves the right to make reasonable changes to any of your terms and conditions of employment and will notify you in writing of such changes at the earliest opportunity and, in any event, within one month of such changes taking effect.

Declaration:

I understand that during the course of my employment it will be necessary for the Company to maintain personnel records in relation to my employment. Any information held concerning my employment which is personal data and which is processed by the Company for these purposes shall be processed only in accordance with the Data Protection Act 1998.

Acknowledgement:

I acknowledge receipt of this Statement. I have been shown the Employee Handbook. I confirm that I have read the Statement and the Employee Handbook which set out the principal rules, policies and procedures relating to my employment and which together with my offer letter form my written contract of employment.

Signed by the employee. ....

Date..

Signed for and on behalf of **ANOTHER COFFEE SHOP LTD**

....

Date...

APPENDIX 2
EMPLOYMENT CONTRACT: PART-TIME STAFF

(This is a copy of the contract document which I used in my coffee shop.)

ANOTHER COFFEE SHOP LTD

STATEMENT OF PARTICULARS OF EMPLOYMENT

COFFEE SHOP: PART-TIME NEW EMPLOYEES

This Statement dated ....………… sets out the main terms of your employment with **Another Coffee Shop Ltd, 125 Broccoli Street, Glasgow G21 9AB** which the Company is required to provide to you under the Employment Rights Act 1996. This Statement together with your offer letter and the Employee Handbook form your written contract of employment.

Employee: ………………………………..

Employee Handbook:
The Employee Handbook is available for you to consult in the Office.

Commencement of Employment:
Your employment with the Company commenced on…………………

Job Title:
The title of the job which you are employed to do is ……………………………

The Company may amend your duties from time to time and may require you to undertake other duties as necessary to meet the needs of the business.

Probationary Period:
Your employment is subject to satisfactory completion of a three-month probationary period. The Company reserves the right to extend this period at its discretion.

The Company will assess and review your work performance during this time and reserves the right to terminate your employment at any time during the probationary period.

During the first month of your probationary period, either the Company or you may give one day's notice to terminate your employment. After one month's service and up to satisfactory completion of your probationary period, the Company or you may terminate your employment by giving one week's notice.

Place of Work:

Your usual place of work is ....

Pay:

Your rate of pay is £.................... per hour, payable weekly on a Friday by credit transfer, in arrears.

Deductions:

The Company reserves the right to deduct any outstanding monies you owe to the Company from your pay or, on termination of employment, from your final pay. This includes any previous error or overpayment, holiday or time off in lieu taken but not yet accrued, the costs of cash shortages from the till, and the cost of personal calls on Company telephones.

Hours of Work:

Your working hours are on a part-time basis between the hours of 10 a.m. and 6 p.m. The hours you are required to work will vary depending on the needs of the business and will be organized according to a rota, which you will be notified of on a weekly basis.

You are entitled to the statutory minimum rest breaks according to the hours you work as set out in the current regulations.

Short-Time Working and Lay-Off:

The Company reserves the right to introduce short-time working or a period of temporary lay-off without pay where this is necessary to avoid redundancies or where there is a shortage of work.   The Company will comply with any statutory guaranteed minimum payment obligations.

Statutory Rights in Relation to Sunday Shop Work:

You have become employed as a shop worker and are or can be required under your contract of employment to do the Sunday work your contract provides for.

However, if you wish, you can give a notice, as described in the next paragraph, to your employer and you will then have the right not to work in or about a shop on any Sunday on which the shop is open once three months have passed from the date on which you gave the notice.

Your notice must:

☐ be in writing;

☐ be signed and dated by you;

☐ say that you object to Sunday working.

For three months after you give the notice, your employer can still require you to do all the Sunday work your contract provides for. After the three-month period has ended, you have the right to complain to an employment tribunal if, because of your refusal to work on Sundays on which the shop is open, your employer:

☐ dismisses you; or

☐ does something else detrimental to you, for example, failing to promote you.

Once you have the rights described, you can surrender them only by giving your employer a further notice, signed and dated by you, saying that you wish to work on Sunday or that you do not object to Sunday working and then agreeing with your employer to work on Sundays or on a particular Sunday.

Annual Holidays:

The holiday year runs from 1st January to 31st December.

Your annual holiday entitlement in any holiday year is four weeks excluding all public holiday entitlement.

Annual holiday entitlement accrues at the rate of one twelfth of the full annual holiday entitlement, on the 1st of each month, in advance in the first year of employment.

Employees with no normal working hours will be paid their average pay in the 12 weeks prior to the holiday.

In the event of termination of employment, you will be entitled to holiday pay calculated on a pro-rata basis in respect of all annual holiday already accrued but not taken at the date of termination of employment.

If, on termination of employment, you have taken more annual holiday entitlement than you have accrued in that holiday year, an appropriate deduction will be made from your final payment.

Public Holidays:

Full-time employees are entitled to ....public holidays each year. Part-time employees are entitled to public holidays pro rata. Where the Coffee Shop closes on a public holiday and the employee has exhausted his or her pro rata public holiday entitlement, the employee will not be paid for this day. If the employee wishes to be paid for this day, he or she should take this time from his or her annual holiday entitlement, or arrange to work on an alternative day, at the sole discretion of the Company in accordance with the needs of the business.

Where a recognized public holiday falls on a Saturday or a Sunday, alternative dates will not be substituted for these. Employees will be advised of these as early as possible.

Sick Pay:

If you are absent from work because of sickness or injury you will be entitled to Statutory Sick Pay, provided you meet the qualifying conditions.

Absence Reporting:

You are required to notify the Company as soon as possible of your sickness absence and the reasons for it. You should do this personally at the earliest opportunity to the coffee shop owner, no later than 10 a.m. on the first day of your absence.

Notice:

Following successful completion of your probationary period, you are required to give two weeks' notice in writing to terminate your employment with the Company.

Following successful completion of your probationary period, you are entitled to receive the following written notice of termination of employment from the Company:

End of probationary period but less than two years' continuous service:	One week.
Two years' continuous service or longer:	One week for each complete year of service up to a maximum of 12 weeks after 12 years' service.

The Company may exclude these notice provisions in the event of dismissal for gross misconduct.

The Company reserves the right to make payment in lieu of notice.

Disciplinary and Dismissal Appeals:

If you are dissatisfied with any disciplinary or dismissal decision taken in respect of you, you have the right of appeal.

Grievance Procedure:

Your employer encourages all employees to settle grievances informally. If, however, you have a grievance relating to any aspect of your employment which you would like to be resolved formally, you must set out the grievance and the basis for it in writing and submit it to the coffee shop owner.

Post-Termination Grievance:

Should you wish to raise a grievance after your employment has ended, you should submit the grievance in writing to the coffee shop owner.

Dress and Appearance:

You are required to dress smartly during working hours and to wear any Company clothing which has been supplied to you. Should you turn up for work dressed inappropriately, the Company reserves the right to send you home.

UNIFORMS:

It is a condition of your employment that you wear a uniform at all times during your working hours.

The Company will supply you with the necessary uniform at the Company's expense. You are expected to take care of this and to maintain it in a reasonable condition.

You are required to return your uniform in reasonable condition upon termination of your employment.

Health and Safety:

You are required to gain an understanding of the Company's health and safety procedures, observe them, and ensure that safety equipment and clothing are always used. The Company's health and safety information is displayed on the Coffee Shop notice board.

Staff Discount:

The Coffee Shop operates a staff discount scheme which you are entitled to take advantage of. Full details of the scheme are available from the coffee shop manager.

Changes to Terms of Employment:

The Company reserves the right to make reasonable changes to any of your terms and conditions of employment and will notify you in writing of such changes at the earliest opportunity and, in any event, within one month of such changes taking effect.

Declaration:

I understand that during the course of my employment it will be necessary for the Company to maintain personnel records in relation to my employment. Any information held concerning my employment which is personal data and which is processed by the Company for these purposes shall be processed only in accordance with the Data Protection Act 1998.

Acknowledgement:

I acknowledge receipt of this Statement. I have been shown the Employee Handbook. I confirm that I have read the Statement and the Employee Handbook which set out the principal rules, policies and procedures relating to my employment and which together with my offer letter form my written contract of employment.

Signed by the employee ....

Date...

Signed for and on behalf of **ANOTHER COFFEE SHOP LTD**

....

Date...

APPENDIX 3
EMPLOYMENT CONTRACT: WEEKEND STAFF

(This is a copy of the contract document which I used in my coffee shop.)

ANOTHER COFFEE SHOP LTD

STATEMENT OF PARTICULARS OF EMPLOYMENT

COFFEE SHOP: WEEKEND NEW EMPLOYEES

This Statement dated .... sets out the main terms of your employment with **Another Coffee Shop Ltd, 125 Broccoli Street, Glasgow G21 9AB** which the Company is required to provide to you under the Employment Rights Act 1996. This Statement together with your offer letter and the Employee Handbook form your written contract of employment.

Employee: ....

Employee Handbook:
The Employee Handbook is available for you to consult in the Office.

Commencement of Employment:
Your employment with the Company commenced on.....................

Job Title:
The title of the job which you are employed to do is ....
The Company may amend your duties from time to time and may require you to undertake other duties as necessary to meet the needs of the business.

Probationary Period:
Your employment is subject to satisfactory completion of a three-month probationary period. The Company reserves the right to extend this period at its discretion.

The Company will assess and review your work performance during this time and reserves the right to terminate your employment at any time during the probationary period.

During the first month of your probationary period, either the Company or you may give one day's notice to terminate your employment. After one month's service and up to satisfactory completion of your probationary period, the Company or you may terminate your employment by giving one week's notice.

Place of Work:

Your usual place of work is ....

Pay:

Your rate of pay is £.................... per hour, payable weekly on a Friday by credit transfer, in arrears.

Deductions:

The Company reserves the right to deduct any outstanding monies you owe to the Company from your pay or, on termination of employment, from your final pay. This includes any previous error or overpayment, holiday or time off in lieu taken but not yet accrued, the costs of cash shortages from the till, and the cost of personal calls on Company telephones.

Hours of Work:

Your hours of work are from 10 a.m. to 6 p.m. on a Saturday and from 12 noon to 5 p.m. on a Sunday.

You are entitled to a daily half hour paid meal break.

The Company may require you to perform a reasonable amount of work outside your normal hours of work, depending on the needs of the business. You are entitled to receive payment for this work at your normal rate of pay.

Short-Time Working and Lay-Off:

The Company reserves the right to introduce short-time working or a period of temporary lay-off without pay where this is necessary to avoid redundancies or where there is a shortage of work. The Company will comply with any statutory guaranteed minimum payment obligations.

Statutory Rights in Relation to Sunday Shop Work:

You have become employed as a shop worker and are or can be required under your contract of employment to do the Sunday work your contract provides for.

However, if you wish, you can give a notice, as described in the next paragraph, to your employer and you will then have the right not to work in or about a shop on any Sunday on which the shop is open once three months have passed from the date on which you gave the notice.

Your notice must:

- be in writing;

- be signed and dated by you;

- say that you object to Sunday working.

For three months after you give the notice, your employer can still require you to do all the Sunday work your contract provides for. After the three-month period has ended, you have the right to complain to an employment tribunal if, because of your refusal to work on Sundays on which the shop is open, your employer:

- dismisses you; or

- does something else detrimental to you, for example, failing to promote you.

Once you have the rights described, you can surrender them only by giving your employer a further notice, signed and dated by you, saying that you wish to work on Sunday or that you do not object to Sunday working and then agreeing with your employer to work on Sundays or on a particular Sunday.

Annual Holidays:

The holiday year runs from 1st January to 31st December.

Your annual holiday entitlement in any holiday year is four weeks excluding all public holiday entitlement.

Annual holiday entitlement accrues at the rate of one twelfth of the full annual holiday entitlement, on the 1st of each month, in advance.

Part-time, weekend employees' annual holiday entitlement accrues on a pro-rata basis.

You will be paid at their normal rate of pay in respect of periods of annual holiday. Overtime will not normally be included in the calculation of holiday pay, except where the overtime is contractually guaranteed.

In the event of termination of employment, you will be entitled to holiday pay calculated on a pro-rata basis in respect of all annual holiday already accrued but not taken at the date of termination of employment.

If, on termination of employment, you have taken more annual holiday entitlement than you have accrued in that holiday year, an appropriate deduction will be made from your final payment.

Public Holidays:

Full-time employees are entitled to …………public holidays each year and part-time, weekend employees' entitlement to public holidays is calculated on a pro-rata basis. Where the coffee shop closes on a public holiday and the employee has exhausted his or her pro rata public holiday entitlement, the employee will not be paid for this day. If the employee wishes to be paid for this day, he or she should take this time from his or her annual holiday entitlement, or arrange to work on an alternative day, at the sole discretion of the owner in accordance with the needs of the business.

Public holidays are in addition to annual holiday entitlement.

Where a recognized public holiday falls on a Saturday or a Sunday, alternative dates will not be substituted for these.

Sick Pay:

If you are absent from work because of sickness or injury you will be entitled to Statutory Sick Pay, provided you meet the qualifying conditions.

Absence Reporting:

You are required to notify the Company as soon as possible of your sickness absence and the reasons for it. You should do this personally at the earliest opportunity to the coffee shop owner, no later than 10 a.m. on the first day of your absence.

Notice:

Following successful completion of your probationary period, you are required to give two weeks' notice in writing to terminate your employment with the Company.

Following successful completion of your probationary period, you are entitled to receive the following written notice of termination of employment from the Company:

End of probationary period but less than two years' continuous service:	One week.
Two years' continuous service or longer:	One week for each complete year of service up to a maximum of 12 weeks after 12 years' service.

The Company may exclude these notice provisions in the event of dismissal for gross misconduct.

The Company reserves the right to make payment in lieu of notice.

Disciplinary and Dismissal Appeals:

If you are dissatisfied with any disciplinary or dismissal decision taken in respect of you, you have the right of appeal.

Grievance Procedure:

Your employer encourages all employees to settle grievances informally. If, however, you have a grievance relating to any aspect of your employment which you would like to be resolved formally, you must set out the grievance and the basis for it in writing and submit it to the coffee shop owner.

Post-Termination Grievance:

Should you wish to raise a grievance after your employment has ended, you should submit the grievance in writing to the coffee shop owner.

Dress and Appearance:

You are required to dress smartly during working hours and to wear any Company clothing which has been supplied to you. Should you turn up for work dressed inappropriately, the Company reserves the right to send you home.

UNIFORMS:

It is a condition of your employment that you wear a uniform at all times during your working hours.

The Company will supply you with the necessary uniform at the Company's expense. You are expected to take care of this and to maintain it in a reasonable condition.

You are required to return your uniform in reasonable condition upon termination of your employment.

Health and Safety:

You are required to gain an understanding of the Company's health and safety procedures, observe them, and ensure that safety equipment and clothing are always used. The Company's health and safety information is displayed on the Coffee Shop notice board.

Staff Discount:

The Coffee Shop operates a staff discount scheme which you are entitled to take advantage of. Full details of the scheme are available from the coffee shop manager.

Changes to Terms of Employment:

The Company reserves the right to make reasonable changes to any of your terms and conditions of employment and will notify you in writing of such changes at the earliest opportunity and, in any event, within one month of such changes taking effect.

Declaration:

I understand that during the course of my employment it will be necessary for the Company to maintain personnel records in relation to my employment. Any information held concerning my employment which is personal data and which is processed by the Company for these purposes shall be processed only in accordance with the Data Protection Act 1998.

Acknowledgement:

I acknowledge receipt of this Statement. I have been shown the Employee Handbook. I confirm that I have read the Statement and the Employee Handbook which set out the principal rules, policies and procedures relating to my employment and which together with my offer letter form my written contract of employment.

Signed by the employee ....

Date..

Signed for and on behalf of **ANOTHER COFFEE SHOP LTD**

....

Date..

JOB DESCRIPTION PRO FORMA

Another Coffee Shop
125 Broccoli Street
Glasgow
G21 9AB

Post: Catering Assistant

Wage ....

Responsible to:

Job Purpose: Undertake duties connected with the preparation, simple cooking and service of food.

Main Duties: Preparation of food and beverages and serving and clearing tables.

General kitchen and coffee shop duties including washing up, serving and clearing tables.

Cleaning duties including the kitchen equipment, the kitchen and the sitting area of the coffee shop.

Duties may include some cash handling.

All duties must be carried out to comply with the Health and Safety at Work Act and Environmental Health Procedures.

Where appropriate training facilities may be provided.

General conditions:

Arrive at work at least 5 minutes before scheduled time to be ready to start your shift on time.

Employees will be provided with and required to wear a clean pressed uniform and protective clothing required for the position.

There is a no smoking policy in force.

Staff cannot make personal telephone calls from the coffee shop phone. All mobile phones must be switched off during working hours.

In the event that you are not well enough to come in to work you must telephone the owner or manager as soon as possible to allow time to get another member of staff to cover your shift.

I understand that failing to keep to any of these policies may result in disciplinary measures.

Employee's signature ....Date....................

EMPLOYEE HANDBOOK

ANOTHER COFFEE SHOP LTD

EMPLOYEE
HANDBOOK

This is a copy of the handbook which I used in my coffee shop. It may appear somewhat excessive for some part-time coffee shop employees. However it is, I believe, prudent to cover as many of the 'bases' as possible.

My experience is that many a problem has been resolved before it had time to grow because of the existence of a detailed employee handbook.

CONTENTS

☐ Holidays

☐ Sick Pay Entitlement

☐ Maternity Leave and Maternity Pay

☐ Paternity Leave and Paternity Pay

☐ Adoption Leave and Adoption Pay

☐ Parental Leave

☐ Time Off for Dependants

☐ Disciplinary Procedure and Action

☐ The Right to be Accompanied

☐ Code of Conduct

☐ Operational Policies and Procedures

☐ Grievance Procedure

Holidays
ANNUAL HOLIDAYS

The holiday year runs from 1st January to 31st December. Employees' annual holiday entitlement in any holiday year is four weeks period, which part-time employees will receive on a pro rata basis.

Annual holiday entitlement accrues at the rate of one twelfth of the full annual holiday entitlement, on the 1st of each month, in advance.

Employees will be paid at their normal rate of pay and salaried employees will be paid their normal salary in respect of periods of annual holiday. Overtime will not normally be included in the calculation of holiday pay, except where the overtime is contractually guaranteed.

On termination of employment, employees will be entitled to holiday pay accrued but not taken at the date of termination of employment.

If, on termination of employment, an employee has taken more annual holiday than he or she has accrued in that holiday year, an appropriate deduction will be made from the employee's final pay.

PUBLIC HOLIDAYS

Full-time employees are entitled to .... public holidays each year:

Public holidays are in addition to annual holiday entitlement.

Sick Pay Entitlement
STATUTORY SICK PAY

Employees who are absent from work because of sickness will normally be entitled to receive Statutory Sick Pay (SSP) from the Company providing they meet the relevant criteria.

Once the criteria have been met, SSP is not normally payable for the first three days of sickness absence, unless the employee has been absent and in receipt of SSP within the previous eight weeks. Thereafter the Company will normally pay SSP at the statutory rate in force for a maximum of 28 weeks.

In order to qualify for SSP the employee must notify the Company on the first qualifying day, and submit a certificate of absence as soon as practicable. The Company reserves the right to withhold payment of SSP where an employee fails to follow the correct procedure. Certain employees are excluded from the SSP scheme, e.g. employees who earn below the lower earnings limit for National Insurance purposes.

Note *The new Fit Note will come into force from April 2010 and will replace the sick note. Further information is available on the fit note pages on the* www.lge.gov.uk *website.*

Maternity Leave and Maternity Pay

Pregnant employees and employees who have recently given birth have a variety of rights under current legislation. This area of law is very complex, and I would advise that you check the most up to date legislation. Therefore the following sections provide only a general guide for employees.

INTRODUCTION

In general all pregnant employees, i.e. those working under a contract of employment, are entitled to take up to 52 weeks' statutory maternity leave (SML) around the birth of their child. This includes surrogate mothers and mothers who have undergone IVF treatment. It does not matter how long the employee has worked for you.

Your employee is entitled to receive the same terms and conditions that they currently receive during ordinary leave in the additional leave period.

For up to date information look at the website www.businesslink-gov.uk as legislation is constantly changing.

It should also be noted that women are legally obliged to take a minimum of two weeks maternity leave after giving birth. This is called Compulsory Maternity Leave.

NOTIFICATION PROCEDURES FOR MATERNITY LEAVE

To qualify for maternity leave the employee must comply with the rules and procedures set out below.

☐ A minimum of 15 weeks before the expected week of childbirth, the employee must give her employer notice of:

(a) the fact that she is pregnant;

(b) her expected week of childbirth, which must be confirmed with the medical certificate MATB1; and

(c) the date on which she intends to start her maternity leave. This must be in writing if requested by the employer.

☐ Within 28 days of the employee giving notice, the employer must respond in writing to the employee, confirming her full entitlement to maternity leave (52 weeks) and the date when she is expected to return to work.

☐ The earliest the employee may start her maternity leave is 11 weeks before the expected week of childbirth. An employee may change her mind about when she wants to start her leave, providing she gives her employer at least 28 days' notice of the change.

☐ The employee does not need to give notice of her return to work if she simply returns at the end of her maternity leave period. However, if she wishes to return to work before her full entitlement to maternity leave has ended, she must give her employer a minimum of 28 days' notice of the date of her earlier return.

☐ If the employee fails to give the required 28 days' notice of an earlier return to work, the employer may postpone the employee's return until the end of the 28 days' notice she should have given, or until the end of her maternity leave period, whichever is earlier.

☐ An employee does not lose the right to return to work if she does not follow the correct notification requirements. However, her employer may take appropriate disciplinary action if she fails to return to work at the end of her maternity leave period.

STATUTORY MATERNITY PAY

All employees who have been continuously employed for at least 26 weeks ending with the 15th week before the expected week of childbirth (the Notification Week), and who satisfy the following conditions, are entitled to receive Statutory Maternity Pay (SMP) from their employer. The employee must:

☐ still be pregnant at the 11th week before her expected week of childbirth or have had the baby by that time;

☐ have average weekly earnings equal to or above the Lower Earnings Limit for National Insurance purposes over the eight-week period up to and including the Notification Week;

☐ give her employee a minimum of 28 days' notice that she intends to be absent from work because of her pregnancy;

☐ provide her employer with medical certification of her expected week of childbirth, normally using form MAT B1.

Statutory Maternity Pay is payable for 39 weeks. The first six weeks are payable at the higher rate which is 90% of the employee's normal earnings. The remaining 33 weeks are payable at a standard rate which changes from time to time. You can download a flowchart illustrating when you must pay Statutory Maternity Pay from the website HM Revenue & Customs at www.hmrc.gov.uk or www.lge.gov.uk

The Government has announced that it will not go ahead with the planned extension of maternity pay from 39 to 52 weeks at this time but this may still be implemented at a later date.

ANTENATAL CARE

All pregnant employees are entitled to take time off with full pay during working hours to receive antenatal care. The employer may require an employee who wishes to take time off for these purposes to provide medical certification of her pregnancy and an appointment card, except in connection with the first appointment.

PREGNANCY-RELATED ABSENCE

An employee's maternity leave will automatically start if she is absent from work for a pregnancy-related absence during the four weeks before the baby is due.

Paternity Leave and Paternity Pay

Currently employed fathers can take up to 2 weeks pay and leave.

The government had intended to increase additional paternity leave and pay by April 2010 but this has been delayed.

Eligible employees (see below) are entitled to take up to two weeks' paid paternity leave following the birth of their child in order to care for the child or support its mother. During paternity leave, most employees will be entitled to Statutory Paternity Pay (SPP), which will be the same as the standard rate of Statutory Maternity Pay (SMP).

ELIGIBILITY FOR PATERNITY LEAVE AND PATERNITY PAY

In order to qualify for paternity leave and Statutory Paternity Pay the employee must:

☐ be the biological father of the child or the mother's husband or partner (male or female);

☐ have or expect to have responsibility for the child's upbringing;

☐ have worked continuously for the employer for 26 weeks leading into the Notification Week (the 15th week before the child is due); and

☐ have average weekly earnings equal to or above the Lower Earnings Limit for National Insurance purposes over the eight week period leading up to and including the Notification Week.

Employers may ask an employee to provide a self certificate as evidence that he or she meets these conditions. The self certificate must provide the information required above and include a declaration that the employee meets the necessary conditions.

TAKING PATERNITY LEAVE

An employee is permitted to take paternity leave in units of either one whole week or two consecutive whole weeks. Leave may start on any day of the week of or following the child's birth but must be completed:

☐ within 56 days of the actual date of birth of the child; or

☐ if the child is born early, within the period from the actual date of birth up to 56 days after the expected week of birth.

NOTIFICATION PROCEDURES FOR PATERNITY LEAVE

An employee who wishes to take paternity leave must notify the employer by the 15th week before the expected week of childbirth, stating:

- ☐ the week the child is due;

- ☐ whether the employee wishes to take one week or two weeks leave; and

- ☐ when the employee wants the leave to start.

CONTRACTUAL BENEFITS DURING PATERNITY LEAVE

An employee on paternity leave is entitled to benefit from normal terms and conditions of employment, with the exception of pay. The employee is entitled to return to the same job following paternity leave.

Adoption Leave and Adoption Pay

Employees who adopt a child may be entitled to adoption leave and Statutory Adoption Pay. This right applies to both men and women. There are special conditions relating to adoption leave and adoption pay. Employees who plan to adopt a child up to 18 years of age should discuss this with the employer, at which time their entitlements can be clarified.

Parental Leave

After one year's service, employees are entitled to a maximum of 13 weeks' unpaid Parental Leave for each of their children under five years old.

Parents of disabled children are entitled to a total of 18 weeks' parental leave, which can be taken at any point until the child's 18th birthday. Where an employee adopts a child under the age of 18, he or she is entitled to Parental Leave during the five years after the adoption, or until the child's 18th birthday, whichever is earlier. Employees who are entitled to parental leave should discuss their entitlements and conditions with the employer.

TIME OFF FOR DEPENDANTS

Employees are entitled to take reasonable unpaid time off to deal with sudden or unexpected problems with a dependant. A dependant is a partner, child or parent who lives with the employee as part of his or her family or any other person who reasonably relies on the employee for assistance.

Reasonable time off will be granted in appropriate circumstances.

The right is only to deal with emergencies and to put care arrangements in place. This means that in the case of a dependant's illness, for example, the employee is not entitled to time off for the duration of the dependant's illness.

Disciplinary Procedure and Action

The primary objective of the Company's Disciplinary Procedure is to ensure that all disciplinary matters are dealt with fairly and consistently.

For employees with 12 months' continuous service or longer, the Company will follow the Disciplinary Procedure set out below.

DISCIPLINARY PROCEDURE

Where appropriate all allegations of potential disciplinary offences will be investigated to establish the facts. A prior investigation may be judged as inappropriate only in very straightforward circumstances, e.g. lateness. The Company will give the employee the opportunity to state his or her case at a disciplinary meeting before taking any disciplinary action. The Company will give the employee reasonable notice of the requirement to attend a disciplinary meeting to allow the employee to prepare his or her case.

Following the disciplinary meeting, the Company may take disciplinary action against the employee. In any event, the employee will be informed of the outcome of the meeting as soon as possible.

Employees have the right to appeal against any disciplinary action taken against them in accordance with the Disciplinary and Dismissals Appeals Procedure.

DISCIPLINARY ACTION

The severity of the disciplinary action, if any, will be determined by the severity of the offence. For relatively minor first offences the Company will normally impose a Verbal Warning. If the employee persists with the offence in question, the Company may, having followed the Disciplinary Procedure in each instance, apply a Written Warning followed by Final Written Warning and eventually dismiss the employee.

For more severe first offences the Company may apply a Written Warning or Final Written Warning. In cases of gross misconduct the Company will normally dismiss the employee summarily, i.e. without notice.

A summary of the disciplinary actions that may be imposed is set out below.

> **Verbal Warning:** The Company will advise the employee that his or her standard of conduct or performance has been unacceptable and that a failure to improve will result in further disciplinary action. The required standard will be outlined. The warning will be given verbally and subsequently confirmed in writing.

> **Written Warning:** As for a Verbal Warning, but normally applied following a second disciplinary offence (but may be applied after a more serious first offence). The employee will be advised in writing that a failure to improve the standard of conduct or performance will result in further disciplinary action.

> **Final Written Warning:** As for a Written Warning, but normally applied following

a third disciplinary offence. The employee will be advised in writing that a failure to improve the standard of conduct or performance will result in dismissal.

Dismissal: The employee is dismissed either with or without notice. Dismissal without notice is referred to as 'summary dismissal' and is normally restricted to cases of gross misconduct.

DISCIPLINARY APPEAL

The employee has the right to appeal against any disciplinary action against them.

THE RIGHT TO BE ACCOMPANIED

Employees are entitled to be accompanied at any formal disciplinary, grievance or appeal meeting. An employee under the age of 18 may choose to be accompanied by a parent or legal guardian.

Code of Conduct
COMPANY RULES
ATTENDANCE AND TIMEKEEPING

Employees are required to comply with the rules relating to notification of absence set out in the Company's Absence Policy and Procedure.

Employees are required to arrive at work promptly, ready to start work at their contracted starting times. Employees are required to remain at work until their contracted finishing times.

Employees must obtain authorization if for any reason they wish to arrive later or leave earlier than their agreed normal start and finish times.

The Company reserves the right not to pay employees in respect of working time lost because of poor timekeeping.

Persistent poor timekeeping will result in disciplinary action.

STANDARDS AND CONDUCT

Employees are required to maintain satisfactory standards of performance at work.

Employees are required to comply with all reasonable management instructions.

Employees are required to ensure the maintenance of acceptable standards of politeness.

Employees are required to take all necessary steps to safeguard the Company's public image and preserve positive relationships with its customers.

Employees are required to ensure that they behave in a way that does not constitute unlawful discrimination.

Personal mobile telephones must be switched off at all times during normal working hours.

FLEXIBILITY

Employees may be required to work additional hours at short notice, in accordance with the needs of the business. Employees may be required from time to time to undertake duties outside their normal job remit.

WORK CLOTHING

Where work clothing or uniforms are provided by the Company, they must be worn at all times during working hours. Employees are responsible for ensuring that all items of work clothing or uniform are kept clean and maintained in reasonable condition at all times and returned to the Company on termination of employment.

HEALTH AND SAFETY

Employees are required to gain an understanding of the Company's health and safety procedures, observe them, and ensure that safety equipment and clothing are always used. Employees must report all accidents, however small, as soon as possible, making an entry in the Company's Accident Book.

GROSS MISCONDUCT

Set out below are examples of behaviour which the Company treats as gross misconduct. Such behaviour may result in dismissal without notice. This list is not exhaustive.

☐ theft, dishonesty or fraud;

☐ smoking on the business premises;

☐ sleeping during working hours;

☐ assault, acts of violence or aggression;

☐ unacceptable use of obscene or abusive language;

☐ possession or use of, or being under the influence of, non-prescribed drugs or alcohol on the premises or during working hours;

☐ wilful damage to Company, employee or customer property;

☐ serious insubordination;

☐ serious or gross negligence;

☐ unlawful discrimination, including acts of indecency or sexual harassment;

☐ refusal to carry out reasonable management instructions;

☐ serious breach of the Health and Safety policies and procedures.

Operational Policies and Procedures

Harassment

Harassment is physical, verbal or non-verbal behaviour which is unwanted and personally offensive to the recipient, and which causes the recipient to feel threatened, humiliated, intimidated, patronized, denigrated, bullied, distressed or harassed.

If an employee is accused of unlawful discrimination or harassment, the Company will investigate the matter fully. Any breach of this rule will be treated as gross misconduct and is likely to result in summary dismissal.

ABSENCE PROCEDURE AND RULES

Employees must ensure that any time off (other than in the case of sickness) is authorized in advance by their manager. Employees should complete an Absence Form on their first day back at work.

Medical and Dental Appointments

Employees are requested to arrange any medical or dental appointments outside working hours. Where this is not possible, employees must obtain permission from management before taking any time off and appointments should be arranged for first thing in the morning or last thing at night to minimize any disruptions to the Company.

Absence Due to Sickness

Employees are required to notify the Company as soon as possible of their sickness absence and the reasons for it. They should do this personally at the earliest opportunity to their line manager, no later than the time their shift starts, on the first day of the absence.

It is essential that employees keep the Company updated on the circumstances of the absence and of its estimated duration.

Where an employee's absence lasts more than seven calendar days a Medical Certificate completed by a medical practitioner must be given to the coffee shop owner.

ALCOHOL AND DRUGS

Consumption of Alcohol on the Premises

Employees are expressly forbidden to consume alcohol when at work or to bring it onto Company premises. Any breach of this rule will be treated as gross misconduct and is likely to result in summary dismissal.

Drug Misuse or Abuse on the Premises

Employees who take, sell or buy non-prescription drugs during working hours or on Company premises will be committing an act of gross misconduct and are likely to be summarily dismissed.

Intoxication at Work

An employee who is under the influence of alcohol or drugs during working hours or on Company premises will be escorted from the premises immediately. The Company will take disciplinary action when the employee has had time to sober up or recover from the effects of drugs. Intoxication at work will normally be treated as gross misconduct and result in summary dismissal.

DRESS AND APPEARANCE GUIDELINES

If a uniform or specified clothing is not provided, employees are required to dress in a manner appropriate to the function in which they are engaged.

All employees are required to attend work each day either in the supplied uniform or in normal smart dress suitable for a working environment which involves regular contact with customers, and to maintain high standards of personal hygiene.

All employees must ensure their clothing is clean, ironed and in good condition, free from rips and tears. Footwear should normally be dark, kept clean and in good condition.

Employees should not wear fingernail varnish, should keep their hair tidy and must ensure that their hands and nails are clean when at work.

UNIFORMS AND COMPANY CLOTHING

It is a condition of employment that employees wear any uniforms or clothing specified by the Company at all times during working hours.

The Company will supply employees with the appropriate uniforms or clothing at the Company's expense. Employees are expected to take care of any such items and to maintain them in a reasonable condition.

Employees must return any uniforms or clothing supplied by the Company at the termination of their employment. The Company reserves the right to deduct from the employee's final pay the cost of any uniforms or clothing that are lost, damaged or not returned.

CASH HANDLING

Only those employees specifically authorized by the Company to do so may have access to or use cash tills. Employees who use or attempt to use cash tills without being so authorized will be subject to disciplinary action.

Employees are not permitted to give discounts on any food or drink without permission of the manager.

FOOD HANDLING AND HYGIENE

Employees must always wash their hands before handling food and particularly after using the toilet.

Employees must inform the owner at once of any skin, nose, throat or bowel conditions.

Employees must inform the owner if anyone at home, or any pet or animal with which they have contact, is suffering from diarrhoea or vomiting.

Employees must ensure that any cuts or sores they may have are covered with a coloured (not skin-tinted) waterproof dressing.

Employees must ensure that protective clothing is clean and worn at all times.

Employees are not permitted to smoke during food preparation or in serving areas during working hours.

Employees should be careful not to cough and sneeze over or near food.

Employees should ensure that all equipment and surfaces are scrupulously clean at all times.

Employees should take care to keep the handling of food to a minimum and should not let their hands touch their clothes, face, nose, mouth or hair while handling food.

Employees must ensure that unused food is disposed of properly.

Employees must ensure that they wash their hands after handling bins and rubbish.

TRAINING

Whenever a new employee joins the Company, it is the employer's duty to ensure that he or she is given a proper introduction to the workplace, colleagues, environmental health and health and safety procedures.

Within the first few days of employment the new employee's training requirements will be assessed and arrangements made for that training to be provided. Training will be met by a combination of 'on the job' and related 'in house' training. From time to time, however, it may be necessary to arrange external training.

Each induction process will be tailored to the individual employee.

REDUNDANCY, SHORT-TIME WORKING AND LAY-OFF

It is the Company's intention to develop its business and to provide security of employment for its employees. However, circumstances may arise when changes in the market will lead to the need for reductions in employees.

Where a redundancy situation arises, the Company will give consideration to alternative options.

Selection for redundancy will be based on criteria drawn up at the time, and will be assessed in an objective manner.

CUSTOMER QUESTIONNAIRE

To help us improve our service and food it would be very helpful if you could answer the following questions and leave your comments and suggestions. Please post the questionnaire into the box on the counter when you have completed it.

POLITENESS AND FRIENDLINESS OF STAFF
☐ Could be improved ☐ Good ☐ Very Good ☐ Excellent

SPEED OF SERVICE
☐ Could be improved ☐ Good ☐ Very Good ☐ Excellent

CHOICE OF FOOD
☐ Could be improved ☐ Good ☐ Very Good ☐ Excellent

CHOICE OF DRINKS
☐ Could be improved ☐ Good ☐ Very Good ☐ Excellent

PRESENTATION OF FOOD
☐ Could be improved ☐ Good ☐ Very Good ☐ Excellent

TASTE OF FOOD (Please say what you had to eat.)
☐ Could be improved ☐ Good ☐ Very Good ☐ Excellent

VALUE FOR MONEY
☐ Could be improved ☐ Good ☐ Very Good ☐ Excellent

GENERAL CLEANLINESS
☐ Could be improved ☐ Good ☐ Very Good ☐ Excellent

Would you come back to the coffee shop?   Yes   ....
Perhaps ....
No   ....

Please give your comments and suggestions in the space below.

Name ....

Address ....

....

....

Telephone number ....

APPENDIX 7
USEFUL CONTACT NUMBERS AND ADDRESSES

The following is an index of useful contact addresses, most of which have been referred to in the text of the book.

Alexandra – www.alexandra.co.uk – 08700 600 200
For aprons, uniforms, white coats and chefs' jackets

Baco – www.baco.co.uk – 01236 733 954 and 0191 378 0088
For all baking ingredients and cake and scone mixes

British Franchising Association – www.british-franchise.org.uk – 01491 578050

Business Debtline – 0800 197 6026

Business Start-ups

England – Business Link: 0845 6009006 – www.businesslink.gov.uk

Wales – Business Eye: 0845 7969798 – www.businesseye.org.uk

Scotland – Small Business Gateway: 0845 6096611– www.b.gateway.co.uk

Northern Ireland – 02890 239090 www.nibusinessinfo.co.uk

Highlands and Islands Enterprise – www.hie.co.uk

Cobweb Information Ltd – factsheet on dismissing staff – www.scavenger.net

Coffee Beans and Coffee Machines – www.matthewalgie.co.uk – 0141 429 2817

Companies House – www.companies-house.gov.uk – 0870 333 3636

Department of Trade and Industry – advice on resolving disputes
www.dti.gov.uk/er/resolvingdisputes.htm

Equal Opportunities Commission – www.eoc.org.uk – 0845 601 5901

Food Safety Management Packs

These packs are available from the FSA.

> **England**: it is known as 'Safer Food, Better Business'. You can contact 0845 606 0667 for a copy or you can view it online at www.food.gov.uk/sfbb

> **Scotland**: it is known as 'Cook Safe' and you can contact 0845 606 0667 for a copy or you can view it online at www.food.gov.uk or you can contact your local authority for more information.

> **Northern Ireland** has produced a guidance pack known as 'Safe Catering' and you should contact your local authority for more information.

> **Wal**es: some Welsh authorities are using 'Safer Food, Better Business' which you can view online at www.food.gov.uk/sfbb or contact your local authority for more information.

Food Standards Agency for publications – 0845 606 0667; email foodstandards @ecgroup.uk.com, www.food.gov.uk

Food Standards Agency for caterers – www.food.gov.uk/cleanup

Franchise Direct – www.franchisedirect.co.uk
If you are thinking of taking on a franchise

Health and Safety Executive – www.hse.gov.uk – 08701 545500
Information Line – 08701 545 500
Book ordering line – 0178 788 1165

Home Office – www.homeoffice.gov.uk – 0845 010 6677
If you are considering employing overseas staff

HM Revenue and Customs – www.hmrc.gov.uk
Working for yourself – The Guide – to order – 0845 9000 404

Inland Revenue – www.inlandrevenue.gov.uk

Job Centre Plus – www.jobcentreplus.gov.uk

Law Society – See local telephone directory for your nearest Law Society

Microfibre cloths – www.micro-pro.co.uk
For information on microfibre cloths for use in the kitchen

National Minimum Wage helpline – 0845 600 0678

New employers' helpline – 0845 607 8787

Nisbets Catering Equipment and work wear – www.nisbets.com – 0845 140 5555

Part-time workers' regulations – www.dti.gov.uk/er/ptime.htm

Paul Wigley breakthrough facilitator – www.howmightwe.co.uk
email paul@howmightwe.co.uk – 0777 805 8026

Performing Rights Society – www.prs.co.uk – 0207 580 5544

Rich Sauces – 02891 819004
For luxury mayonnaise and different-flavoured mayonnaise

Royal Institute of British Architects – www.architecture.com

Royal Institute of Chartered Surveyors – www.ric.org

Supplier of Scottish Smoked Salmon, smoked duck etc. – 01292 442 773;
 email hello@burnsmoke.com

VAT registration – 0845 010 9000

XS Stock Ltd – www.xs-stock.com – 01294 204 004
For microfibre cloths etc.

INDEX

A

absence, 215
absenteeism, 87
adoption leave, 211
advertising, 108, 109, 114, 115
annual holidays, 187, 193, 199
appearance (staff), 83
apple spice chocolate chip cake, 159
atmosphere, 26
attracting customers, 111
aunt Isa's custard creams, 167

B

bain-marie, 51
baked potatoes (toppings), 143–7
banoffee pie, 178
breakfast casserole, 135
breakfast, 40
business agreement, 3
business plan, 21
butter icing, 162

C

cakes, 41, 150
caramal butter icing, 160
carrot cake, 155
cash and carry, 65
cash handling, 216
cash register, 59
catering equipment, 46
chairs, 60
charity fund raising, 115

cheesecake, 179
cheesy chilli pasta, 141
chicken and mushroom casserole, 139
chicken casserole, 140
chicken (coronation), 147
chicken curry, 146
chicken tikka, 145
children, 41
chilli con carne, 144
chocolate cake, 165
chocolate coconut squares, 175
chocolate shortcake, rich, 170
chopping boards (colour coded), 54, 55
cleaning schedule, 91, 92, 93, 94
cleaning tips, 93
coconut slice, 151
code of conduct, 213
coffee grinder, 48
coffee stall, 7
cold filled snacks, 35
competition prizes, 114
cooker, 51
cornflake crunch, 173
coronation chicken, 147
cream cheese icing, 156
crispy date cake, 174
crispy surprise, 177
croutons, 134
cupcakes, 162
customer feedback, 113
customer loyalty, 112
customer relations, 83

customers (difficult), 84
cut price beverages, 112
cutlery, 58

D
delivery service, 8
disciplinary procedure, 212
dishwasher, 49
dismissing staff, 75, 76, 77, 78, 79
dress and appearance, 216
drinks, 44
drugs and alcohol, 215

E
empire biscuits, 167
employee handbook, 205
employment contract:
    full time staff, 185
    part time staff,191
    weekend staff, 197
environmental health, 95–102, 217
expresso coffee, 48

F
filter coffee, 48
first aid kit, 105
flexibility, 214
fly killer, 56
flyers, 110, 111
food labelling, 104
food safety, 65, 91, 99, 100, 101, 102
food suppliers, 61–65
    ordering, 63
    relationships, 62
food temperature, 103
franchise, 7, 8
free coffee, 110, 113
free refills, 112
free samples, 112, 114

freezer, 50
frozen food, 104
fruit loaf, 156
fudge (vanilla), 181
fudge slices, 169

G
gingerbread, 163
good employer, 87, 90
griddle, 52
grievance procedure, 189, 195, 201
grill, 51
gross misconduct, 214

H
harassment, 215
hazards, 105, 106, 107
health and safety, 104, 105, 107, 189,
    195, 201, 214, 217
holidays, 187, 193, 199, 207
hot filled snacks, 28
hours of work, 186, 192, 198
hygiene (food), 101, 216, 217
hygiene (staff), 99, 100

I
ice cream, 41
immigrant employment, 67, 68
insurance, 105
interviewing, 73, 74

J
job centre, 70, 71, 72
job description – proforma, 203
job description, 73

L
leek and smoked haddock quiche, 138

lemon meringue pie, 168
lemon squares, 171
licences, 21
loaves
   apple spice loaf, 158
   cranberry nut loaf, 157
   fruit loaf, 156
location (buy or lease), 5
location (choice of), 4
logo design, 26

M
marketing strategies, 108
Mars bar squares, 171
maternity leave, 208–10
meals (home cooked), 40
meat loaf, 136
menus, 30–38
microwave, 52
millionaire shortbread, 172
mince, mushroom and pasta casserole, 141
misconduct, 76, 77, 78
muffins, American style, 154

N
name (business), 25
negative feedback, 113
notice, 189, 194, 201

O
opening hours, 34

P
paninis, 62, 149
partnerships (advantages and
   disadvantages), 2
partnerships, 1
pastry, 136
paternal leave, 211

paternity leave, 210–11
peppermint slice, 182
portion sizes, 41
premises, 11–14
professional advice
   accountant, 16
   advice agents, 20
   architect, 18
   banks, 18
   insurance, 19
   solicitor, 15
   surveyor, 17
public holidays, 188, 194, 200

Q
questionnaire (customer), 113, 218
quiche, 136
   leek and smoked haddock quiche, 138

R
recruitment of staff, 68
redundancy, 217
references, 69
refrigerator, 50
research, 9, 10
risk assessment, 105
robot coupe, 54
rubbish bin, 55

S
sandwiches, 148
sandwiches (toasted), 149
savoury recipes, 135
scones, 152, 153
Scottish tablet, 180
self service, 33
short time working and lay-off, 186, 192,
   198
shortbread, 166

shortbread (millionaire), 172
shortcrust pastry, 150
sick pay, 207
skills – essential, 184
smoked fish crumble, 142
soup, 38, 39, 40, 119
  chicken and rice soup, 122
  cream soup, 119
    carrot and coriander soup, 129
    carrot and ham soup, 130
    cauliflower and stilton soup, 127
    celery soup, 128
    mushroom soup, 130
    tomato and basil soup, 132
  cullen skink, 131
  French onion soup, 125
  Italian sausage soup, 134
  leek and potato soup, 122
  lentil soup, 124
  minestroni soup, 121
  parsnip and chilli soup, 128
  scotch broth, 126
  split pea soup, 123
  tomato and basil soup, 133
  vegetarian soups, 119
soup kettle, 53
sponge (plain), 164
staff
  employment, 67, 69, 70, 71, 72, 73
  keeping good staff, 88
  manual, 82
  meetings, 86
statutory rights, 186, 192, 198

sticky toffee buns, 160
stock rotation, 66, 102
stock rotation, 66, 102
strawberry and vanilla cheesecake, 179
strawberry tarts, 173
supermarkets, 65

T
table service, 33
tables, 59, 60
tablet (Scottish), 180
takeaway service, 112
thermometer with probe, 54
time keeping, 83
toaster, 53
toffee sauce, 161
toffee tarts, 173
training, 81, 101, 217
tray bakes, 119, 150
truffles, 183

U
uniforms, 28–30, 189, 195, 201, 216
useful contacts, 220–2

V
vouchers (complementary), 109, 110, 102

W
wash hand basin, 55
waste disposal, 50
water boiler, 49
work clothing, 214

UNIVERSITY OF
WOLVERHAMPTON
KNOWLEDGE • INNOVATION • ENTERPRISE

KT-158-257

...entre
City Campus
University of Wolverham...
St Peter's Square
Wolverhamp...
WV1 1...
Onli...   Telep...

UNDERST...
MASCULIN...

WITHDRAWN

WP 2033982 8

UNDERSTANDING MASCULINITIES

SOCIAL RELATIONS AND CULTURAL ARENAS

Edited by
Máirtín Mac an Ghaill

UNIVERSITY OF WOLVERHAMPTON
LIBRARY

Acc No. 2033982

CONTROL 0335194613

DATE 12. DEC. 1996

CLASS 305. 32

SITE UND

Open University Press
Buckingham · Philadelphia

Open University Press
Celtic Court
22 Ballmoor
Buckingham
MK18 1XW

and
1900 Frost Road, Suite 101
Bristol, PA 19007, USA

First Published 1996

Copyright © The Editor and Contributors 1996
Poetry © Richard Johnson 1996

All rights reserved. Except for the quotation of short passages for the purpose of
criticism and review, no part of this publication may be reproduced, stored in a
retrieval system, or transmitted, in any form or by any means, electronic,
mechanical, photocopying, recording or otherwise, without the prior written
permission of the publisher or a licence from the Copyright Licensing Agency
Limited. Details of such licences (for reprographic reproduction) may be obtained
from the Copyright Licensing Agency Ltd of 90 Tottenham Court Road, London,
W1P 9HE.

A catalogue record of this book is available from the British Library

ISBN   0 335 19460 5 (pb)   0 335 19461 3 (hb)

Library of Congress Cataloging-in-Publication Data
Mac an Ghaill, Máirtín.
    Understanding masculinities: social relations and cultural arenas Máirtín Mac an
    Ghaill.
        p.   cm.
    Includes bibliographical references and index.
    ISBN 0-335-19461-3. — ISBN 0-335-19460-5 (pbk.)
    1. Men — Psychology. 2. Masculinity (Psychology) I. Title.
    HQ1090.M325   1996
    305.31—dc20   95-32050
                                                                                            CIP

Typeset by Type Study, Scarborough
Printed in Great Britain by Biddles Ltd, Guildford and Kings Lynn

To

Cameron,
Catherine,
Howard,
Jason,
Lawrence,
Martin,
Meredith,
Patrick,
Saul
and
Scott.

Contents

Notes on contributors   ix
Acknowledgements   x

Introduction
Máirtín Mac an Ghaill   1

Part 1   Social relations of masculinities

   Hard rulers   *Richard Johnson*   17

1 'Feckless fathers': masculinities and the British state   21
   Sallie Westwood

2 Masculinities and families   35
   Christine Heward

3 Schooling masculinities   50
   Christian Haywood and Máirtín Mac an Ghaill

4 'Men' at 'work': multiple masculinities/multiple workplaces   61
   David Collinson and Jeff Hearn

5 Men, masculinity and the challenge of long-term
   unemployment   77
   Sara Willott and Christine Griffin

Part 2   Cultural arenas of masculinities

   Freedom: poem for a secular Passover feast   *Richard*
   Johnson   95

6 Masculinity, power and identity   97
   Nigel Edley and Margaret Wetherell

7   'One thing leads to another': drinking, fighting and working-
class masculinities   114
Joyce E. Canaan

8   Sporting masculinities: gender relations and the body   126
Andrew Parker

9   Are you sitting comfortably? Men's storytelling, masculinities,
prison culture and violence   139
Richard Thurston

10   From 'little fairy boy' to 'the compleat destroyer': subjectivity
and transformation in the biography of Mike Tyson   153
Tony Jefferson

11   'Empowering men to disempower themselves': heterosexual
masculinities, HIV and the contradictions of anti-oppressive
education   168
Peter Redman

Part 3   Critical evaluations of masculinities

White fright   *Richard Johnson*   183

12   Reading black masculinities   185
David Marriott

13   Is masculinity dead? A critique of the concept of masculinity/
masculinities   202
Jeff Hearn

Author index   218
Subject index   222

of slavery, colonialism and imperialism, black feminists have consistently argued against parochialism and stressed the need for a feminism sensitive to the international social relations of power.'

A fragmentary literature has begun to suggest a more complex conceptualization of masculinity. Most specifically there has been a shift to the notions of hegemonic masculinity and multiple masculinities (Brittan 1989). Clatterbaugh (1990: 2), in his book written within the context of contemporary North American society, identifies six major perspectives that dominate discussion of men and masculinity: the conservative, pro-feminist, men's rights, spiritual, socialist and group-specific perspectives. In Britain during the 1980s, particularly, as a result of feminist, gay, and lesbian writing, and AIDS activism, the changing nature of men's lives and their experiences were much debated within a range of literatures, drawing upon sex-role, psychoanalysis and gender and power theories (Weeks 1981, 1989; Watney and Carter 1989; Dollimore 1991; Sedgwick 1991; Plummer 1992; Sinfield 1994). The contributors to *Understanding Masculinities* reflect a similar wide range of theoretical backgrounds, including sociology, criminology, social psychology, psychoanalysis, anthropology, history and cultural studies. The book takes account of these different perspectives, locating them within broader theoretical problems, including the structure/ agency, macro/micro, society/individual and social order/social change divisions (Giddens 1979). At the same time, different chapters in the book draw upon theoretical work that focuses, at a time of high modernity, upon interconnections between and within gender, sexuality, class, 'race', ethnicity, nation, age relations and 'the more subtle inflections of those positions in . . . people's lives' (Cohen 1989: 12; see Mercer and Julien 1988; Harvey 1990; Giddens 1991; Anthias and Yuval Davis 1992; Bauman 1992; Brah 1992).

A specific feature of the book is to bring together recent historical and contemporary theoretical and empirical work to allow a critical reflection on the relative adequacy of different perspectives on masculinity, while at the same time highlighting the different problematics which make different assumptions about men and masculinity. In turn this may suggest different political interventions within the context of the rapid transformation of British society. The book builds on earlier work, such as Tolson (1977), Connell (1987) and Segal (1990), and their starting point that masculinities are problematic, negotiated and contested within frameworks at the individual, organizational, cultural and societal levels.

The book has a number of interrelated aims in providing up-to-date accounts of research on masculinity in key social and cultural arenas. First, to highlight the complex relationship between masculinities, sexualities and power relations. Second, to highlight the active cultural production of masculinities within local institutional sites. Third, to explore the contextual contingencies, confusions and contradictions of contemporary forms of

Notes on contributors

Joyce E. Canaan, School of Sociology, University of Central England
David Collinson, School of Industrial and Business Studies, University of Warwick
Nigel Edley, Faculty of Humanities, Nottingham Trent University
Christine Griffin, Department of Psychology, University of Birmingham
Christian Haywood, School of Education, University of Birmingham
Jeff Hearn, School of Applied Social Studies, University of Bradford
Christine Heward, Department of Education, University of Warwick
Tony Jefferson, Department of Law, University of Sheffield
Richard Johnson, Faculty of Humanities, Nottingham Trent University
Máirtín Mac an Ghaill,* School of Education, University of Birmingham
David Marriott, African and Asian Studies, University of Sussex
Andrew Parker, Department of Sociology, University of Warwick
Peter Redman, Faculty of Social Science, The Open University
Richard Thurston, Mid Glamorgan Probation Service, Pontypridd
Sallie Westwood, Department of Sociology, University of Leicester
Margaret Wetherell, Faculty of Social Science, The Open University
Sara Willott, Department of Psychology, University of Birmingham

The editor

* *Máirtín Mac an Ghaill* currently works in the School of Education, at the University of Birmingham. He is the author of *The Making of Men: Masculinities, Sexualities and Schooling.* He is currently researching with Christian Haywood around issues of working-class masculinities, changing work and family forms, funded by the Leverhulme Trust.

Acknowledgements

I am indebted to a number of people for their help, support and encouragement; to all the contributors to the book; to Beverley Burke at Birmingham University; to Nick Evans, Joan Malherbe, Pat Lee and Jacinta Evans at Open University Press. I am particularly grateful to Christian Haywood for his continuing emotional and intellectual comradeship.

Introduction

Until recently masculinity has tended to be absent from mainstream academic research. Earlier studies of gender relations, in which a unitary notion of musculinity was often employed, largely concentrated on women and girls. In much of this work, masculinity was assumed to be a monolithic unproblematic entity, with patriarchy attaining a universal status as the single cause of the oppression of women. From the late 1970s a continuing debate from different perspectives within feminism and pro-feminism has challenged this theoretical position (Rowbotham 1979; Bhavnani and Coulson 1986; Gilbert and Taylor 1991; Davies 1993). For example, Walby (1986) has identified a range of key patriarchal structures including capitalist work, the family, the state, violence, sexuality and culture. Connell (1987) also critiques the notion of patriarchy, claiming that it oversimplifies the structures of gender. He talks of a gender order and presents three majo structures, focusing upon the division of labour, power relations betwee men and women and sexuality (see also Roman and Christian-Smith 198 Griffin 1993). From a pro-feminist position, Hearn (1992) has illustrated t more complex picture of male domination, examining the shift from pri to public patriarchies. These studies maintain that we need to move a from categorical theories that emphasize that gender/sexual relation shaped by a single overarching factor. Rather, they suggest that relations are multidimensional and differentially experienced and resp to within specific historical contexts and social locations. As (1988: 11) points out: 'differentiated forms of male power can accounted for by analysis which takes into consideration the conditions that give rise to these situations'. An important aspect of t complex view of power is a critical focus on the multidimensior subject, involving an exploration of interactions and intersections v between different sets of social relations. For example, Brah (1992 argued that 'As a result of our location within diasporas formed by masculinity. And finally, to make problematic dominant forms of hetero-sexuality in a male-dominated (patriarchal) society.

Currently, there are competing representations of reconstructed and unreconstructed man (Chapman and Rutherford 1988; Craig 1992; Middleton 1992; Dyer 1993 and Edwards 1994). It is important to note that the new interest in the masculinity and sexuality of the gender majority is taking place within a broader context of the cumulative effects of the globalization of capital and communication systems, the changing nature of labour processes and new work technologies, the collapse of manufacturing and the accompanying suggested feminization of local labour markets, changing family forms and an increasing range of contradictory representations of men and masculinity. At the same time it is important to note the current backlash against feminism taken up in the popular media. A recent television programme asked the question: 'Is the future female?' If it is, for many working-class young women it is a future of low paid, non-unionized part-time work combined with a continuing responsibility for domestic labour. Hence the increased interest in masculinity and its deconstruction within the academy does not necessarily mean that gender relations are being transformed (Mac an Ghaill 1994a). It may be as Brittan (1989: 2) has suggested, that 'what has changed is not male power as such, but its form, the presentation and the packaging'.

During the last decade masculinity has gained increasing popular and academic interest. At one level, the 'football hooligan', the 'absent father', 'Essex man' and the 'new man' are regular popular media features. At the same time, a number of high quality theoretical accounts are now available that offer fresh insights into the making of masculine formations. By the early 1990s we have been provided with theoretical frameworks that enable us to analyse systematically and document coherently the material, social and discursive production of masculinities (Cockburn 1984; Metcalf and Humphries 1985; Weeks 1989; Hearn and Morgan 1990; Segal 1990; Brod and Kaufman 1994). These texts reveal a tension between materialist, deconstructionist and psychoanalytic critiques of sexual/gender identity formation. In materialist accounts, gender and sexuality are viewed as a matrix of power relations. In contrast, deconstructionist theorists have emphasized that the living of sexual/gender categories and divisions is more contradictory, fragmented, shifting and ambivalent than the dominant public definitions of these categories suggest. As Davies and Hunt (1994: 389) assert, 'Deconstruction is a strategy for displacing the hierarchy, for revealing the dependence of the privileged or ascendant term on its other for its own meaning: deconstruction moves to disrupt binary logic and its hierarchal, oppositional constitutive force.' Psychoanalysis has developed highly productive accounts of the complex psychic investments that individuals have in dominant sexual and gendered discourses (Hollway 1989; Butler 1990; Middleton 1992). At the same time, psychodynamic explanations illustrate

the limits of overrationalist accounts of sexual politics that fail to acknowledge that what we *feel* is as important as what we *know* in relation to the
maintenance of dominant gendered and heterosexual discourses and social
practices. Sexual/gender categories can be seen as being shaped by and
shaping the processes of colonization, of racism, of class hegemony, of male
domination, of heterosexism and other forms of oppression. In short,
masculinity can be seen as a crucial point of intersection of different forms of
power, stratification, desire and subjective identity formation (Fanon 1967;
Hemphill 1991; Jefferson 1994; Mac an Ghaill 1994b).

As Kessler *et al.* (1985) argue, in placing power at the centre of an analysis
of masculinity, it is important to comprehend fully the complexity of its
dynamic within institutional cultures. The conceptual difficulties involved in
moving beyond monocausal explanations that employ 'simple' models of
power are highlighted in the attempt to hold on to the tension between
materialist, deconstructionist and psychoanalytic accounts of masculine
identity formation. Deconstructionist theory has been important in moving
beyond both role model and social reproduction theories that often assume
that men and women are unitary, rational subjects occupying predictable
power positions. The suggestion that there are a range of subject positions
that may be occupied within different contradictory discourses is useful; it
helps in understanding the local social and cultural contextual specificity in
the production and reproduction of masculine identity formations that are
explored in this book (Henriques *et al.* 1984; Walkerdine 1991). On the other
hand, the development of masculine and feminine identities takes place
within the materially structured asymmetrical relations of power that
constitute hegemonic gender divisions and heterosexual arrangements
(Walby 1986; Kitzinger 1990). For example, this is currently made highly
visible in relation to Section 28 and the age of consent debate. As Collinson
and Hearn (1994: 3) argue in their study emphasizing the importance of
analysing the gendered nature of power relations in organizations: 'various
current debates . . . throw up certain unresolved analytical difficulties,
particularly regarding the understanding of gendered power relations and
multiple masculinities'.

Currently what is missing from this field of study in Britain is an
introductory text that provides a general overview (see Connell 1995, and
Edley and Wetherell 1995). Masculinity is an unclear field of study in which
highly complex theories are being developed that fail to connect with
individuals' experiences (see Wood 1984). Another aspect of the complexity
of researching and writing in this area is that of the question of the
elusiveness, fluidity and complex interconnectedness of masculinity in
modern societies. The book brings together main theorists, key concepts and
major debates. While in no way simplifying its complexities or understating
the challenge it presents, this book sets out to make the study of masculinities
more accessible to a wider readership. The 'second wave' feminist movement

of the 1960s and 1970s provided a vocabulary of sexual politics, patriarchy, sexual division of labour, etc. More recently gay and lesbian writers, AIDS activism and the influence of 'new queer theory' have made popular a language around heterosexual oppression employing notions of homophobia and heterosexism. In *Understanding Masculinities* every effort is made to translate the abstractness of current theorizing of gender and sexuality and to enable us to develop a language to talk about men, masculinities and sexualities. The chapters may be read as an attempt to jostle the imagination of the reader, 'by providing some more metaphors for living life, some more complexities to disturb old routines, some more politics to disrupt the functions of the past, some more views to punctuate the now crumbling view of a unified social order' (Plummer 1992: xviii–xix).

Bob Connell remains one of the most influential and creative theorists on men and masculinity. In his recent writing, he speaks of the need for a shift 'in the strategic conception of research and in our understanding of the object of knowledge' (Connell 1993: 598). He argues against reified conceptions of masculinity, suggesting that the object of knowledge is men's places and practices in gender relations. Pointing to the urgency of constructing a new framework of what he calls a political sociology of men in gender relations, he highlights the need to emphasize the institutionalization of masculinity, particularly in relation to the state, the workplace/labour market and the family. Elsewhere Connell (1989) has noted that schools are of strategic importance in the making of masculinities. In the first section of *Understanding Masculinities* each of these social arenas are critically explored by contributors.

Each section opens with a poem from Richard Johnson. They deal with issues around ruling – class masculinities and problems of personal and political change. The first deals with the intransigence and ultimately self-defeating character of forms of masculinity associated in Britain with upper-middle-class backgrounds and powerful social positions. The remaining two poems consider the dynamics of change, especially dialogues, of friendship or intimacy, across major power relations. The sequence poses a question: how far can men cease to mourn the loss of power and welcome the social benefits and personal pleasures of changing? In Chapter 1 Sallie Westwood examines the complex relationship between masculinities and the state through a concentration on one site – the Child Support Agency. In an analysis of the politics surrounding the agency, this chapter highlights the way in which ethnicity and class are articulated via masculinity providing a key moment in the generation of a collective subject in opposition to the state apparatus.

In Chapter 2 Christine Heward takes up how heterosexual masculinities are initially constructed within families. Substantive work is drawn upon to examine the dynamics of sex/gender identity formation, illustrating the processes of constructing masculinities within economic, political and emotional relations of particular families with different dominant ideals of masculinities. In Chapter 3 Christian Haywood and Maírtín Mac an Ghaill explore the claim by Connell (1989) that schools are strategically significant in shaping masculinities. They argue that earlier sex-role theories are inadequate to explain the complex social and psychological processes involved in the development of students' gendered subjectivities; subjectivities that are underpinned by institutional and wider material powers. They maintain that in order to understand the complex articulation between schooling, young people's cultural formations and masculinity, it is necessary to reconceptualize masculinities as situational, relational and dynamic, being constituted by and constituting various arenas within the school. It is suggested, through a focus on teacher cultures, the curriculum and student relations, that the school should be seen as a gendered/sexual regime, manifesting a range of competing masculinities and femininities. The chapter includes the findings of ethnographic studies that they have recently carried out, investigating the construction and maintenance of masculinity and sexuality within state schools.

In Chapter 4 David Collinson and Jeff Hearn make explicit a key theme in *Understanding Masculinities*: the tension between the recent interest in multiple masculinities and the continuing patterns of patriarchal domination. They begin their chapter by reviewing recent critical literature, inspired by feminist analysis, that has focused upon the gendered nature of 'men' at 'work'. This involves not only naming men as men but also critically examining the multiple conditions, processes and consequences of the continued domination of men and masculinities in various workplaces. The latter part of the chapter examines multiple masculinities within multiple workplaces, namely the home, the shopfloor, the office and management. In particular, five discourses of masculinity within organizations – authoritarianism, paternalism, entrepreneurialism, informalism and careerism – are analysed, before concluding on the need for further empirical and theoretical work on multiplicity, difference and unities in men, masculinities and workplaces.

In addition to the key social sites identified by Connell as of central significance in understanding the institutionalization of masculinity, we need to add unemployment. In Chapter 5 Sara Willott and Christine Griffin examine patterns of discourse around masculinity and unemployment. They do this with reference to existing literature and to a recent empirical study carried out in the West Midlands. The construction of traditional working-class masculinities relies heavily on the husband–father going out to earn a living through paid employment. It seems probable that unemployment constitutes a challenge to this hegemonic definition. For example, in a situation of limited resources, an unemployed man may talk about a conflict between public consumption and domestic provision. However, a challenge to the hegemonic does not necessarily lead to the construction of alternative identities which are less oppressive to women. They therefore explore discursive strategies used to resolve these dominant discourses of masculinity.

Part 2 identifies a number of cultural arenas in which specific institutional dynamics produce a particular interplay between masculinities, sexualities, power relations and identity formation. Nigel Edley and Margaret Wetherell's chapter looks at the theorization of male power. They begin with the feminist premiss that any adequate theory of men and masculinity has to have the concept of power at its centre, and from there move on to provide critical evaluations of psychoanalytic theory, role theory and social relations perspectives on men. Edley and Wetherell argue that whilst these different perspectives have their own contributions to make to any comprehensive social scientific understanding of men and male experience, when it comes to explaining the fact of men's privileged position in society, the burden of responsibility is best carried by a different approach, namely, cultural theory. Edley and Wetherell argue that male dominance is in part underpinned by their relative success in controlling the *meaning* of masculinity and (femininity). By managing to get their versions of the concept privileged above all others, men have been able to secure a dominant place in society. According to Edley and Wetherell, viewing masculinity as a contested territory or ideological battlefield not only has the advantage of providing a thoroughly social explanation of male dominance, but it also allows for the possibility of change. At the end of their chapter the authors provide an illustration of what these ideological battles look like in practice. In doing so, they draw upon data taken from a series of interviews with a number of 17 to 18-year-olds attending a Midlands single-sex independent school.

Joyce E. Canaan also addresses issues around hegemonic masculinity in Chapter 7. She considers how the working-class Midlands young men she interviewed enacted key signifiers of traditional hegemonic working-class masculinity in one of two ways in leisure, depending on whether they were younger and employed, or older and unemployed. She evaluates how each of these enactments of masculinities offers a different response to the recent post-Fordist structuring of the workplace, which has resulted in the employment of significantly fewer men, particularly those like the young men she interviewed who perform or would have performed predominantly unskilled manual labour jobs. Whilst the younger, employed young men had little problem in deeming drinking and fighting the means of affirming the 'hardness' of traditional working-class hegemonic forms of masculinity in their local territory – as well as in social contexts extending as widely as the city – the older young men lacked the money to go to pubs, clubs and football matches where they had formerly affirmed this same form of masculinity as those younger than themselves. These older young men seemed to shift their investment in traditional forms of masculinities from fighting to relationships with young women. Both groups of young men appeared to accept their position in society; whereas the younger men celebrated it, the older ones seemed worn down by it. Canaan places her analysis in the context of the cultural studies youth subcultures literature. She shows how its understandings of masculinities have been radically transformed since the 1970s, particularly as a consequence of insights from feminist, black and post-structuralist theories. She suggests that analyses of working-class men's masculinities are forged in the context of the wider social institutions and must consider how multiple factors like gender, age, class, and employment play key roles in particular versions of masculinity that young men elaborate.

In Chapter 8 Andrew Parker describes how, historically, feminist analyses of sport have been scarce, but that more recently a broad feminist critique has emerged, exposing sport as a bastion of male domination. Additionally encompassing notions of physical education and leisure, such an analysis has concentrated on women, thereby promoting monolithic constructions of masculinity within the confines of patriarchy. Accordingly, sport has also attracted the attention of those within the men's studies tradition and, as a consequence, the multifaceted nature of masculine identity has been addressed. The chapter identifies the main contributors within the sport/masculinity debate, and traces its historic development in terms of the shift from stringent, functionalist notions of masculine formation to more complex conceptualizations concerning the existence of a gender order. More specifically, substantive material from qualitative research that he is currently engaged in will illustrate the changing nature of sport as a cultural site in which a range of heterosexual masculinities are produced. He maintains that a dominant element of the current change are the powerful discourses around health and the male body.

In Chapter 9 Richard Thurston explores the relationship between heterosexual men's investments in particular formations of masculine identities relating to violence within the cultural arena of prison. He looks at some of the strategies men employ in prison in the production and reproduction of gendered power relations through discursive practices, violent interactions, and telling stories. Indeed, storytelling emerges as a key process by which heterosexual men relocate and reproduce their power and identities within prison. Importantly, this analysis is not limited to the traditional focus in prison sociology of men as inmates, but is extended to include more or less powerful men throughout the prison regime, including governors and prison officers. Furthermore, the stories told in prison are linked to wider discursive networks of identity production, power relations, and personal and social investments in violence, across cultural arenas or 'lifespheres', and across lives, or more specifically, life histories. As a necessary strategy for this approach, the analysis or cultural decoding of the material is told within and is integral to the 'story of the research' itself. Thus the chapter includes material relating to researcher–researched relations, and the outcomes of the research within practical, political and social policy contexts. The focus here is on the possibility and desirability of bringing about transformative practices in order to challenge men's personal, material and institutionally located investment in particular identities and social action strategies involving violence. The life story method is offered as an example of how a research method can be used dynamically and creatively both as a challenging and insightful way into studying men and masculinities, and as a practice technique for re-educational and challenging work with men.

In Chapter 10 Tony Jefferson describes how as a young child living in the slums of Brooklyn, Mike Tyson was known as 'little fairy boy' and was the object of neighbourhood bullying. He went on to become a bully and a thief; a boxing prodigy; the youngest-ever heavyweight boxing champion of the world widely referred to as 'Iron' Mike or 'the compleat destroyer'; a superstar millionaire; married; divorced inside a year; and finally a convicted rapist. In thinking particularly about two of these dramatic changes in Tyson's short life to date, namely, becoming a bully boy and then a boxer, this chapter explores the role of masculine desire in Tyson's downfall. Was he, as some would have it, the archetypal ghetto child, a product of social circumstances beyond his control? Jefferson argues the need for a more complex account combining insights drawn from post-structuralist, feminist and psychodynamic theories. This is necessary to do justice to both the psychic and the social levels involved in thinking adequately about subjectivity. Specifically, he argues that anxiety fuelled the desires behind the particularly hypermasculine subject positions Tyson adopted, which helps explain a series of choices which seem otherwise highly counterproductive. He also touches upon the role of memory in the historical construction of the relevant discursively based subject positions.

In Chapter 11 Peter Redman argues that the history of popular response to HIV and AIDS reveals a profound anxiety about heterosexual masculinity. Redman argues that widespread attempts to blame gay men for the virus, to construct them as a threat to the 'mainstream population', and to deny the reality of heterosexual transmission of HIV, represent attempts to police the psychic and social boundaries of hegemonic heterosexual masculinities and to preserve their hegemonic position in both the field of representation and social relations of power. The chapter's central argument is that sex education, youth work and other allied fields have largely failed to address the ways in which hegemonic heterosexual masculinities have been actively reproduced, secured and reinforced in the struggles over the HIV epidemic. In this light, Redman attempts to unravel some of the complexities and contradictions that are involved in developing anti-sexist, anti-heterosexist and anti-homophobic strategies aimed at heterosexual men and boys. The chapter suggests a need for strategies that grapple with the realities of heterosexual mens' and boys' lives and that address the investments that heterosexual men and boys have in the forms of masculinity that they occupy. To this end, the chapter explores the limitations of some of the approaches currently available in this area, and suggests the basis for an alternative model is to be found within recent debates in subcultural theory, 'queer studies', and in critical feminist social psychology.

The third part of the book presents two critical evaluations of the study of masculinities. In Chapter 12 David Marriott examines how critical notions of black masculinity have changed over the last two decades. He points out that social and psychological analyses of black men have sought to explain their masculinity in terms of 'internalization', 'castration' and 'emasculation', situating the 'problem' of black masculinity within the framework of the black family. These social psychological explanations have tended to work with functionalist accounts of gender role formation. Marriott suggests that recent studies of black masculinities have shifted the debate. Black feminists and writers and black gay men and activists interrogate how the political and cultural strategies of ideological resistance in black communities has operated historically to offset white and black racism and sexism. This body of criticism has challenged the account of black men as pathological and socially dysfunctional via non-functionalist theories of race, gender and representation. Both black feminists and cultural theorists have objected to the perceived phallocentric bias of functionalist theories. The blaming of the black mother in the sociology of race relations accounts of emasculation, according to these theorists, represents a signal failure to interrogate the phallocentric and patriarchal notions of masculinity itself. The issue of black 'manliness' is tied up with white masculinity. In an attempt to move discussion beyond claims that black masculinity is a monolithic and homogeneous identity (and is therefore to be identified with an unsuccessful version of white masculinity), recent theorists have concentrated on the ambivalent and racial dialectic between fantasy and desire in identity formation. These critics draw on discourse analysis and psychosocial accounts of gender formation, and argue for an understanding of black masculinities from within a radical sexual politics of the cultural arena.

Finally, Jeff Hearn's chapter concludes the book with a focused critique of the concept of masculinity/masculinities. A number of fundamental issues are raised, including the frequent imprecision of the concept, the attribution of causal power to masculinity/masculinities, and the obscuring of the power of men's material practices.

As these chapter outlines indicate, a major concern of this book is a critical examination of the way in which dominant definitions of heterosexual masculinity are affirmed and authenticated within social and cultural arenas, where ideologies, discourses, representations and material practices systematically privilege men and boys. Empirical findings and theoretical arguments are integrated to propose a more comprehensive understanding of the social and psychic investments that males make and remake in a range of socially and culturally located masculinities and the accompanying power relations. Such an account involves the attempt to work through a multilevel analysis that incorporates explanations at the level of state discourses, institutions, social groups and individuals. The book is written at a time of a political and cultural interregnum in which 'the old politics and identities have been in decline, but the new have still to emerge. In this sense the book describes a transition, rather than offering a definitive new position' (Rutherford 1990: 23).

References

Anthias, F. and Yuval Davis, N. (1992) *Racialized Boundaries: Race, Nation, Gender, Colour and Class and the Anti-Racist Struggle*. London: Routledge.
Bauman, Z. (1992) *Intimations of Postmodernity*. London: Routledge.
Bhavnani, K.K. and Coulson, M. (1986) Transforming socialist feminism: the challenge of racism, *Feminist Review*, 23: 81–92.
Brah, A. (1992) Difference, diversity and differentiation, in J. Donald and A. Rattansi (eds) *'Race', Culture and Difference*. Milton Keynes: Open University/Sage.
Brittan, A. (1989) *Masculinity and Power*. New York: Blackwell.
Brod, H. and Kaufman, M. (1994) *Theorising Masculinities*. London: Sage.
Butler, J. (1990) *Gender Trouble, Feminism and the Subversion of Identity*. London: Routledge.
Chapman, R. and Rutherford, J. (eds) (1988) *Male Order: Unwrapping Masculinity*. London: Lawrence and Wishart.
Clatterbaugh, K. (1990) *Contemporary Perspectives on Masculinity: Men, Women and Politics in Modern Society*. Oxford: Westview Press.
Cockburn, C. (1984) *Brothers: Male Dominance and Technological Change*. London: Pluto Press.
Cohen, P. (1989) *Really Useful Knowledge: Photography and Cultural Studies in the Transition from School*. London: Trentham.
Collinson, D. and Hearn, J. (1994) Naming men as men: implications for work, organization and management, *Gender, Work and Organization*, 1(1): 2–22.
Connell, R.W. (1987) *Gender and Power*. Cambridge: Polity Press.
Connell, R.W. (1989) Cool guys, swots and wimps: the interplay of masculinity and education, *Oxford Review of Education*, 15(3): 291–303.
Connell, R.W. (1993) The big picture: masculinities in recent world history, *Theory and Society*, 22(5): 597–624.
Connell, R.W. (1995) *Masculinities*. Cambridge: Polity Press.
Craig, S. (ed.) (1992) *Men, Masculinity and the Media*. London: Sage.
Davies, B. (1993) *Shards of Glass: Children, Reading and Writing Beyond Gendered Identities*. Sydney: Unwin and Allen.
Davies, B. and Hunt, R. (1994) Classroom competencies and marginal positionings, *British Journal of Sociology*, 15(3): 389–408.
Dollimore, J. (1991) *Sexual Dissidence: Augustine to Wilde, Freud to Foucault*. Oxford: Clarendon Press.
Dyer, R. (1993) *The Matter of Images: Essays on Representation*. London: Routledge.
Edley, N. and Wetherell, M.S. (1995) *Men in Perspective: Practice, Power and Identity*. Hemel Hempstead: Harvester Wheatsheaf.

Edwards, T. (1994) *Erotics and Politics: Male Sexuality, Masculinity and Feminism*. London: Routledge.

Fanon, F. (1967) *Black Skins, White Masks*. London: Paladin.

Giddens, A. (1979) *Central Problems in Social Theory*. London: Macmillan.

Giddens, A. (1991) *Modernity and Self-Identity*. Cambridge: Polity Press.

Gilbert, P. and Taylor, S. (1991) *Fashioning the Feminine: Girls, Popular Culture and Schooling*. Sydney: Allen and Unwin.

Griffin, C. (1993) *Representation of Youth: The Study of Youth and Adolescence in Britain and America*. Cambridge: Polity Press.

Harvey, D. (1990) *The Condition of Postmodernity*. Oxford: Blackwell.

Hearn, J. (1992) *Men in the Public Eye: The Construction and Deconstruction of Public Men and Public Masculinities*. London: Routledge.

Hearn, J. and Morgan, D. (eds) (1990) *Men: Masculinities and Social Theory*. London, Hyman and Unwin.

Hemphill, E. (ed.) (1991) *Brother to Brother: New Writings by Black Gay Men*. Boston, MA: Alyson.

Henriques, J., Hollway, W., Urwin, C., Venn, C. and Walkerdine, V. (1984) *Changing the Subject: Psychology, Social Regulation and Subjectivity*. London: Methuen.

Hollway, W. (1989) *Subjectivity and Method in Psychology: Gender, Meaning and Science*. London: Methuen.

Jefferson, T. (1994) Theorising masculine subjectivity, in T. Newburn and E. Stanko (eds) *Just Boys Doing Business? Men, Masculinities and Crime*. London: Routledge.

Kessler, S., Ashenden, D.J., Connell, R.W. and Dowsett, G.W. (1985) Gender relations in secondary schooling, *Sociology of Education*, 58: 34–48.

Kitzinger, C. (1990) *The Social Construction of Lesbianism*. London: Sage.

Mac an Ghaill, M. (1994a) *The Making of Men: Masculinities, Sexualities and Schooling*. Buckingham: Open University Press.

Mac an Ghaill, M. (1994b) (In)visibility: sexuality, masculinity and 'race' in the school conext, in D. Epstein (ed.) *Challenging Lesbian and Gay Inequalities in Education*. Buckingham: Open University Press.

Mercer, K. and Julien, I. (1988) Race, sexual politics and black masculinity: a dossier, in R. Chapman and J. Rutherford (eds) *Male Order: Unwrapping Masculinities*. London: Lawrence and Wishart.

Metcalf, A. and Humphries, M. (eds) (1985) *The Sexuality of Men*. London: Pluto Press.

Middleton, P. (1992) *The Inward Gaze: Masculinity, Subjectivity and Modern Culture*. London: Routledge.

Plummer, K. (ed.) (1992) *Modern Homosexualities*. London: Routledge.

Roman, L. and Christian-Smith, L. (eds) (1988) *Becoming Feminine: The Politics of Popular Culture*. London: Falmer Press.

Rowbotham, S. (1979) The trouble with patriarchy, *New Statesman*, 98: 970–1.

Rutherford, J. (1990) 'A place called home: identity and the cultural politics of difference', in J. Rutherford (ed.) *Identity: Community, Culture and Difference*. London: Lawrence and Wishart.

Sedgwick, E.K. (1991) *Epistemology of the Closet*. London: Harvester Wheatsheaf.

Segal, L. (1990) *Slow Motion: Changing Masculinities, Changing Men*. London: Virago.

Sinfield, A. (1994) *Cultural Politics: Queer Reader*. London. Routledge

Tolson, A. (1977) *The Limits of Masculinity*. London: Tavistock.

Walby, S. (1986) Gender, class and stratification: towards a new approach, in R. Crompton and R. Mann (eds) *Gender and Stratification*. Cambridge, MA: Harvard University Press.

Walkerdine, V. (1991) *Feminism and Youth Culture: From 'Jackie' to 'Just Seventeen'*. London: Macmillan.

Watney, S. and Carter, E. (eds) (1989) *Taking Liberties: AIDS and Cultural Politics*. London: Serpent's Tail.

Weeks, J. (1981) *Sex, Politics and Desire*. London: Longman.

Weeks, J. (1989) *Sexuality and its Discontents: Meanings, Myths and Modern Sexualities*. London: Routledge.

Wolpe, A.M. (1988) *Within School Walls: The Role of Discipline, Sexuality and the Curriculum*. London: Routledge.

Wood, J. (1984) Groping towards sexism: boys' sex talk, in A. McRobbie and M. Nava (eds) *Gender and Generation*. London: Macmillan.

Part I

Social relations of masculinities

Hard rulers

Richard Johnson

We are Reason's
evident efficiencies
its proper beneficiaries.
We make the histories happen, patterns
fall our way and
all the best eventualities
are games we play.
We are confident
of our entitlement
to rule you.

        *   *   *

We took them
from their mothers', sisters' sides
for undomesticated Missions,
joined them to the other
accidental aristocrats
according
to the sad
subordinate
ambitions
of their fathers.

Our kindest cuts
have hollowed out
the vital parts of
caring unconditional,
for self included,
all feminine affinities,
love for other boys,
and gifts for intimacy.
Of course we had to cauterize
the tender parts
against infectious sympathies
and make for every one

a wood and iron cask
to hold
the personal substance
tight inside
including half each word.

Then they could join
the hearty-hard contingents
of our ruling men
whose loyalty
in company
is gross un-relativity,
greater betrayal.

*   *   *

We do not have to feel
the weight of others' faces
on our fists.
To men and engines
tuned to this
the vicious twist
of power
reduces.

A softer manhood
our indulgence marks,
immunity from every common rule
of scarcity enforced.
Our work is will imposed
as to your need
(whose terms we deem);
as to the law
(we camber to our use);
as to the secrets held from you
of what we do
and what decree
that you shall be.

*   *   *

Dependence they denied
dizzies the hard clear vision
they once had,

fumbles their hold
on scheduled happenings,
prompts history's little accidents
and honest justifiable mistakes,
turns freedom
into anarchy
that wakes them trembling
in the early hours
to press desperate
against our backs.

The people even
earth itself
rebels degenerate
beneath their touch
unrecognized from what they
thought they made,
no longer theirs
and now ungovernable.

So in exclusion zones
which are our homes
among the prizes seized
from other people's lives
they come to us
their co-exploited wives,
and mothers, sisters lost
and shrink to persons isolate
their theories recommend.

The wrecked foundations
of these fortress selves
show seawards
sliding over groynes
they built of bones
still washing red
with every wave.

                    *   *   *

We were schooled
to rule
We were ruled
to rule.

Too late to take
a warm
and calming hand,
joining wth the .
vulnerably
powerful now.

(June 1994 to January 1995)

**Sallie Westwood

'Feckless fathers': masculinities and the British state

Introduction

The articulation between forms of masculinity and the state is an old story, conjuring images of the military and tied to conceptions of the nation and national destinies. These very visible signs of the relationship between masculinities, the state and the nation are organized around 'fictive ethnicities' (Balibar and Wallerstein 1988) and racialized conceptions of national identity – the 'freeborn English man', for example, who fights for Queen and Country. Although imperial in tone, it is a vision regenerated within the racial formation of Britain in the 1990s and expressed, in its most visible moments, through the politics of the British National Party on the streets and at football matches. These events generally produce a counter from the police which offers another image of the encounter between masculinities and the state. These pictures of fascists, the military and the police all suggest the link between masculinity and violence that has been a central motif of some radical feminist writings on men and masculinities. This account has privileged male violence, especially against women, by seeing men as all-powerful and women as victims. Such an account, with its monolithic categories of 'men' and 'women' does not assist the theorization of violence or masculinities. Similarly, in understanding the state, one common view of the state (from the work of Max Weber) regards the state as the legitimate keeper of the means of violence. In this chapter I want to suggest some alternative ways in which we can understand the articulation between masculinities and the state.

The state, sociology and social policy

There are a variety of ways in which 'the state' has been understood in sociological discourses. One of these is as the legitimate source of power and the means of violence. This account, like many of the others, suggests that the state is a unitary, single entity and this has led to the use of 'the state' to imply that the state is an actor, a visible and invisible hand in all our lives. This constructs an all-powerful state and is often allied with a conspiratorial view of how the state 'acts' in relation to society and citizens. An alternative and early Marxist view presents us with the opposite: the state denuded of its power and a mere agent of specific class interests. An early feminist view nudged the class interests out of the way and inserted 'male' interests, coining the term 'patriarchal state' as a way of signalling the relationship between masculinity and the state (Walby 1990). More generally in sociology, the state is understood as a nexus of institutional arrangements, for example, in terms of national identity the state sets the legal limits of nationality and citizenship, defining who is a national and who is an alien.

Clearly, the state operates in complex and multifarious ways that impact on our daily lives to the extent that the state seems to be everywhere at all times. One attempt to delimit the boundaries of the state has come from Antonio Gramsci (1985), who made the distinction between the state and civil society that was reworked in the famous Althusserian notion of repressive and ideological state apparatuses (Althusser 1977). Althusser reproduced notions of the military, the police and the courts as RSAs, while education, the media and trade unions were considered as ISAs. Thus very little space was left for civil society, which was understood by Gramsci to include trade unions and political groupings and forms of education. The distinction between the state and civil society is an important one analytically and politically. More recently, following the work of Michel Foucault (Foucault 1977) there has been an attempt to understand the state in a disaggregated way as a complex of discourses and practices infused with power relations that are not located in one place or one specific form of the state but are suffused throughout social formations. Foucault has also used the notion of governmentality to foreground his critique of the state as an actor and to emphasize the ways in which the complex structures of the state, professional bodies and welfare practices generate the 'management of populations'. Although Foucault is notorious for his lack of attention to the entity of the state, his institutional studies provide an account of the rise of the modern state, but understood in very novel ways. One very interesting account which uses Foucault's insights on governance and the 'management of populations' is offered by Zygmunt Bauman.

Sociology and social policy are both currently in crisis but of a very creative and productive kind. In order to understand these crises it is necessary to step back and to consider the moment in which sociology was called into being. Thus I would argue that these are crises born out of the crisis of modernity which is the frame in which sociological knowledges have been generated. Bauman (1992: 81) notes: 'Sociological discourse was formed within the perspective of managed social processes' – the social engineering account of sociology remains an always present and continuing rationale within the discipline. It was allied with the 'management of populations' through the rise of welfarism and what Bauman calls the 'gardening state' – a nice metaphor for the ways in which the state intervened to classify, counter and set apart the useful and useless plants, the flowers and the weeds. But, the gardening state is in trouble not only in Britain but across the metropolitan core. It was founded upon the underlying premiss that Keynes had solved the problems of production and this allowed Beveridge to put in place a system of care and benefits – the welfare state – built upon an economic strength that no longer exists. It was also, of course, a gendered account of welfare which assumed that women's place was in the home and that male breadwinners actually existed. The myth of the male breadwinner has been long exposed but is now foregrounded by the high levels of male unemployment while women make up 50 per cent of the workforce and 90 per cent of single-headed households claiming benefits. Childcare was not an issue with the Beveridge model and its foundation upon the eugenicist call for white women to reproduce. 'In the next thirty years housewives as mothers have vital work to do in ensuring the adequate continuance of the British race and British ideals' (Beveridge Report 1942: 52).

The means to pay for the welfare system was solved by the conventional means of direct taxation. Now both childcare and paying for the system are on the agenda and have generated new models, one of which is of concern in this chapter: the Child Support Agency (CSA). Equally, the racialization of welfare, especially of the healthcare system, was not considered. A post-colonial state like Britain simply imported the labour it needed to fuel the economy and staff the health service. The deepening crisis of welfare in Britain is never solely a story of economics devoid of questions of racialization and gender.

It is what is conventionally called the welfare state that is at issue here. The juxtaposition of welfare/state is itself worthy of note in terms of the development of modernity in Europe and the generation of forms of discipline and individuation that seek to establish a consensus and moral order within the social formation through dispersed power relations. The complex of discourses and practices that add up to a system of welfare is a contested terrain, subject to organized politics, scrutiny, comment and debate as much as any other areas of the state. In the 1990s we have witnessed struggles around the Criminal Justice Bill, the health service, immigration rules in relation to EU regulations, education, and so on. These arenas are 'sites' of struggle which are part of a larger picture but have a specificity as well. Within all of these sites as aspects of the state there are generated and sustained accounts of social, economic and legal life, all of which involve conceptions of masculinity and femininity. In its most transparent form the debates around the family bring these accounts together at the same time that 'the family' as an imaginary organizes accounts of the public and the private.

At the commonsense level the state equals the public and the family the private domain. However, it is clear that this binary division is constantly transgressed; the state through the law, health social work and educational professionals intervenes in family life and by so doing deconstructs the division between public and private while similarly reinventing the relations between civil society and the state. 'The family' has itself become an important site of struggle and gendered and racialized identities are central to this. Thus the model of the white two-parent and two-children nuclear family is held up as a model of family life while the *Daily Mail* (6 April 1990) declares the Asian family is the typical British family, the survivor in the breakdown of family life in Britain. The *Daily Mail* omits from its pages the immigration rules that ensure that many British Asian and African-Caribbean families in Britain remain separated by immigration officials and British immigration law. These legal interventions are a classic encounter with the gardening state as it seeks to categorize and police families within the developing diversity of Britain. Thus through the discourses and practices of the state, families are simultaneously generated, sustained and destroyed. In recent years the politics of the family has condensed around issues of one-parent families and child support represented by the Child Support Agency. But before I elaborate further on these issues let me turn briefly to a discussion of masculinities.

Masculinities and gender politics

Masculinity, like the state, exists in a plurality of forms. There is no fixed set of attributes that can be labelled masculinity. Instead, masculinity is theorized in this essay as unstable and multiple, as decentred and subject to changing contexts, in a constant play of reproduction and innovation. Masculinity shifts and is constantly in the process of being remade through 'gender identity work' (Brittan 1989). Such a view is at odds with earlier accounts from sociology of 'the male role' which has been the subject of several critiques. Most notably, Carrigan, Connell and Lee (1987: 80) comment: 'let us be blunt about it. The "male sex role" does not exist. It is impossible to isolate a "role" that constructs masculinity or another that constructs femininity.' Thus it has been possible within the last decade for the conception of the 'new man' to be generated and sustained through the media and patterns of consumption that have offered alternative accounts of masculinity (Chapman 1988). Equally, queer politics has consistently offered alternative accounts of men and masculinity. The media, once thought to reproduce simply conventional accounts of masculinity and femininity, instead present a complex series of accounts of masculinity from the safety of the 'boy next door' to the machinations of power, sporting prowess, buddies and hitmen. But within popular television like the soaps and comedy programmes, fathers and fatherhood are explored in complex and nuanced ways. Thus, as I have suggested elsewhere (Westwood 1990), masculinity does not simply have its own history on a linear model but is constantly reconstructed in relation to social, political and cultural developments. Consequently, like the state, masculinities are contested terrain and subject to instability and change. There is clear evidence of this in relation to one of the major signifiers of masculinity, fatherhood, which was seized upon by advertisers following the photograph of the great Caribbean cricketer Viv Richards with a baby on his back. The suggestion was, and is, that fatherhood is 'back in fashion' and it will sell products as diverse as Flora margarine and Armani suits and cologne. But beyond this rather cynical view there are some developing social trends which are in part born of the interaction between changes in men's employment, the growth of male unemployment and women's employment and the complexities of family life in Britain today. These changes are expressed in current research findings (Sianne and Wilkinson 1995) generated by Demos, the independent think-tank, which suggest 'Young men are less attached to their status as breadwinner and see it in the context of other goals, such as being a good father and a loving companion. Women, meanwhile are becoming more attached to their working lives' (Guardian 6 March 1995). This, in part, reflects the changing employment opportunities for women and men but it also signals the ways in which the work ethic has shifted and the link between masculinity and the wage has been eroded. Instead, some men are more inclined to define interpersonal relations as the most important area of their lives, often citing the family. It has become a familiar call from politicians when they decide to resign from government; 'to spend more time with my family' is probably the most overused phrase in politics today.

This is one part of a very complex series of shifts in family life and gender relations which writers like Anthony Giddens (1994) have tried to conceptualize in terms of the changing nature of intimacy and the growth of reflexivity in later modernity. Giddens has emphasized the complexities of life at the end of the twentieth century and the ways in which people individually and together find ways of talking about the self, life and contradictions – what Foucault would call 'technologies of the self'. The rise of therapy culture, especially among the white middle classes, is part of this but it has popular variants in women's magazines, in men's magazines and through popular television. On the other hand, however, the ruling Conservative party has set a very different agenda, calling up 'family values' that even they find it hard to live by with a vision of a settled 1950s world in which men worked and women baked cakes – a vision at odds with the employment patterns of the time – and which itself generated enormous anxieties about the family and children. It was in the 1950s that studies of delinquency suggested that deviancy in children was prompted by mothers who worked outside the home: the notion of the 'latchkey child' was born. Sociological studies undertaken at the time disputed this account, suggesting the opposite effects on children (Jephcott 1962). Central to official discourses was an account of motherhood fashioned on a model of white middle-class domesticity against which working mothers were judged. Working mothers were constructed in official discourse in ways which generated an account of the 'feckless mother'. It was a discourse familiar from the Victorian era, when the health of the nation was laid at the feet of women as mothers, whose morality and mothering were subject to public scrutiny and increasingly the intervention of state agencies through the 1940s and into the post-Beveridge 1950s. The feckless mother re-emerged in the 1980s in the debates around single parents and state benefits.

Family values

The statistics of family life in Britain belie the attention given to both the 2.4 nuclear family and the numbers of single parents. What is clear is that the lived reality of family life is increasingly diverse with less marriage, more divorce and more women as lone parents. The suggestion from government rhetoric is that single parents with children are a category apart from 'the family' rather than one instance of the increasing diversity of family forms in Britain. Statistically the classic nuclear family accounts for only 24 per cent of households, while lone parent families now constitute 9 per cent of families; and with the growing age of the population 26 per cent of households are single person households (General Household Survey 1993). Fertility rates have fallen and women, on average, have their first child at 28. But the patterns are not uniform: fertility rates are higher among those of Asian descent overall but differentiated by class and ethnicity, and similar to white women among those of African-Caribbean descent. The government assumed the high moral ground suggesting that there were too many lone parents and too many – one in four children – born outside marriage. In fact, most of these babies are born to cohabiting couples. The rise of cohabitation means that while in 1979 74 per cent of women aged 18–49 were married, in 1993 it was 59 per cent. The trends are strikingly similar to those in the Scandinavian countries but British women are supported by far fewer state benefits.

Faced with the changing demography of Britain and armed with 'family values', the Conservative government, eager to cut the mounting benefits bill, targeted the family as a terrain of action. The welfare benefits bill had increased in relation to the age profile of the country but, more importantly, in relation to the steady growth in unemployment through the 1980s and 1990s. However, the withdrawal of government support was never solely an economic project; it was a political/ideological intervention in which the notion of the individual and citizen as responsible for their own welfare replaced the earlier settlement based on welfare as part of a collective responsibility and social wage. What emerged from the ensuing debate was in part a vilification of lone parents, most especially mothers; the familiar story of 'feckless mothers' and irresponsible women was rerun. But a new twist entered the tale. I have already noted the re-emergence of fatherhood as part of the redefinition of masculinity in the last 20 years, a new chapter in the histories of fatherhood (Morgan 1985; Brittan 1989). In keeping with conceptions of the new man, the emotional and caring lives of men were centred around the refashioned notion of the father, no longer the distant wage-earner but a co-carer and parent in the work of raising a child, now emotionally involved with children in ways not previously expected or acknowledged. The government – eager to both cut the welfare bill and recover the moral high ground of the family – seized on the new fatherhood but recast it in a previous incarnation. The problem was no longer simply 'feckless mothers' but 'feckless fathers' who abandoned their material responsibilities towards their children and who should be accountable to the state and required to pay up – enter the Child Support Agency.

The politics of the Child Support Agency

The Child Support Agency initially received all-party support, but from the time it started to work in April 1992 it was controversial. It was created as a novel approach to the problems of maintenance orders made against absent fathers that were often minimal in their effect and the income they generated for mothers and children. Instead, the new agency was charged with the responsibility for generating and enforcing adequate maintenance from fathers living apart from their children in the hope that this would offset the amount of income support paid to some mothers. Thus, a maintenance order for £25 a week was re-examined and could generate a new figure of £150 based on a rigid formula that was part of an overall grid of assessment. When the agency started work there were 895,000 one-parent families, mostly headed by women, drawing income support. The agency had a staff of 5000 and was headed by Ros Hepplewhite who, when interviewed in the *Guardian* (30 December 1992) said: 'This is not an agency which is dealing with a small and irresponsible element of society; this is a major social change', and she continued: 'Paying maintenance will become like paying income tax. It will become a feature of life for very many people, particularly given the social trend of serial relationships.'

The agency was given far-reaching powers to track 'errant' fathers and to secure deductions from wages and salaries at source following settlement of entitlements. These powers proved some of the most controversial and Ms Hepplewhite in the same *Guardian* article was anxious to overcome the expressed disquiet. As she commented: 'One of the big misconceptions that I am fighting is that the agency is engaging in some moral crusade to punish feckless fathers or punish irresponsible behaviour. In fact the agency makes no moral judgements whatsoever. Many fathers who have been entirely responsible in paying maintenance under existing arrangements will find that their bills are significantly increased; many so-called feckless fathers, who perhaps have re-partnered or have low incomes will not have to pay at all.' From the outcry that hailed the new agency no one, it seemed, believed in these reassuring words.

In the early part of 1993 Panorama broadcast a programme which let single mothers respond to the regulatory powers of the Child Support Agency. There was universal condemnation, especially in relation to the punitive suggestion that mothers who did not cooperate with the CSA in finding errant fathers would be penalized by cuts in their income support. Many of the women told stories of strength and pain, the outcome of which was that they preferred to leave absent fathers absent and rely for support on the state and their own considerable ingenuity. The programme was contested by the government and the CSA, but was quickly followed by a series of discussions on the civil rights issues raised by the powers of the agency to intervene in the lives of women and men. What followed these early contestations started as a shout and became a deafening roar from the voices of fathers, most especially white middle-class fathers. These were the fathers who with ex-partners had arrived at a legally binding division of resources and an agreement on child maintenance. Both women and men from the middle classes protested the intervention by the state in an arena where arrangements had been worked out over a period of time. Those most at risk were the couples who had opted for a 'clean-break' settlement which had divided houses and goods, pension rights and entitlements in relation to notions of responsibilities which both parties accepted. The agency intervened to start what was often a painful process all over again, and an articulate, well-educated constituency was on course for confrontation with the state in the guise of the CSA.

The Child Support Agency was a classic example of the Foucauldian notion of governmentality and the power of surveillance in postmodern societies. It was constructed out of a series of discourses that generated a specific subject/object, one of which was the 'feckless father', who was to be the subject/object of surveillance, tracking and intervention at both the economic and moral moments. The feckless father had already forfeited his rights as a moral person to engage in self-regulation. Instead, a refashioned state agency would regulate him and the woman and the children to whom he was to be forcibly attached.

As an account of masculinity and fatherhood it is one that denies the commonsense and understanding of fatherhood which privileges responsibility and power and the control a man may exercise over the sale and rewards of his labour power. Instead, in the state reconstruction of masculinity and fatherhood the state has power and power is not an attribute of either masculinity or fatherhood. But, as Foucault suggests, where there is power there is resistance and power is not unitary nor the state a simple agent for the voluntaristic exercise of power. Power on this model is exercised in complex ways through the discourses generated and sustained in the discursive practices of one site – the Child Support Agency. The resistance encountered was widespread and, more importantly, it very soon became an organized campaign which generated a collective subject in opposition to the agency. White middle-class fathers and mothers demonstrated, took legal action, consulted their MPs and generally harassed the new agency, refusing to cooperate with procedures and investigations and actively publicizing the injustice of the agency as they understood it.

Action around the Child Support Agency united men as fathers against the state, but it was a specific white middle-class group who organized and led the protest. Here were men with considerable economic and cultural resources organizing on a nationwide basis to rally support for opposition. These were men used to a degree of power and control in their lives who fiercely resented the surveillance of the CSA and further refused to be identified with the moral category 'feckless father'. Their accounts of themselves were based on their ability to secure rational solutions to problems including dissolved marriages and the care of children in responsible ways. The CSA was an assault on the self-conceptions and dignity of these specific men. Often they received the support of current partners and former wives or partners with whom they had 'settled'. Equally, these were the men in the higher income bands who stood to lose most from CSA settlements. The bands allowed for those earning £20,000 to pay £105.51 a week for a child between the ages of 11 and 15, rising to £166.10 for those with earnings in excess of £40,000. This was serious money, especially in the context of serial relationships which required a resource base.

By February 1994 the Commons was already debating revised regulations for the CSA, and as Polly Toynbee commented:

> But besieged by the press, abused for its severity, mocked for its errors, assaulted by the legal profession, under battery from men everywhere, can the CSA hold out? Will today's minor changes hold the line or will the Government have to give way again? If so the silent battalions of divorced and single mothers who stand to gain so much from the CSA will have to get themselves organised quickly to do battle with the swelling ranks of angry men. For the silence of women has been conspicuous. Already, 90,000 have benefited yet it is hard to find many who will hymn its praises in public.
>
> (*Guardian* 2 February 1994)

Yet it was clear that women had gained, on average, £50 a week via the CSA and this, it was suggested, enabled them to consider returning to work.

Others could not see the benefit because it was deducted from income support – the purpose of the scheme – and some women preferred to collect from the state rather than the father of their children. Was this the reason for the salience of women? Certainly they were not united against the CSA 'but the silence was also sustained by the peripheralization of the multiplicity of women's accounts which did not receive media attention – the men made the running. For out there now are 120 different father's groups, bristling with rage at rallies up and down the country. It is a rare political phenomenon to see a spontaneous eruption of men who have nothing else in common' (*Guardian* 2 February 1994). Polly Toynbee in part misses the point – the eruptions were far from spontaneous, and shared economic interests and a collective self-image as fathers is more than 'nothing in common'.

The turbulent history of the CSA continued throughout 1994, and by January 1995 the Ombudsman produced a special report following complaints from 95 MPs – the complaints a product of the fathers' campaign. The report was consistently negative concluding:

> Maladministration leading to injustice is likely to arise when a new administrative task is not tested first by a pilot project, when new staff, perhaps inadequately trained, formed a substantial fraction of the workforce; where procedures and technology supporting them are untried; and where quality of service is subordinated to throughput.
>
> (BBC 1995)

The chief executive, Ann Chant, replacement for Ros Hepplewhite, responding by letter, wrote:

> I do not think it was fully appreciated that the agency's intervention into the most personal and sensitive areas of people's lives would make such a negative impact; nor was it realised how many people would actively resist or reject prioritising child maintenance above all other financial commitments.
>
> (*Guardian* 19 January 1995)

This statement is either naive or political-speak because it was obvious that an intervention like the CSA was going to encounter the class interests and conceptions of self that construct masculinities in Britain and that this assault would not go uncontested for these precise reasons. Error piled upon error and what were to become famous cases emerged. In one case a man was accused of fathering a child and received a maintenance order. The accusations then proved unfounded. In between times, however, another marriage or partnership was wrecked. The Ombudsman recommended compensation be paid in this case. Most importantly critics emphasized the way in which the CSA tracked fathers who were already paying maintenance rather than the 'feckless fathers' who were the much-trumpeted and initial target of the agency.

By the time of the Ombudsman's report the government was in retreat. The protest from white middle-class fathers had proved enormously successful and the government deferred assessments for some 350,000 'absent' fathers where welfare benefits were not involved. The decision was a political one because the government now feared the further alienation of middle-class voters whose tactics had included leaflets with 'Child Support Agency – Murderers' and the declaration that those who worked for the CSA were 'government spies and lackeys'. The Commons Committee set up to investigate reported a degree of sympathy for the fathers until they met them, when one member said: 'You cannot have a proper conversation with these blokes . . . They are almost exploding with rage' (*Guardian* 17 January 1995). The stories of the agency continue; as I write in March 1995 the East Midlands news features a white working-class man who has been in dispute with the agency for the past six months because his child support payment was assessed as £110 and his net earnings are £105 per week. When interviewed, he said his arrangement with his wife was 'perfect' – the children are with his wife during the week and with him at weekends. He now has a huge deficit running into thousands of pounds that he cannot pay and he suggested his only option was to leave work and 'go on income support' – where, of course, the CSA entered the contested terrain of economic and family life in the 1990s. The response to this case from the CSA was that it was the outcome of a 'bureaucratic error'.

The government bowed to pressure in January 1995 with Peter Lilley, Social Security Secretary, admitting that 'The CSA has performed less well than I would wish, in spite of hard work by its staff' to jeers in the House of Commons. Peter Lilley was introducing a white paper outlining changes to take effect in April 1995. The reformed CSA would now be able to depart from the original rigid formula for the assessment of child maintenance. In addition, no maintenance order would exceed 30 per cent of net income; clean-break settlements would be acknowledged; the cost of travel to work would be included; pre-1993, non-benefit cases would be deferred indefinitely; lone parents on benefit would be able to earn £5 a week maintenance credit; a new appeals tribunal would have powers to override the assessment and the formula. The credit system would enable parents to save money and receive it as a lump sum if they returned to work.

The response from the Network Against the Child Support Act formed and organized by mostly absent fathers was not an encouraging one for the government or the CSA. The comment released to the press was: 'Although some of the proposals seem like a step in the right direction, Mr Lilley has not gone nearly far enough' (*Guardian* 24 January 1995).

The banners in the protests around the CSA read: 'Dad Tax', 'I am Innocent' while divorced fathers tell stories of depression, economic hardship and suicide in the face of financial ruin. Women, seldom heard, tell stories of economic hardship and bureaucratic bungles which make life harder all round. We cannot yet know what the successes and failures of the CSA actually are but the vehement opposition to the agency – ill-founded or otherwise – does tell us something about the ways in which citizens regard the state and state interventions into an arena constructed mythically as a 'private sphere'. In part the protest from women and men is due to the powers afforded the CSA. As Simon Hoggart, commenting on the changes introduced, notes:

> The CSA is a bureaucrat's dream. It reminds me of Sim-City, the computer programme which allows you to play God by creating your own city. Raise taxes, change the rules for planning permission, put extra policemen on the streets; every decision you make has tremendous consequences, few of them predictable. It creates a fantasy world for sad and lonely people. In the same way, Mr Lilley has fashioned a Sim-City for separated couples with children. Every aspect of their life is covered. There are 'set allowances in the formula falling into three broad bands'. 'I intend to have the maximum additional amount payable above basic maintenance' . . . Live more than fifteen miles from your children and you get another 'broad brush allowance'. Live 14 miles, 1500 yards and you don't. He almost admitted that he was inventing his own fantasy world while answering one question, describing the 'simulations that were done before the agency began its operations'.
>
> (*Guardian* 24 January 1995)

Clearly, the simulations to which Peter Lilley made reference did not take into account the increasing complexities of family life in Britain today. The myriad of forms of family and interpersonal relations now part of people's lives are far from the formulaic interventions of the CSA. It did recognize, as I have suggested earlier, the issue of divorce but it then proceeded to reassert the two-parent nuclear family mode. Yet, the evidence consistently works against the reassertion. The Rowntree Report (Utting 1995) emphasizes the transitions within the family and family life and suggests ways in which state agencies could support these changes through progressive taxation, benefits and supports for lone parents and easier mechanisms for settlements. But the family values lobby, exemplified in the *Mail* and *Express*, accused the report of supporting lone parents against 'real' families of the two-parent, two-children variety. The familialism of these interventions stops the debate and disallows a discussion of the ways in which the lived experience of family life in all its variety can be valued and supported. There is never any discussion of the problems and pains of life in these idealized nuclear families – why else is psychotherapy booming, child registers in operation and so on.

The CSA misjudged the politics of the family in other ways too. The intervention of Thatcherism, with its emphasis on individualism and strategic approaches to resources, careers, mortgages and the economics of family life, has become the frame in which many of those targeted by the CSA have organized their lives. As the study by Jordan, Redley and James (1994) demonstrates among the white middle-class families they interviewed, the message of the Conservative government on self-reliance and economic investments and opportunities has been taken very seriously and used as a basis for decision-making around the resource base of the family. This new individualism coupled, within these families, with economic success in the 1980s is at odds both with the intervention of the state into the family sphere and with a redefinition of citizenship rights articulated in an individualist mode. The void between these discourses and the discourses and powers of the CSA was enormous but it was filled by the 'active citizens' encouraged by the government's attention to redefinition of citizenship. The contradictions could not hold.

Not yet concluded

The analysis presented here speaks to the current contradictions of masculinities and the complex interface between forms of masculinity and forms of the state. It has been suggested that there is no single unitary masculinity and no single unitary state. Instead, using a deconstructed notion of the state, we can see the state sectors as sites constructed within discourses and practices part of the 'management of populations' and whose forms of power are generated by these. One site in which struggles especially relevant to the analyses of masculinities have been conducted most recently is the Child Support Agency. According to its title, it supposedly privileges the lives and well-being of children; but children have been mostly absent from the debates and politics of the CSA. Instead, it has been the politics of class, ethnicity and masculinity which has been at issue in a debate over family life. What the CSA produced was a determined, well-organized campaign from white middle-class fathers. It is easy to regard this as economic in its motivation – and certainly this is at issue – but what has fuelled the vehemence of the action has been the affront to masculine dignity in terms of the state's construction of the 'feckless father'. Men have embraced the new fatherhood ideologically if not practically and taken this imaginary as part of the gender identity they present to the world. The public shaming exercise of the CSA in relation to absent fathers was a body blow to the self-conceptions of men who created an image of themselves as loving, responsible fathers. 'I am Innocent' speaks volumes for the anger and the desire by many men to distance themselves from the frame of the CSA. Thus two imaginaries clashed and the fathers proved a well-organized and persistent opponent. But, the poverty of children will continue, the difficulties of women to secure adequate resources for childcare will continue and so on. As a case study on the relations between masculinities and the state, the CSA is fascinating for it tells us something

about the power of discourse and the contradictions involved in the
encounter between men and the state.

References

Althusser, L. (1977) *Lenin and Philosophy and Other Essays*. London: New Left
Books.
Balibar, E. and Wallerstein, I. (1988) *Race, Nation, Class: Ambiguous Identities*.
London: Verso.
BBC (1995) *East Midlands News*. 15 March.
Bauman, Z. (1992) *Intimations of Postmodernity*. London: Routledge.
Beveridge Report (1942) *Social Insurance and the Allied Services*. London: HMSO.
Brittan, A. (1989) *Masculinity and Power*. Oxford: Blackwell.
Carrigan, T., Connell, R.W. and Lee, J. (1987) Toward a new sociology of
masculinity, in H. Brod (ed.) *The Making of Masculinities: The New Men's Studies*.
London: Allen and Unwin.
Chapman, R. (1988) The great pretender: variations on the new man theme, in R.
Chapman and J. Rutherford (eds) *Male Order: Unwrapping Masculinity*. London:
Lawrence and Wishart.
Foucault, M. (1977) *Discipline and Punish*. London: Allen Lane.
Giddens, A. (1994) *The Transformation of Intimacy*. Cambridge: Polity Press.
Gramsci, A. (1985) *Prison Notebooks: Selections*. New York: International.
Jephcott, P. (1962) *Married Women Working*. London: Allen and Unwin.
Jordan, B., Redley, M. and James, S. (1994) *Putting the Family First: Identities,
Decisions, Citizenship*. London: University College London Press.
Morgan, D.H.J. (1985) *The Family, Politics and Social Theory*. London: Routledge
and Kegan Paul.
Office of Population Censuses and Surveys (1993) *General Household Survey*.
London: HMSO.
Sianne, G. and Wilkinson, H. (1995) *Gender, Feminism and the Future*. London:
Demos.
Utting, R. (1995) *Family and Parenthood: Supporting Families, Preventing Break-
down* (The Rowntree Report). London: The Rowntree Trust.
Walby, S. (1990) *Theorizing Patriarchy*. Oxford: Blackwell.
Weber, M. (1982) Selections, in A. Giddens and D. Held (eds) *Classes, Power and
Conflict*. Berkeley, CA: University of California Press.
Westwood, S. (1990) Racism, black masculinity and the politics of space, in J. Hearn
and D.H.J. Morgan (eds) *Men, Masculinities and Social Theory*. London: Unwin
Hyman.

Masculinities and families

Introduction

Until the 1970s scholarly work on masculinities in families was confined to two approaches: Freudian psychoanalysis and Parsonian sex-role theory. Freud's analysis focuses on the 'Oedipal' conflict, 'the fateful combination of love for one parent and simultaneous hatred for the other as rival' which emerges in the erotic lives of children between four and six (Connell 1987: 204). In Sophocles's tragedy *Oedipus the King*, Oedipus unwittingly kills his father, destroying the model he should most revere and marries his mother, the woman he should never desire. Freud's theory accounts for sons' gender identity by means of their identification with their fathers in fear and anger. To overcome the fear of castration resulting from the Oedipal desire for the mother, sons convert their rivalry with their fathers into angry emulation (Richards 1990). The most well known of Freud's popularizers in the UK, Bowlby and Winnicott, have concentrated on pre-Oedipal relations, emphasizing the initial nurturing function of mothers. Later feminist re-examinations of the Oedipal conflict by Dinnerstein (1976) and Chodorow (1978) have attempted to re-evaluate mothering. These theories are about universal essential psychic drives and relations within families, the meanings of which are seen as independent of their cultural and historical context. A model of parenting in which both parents are loved, loving, protective and facilitating remains elusive (Richards 1990).

One theory which links gender roles within the family firmly to their social context is Parsonian sex-role theory. For Parsons identification of daughters with mothers and sons with fathers is essential in reproducing the gendered division of labour within the western family. Parsons' theory thus ossifies a particular normative understanding of family relations as a theoretical ideal. Other variations are seen as deviant.

None of these theories conceptualize personality in terms of its biographical development, nor do they link different levels of personality with their social and cultural context. This chapter examines the relation of male personality and society in the construction of masculinities in families within their social and historical contexts. It considers subjectivity, intimate emotional and sexual relations and institutionalized structures in the biographies of seven men. It investigates the way individual men have negotiated their masculinities in the course of their biographies. An alluring source of evidence of the construction of masculinities among a variety of periods, social and cultural settings is life history, including published autobiographies. While such sources are the authentic testimony of experience, they are also highly selective, produced for public consumption by men from more literate and articulate groups, often for specific reasons. Despite these limitations, this type of life history can sensitize us to important issues in the construction of masculinities.

These personal accounts – with evidence from the study of the construction of masculinities among parents who sent their sons to a minor public school – illustrate the most significant problems for theorizing the construction of masculinities in families. First there is the problem of the relation of self to structural constraints. Contexts such as the labour market, ethnicity, culture and religion may be complex and potentially contradictory. The problem of the integration of sexuality and emotion within the self is the second problem of equal or greater significance. The third is the power relations within families and their relations to the oppositional gender categories of masculinity and femininity. The relations among parents and sons and their significance for emotional attachments is perhaps the problem that is most frequently ignored in the literature.

A classic working-class masculinity?

One of the first analyses to consider the significance of social and historical contexts on the construction of masculinity was Tolson (1977). He maintained the Freudian emphasis on father–son relations while emphasizing social class. He saw work and father's position in the labour market as an important differentiator in the construction of masculinities. He stressed the problematic aspect of father–son relationships. Tolson argues that 'A boy's identification with his father is the basis of his future experience.' Fathers legislate and punish yet their 'masculine presence' is realized in their absence from home while at work. For a son, masculinity is a 'promise of the world of work and power'. The ambivalence and alienation which characterize father–son relations are rooted in the vast range of complexities of the power, emotion and sexuality nexus within families.

One of the best-known autobiographies of men from the working class is that of Robert Roberts (1978), born in 1903 in Salford. Robert constructed his masculinity amid the intense ambivalence of his identification with his father. Roberts senior was a patriarch, who assumed his right to control his family's lives was justified by the significance of skilled manual work in local labour markets. For him all men who did not work with their hands were somehow emasculated. He told his son from an early age that he 'wasn't bringing up his lads to be stool arsed jacks – sitting all their days in a bloody office' (p. 25). They were going to do a man's job – engineering – 'finest work in the world'. Although his father raised no objection when Robert Roberts decided to enter for the technical school bursary, he greeted the news that his son had come top with a roar, 'Go out and find work!' At the Labour Exchange Roberts junior entered 'journalist' as his chosen occupation. 'Journalists weren't in demand. They wanted a lad in the brass finishing shop. I took that.' On the way home he scattered the headmaster's testimonial to the four winds. 'That was school done. I was entering the world of men' (p. 158). In the Roberts family, patriarchy was a facade, for Roberts senior was in and out of work. He was given to hopelessly optimistic schemes to improve the family's lot at a stroke. His family managed to survive because his wife kept a shop, bought shortly after their marriage without his wife's knowledge on borrowed money. He saw it as a potential 'gold mine' in which their stay would be short. The area was so poor that only very long hours and his wife's constant vigilance over customers' debts prevented bankruptcy.

Patriarchal authority was unstable in the Roberts household, maintained by means of his father's fierce temper. There were frequent rows when he attempted to bully his wife and children into submission. In the emotional relations within the family, Roberts junior rejected his father's bullying, temper and drunkenness, forming close, loving and supportive relationships with his mother and sisters. Robert Roberts believed that the work in the shop and the seven children she bore above it contributed to the breakdown of his mother's health and early death from cancer. How far he rejected his father's exploitative sexuality is unclear. In Robert Roberts we have an account of the construction of a masculinity in which power, emotion and desire were in continual conflict behind a patriarchal facade. While his relationship with his father dominated his early construction of a gender identity and his father imposed his view of 'men's work', Robert Roberts successfully negotiated a very different masculinity with his mother and sisters. His biography shows a long journey away from his father's model of masculinity in which he established a career as an extramural tutor and writer.

This example suggests that families are the first site in which masculinities are constructed. While fathers are the first role models for their son's masculinities and take an active part in shaping their sons' construction of masculinity, outcomes are problematic, negotiated and contested. Theorizing focuses on oppositional categories of masculinity or femininity, fathers or mothers, identification or rejection. These categories do not allow for the rejection of fathers except as a deviant, pathological response. Roberts's evidence suggests that lived experience transcends these oppositional categories. It suggests that mothering has greater importance than as simply an anti-model. It supports the arguments of Chodorow and Donnerstein about mothers' significance in the integration of emotion in the self and its relations to structure. The importance of mothers in the process of identity formation should be acknowledged rather than dismissed as anti-models who have performed their initial nurturing function. A theory about the construction of a masculine identity in relations with fathers and mothers, identifying and rejecting features of both within a historical and social context is needed.

Parents and sons negotiating masculinities

Tolson argues that the construction of masculinity in the middle classes is characterized by psychic hardening within a competitive hierarchy epitomized in the public schools. At Ellesmere College, a minor public school, between 1929 and 1950 the school power structure was clearly defined as a series of competitive hierarchies (Heward 1988). The first hierarchy was that of age, distinguishing lowly first formers from the lordly sixth. The school was streamed into A, B and C forms. Each boy had a precise place in the academic hierarchy determined by his performance in tests and examinations and his consequent place in class and its place in the age and ability hierarchy. In the social organization boys ascended the ladder from 'grub' to prefect within their houses. Games and a boy's position in the hierarchy of teams was also very important. In the fierce competition for a place at the top of these hierarchies at Ellesmere, the fittest survived, the weak suffered in silence and the weakest were eliminated.

The parents who sent their sons to the school in the period before and during the Second World War saw such a boys public school as the ideal environment for their sons. The socialization process was intensive and sustained, insulating the boys from all influences from girls and the working class. Masculinities and femininities were defined antagonistically. There was a varying but rigid division of labour within these families, with mothers taking care of domestic matters like the uniform and worrying about their sons' emotional and physical well-being at school, while fathers were responsible for the fees and planning their careers. This opposition of masculinity and femininity was also strongly institutionalized in the school, with the only women present dedicated to the service of boys and men. They were confined to one part of the building segregated from the masters and boys.

Fathers directed their sons' education and future careers, acting as their sons' role models. They wanted their sons to enter occupations with a high, secure income and a respected position in the community, thus ensuring their future among the middle classes. The professions were their desired goal, entailing prolonged study and examination success. There were a number of competing models of masculinity in the school. The captain of rugger was the most prestigious. In the C forms rebel and prankster reigned supreme. These understandings of masculinity and the power relations among them were not shared by parents. They caused considerable conflicts between parents and their sons.

The evidence of the construction of masculinities in the school supports Connell's theory that gender involves multilayered relations among the levels of personality, institutions and society. Each is characterized by particular gender regimes. He argues that within these complex power relations, certain hegemonic masculinities and emphasized femininities are institutionalized. Connell defines structure as 'the pattern of constraint on practice inherent in a set of social relations' and argues that three structures – the division of labour, power and cathexis (personal emotional attachments) – are the major elements of any gender order or regime (Connell 1987: 97–9). Connell rejects the notion of patriarchy as a universal phenomenon characterizing and explaining all power relations between the gender groups. He maintains that four power structures preserve hegemonic masculinity: the hierarchies and workforces of institutionalized violence like the police; the hierarchies and workforces of heavy and high tech industries; the planning and central control machinery of the state; working-class milieus which emphasize physical toughness and men's association with machinery. For Connell one of the most important theoretical tasks is to explain the hegemony of heterosexual desire and its implications.

The study of masculinities at Ellesmere College demonstrates the way individual boys constructed their masculinities as practical daily accomplishments within structures that can be inspected through life histories (Connell 1991). Sending a boy to a boys public school is an ideal as it insulates him from gender and class influences. However, even in an apparent masculinity factory, the outcome is very uncertain. Sons constructed their biographies and masculinities in terms of their previous experience and the range of hegemonic masculinities in the school. Gender categories are realized in particular cultural and historical situations. They are problematic, shifting and contradictory. The relation of gender regimes to the construction of sexualities and the preservation of the hegemony of heterosexual desire are unclear. Major changes like the war disrupted gender regimes and parental strategies.

The hegemonic masculinities to which boys could aspire were redefined during the Second World War, exacerbating the conflicts between parents and sons. After the Battle of Britain and Churchill's glorification of 'the few', joining the 'boys in blue' became every schoolboy's dream. The school's VC, J.C. Brunt, 'a duffer with bags of guts', according to a contemporary, rivalled the captain of rugby as a model of the school's hegemonic masculinity. Parents, especially mothers, were bewildered. 'Why he wants the navy after the *Hood*, I do not know', said one woman reflecting on the fate of the 1400 men who lost their lives when the *Bismarck* sank HMS *Hood* in May 1941. While the school and its structures manifested readily identifiable hegemonic masculinities, individual masculinities and biographies were diverse, reflecting the interaction between boys' family backgrounds and the labyrinthine web of school, society and polity in the daily choices made during a boy's school life.

Complex diverse contexts

While the experience of school had a measure of uniformity, the boys came from a diversity of cultural, social backgrounds. There was a variety of religious and ethnic heritages including Jews, who had fled Hitler's pogroms, and others whose parents were expatriates in the furthest corners of the British Empire. Some of the families experienced tumultuous change. The construction of masculinities for such boys could involve intense ambiguities and conflicts among a number of cultural and social structures.

The best account of the construction of a masculine identity in the period of the Ellesmere study amid all the complexities and ambiguities of colonial society in the 1940s and 1950s is that of Dom Moraes. His masculinity was constructed in a family where religion and gender were sources of persistent conflict and anguish exacerbated by the power struggles of Indian independence. He wrote his autobiography *My Son's Father* (Moraes 1990) when he was 30 for his newly born son to give him an insight into his own feelings as he grew up. He was born in 1938 in Bombay. His parents were Indian Christians in the highly privileged professional middle class. His mother was a pathologist, daughter of the first woman doctor in India and a devout Roman Catholic. His father was a barrister, educated at Oxford and Lincoln's Inn, who enjoyed a brilliant career as a journalist. Unusually among their social circle, they were keen supporters of the Indian Nationalist cause.

His masculinity was constructed amid the disintegration of his parents' relationship as his father's career developed and his mother became seriously mentally ill and violent to the servants and her son. From an early age Dom Moraes's model was the nineteenth-century visionary poet, Rimbaud. He constructed a masculine identity about the single-minded pursuit of literary prizes. He met Auden and Spender when they visited India, both of whom encouraged him. His earliest memories are of his father's absence from home while serving as a war correspondent in Burma. After the war the family moved as his career progressed. He became editor of the *Ceylon Times* and then the *Times of India*.

Gender divisions for Dom Moraes were categorical and oppositional. Women were subordinate and femininity increasingly despised. He recalls his mother, dressed attractively for parties, but then charts his growing disgust and mistrust of her as she neglected her appearance and began to sit on his bed weeping for his father's return. When he was 6 she took him to visit Gandhi, whom she was attending professionally. Gandhi told Dom Moraes that 'you must look after your mother, beta. Take care of her. Till your father comes back she is your responsibility.' He identified more and more with his father, who increasingly used subterfuges to ensure that Dom Moraes spent his time with him rather than his unpredictable and violent mother. After a particularly violent frenzy, when she threw the furniture out of the window, she was certified and institutionalized. Like the fathers who sent their sons to Ellesmere College, Moraes senior had a plan for his son which he revealed when Dom was 16. He was to be prepared for Oxford. There he established himself as a precocious literary talent.

His masculinity was constructed within a context of patriarchal gender categories and power relations in which contradictions were seen as deviance and excluded. While his father's patriarchal authority in the family and élite class position enabled him to resolve any contradictions and dilemmas, Dom's account records the inner turmoil of his feelings for his mother. His sexuality was constructed in the contradictions of literary romanticism, heterosexual desire and the tensions of power, emotion and sexuality in his family. He recounts how he became aware of the meaning of Gandhi's words. When he chided his mother for sitting weeping on his bed after his father had left for Burma, she slapped him on his face for the first time. 'I could not understand it, till years later, with slow strokes on a bed I nailed a woman to her cross' (Moraes 1990: 10). While male dominance and female dependence and subordination may have been his ideal, his account shows clearly that his lived experience was contradictory and emotionally costly.

His account shows the importance of ethnicity and religion. Contexts may be very complex in their ambiguities and contradictions. Power relations are crucial to the negotiation of a masculine identity within them. It emphasizes the problem of cathexis, the emotional attachments identified by Connell. Moraes's account also draws attention to the central importance of sexuality for the understanding of gender identities and the continued hegemony of heterosexuality. Once again relations with mothers are problematic both in the sense of lived experience and theoretical understanding.

Challenging the structures to construct an alternative identity

Perhaps the most difficult problem for theoretical understandings of the constructions of gender identities is that of self and structure – the extent to which individuals are constrained by their structural contexts and how far they can build alternative identities despite their stigma. A very different account from this period illustrating this issue is written by Paul Bailey

(1991). Dom Moraes describes a disintegrating family amid deeply fractured structures which were made coherent by his father's ability to impose the dominant values of colonial and patriarchal society. Paul Bailey's father eschewed power and the immutable verities of class and gender relations so dear to his wife. Paul Bailey was born in south London in 1937, the son of a road sweeper who had fought in the First World War. He won a scholarship to the local grammar school – the passport to upward social mobility. Paul was also developing an identity in the arts, initially as an actor. His mother viewed his aspirations with suspicion. She, like Robert Roberts's father believed in oppositional gender divisions and constantly reiterated their natural origins. Paul questioned her rigid categorization of the world with the tacit support of his father. He remained passive, any basis for assertions about masculinities brutally shattered in the carnage in the trenches in Flanders. Bailey became a writer and critic, constructing a masculinity in which a gay sexuality was central.

Like Dom Moraes, his account demonstrates the centrality of sexuality. Like Connell it raises the issue of the maintenance of heterosexuality as the hegemonic type. It demonstrates that heterosexuality is not an unproblematic outcome. Paul Bailey makes clear that individuals construct their masculinities and sexualities. Like Robert Roberts he rejected the model his more vociferous parent – in this case his mother – attempted to impose. The power relations in the family and the models it supplied were successfully subverted by an alternative.

The contemporary context

In the second half of the twentieth century, the period since the events related in the autobiographies, there has been widespread radical change in families in Britain. Households and families are increasingly diverse in composition, culture and domestic economic organization. Over the last 30 years the number of marriages has fallen by a third while the divorce rate has risen sixfold. For every two marriages in 1991 in Great Britain there was one divorce. Almost one in five families with dependent children is headed by a lone parent (Central Statistical Office 1994). There has been a sexual revolution. Abortion has been legalized. Contraception is available on demand to single people. Homosexuality has been legalized. The age of legal majority has been lowered to 18. A rising number now estimated at one in three couples live together before they marry. Birth rates have fallen steadily, particularly since the advent of the contraceptive pill in the 1960s. The number of male manual jobs has shrunk dramatically, while the professions and service industries have continued to expand. Women have increased their participation in the workforce to 47 per cent. Part-time and home working are increasing. A further source of diversity is mobility and migration. The migration to Britain of Asian and Afro-Caribbean groups in the 1950s and 60s was a contribution to an increasingly ethnically diverse population. Since the 1960s there have been significant movements seeking improved rights for women, ethnic minorities, gays and the disabled.

In Britain successive Conservative administrations have resisted these pressures, doggedly attempting to impose a white heterosexual patriarchal hegemony in such deeply unpopular policies as the Child Support Agency (CSA), withdrawing benefit from 16 to 18-year-olds and resisting voluntary paternity leave. Britain has the poorest childcare provision in the EU. The CSA has had to be modified; and after 13 unsuccessful attempts, feeble anti-discrimination legislation in relation to the disabled population will reach the statute book, probably late in 1995. Britain's partners in the EU have reacted somewhat differently, bringing social provision into line with changing lifestyles and mores. Sweden is the most advanced. There female earnings are 87 per cent of male earnings and childcare and parental leave is generous. The Swedish Marriage Act of 1987 specifies that childcare and domestic tasks must be shared equally. Nevertheless, manual work is strongly sex segregated and individualist competitive masculinities remain dominant in masculine discourse. For men and women attempting to reconstruct the relations of work, family and intimate relations remain problematic (Segal 1990).

A number of these changes in gender and sexual relations impinged on the construction of masculinities at Ellesmere College in the 1980s. The situation began to change in the 1970s with the admission of girls to the sixth form. Gradually a heterosexual relationship with a sexually attractive girl became an additional aspect of hegemonic masculinities at the school (Heward 1990). By the 1980s the hegemonic masculinity had been redefined. It was no longer adequate to be simply the captain of rugger to be the principal idol of younger boys; a highly visible relationship with an attractive girl was also necessary.

Contemporary theorizing

The formation of identities within contemporary society is a prominent area in postmodernist theorizing and empirical research (Giddens 1991). Much of this work has emphasized the individualization of society and reduced the emphasis on structures. It suggests that experience is problematic, and that contextualizing dominant ideologies are fractured and more akin to distant myths than deterministic structures. It looks at individual lived experience, emphasizing choice and risk-taking within the myriad opportunities presented by highly ambiguous contexts. Ulrich Beck's (1992) 'individualization thesis' suggests that a fragmentation in traditional institutions of reproduction like the family, education and work has obscured individual social roles, increasing risks at all levels. Giddens also refers to a risk society. Whereas Beck argues that individuals now attempt to achieve their personal ambitions in individualized ways, Giddens sees men and women involved in actively constructing alternative forms of family and other institutions. Life histories are thus reflexive processes in which individuals connect the self, the personal with social change. They actively construct their identities – the self – as part of an active involvement with social change in their social relations at all levels, in their family, education and work.

The study of men and masculinities has been one of the most vigorous in contemporary postmodernist scholarship as writers have begun to explore the diversity of men's experience, conceptions of masculinities and their power relations (Hearn and Morgan 1990).

Masculinities are individual practical daily accomplishments, constructed, negotiated and often contested within the complex power relations of families, schools and related structures. All experiences are constrained by structural assumptions about masculinities and femininities and their interrelations. It shows how masculinities and their relations with femininities are consistently differentiated at many levels and are experienced by individuals as problematic, shifting, even contradictory. Masculinities are constructed in many sites within which and between which there may be competing understandings. The power relations among these definitions may be confused and shifting.

Competitive hierarchies

James grew up in a farming family. There was a rigid gender division of labour between his mother and father. His mother maintains an active Christian faith and morality, which has influenced James strongly. At ten his father introduced him to the men's world of stock, crops and markets, making an Oedipal-like break with the maternal domain of home. He learned to drive a tractor, spending more time and identifying with his father. He went to a traditional boys public school, a competitive hierarchy which he climbed. With good science A levels he gained a place to read Engineering at a Midlands university. He experienced university as a competitive hierarchy, essentially similar to the public school. In his second year he fell in love and for a while this absorbed his life and feelings. When his girlfriend ended the affair in his final year the emotions unleashed by this rejection and loss became almost unbearable. After graduation he joined a multinational company as a graduate apprentice moving between North America and Europe, gaining promotion rapidly. For him the passage through a succession of individualized competitive male hierarchies is something that has happened without any active choices on his part. It is entirely taken for granted. For him masculinity and its choices is about inner consciousness and the way to be from moment to moment. He sees himself as 'the people manager', orientated towards human needs within the structure of the multinational organization which is beyond his control. He thinks that the next decision in his own life will come in two years when he will finish his apprenticeship and become a chartered engineer. He does not regard further progress up the competitive hierarchy as simply inevitable. He believes that in the long term it may not be very satisfying, concluding 'maybe I'll do VSO'.

This case study suggests that while patriarchy may not be universal and immutable, as Connell argues, patriarchal structures remain none the less pervasive and prestigious in educational and work organizations in late twentieth-century Britain. While these patriarchal relations give a coherent context to James's experience, his identity – the reflexive biographical narrative, in Giddens's conceptualization – is problematic. The importance of his relationship with his mother is unclear. The integration of emotion and sexuality into the self are unresolved. These issues continually reappear because of the inadequacy of sociological and psychological theorizing to encompass them except in terms of oppositional categories of masculinity and femininity, fathering and mothering; emotion, as an aspect of femininity and mothering, has to be eschewed in constructing masculinities.

Integrating maternal and paternal models

Nick comes from a household where both his parents are professional. His father does not cook but the division of labour is perceived as fair among them. His father reads a great deal. He is an engineer and Nick read engineering in his first year but transferred to teaching, his mother's profession, which he enjoys more. He has spent time with outdoor pursuits people, becoming a 'doer' rather than a thinker like his father. His girlfriend has travelled extensively and sees the world differently from his parents. He is taking a course on the Third World specifically because it confirms his view of the world as a wider place than his background. He and his girlfriend share all the domestic chores equally, washing, ironing and cooking for each other. He considers he would not want a girlfriend who expected to do all the chores, who wasn't a person in her own right with a point of view and something to contribute. In his view the family was only the first arena in which a masculine way to be was worked out. Doing an initial teacher education course has raised his awareness. Women are in the majority by far and gender issues are raised all the time – almost to the point of tedium. There is also a great interest in people – their activities and reactions – which makes gender and sexuality problematic rather than taken for granted and immutable. He thinks this contrasts with engineering where traditional masculinities are not questioned.

Nick sees himself constructing a masculinity which integrates his mother's propensity for doing with his father's studious ways of acquiring the necessary knowledge so that actions are based on reflection on the available evidence. He wants to make a career in outdoor pursuits. He is a rock climber, a 'macho' activity which is becoming more accessible and being redefined as a sport. He sees himself as an enabler and facilitator rather than a 'hard man' who does all the severest routes in the toughest conditions. He is well aware that changing intimate relations with his girlfriend is easier than changing the structures like outdoor pursuits. He is also aware that he constructs his masculinity within particular contexts. When he goes home he reverts to 'slob mode', leaving the domestic chores to his mother.

This case study suggests that constructing a masculine identity in the 1990s is not necessarily about identifying with father and rejecting mother. It can involve building on both models. It supports Giddens's view that individuals are collaborating to construct new social arrangements and groupings. It suggests strongly that change is easiest and consequently most common in intimate relationships. While some institutions appear immutable, particular areas of others are more open and questioning.

Moving beyond the family

Colin was born in 1965. From the age of 9 he began challenging authority at school and at home. His father became increasingly domineering with two young men growing up beside him. Colin developed strategies to divert his father's anger from his mother to himself, more and more rejecting his father as a model and seeking alternatives in his sixth-form college. There he began to develop an identity, seeking to be different from conventional masculinities. At university he read economics. From the outset he made a circle of friends in his residence who stayed together as a mixed social group throughout the first year. He continued to build a distinctive masculinity, doing aerobics and finding a career about people rather than accountancy, the choice of most of his fellows. He did an MA, choosing gender issues as his thesis topic. Gradually he developed a career as a researcher, moving steadily towards research on controversial social issues. His ability to maintain a continuous career in the insecure world of contract research, the growing respect and academic reputation that he experiences and a stable and supportive network of friends has given him increasing confidence. This has enabled him to move beyond the oppositional gender categories experienced in his family. Ending his unsatisfying relationship with his girlfriend and coming out in a gay relationship was a complete redefinition of his sexual identity, which his close friends understood but his parents found upsetting and bewildering.

This case study supports Connell's argument that patriarchal control is being weakened by decades of bargaining and negotiation. In consequence the family is becoming increasingly peripheral to gender regimes in contemporary society. Such changes are not acknowledged publicly. A facade of male authority is preserved in many families. Such a view contrasts with feminist writing in the 1970s which saw the family as the heart of patriarchal power.

Men and women remaking masculinities

Barry was born when his parents were both 19, the eldest of four brothers. From about 9 he felt that he was mature enough to take much more control and responsibility for his own life than his parents allowed. When he was 13 he and his girlfriend – 'the love of his life' – planned their lives together. She was his 'best friend' and they told each other everything. He took charge of his own life, rebelling against his father's 'shouts and clouts' regime. His was an anti-model. In the family his mother was the mediator, keeping a light control of the situation. It caused enormous problems between his parents, who subsequently separated. He was at a boys secondary school, where he increasingly saw bullies and 'macho men' as 'a pretence' and a 'turn off'. He believes that friends are very important in providing models of the way to be from an early age. His best friends are women. His present girlfriend is 'assertive', 'not a girlie girl'. 'Everything works', in their relationship – intellectual, social, sexual and emotional. He has remade his relationships with his parents. He has an 'open' relationship with his mother who is now a good friend. Barry admires her: she has gone back to college while bringing up his brothers and working part time. He sees his self-identity in terms of self-confidence, kindness, fairness and independence, stressing that he emulates aspects of women and men, finding stereotypical 'macho' men and 'girlie' women unattractive.

This case study exemplifies the argument in postmodernist theory about individuals being involved in risk-taking amid increasingly fractured structures. Importantly it raises issues of the significance of gender for the construction of self-identity, which postmodernist theorists do not address. It suggests that the rigid oppositional categorizations of masculinity and femininity are increasingly inadequate for understanding the construction of gender identities. It further raises the issue of the importance of women in the construction of masculinities. The work of Brannen *et al.* (1994) on families and young people's health shows that it is mothers who continue to communicate with young people about health, including sexual relations, while fathers dismiss this as their wives 'worrying'. Shere Hite (1988) has argued that women are creating a cultural revolution by turning away from exploitative male heterosexualities. Women may also be collaborating with men to change intimate relations, enabling them to redefine masculine sex gender regimes towards pluralism and 'androgyny'.

Conclusions

Freudian and Parsonian theories assume oppositional sex gender categories represented in 'the family' by mothers and fathers, which are transmitted by identification of sons with fathers and daughters with mothers. The evidence suggests that identification is problematic, that individuals construct their masculinities actively within complex and changing family and other contexts constrained by gendered structural power relations. Families and societies are changing, becoming increasingly diverse. While individual experience is ambiguous or even contradictory, competitive hierarchies – which are apparently immutably patriarchal – remain pervasive and powerful. Intimate relations are the site of sometimes tumultuous change, while the UK state attempts to impose patriarchal relations. Women and relations between men and women are a potent source of change in intimate relations. Postmodernist theory is about the self and structure, neither of which is conceptualized as gendered. Theories which transcend the tired oppositional gender categories and identifications are needed to understand intra- and interfamily gender relations within their structural contexts. This would permit a wider variety of outcomes to be envisaged and make mothers integral rather than peripheral to the process of constructing masculinities in families.

Acknowledgements

I wish to thank my respondents, including Adam, whose evidence I did not use, for their patience and Máirtín Mac an Ghaill for his encouragement.

References

Bailey, P. (1991) *An Immaculate Conception: Scenes from Childhood and Beyond*, 2nd edn. Harmondsworth: Penguin.

Beck, U. (1992) *Risk Society: Towards a New Modernity*. London: Sage.

Brannen, J., Dodd, K., Oakley, A. and Storey, P. (1994) *Young People, Health and Family Life*. Buckingham: Open University Press.

Central Statistical Office (1994) *Social Trends 24*. London: HMSO.

Chodorow, N. (1978) *The Reproduction of Mothering: Psychoanalysis and the Sociology of Gender*. Berkeley, CA: University of California Press.

Connell, R. (1987) *Gender and Power: Society, the Person and Sexual Politics*. Oxford: Polity.

Connell, R. (1991) Live fast and die young: the construction of masculinity among young working class men on the margins of the labour market, *Australia and New Zealand Journal of Sociology*, 27(2): 141–71.

Dinnerstein, D. (1976) *The Rocking of the Cradle and the Ruling of the World.* New York: Harper Row.

Giddens, A. (1991) *Modernity and Society: Self and Society in the Late Modern Age.* Oxford: Polity.

Hearn, J. and Morgan, D. (eds) (1990) *Men, Masculinities and Social Theory.* London: Unwin Hyman.

Heward, C. (1988) *Making a Man of Him: Parents and their Sons' Careers at an English Public School 1929–1950.* London: Routledge.

Heward, C. (1990) Public school masculinities: an essay in gender and power', in G. Walford (ed.) *Private Schooling: Tradition, Change and Diversity.* London: Paul Chapman.

Hite, S. (1988) *Women and Love.* London: Viking.

Moraes, D. (1990) *My Son's Father: an Autobiography*, 2nd edn. Harmondsworth: Penguin.

Richards, B. (1990) Masculinity, identification and political culture, in J. Hearn and D. Morgan (eds) *Men, Masculinities and Social Theory.* London: Unwin Hyman.

Roberts, R. (1978) *The Classic Slum: Salford Life in the First Quarter of the Century.* Harmondsworth: Penguin.

Segal, L. (1990) *Slow Motion: Changing Masculinities, Changing Men.* London: Virago.

Tolson, A. (1977) *The Limits of Masculinity.* London: Tavistock.

Schooling masculinities

Introduction

In recent years we have witnessed a radical restructuring of English state schooling. This restructuring is located within the more fundamental sociopolitical changes following the breakdown of the postwar educational settlement, with its main tenet that the role of education was of central strategic importance to the development of economic growth, equality of opportunity and social justice. Currently schools are in the process of being restratified with the accompanying privatization, commercialization and commodification of institutions located within competitive local markets. This New Right agenda has served to marginalize the quest for social justice; in the process the social subject has tended to be discarded. It is against this background that studies of schooling and masculinities are starting to be produced, albeit in a rather sketchy and indirect way. The school is a social process, a set of social relations charged with formal and informal meanings. All aspects of schooling are subject to these meanings and they are deployed across a diversity of areas, including discipline and control, the formal and hidden curriculum, streaming and prefectorial systems, teaching staff appointments, and auxiliary staff. Work on masculinities has suggested that schools through these meanings offer interpretations about what it means to be 'male' or 'female'. More specifically, schooling processes can be seen to form gendered identities, marking out 'correct' or 'appropriate' styles of being (Butler 1993).

Integral to this understanding of the practice of making masculinities is the demand for theoretical and conceptual clarity of its use in the sociology of education. Second-wave feminism has provided the major contribution to our understanding of gender in the schooling arena, providing a stimulus for the theoretical and conceptual developments of 'multiple masculinities' and 'hegemonic masculinities'. We will use these conceptual and theoretical tools to consider empirical examples of the ways that schools shape masculinities. First, we shall concentrate on the teachers' social world and their responses to the changing labour process of teaching as work. Equally important, the use of discipline in their labour process can be seen as another terrain where masculine identities are contested. Second, we shall explore the ways, through the use of language, that students among themselves police and regulate their masculinities. The curriculum has been seen as a direct producer of masculinities. Through the stratification of knowledge, the curriculum provides the resources to make and convey masculine identities. As part of this stratification, sexuality as a subject is an area which has been systematically organized, providing critical implications for legitimizing styles of male behaviour. Furthermore, we shall consider student responses to the curriculum and the ramifications of the rise of the new vocationalism.

As was pointed out earlier, work on masculinities and schooling is very sketchy and sporadic. As a result the choice of these areas is informed by previous work done in this area by others and by ourselves.

Gendering roles: (re)conceptualizing male–female relations in schooling

Prior to feminist studies highlighting the gendered nature of schooling, masculinity appeared as unproblematic. A wide range of feminist perspectives began to make visible the gendered nature of education (see Deem 1984). Recent research in education has opened up the discussion of masculinity and sought to contextualize its constitution by grounding it in the different social contingencies within which it is manifest (Connell 1987, 1989; Mac an Ghaill 1991). These studies indicate that the social, ethnic, class and sexual specificities of male identities within local sites influence the range of masculinities that are inhabited. As Connell (1992: 736) claims: 'Different masculinities are constituted in relation to other masculinities and to femininities through the structure of gender relations.'

Masculinities, it is argued, should be conceptualized in terms of *relationships*. Moving away from the singular 'role' based on gender, masculinities need to be conceptualized in relation to their class, sexual and ethnic locations (Thorne 1993). This has led to the theorizing of masculinity in terms of multiple masculinities (Brittan 1989). Masculinities do not have a one-dimensional identity, rather they embody multiple dimensions. For example, there are white working-class gay masculinities alongside Asian middle-class heterosexualities. An important development in the theorization of masculinities and schooling is to see that these social locations create the conditions for relations of power. There are different masculinities with differential access to power, practices of power and differential effects of power.

Connell (1987) has provided one of the most productive accounts of how to incorporate power into an analysis of masculinity. Translating Gramsci's notion of hegemony that was used in the context of class relations into the realm of gender relations, Connell has produced valuable analytic insights about the nature of masculinity. Not only are different masculinities worked out in relation to other masculinities. These relations as part of a hegemony are mediating oppression and domination. Power is differentiated so that particular styles of masculinity become ascendant or dominant in certain situations. Their ascendancy is achieved through processes of persuasion, having the power to define what is normal and 'ordinary' male behaviour. Power is linked to material practices, so that various social and cultural arenas provide the potential for the ascendancy of masculinities. In relation to the school, the ascendancy of a specific masculinity is contextually contingent. There are various spaces, such as the staffroom, classroom, the playground, or the common room, where different styles of masculinity onset 'normality'. Hegemony is a social and historical phenomenon, where the constitution of what is defined as 'normal' masculinity is a process of production. There is a need critically to examine hegemonic masculinity as an analytic tool. Such an examination might explore how fluid or unstable hegemonic masculinity is and how this structure might be linked to the spaces of empowerment. Nevertheless, hegemony remains a highly useful concept with incisive analytic scope to examine the asymmetric nature of gendered power relations, while at the same time arguing that dominance is never secure but must always be won.

In order to examine how masculinity in education has been theorized, it is necessary to turn to schooling processes themselves and to explore theoretical contributions within the context of empirical studies.

Schooling masculinities: making men

Corresponding to theoretical arguments about masculinity, schools exist as sites where styles of masculinities are produced and used. Within the school there are particular spaces where 'masculinity-making' appears both explicit and abundant. One of these spaces is the interrelations of teachers. It is that area which we will now address.

Teacher culture: relationships to the labour process and the implications for masculine styles

There are two interlinked areas that illustrate the ways in which teachers' masculinities are produced. The first concerns teacher ideologies and their relationship to the labour process. The second concerns the use of discipline in teaching styles. Although research in this area has predominantly concentrated on students, there is evidence to suggest that relations between teachers are also part of a process of making the spaces for particular styles of gender to predominate. Work as a site of inequality has been extensively examined from a number of perspectives (see Phizacklea 1990). Teachers' work manifests and reflects the inequalities operating within other work arenas. It has been argued that teachers' institutional responses and resistances shape the forms of gender relations to the labour process.

As we have pointed out above, teaching has undergone a process of reconstruction, which has involved degrees of specialization, deskilling and increased alienation. This reconstruction has crucial implications for the way teacher masculinities are worked out. Mac an Ghaill (1994) presents a range of male teacher styles which are located around certain ideologies of teacher labour. These ideologies embody assumptions and expectations about the labour process. Attitudes to the labour process are closely worked into personal desires and fears, with major personal investments. He outlines three particular groups: the Professionals, the Old Collectivists and the New Entrepreneurs. At one level, these groups are based on their responses to the political organization of schooling. More specifically, the groups' identities are acted out in relation to their different responses to recent educational reforms. These differences created conflicts. The groups' strategic political positioning was underpinned by their collective impressions of what constitutes the labour process. At another level, sexual politics is also at work here, involving the contestation of masculine styles. These styles are not totally cohesive, but rather contain multiple and contradictory elements. Nevertheless, the Professionals tended to advocate a masculine style that revolved around authority, discipline and control. This was a masculinity that appeared to draw on themes of paternalism. The Old Collectivists attached significance to an education system which emphasized equality, meritocracy, anti-sexist and anti-racist practices. This can be seen as a masculine style that was drawing on liberal pluralist and feminist ideas. The third group, the New Entrepreneurs were in favour of recent central government interventions and welcomed a labour process which was redefining teachers' work in terms of appraisal, accountability and effective management. This type of masculinity worked with ideas of a conventional upwardly mobile industrial and business-like masculinity.

Importantly, these ideological positions and styles manifested themselves in working relations and, more specifically, in their responses and resistances to changes in the school organization. The potential for conflict becomes heightened as teachers are not only acting out their micropolitical interests in response to curriculum changes, they are simultaneously acting out their sexual politics through the deployment of masculinities. In other words it is the teachers' relationship to the labour process which mediates their masculinity.

Discipline

A second area where teacher relations reinforce 'normal' masculinity is through the legitimation of different teaching styles. Masculinities have to operate or be competent at operating some degree of power and authority (Brittan 1989). An inability to be powerful and authoritative is a code for an inability to be a 'proper man'. Signs of 'weakness' in many public arenas is associated with femininity. Masculinities in the workplace have competence as an essential feature, while incompetence is deemed as failure, weakness or 'womanly'. In Robinson's (1992) school a competent teacher could keep a class quiet. A quiet class was deemed a class that could be managed, therefore learning could be achieved. The most common way of keeping a class quiet was the use of discipline and force. It was expected that males were able to use this discipline. Although violence in terms of corporal punishment in state schools has been abolished, other forms of physical force were often used to control male pupils. Beynon's (1989) ethnography of 'Lower School', a school for 11 to 18-year-olds in South Wales, highlights the ways that coercive methods used in the classroom represented 'good' teaching. Physical coercion through shaking, cuffing and pushing were seen as acceptable everyday forms of discipline. This discipline complemented the ethos of a 'school for boys and men'. As Beynon (p. 194) points out, the headteacher believed that there was no place for women and children: 'Men and boys were expected to behave in a certain kind of way, put in a certain kind of manly performance, if they were to win the accolade of being a "good teacher" or a "good lad", whether that was a praiseworthy "rough diamond" or "playground hard".' Teachers' awareness of other teachers' pedagogical styles – informed by notions of gender – judged whether teachers were 'good' or 'bad'. As a result 'good teachers' were 'real men' and 'bad teachers' had 'problems' (Wolpe 1988).

There are pressing implications about the use of violence in Beynon's school. First, there is pressure on the teacher that in order to be competent, violence has to be issued. Second, if a competent teacher is a male who can display violence, what part do women play in the school? Third, if violence is appropriate for teaching, what does this mean for theories of child-centredness and the ability to create positive working relations (Robinson 1992)?

By presenting the teachers' labour process as embodying ideas about what it means to be a man, we have illustrated that teachers' work is a set of relations in which masculinities are worked out. Teachers' work exists as another space where gender relations are producing masculine forms. Teachers' identities, ideologies and pedagogical styles demonstrate a particular purchase on certain masculinities. It is a purchase on what kind of men they are.

Student–student relations: the use of language

Male peer group networks are one of the most oppressive arenas for the production and regulation of masculinities. Using ideas about what it means to be male and informed by some of the school processes indicated above, students deploy techniques to legitimize and regulate those meanings. As schools create the conditions for a hegemonic masculinity, differing meanings of masculinity will compete for ascendancy. The curriculum offers male students a resource to develop their masculinity, through a range of responses to it. At the same time, relations of domination and subordination become apparent, as some groups are able to define their meaning of masculinity over others. These definitions create boundaries which serve to delineate what appropriate maleness should be within this social arena. Transgression of these boundaries activates techniques of normalization, ranging from labelling through to physical violence, that ultimately act to maintain differences embedded in the ascendant definitions of masculinity.

As indicated below in the study by Willis (1977), mental work and having girls as friends were defined by the working-class Lads as effeminate. They asserted definitions of masculinity that required men to be strong and powerful and not express any weakness. Language can express such definitions of appropriate masculinities which in effect regulate and actively police male behaviour. In his ethnography of a school unit for disruptives, Wood (1984) points out that the use of language, particularly sexual slang, is also used in a process of expelling male sexual anxieties, self-doubts and confusions. Wood helps us to conceptualize male sex talk as embodying more than a simple process of sexual harassment (see Lees 1986). The use of terms of abuse by males may also help us to understand how they draw upon certain discursive resources to consolidate masculine subjectivities. One way in which males within peer group networks normalize masculine identities is by directing terms of abuse at other males' sexuality. It should be noted that sexuality as a target for terms of abuse is not arbitrarily chosen because sexuality is systematically selected as a critical component in the constitution of masculinities (Brittan 1989).

Haywood (1993) provides an example of how male pupils use language to regulate masculinities through the policing of sexuality. The lack of heterosexual experience by the Academic Achievers, a middle-class group of hard-working A level students became a resource for other males in the school to impose legitimate definitions of masculinity. The other groups of males included the Dominant Heterosexuals, a group which believed in schooling but also believed that heterosexual relationships were as important and the Hyper-Heterosexuals, who tended to reject schooling and concentrated on developing their heterosexual career. These groups interpreted and represented the Academic Achievers' heterosexual inexperience as illustrating childlike behaviour. The use of the term 'wankers' and other terms of homophobic abuse such as 'bum bandits', 'gays' and 'poofs' mediated to Academic Achievers their position in the school as underdeveloped and abject masculinities. These terms were usually spoken outside the classroom in a public arena such as the student common room. By doing so, males consolidated their masculine identities by making alternative/contradictory masculinities problematic. Terms of abuse here represented ways in which certain heterosexual males publicly distanced and expelled from themselves behaviours such as homosexual relations or masturbation, which they felt contradicted their ideas about what their own masculine identities consisted of.

This process of making masculine identities is also evident in the terms of abuse used by the Academic Achievers. Such terms as 'cripple', 'cabbage', and 'spanner' were used to describe male pupils' inadequacy, representing something inanimate, inarticulate and stupid. They were commonly used when male pupils, particularly the Dominant Heterosexuals and the Hyper-Heterosexuals, answered teachers' questions incorrectly within the context of the classroom. For the Academic Achievers, these terms were a method of validating a masculinity based on academic competence, while serving to ridicule other masculine styles. Yet the Academic Achievers' language generally failed to maintain the other groups as subjects in their abuse and legitimate the Academic Achievers' masculinities. This was mainly because the terms of abuse used by the Academic Achievers corresponded to the Hyper-Heterosexuals' and the Dominant Heterosexuals' perception that the Academic Achievers were 'childlike', thus reinforcing and amplifying their own inferiority. Rather than the terms of abuse being a form of cultural resistance, as abuse was for the other males, the Academic Achievers' language colluded with a schooling system which desexualized students and emphasized students' immaturity; a schooling system which restricted their access to certain masculine subjectivities.

Curriculum: mediating masculinities

The curriculum is an area of strategic importance for the production of masculinities. The curriculum – combined with the disciplinary procedures, normalizing judgements and the examination – represents an institutional-ized structure (Foucault 1982). It is the relationship between the curriculum and students that contributes to the conditions for the emergence of particular masculinities (Connell 1989). Hierarchically organized know-ledges legitimate the spaces for hegemonic masculinities to exist. It is important to stress that schools proscribe and prescribe *particular* kinds of knowledges. Furthermore, the spaces available for certain masculinities to occupy are not necessarily conditional upon the acceptance of the hierarchy of knowledges, but can also be shaped through a range of responses, including resistance to those knowledges.

Resistance
Connell (1989) proposes that masculinities are produced in relation to the curriculum, through the sorting of students into academic hierarchies. As

schools actively fail students, they are deprived of a certain source of power and status. Connell argues that students, when formally proclaimed failures by the school, take up alternative resources to validate their masculine identities. One form of validating masculinity has been through resisting school demands and expectations. Willis (1977) has provided one of the early key texts dealing with masculinity and the forms of resistance it entails within the social arena of the school.

During the 1970s Marxist theorists, such as Bowles and Gintis (1976), developed theoretical frameworks suggesting that schools reproduced the social relations of the wider society. In critiquing these theories, Willis (1977) presented a more complex picture, arguing that working-class students – in actively resisting the schooling process – reproduce themselves inside social class relations. His ethnography focused on a group of anti-school working-class males. He identifies certain cultural practices of this group which transgressed the schools' expectations and normative judgements. These practices – which included 'havin' a laff', 'dossing' and 'blagging' – also represented pupils' strategies to deal with the vicissitudes of a schooling system that alienated them. Willis suggests that a process of differentiation occurs between the 'Lads' and the school. Differentiation embodies the separation of the institutional interests and that of the working class. Part of the resistance to schooling was the rejection of the legitimacy of school-sanctioned knowledges. The academic disciplines presented to the lads had no relevance for the type of jobs that they wanted/expected to get. This resistance to schooling paralleled the 'Earoles' who accepted the legitimacy of schooling. A central feature of the Lads' rejection of learning was that it was associated with mental work. According to Willis, enveloped in male working-class culture is a perception that 'real work' is physical. Significantly, the Lads' rejection of knowledges was not solely defined in terms of class but also existed along gendered lines, with mental work deemed effeminate. In other words, mental work is contrasted to manual work, with the latter representing a province of masculinity.

Critics of the above study have suggested that Willis romanticizes the position of the working class. Also, he is seen to celebrate a coercive form of masculinity as a response to the middle-class schooling system. Furthermore, there is no indication that the Lads' sexual domination results from their privileged position in an oppressive masculine regime. At the same time Willis assumes that the processes that boys go through will also be experienced by girls. Evidence suggests that female students' oppression is reproduced in different ways (McRobbie 1991). Apart from these general criticisms, there is a sense that resistance appears to take on a particular masculine style. In overemphasizing the Lads' responses, there is a failure to conceptualize the range of masculine identities that is occupied across the school. Other forms of counterschool cultures may require a more sophisticated analysis of the production of masculinity through resistance to schooling.

Changing curriculum: changing masculinities
If we assume that the curriculum produces the spaces in which masculinities are produced, it follows that as the curriculum changes, so will masculinities. It should be added that the interplay between the curriculum and masculinity does not work in a deterministic way; students can effectively renegotiate curriculum agendas (Davies and Hunt 1994). They do, however, represent a structure, a technique or practice of power which is relatively fixed, closing off and opening up potential masculine subjectivities. At different times dominant institutional orders impose their versions of hierarchical knowledge that serve to stratify the curriculum.

The renegotiation of the hierarchy of subject areas is also present in contemporary English schools. Mac an Ghaill (1994) has argued that until recently, schools were divided along a high status/academic and low status/vocationalist binary. He suggests that currently this division is being challenged and is in the process of being reconstructed. The impetus for reconstruction has been the increased funding for vocation- directed projects, marking a shift from a liberal-humanist schooling paradigm to a technical training paradigm. New resources for the fulfilment of career aspiration emerged as students entered subjects such as business studies, technology and computer studies. He found that the emergence of the new vocationalism has signalled the change in the constitution of stratified knowledge. In turn, as a result of the restratification of knowledges, male student identities take on new dimensions. Rather than seeing male groups in terms of a simple pro-school or anti-school dichotomy, Mac an Ghaill proposes a more sophisticated approach in order to capture these new dimensions. In his study he identifies four groups of male student types, who represent the styles of masculinity that were present at the secondary school: the Macho Lads, the Academic Achievers, the New Entrepreneurs and the Real Englishmen. The groups of students were positioning their masculinities in relation to the school organization, and in particular in relation to the curriculum. The working-class Macho Lads rejected formal schooling. In contrast, the Academic Achievers legitimized and affirmed the schooling process, locating themselves within academic subjects. Meanwhile the working-class New Entrepreneurs located themselves within the newly high status technical and vocational subjects as a resource to develop their masculinities. The Real Englishmen represented a group of middle-class students who, like the Macho Lads, rejected schooling but remained ambivalent to its significance. Key elements of their masculinity included honesty, being different, individuality and autonomy, which they claimed were absent from the school's middle-class culture. Significantly, it is within these peer group networks that masculinities were collectively regulated, maintained and contested. Each group attempted to impose its own definition of masculinity, thus reinforcing their own social position. In doing so, the form and content of the students' schooling experiences became mediated.

Conclusion

Throughout this chapter we have tried to illustrate that schools act as 'masculinity-making devices'. By theoretically examining masculinity and offering empirical examples of the way masculinities are shaped in the context of schools, an attempt has been made to address the notion of the 'schooling of masculinities'. It has to be emphasized that schools do not exist on their own as locations for the creation and contestation of masculinities; rather, they complexly interrelate with other social and cultural sites, including the family, labour markets, media representations, and the legal system. However, perhaps contemporary schooling is the most strategic site, as it offers a condensed range of experiences in a sustained and mandatory fashion. It is also necessary to emphasize that schools do not produce masculinities in a direct, overly deterministic way, but that the construction of students' identities is a process of negotiation, rejection, acceptance and ambivalence. Finally, it should be noted that studies of school masculinities have the potential to collude in the current backlash against feminism by implicitly suggesting that boys are now the 'real victims'. In response, it is intended that this chapter builds on feminist, gay and lesbian scholarship and activism, contributing to the political deconstruction of masculinities. In turn, it is hoped that this will generate fresh insights into what constitutes masculinities. More specifically, this chapter has argued for the need critically to examine heterosexual masculinities and, in the process, to destabilize the assumed naturalness and inevitability of sex/gender schooling regimes.

References

Beynon, J. (1989) A school for men: an ethnographic case study of routine violence in schooling, in S. Walker and L. Barton (eds) *Politics and the Processes of Schooling*. Milton Keynes: Open University Press.

Bowles, S. and Gintis, H. (1976) *Schooling in Capitalist America. Educational Reform and the Contradictions of Economic Life*. London: Routledge and Kegan Paul.

Brittan, A. (1989) *Masculinity and Power*. Oxford: Blackwell.

Butler, J. (1993) *Bodies that Matter: On the Discursive Limits of 'Sex'*. London: Routledge.

Connell, R.W. (1987) *Gender and Power*. Cambridge: Polity Press.

Connell, R.W. (1989) Cool guys, swots and wimps: the inter-play of masculinity and education, *Oxford Review of Education*, 15(3): 291–303.

Connell, R.W. (1992) A very straight gay: masculinity, homosexual experience, and the dynamics of gender, *American Sociological Review*, 57(6): 735–51.

Davies, B. and Hunt, R. (1994) Classroom competencies and marginal positioning, *British Journal of Sociology of Education*, 15(3): 389–408.

Deem, R. (ed.) (1984) *Co-Education Reconsidered*. Milton Keynes: Open University Press.

Foucault, M. (1982) *Discipline and Punish*. London: Peregrine Books.

Haywood, C.P. (1993) 'Using sexuality: an exploration into the fixing of sexuality to make male identities in a mixed sex sixth form', unpublished MA dissertation, University of Warwick.

Lees, S. (1986) *Losing Out: Sexuality and Adolescent Girls*. London: Hutchinson.

Mac an Ghaill, M. (1991) Schooling, sexuality and male power: towards an emancipatory curriculum, *Gender and Education*, 3: 291–309.

Mac an Ghaill, M. (1994) *The Making of Men: Masculinities, Sexualities and Schooling*. Buckingham: Open University Press.

McRobbie, A. (1991) *Feminism and Youth Culture: From 'Jackie' to 'Just Seventeen'*. London: Macmillan.

Phizacklea, A. (1990) *Unpacking the Fashion Industry*. London: Routledge.

Robinson, K.H. (1992) Classroom discipline: power, resistance and gender. A look at teacher perspectives, *Gender and Education*, 4(3): 273–87.

Thorne, B. (1993) *Gender Play: Girls and Boys in School*. Buckingham: Open University Press.

Willis, P. (1977) *Learning to Labour: How Working Class Kids Get Working Class Jobs*. Aldershot: Saxon House.

Wolpe, A.M. (1988) *Within School Walls: The Role of Discipline. Sexuality and the Curriculum*. London: Routledge.

Wood, J. (1984) Groping towards sexism: boys' sex talk, in A. McRobbie and M. Nava (eds) *Gender and Generation*. London: Macmillan.

'Men' at 'work': multiple masculinities/multiple workplaces

Introduction

Throughout the twentieth century, researchers and writers on organizations have talked about 'men' at 'work'. Yet it is only relatively recently that men have actually been recognized as a gendered category requiring detailed critical analysis. Without problematizing gender, men or masculinity in any explicit way, classic texts of the 1950s, for example, referred to *Men who Manage* (Dalton 1959), *The Man on the Assembly Line* (Walker and Guest 1952) and *Organization Man* (Whyte 1956). Although these studies actively dealt with men, they did not explore either men's social construction or the specific implications for the reproduction of men and masculinity of being a manager, working on the assembly line or being trapped in the organization. It was as if men's pervasiveness gave their dominance a universality that precluded the need for further analysis: an assumption that was taken for granted not only in language, but also in analytical categories.[1] In many ways these assumptions mirrored those of everyday workplace life where, typically, the authority, power and dominance of men at various hierarchical levels was simply accepted and unquestioned by organization members.

Inspired by feminist analysis, a more critical literature has emerged that seeks to critique the gendered nature of these assumptions as well as the conventional power, practices and relations of men and masculinity/ies in various organizational positions and settings (e.g. Morgan 1992; Roper 1993). In this chapter we seek to review these arguments, not only to '*name* men [at 'work'] as men' (Collinson and Hearn 1994) and therefore to question the way in which these issues have often been taken for granted in the past, but also to examine critically the multiple conditions, processes and consequences of the continued domination of men and masculinities in various workplaces. We suggest that men and masculinity/ies continue to dominate many of the structures, cultures and practices of routine organizational life and that this in turn has significant implications for our understanding of the great diversity of workplaces that exist as well as the potential for their transformation. In the first half of the paper we briefly review some of the more theoretical issues that have been raised regarding the power/social relations of 'men' at 'work', while in the second half we draw upon empirical research to illustrate the multiplicity of men, masculinities and workplaces by identifying key aspects of this diversity within both manual and non-manual labour.

Analysing 'men' at 'work'

The analysis of 'men' at 'work' raises considerable conceptual difficulty, not least regarding what do we mean by 'men' and what do we mean by 'work'? First, while certainly existing in relation to the category 'male(s)', 'men' are not necessarily 'males', and vice versa. There are a number of reasons for this, including: cultural specificities in 'men' and 'males'; distinctions between 'boys', 'men', 'young males' and 'males'; the various physiological and cultural forms of gender change, whether 'temporary' or 'permanent'; and the differential relation of 'men' and 'males' to history and trans-history, respectively. We find it helpful to see 'men' as a gender that exists or is presumed to exist in most direct relation to the generalized male sex, that being the sex which is not female, or not the sex related to the gender of women (Hearn 1994). Second, feminist analyses have problematized the meaning of 'work'. They have criticized the way that in theory and everyday practices the home is often not recognized as a workplace at all and domestic tasks have failed to be acknowledged as 'work' for women and/or men. In so doing, feminist studies have highlighted the importance of unpaid domestic labour as an important site of gendered 'work' and of men's domination of women.

Feminist studies of men, work and workplaces have revealed how 'most organizations are saturated with masculine values' (Burton 1991: 3). By highlighting the embeddedness of masculine values and assumptions in the structure, culture and practices of organizations, such studies (e.g. Pringle 1989; Cockburn 1991) have encouraged the development of a critical perspective on 'men' at 'work'.[2] Critically analysing the centrality of the masculine model of lifetime, full-time, continuous employment and of the family breadwinner for the organization of paid work, these studies have emphasized the importance of men's continued domination of power relations in contemporary organizations. Relatedly, they have revealed the importance of paid work as a central source of masculine identity, status and power. For many men, employment provides the interrelated economic resources and symbolic benefits of wages/salaries, skills and experience, career progress and positions of power, authority and high discretion.

Typically, it seems, men's gender identities are constructed, compared and evaluated by self and others according to a whole variety of criteria indicating personal 'success' in the workplace. The foregoing studies also demonstrate how these organizational resources of power and status are less accessible to women employees. Many of these feminist writers have used the concept of patriarchy to delineate the recurrent and pervasive nature of men's workplace power.

Patriarchy, dual systems and their limitations

Patriarchy has become an important concept in the critical analysis of men's power and identity in the workplace. Feminist analyses contend that any adequate understanding of 'men' at 'work' needs to consider the social relations of men in the wider society. The term, 'patriarchy', has become the usual shorthand for the kind of society founded on men's gender domination. However, a number of feminist critiques (e.g. Beechey 1979; Rowbotham 1979; Acker 1989) have suggested that patriarchy is too monolithic, ahistorical, biologically overdetermined, categorical and dismissive of women's resistance and agency. In the light of this, greater attention has been given first, to the historicizing and periodizing of patriarchy and second, to the presence of multiple arenas, sites and structures of patriarchy. Studies have addressed the historical movement from private (domestic) to public (capitalism and the state) forms of patriarchy. There have also been attempts to identify the various sites or multiple bases of patriarchy (e.g. Walby 1986, 1990; Hearn 1987, 1992).

Many writers who have used the concept of patriarchy have also adopted a critical perspective on capitalist work organizations, usually deriving their approach from a neo-Marxist focus upon the underlying conflicts and contradictions of economic interests in the workplace. However, these attempts to develop a 'dual systems' theory (e.g. Hartmann 1981) by integrating a critical gender (patriarchy) and class (capitalism) analysis have been less than fully successful. The problem here is that dual systems theory must inevitably treat patriarchal and capitalist relations as somehow outside each other. As Acker (1989: 237) argues, dual systems theory 'leaves intact the patriarchal assumptions buried in theories about the other systems to which patriarchy is related'. By pointing to analytically independent structures it is difficult, if not impossible, to capture the way that gender 'is implicated in the fundamental constitution of all social life' (p. 238).

The main conclusion to be drawn from these analytical difficulties is that notions of patriarchy need to be treated with considerable caution. At minimum they may be better understood as diversified and differentiated rather than unified and monolithic. Equally, in the case of paid work, they are likely to be interwoven in complex ways with other features of organization such as hierarchy, managerial control, culture, subordination, resistance and a diversity of different inequalities. The complexity of men's power in 'work', highlighted by these debates, is reinforced by a growing concern with sexuality and subjectivity, which in turn has further stimulated awareness of the multiple and diverse nature of gendered power relations.

Sexuality, subjectivity and multiplicity

The growing interest in the analysis of sexuality(ies), which has come to be seen as a central feature of men's domination, has developed not only from feminist and gay theory and practices but also from post-structuralist and psychoanalytic work. Men's sexuality first became a topic of major interest in organization studies through a concern with sexual harassment. From the late 1970s, numerous studies have documented the extent, frequency and variability of workplace sexual harassment (Farley 1978; MacKinnon 1979; Hearn et al. 1989). Often studies have focused on the occurrence of 'individual' incidents, though there is increasing attention to sexual harassment as a structural, 'normal' or all-pervasive phenomenon (Hearn and Parkin 1987; Wise and Stanley 1988). Analyses of sexual harassment raise a number of paradoxical questions for men and men's sexualities. On the one hand, sexual harassment is usually an instance or a commentary on men's sexualities; on the other, sexual harassment is often understandable as about violence, power, authority, labour-power, protection of space and wage levels, economic discrimination, rather than just sexuality in any kind of isolation.

Focusing particularly upon male-dominated workplaces, Di Tomaso (1989: 72) argues that men often 'engage in a type of power play by which they use sexuality to put women in their "proper" subordinate role in relation to men'. She suggests that the paid work context seems to provide a licence for men's offensive behaviour and their attempts to take advantage of many working women; as one of her respondents stated, 'The men are different here than on the street. Its like they have been locked up for years' (p. 80). Masculinity can also be implicated in the organizational processing of sexual harassment claims. Where men as managers and/or trade union officials prefer to deal with claims of sexual harassment in an informal way, its significance is often downplayed and there is a tendency to redefine perpetrators of sexual harassment as victims and victims as perpetrators (Collinson and Collinson 1992). The anticipation by women that their claims will not be dealt with sympathetically by men in senior positions is an important barrier to their disclosure of sexual harassment.

Furthermore, 'heterosexual' sexual harassment is also often understandable in terms of relations (sometimes homosocial/homosexual relations) *between men*. This is most clearly the case in the use of pin-ups and pornography by men in workplaces and other organizations. Women are here displayed as signs for contact between men, just as women may figure as currency of conversation, jokes and put-downs in men's socializing (Cock-burn 1983; Collinson 1988). This general perspective can also apply to 'individual' harassments of women, as exchanges between men. There are two major, again apparently contradictory, aspects to such sexual dynamics: the organizational pervasiveness and dominance of men's heterosexuality (Collinson and Collinson 1989); and the organizational pervasiveness and dominance of men's homosociability/homosexuality (Hearn 1992). The contradiction of these aspects is clearest in such practices as horseplay, often performed by and between heterosexually identified men, in the form of (parodies of) homosexuality. More generally, gendered organizations are sites of both 'normal' heterosexuality for men, and men's homosociability in their preference for same gender company and spaces (Kanter 1977; Hearn 1985).

In addition to focusing upon men's sexuality, recent studies have examined the way that gendered/patriarchal workplace relations are reproduced, which in turn has led to an increasing concern with subjectivity/ies and their complex interrelations with power dynamics, and with multiplicity and diversity. For example, Henriques *et al.* (1984) critiqued the unitary and rational subject found in much social science. They conceptualized subjec-tivity as embedded in prevailing power relations, discourses and practices, and as a specific, historical product that is ambiguous, fragmentary, discontinuous, multiple, sometimes fundamentally non-rational and fre-quently contradictory. This approach is particularly relevant to the analysis of gendered power, men and masculinities, not just in the sense of acknowledging subjective variation, for example in the different 'types' of men and masculinities (or women and femininities), but also in the way that these are perceived and experienced and may shift over time and place.

Increasingly research has highlighted the way that men often seem preoccupied with the creation and maintenance of various masculine identities and with the expression of gendered power and status in the workplace (Willis 1977; Collinson 1992a). Men's search to construct these identities often draws upon a whole variety of organizational resources, discourses and practices and appears to be an ongoing, never-ending project that is frequently characterized by ambiguity, tension and uncertainty (Brittan 1989). Like all identities, masculine selves constantly have to be constructed, negotiated and reconstructed in routine social interaction, both in the workplace and elsewhere, through simultaneous processes of identifi-cation and differentiation (Collinson and Hearn 1994). Various studies have highlighted the fragility and precariousness underpinning and surrounding these recurrent attempts to construct masculine identities that superficially appear strong, authoritative and self-assured. Masculine identities have been shown to be threatened by social and economic forces such as new technology (Cockburn 1983; Baron 1992), unemployment (Walter 1979), feminism/equal opportunity initiatives (Cockburn 1991) and by class and status divisions (Sennett and Cobb 1977). In addition, men's tendency to become preoccupied with seeking to secure clearly defined and coherent identities may in itself, paradoxically, further reinforce, rather than resolve, their sense of insecurity and threat (Collinson 1992a).

It is against this background of a growing recognition of analytical difficulties with patriarchy that a more detailed interest has developed in men, masculinities and gendered power. In the second half of the chapter, we now discuss the findings of empirical studies that reveal the various ways in which these multiple masculinities are frequently reproduced in diverse workplace settings.

Multiple masculinities

The concept of multiple masculinities (Carrigan *et al.* 1985) has been used to refer to the temporal, spatial and cultural diversity of masculinity. It tries to convey the way in which specific forms of masculinity are constructed and persist in relation both to femininity and to other forms of masculinity. Different masculinities are embedded in relations of power, and particular forms may be characterized as 'hegemonic' or 'subordinate' in relation to one another (Connell 1995). In turn these masculinities are not fixed, but continually shifting. Multiplicity and diversity are relevant not only to the analysis of masculinity, but also to the different forms and locations of workplaces – the sites of work and of masculinity. These sites will vary, for example, according to occupation, industry, culture, class and type of organization. Thus multiple masculinities interconnect with multiple sites. We will now briefly consider four such sites: the home, the shopfloor, the office and management. Rather than operate in a simple or discrete way, these sites overlap with each other, and there may well be significant interstices between them which might reinforce their complex and ambiguous nature.

The home

Feminist analysis has argued that notions of 'work' and 'the workplace' are ideological because they reduce the meaning and status of 'work' to the organizational or 'workplace', the employed, the public. For men in particular, work and workplaces still refer primarily and overwhelmingly to the organizational, to employment and to what happens in 'public'. This even applies negatively in the sense of men being 'out of work' and being unemployed (see also Willott and Griffin in this volume). Accordingly, the home is often not seen as a workplace at all. This may apply to both women and men, albeit for different reasons. For women, this is one of the many ways in which they and their contribution remain invisible and undervalued; for men, this may be because of their persistent avoidance of domestic tasks and responsibilities. Research suggests that women are mainly or solely respon-sible for three quarters of all housework (Henwood *et al*. 1987) and that there are also major differences between the kind of domestic tasks performed by men and women. The former tend to 'specialize' in putting children to bed, taking out/playing with children, waste disposal, household repairs and do-it-yourself. Such tasks are generally 'preferred' by men over the much more time-consuming, supposedly mundane and indeed socially subordi-nated tasks of cleaning, daily shopping, washing, ironing, cooking and the routine care of children (Oakley 1985).

These dominant masculinities in the home complement, albeit often in difficult and contradictory ways, the masculinities of employment. On the one hand, the very physical/geographical separation of paid work and domestic life may reflect and reinforce specific masculinities both at home and in the public workplace; on the other hand, for some men, paid work may take over the house and the home. This may apply to vicars, doctors, computer workers, research scientists, and particularly academics! Such masculinities may be constructed around a life vocation, an obsession with technology, the working of long hours or the need to maximize earnings. For example, in demonstrating men's obsession with computers in a Cambridge high tech company, Massey (1993) discusses how paid work dominates home and family life in terms of space, time and interaction. Even when wives persuaded their husbands to spend more time with their children, the most frequent outcome was that games were played by fathers and children on home computers! The domination and erosion of the private sphere of home by the public world of paid employment is likely to increase as new technologies and corporate concerns with the reduction of costs and overheads results in greater homeworking and teleworking, where distinc-tions between domestic and occupational tasks become increasingly blurred and difficult to manage (Collinson 1992b). This is also a growing reality for many managerial and professional workers who are employed by 'greedy organizations' demanding more and more of the domestic time and space of employees. By contrast, as the following section discusses, some groups of men workers make a highly conscious effort to retain a clear psychological and symbolic separation between the spheres of paid work and home.

The shopfloor

A key issue, particularly in the UK, which reinforces and indeed structures the multiplicity of masculinities, is the deep-seated nature of economic class inequalities, subcultures and identities that continue to be reproduced in and through routine workplace practices. There is now a considerable literature highlighting the way in which working-class masculinities are frequently embedded in the 'productive' manual skills, experience and relations of all male shopfloor life. Cockburn's (1983) study of printers reveals some of the ways that manual skills can be defined and widely accepted as highly masculine. She shows how the hot-metal skills of linotype compositors have historically been treated and protected as the exclusive province of men. Willis (1977) describes the ways in which masculinities are often central features of working-class countercultures both in schools and in paid work. He examines how working-class lads resist school authority by 'celebrating' the so-called 'freedom' and 'independence' of manual work only to realize the reality of class subordination once they reach the factory with no educational qualifications and therefore little chance of escape.

These themes are developed by Collinson (1988, 1992a), who argues that the complex and sometimes contradictory amalgam of resistance, compliance and consent that simultaneously comprises shopfloor sub/countercultures is frequently expressed in highly masculine discourses and practices. The study focused on examines the interwoven class- and gender-specific values of men manual workers and their subcultural reproduction of masculine identities through, for example, the negation of management (as effeminate and ignorant about the processes of production); middle-class office workers (as unproductive 'pen pushers'); and women (as manipulative and exploitative). Within organizational conditions that treat manual workers as second-class citizens, working-class men may tend to redefine their sense of self, dignity and respect within the counterculture. They not only negate others, but also seek to elevate themselves through specifically masculine values of being, for example, a family breadwinner, 'practical', 'productive', 'having common sense', and being 'able to swear when you like' and 'give and take a joke like a man'. Informal shopfloor interaction between men manual workers is often highly aggressive, sexist and derogatory, humorous yet insulting, playful but degrading. New members are teased incessantly and tested to see whether they are 'man enough' to take the insults couched in the humour of 'piss taking' and the embarrassment of highly explicit sexual references. Those who display a willingness to 'give it and take it' are accepted into the masculine subculture, while those who 'snap' have failed this particular test of manhood and are likely to be kept at a distance.

Typically, masculine shopfloor values emphasize workers' 'honesty', 'independence' and 'authenticity'. In many cases rejecting even the very idea of promotion because it would compromise their sense of masculine 'independence' and 'freedom', men manual workers often insist that this would require them to change and become conforming 'yes men'. Office work is seen as an unacceptable limit on one's freedom and (gender) identity, as one worker stated, 'You can't have a laugh and a joke in the offices. They're all twats and nancy boys there' (Collinson 1992a: 87). Similarly, shopfloor workers know that supervisors and managers are expected to take their work home and 'worry about it' in the evening and at weekends. By contrast, they seek to maintain an impenetrable psychological wall between 'public' and 'private' life, as one engineer explained: 'I leave here at 4.30 and I'm not taking my work home. I'm not getting home at seven o'clock with a briefcase full of notes'; and another added 'Work does not affect my social life, I won't let it. It's 8.00 to 4.30 and that's it' (p. 95). Together, the foregoing studies of shopfloor dynamics reveal how highly male-dominated working-class cultures often symbolically invert the values and meanings of class society, but in ways that often unintentionally reinforce the status quo.

The office

Compared to the shopfloor, the office has been relatively little explored as a site of masculinities. Until the late nineteenth century, office jobs tended to be very much men's preserve. Then, with the expansion of the state and private sector bureaucracies, there was a rapid growth of women's clerical employment to the extent that much clerical and secretarial work became sex-typed as women's occupations (Barker and Downing 1980). 'Women's clerical work' in contemporary organizations is not only downgraded and undervalued but also frequently reflects stereotypical 'homemaker' tasks within the workplace (Pringle 1989). Men, by contrast, are often employed in well-paid and high discretionary positions that sometimes reflect and reinforce an inflated status based on their defined role as organizational 'breadwinners'.

In the UK, insurance sales is one such occupation where men often elevate and exaggerate their contribution in ways that reinforce their power, status and identity within the workplace (Collinson *et al.* 1990). Despite the work involving predominantly mental rather than manual skills, a certain masculine mystique abounds in the selling of insurance. The task is often described in terms of a heroic drama in which 'intrepid' and 'valiant' men venture out into the 'dangerous' world of finance and commerce and, 'against all the odds', return with new business: winning 'bread' for their organization. Men in selling frequently construct an image of self-control and resilience to 'take the knocks' in the aggressive financial market-place. The images of intrepid middle-class masculinities crucially impact on selection criteria and practices in ways that frequently exclude women.

Yet closer analysis of insurance sales reveals that this masculine imagery may be misleading. Much of the work consists of establishing long-term 'business relationships' with intermediaries and agents who then recommend the company's products to customers. Far from aggression and toughness, the nurturing of this business rapport requires a high degree of interpersonal skills. After-sales service is a central and key part of the sales process and it is women working in the offices who frequently play a crucial role in resolving clients' difficulties and thereby retaining their product loyalty. Where selling is conducted direct to the public, a more aggressive style is frequently adopted by 'financial consultants', who are self-employed and thus remunerated according to performance (Collinson *et al.* 1990). Yet in this part of the market the encouragement of a more 'macho' and entrepreneurial approach to selling, particularly in the 1980s, has led to major scandals throughout the UK financial services industry because of the high-pressure, unethical sales practices that have sometimes ensued. Various research studies suggest that other middle-class, male-dominated professions and technical occupations such as doctors, computer specialists, lawyers and academics are equally characterized by gender divisions and highly masculine values and assumptions (e.g. Podmore and Spencer 1987; Massey 1993). It is to the middle-class masculinities of management that we now turn.

Management

It is truly amazing that men's domination of management has not become a serious topic of concern even in critical social science. Yet it is managers who exercise formal power in the workplace and men who frequently exercise power over women. While labour process perspectives have critically examined management as part of a general critique of capitalism (with little consideration of gender issues), feminist analyses have been more concerned with the gendered power of trade unions (with little consideration of management). This neglect is even more evident in mainstream/malestream management theory and indeed management ideology and practice. Yet a closer analysis reveals innumerable ways in which management, both in theory and practice, implicates 'men' and 'masculinities'. This applies in the construction of dominant models of management, styles of management, the language of management (often using militaristic and/or sporting metaphors), management culture, managerialism, and so on.

A few, more recent studies have begun to take up these themes of the simultaneous deconstruction of 'men'/'masculinities' and management in the context of patriarchy (e.g. Rogers 1988; Cockburn 1991; Roper 1993). They provide the basis for a more detailed assessment of the variety of inter-relations between 'men', 'masculinities' and management. In one sense, this approach extends the labour process tradition (e.g. Knights and Willmott 1986) by attempting to retrieve the agency of management from an exclusively structuralist analysis, and by rejecting assumptions of managerial omniscience and unity in favour of a focus on the contradictions that characterize managerial control. These contradictions are embedded, first in the relationship between management/labour, and men/women, second within management itself and third within and between different men and masculinities. Each of these is now examined in turn.

First, management is set within complex tensions between ownership and control, the market and the institution, technological relations and social relations. Alongside the antagonistic relations between capital and labour, based on the material conflict between wages and profit, is a coexisting and contradictory interdependence which limits managerial power (Cressey and Macinnes 1980). Retaining a continued dependence on workers' skills, commitment and consent, management – particularly in certain labour and product market conditions – will have to relax its control and seek a relatively cooperative relationship with labour (Friedman 1977). Employers' contradictory demands for both dependable yet disposable workers result in a changing emphasis, first upon managerial prerogative and coercion (scientific management) and second upon worker cooperation and consent (human relations) as product and labour market conditions shift. Yet neither of these strategies can fully reconcile the contradiction between control and coordination in the capital/labour relation (Hyman 1987). Management control is therefore constrained by its contradictory relationship with labour. It is also highly gendered and reflects specific masculinities. Kanter (1977: 22) has argued that scientific management, with its emphasis on rationality and efficiency, is infused with an irreducibly 'masculine ethic'. She also suggests that despite its emphasis on the social group rather than economic remuneration, human relations theory still rests on the image of the rational/masculine manager who remains, 'the man who could control his emotions whereas workers could not' (p. 24).

A second contradictory element is the variety of divisions and differences within management itself, in terms, for example, of hierarchical, spatial and functional differentiations. By no means a completely integrated and cohesive function, management is rather a set of arenas for diverse, hierarchically orientated careers, promotions and power struggles (Dalton 1959; Jackall 1988; Watson 1994). Internal divisions within the managerial structure can also emerge in the possible attenuation between the formulation of corporate policy and its implementation at grassroots level, between the core and the periphery, and through extensive interfunctional rivalry. For example, Armstrong (1984, 1986) has explored the conflicts and competition between the managerial professions of accountancy, engineering and personnel to secure ascendancy for their own approach to the control of the labour process. Strategic solutions to management's 'control problem' might therefore be competing and internally fragmented. The division between line and personnel managers is often reinforced by stereotyped assumptions of the line manager as 'producer', 'provider' and breadwinner for the organization and the personnel manager as dependent, domestic and organizational 'welfare worker' (Collinson *et al.* 1990).

Third, there are contradictions between different men and masculinities. We have already noted how management differentiates men, both between managers and non-managers, and between different types of managers. Thus 'managerial masculinity/ies' might be understood as a form (or forms) of hegemonic masculinity. Equally, contradictions may exist between hegemonic managerial authority and diverse managerial masculinities. They may also exist between ambitious male managers seeking to purchase their career progress at the cost of others. Such differences between management, men and masculinities may be interrelated and intertwined with other social differences, around age, class, ethnicity, locality, nationality, religion, sexuality, and so on.

These three interwoven contradictions highlight the complex conditions, processes and consequences of managerial control in the workplace. They question conventional assumptions regarding managerial power and reveal the analytical importance of similarities and differences between men, masculinities and managements. Equally, they demonstrate that the power of men as managers and managers as men is circumscribed in various ways. Yet despite the contradictory conditions and consequences of the exercise of gendered and hierarchical power, research suggests that men managers' preoccupation with control over women and labour continues to characterize many routine workplace practices. This preoccupation can be expressed and reproduced through various discourses of managerial masculinity such as authoritarianism, paternalism, entrepreneurialism, informalism and careerism (Collinson and Hearn 1994).

Conclusion

Focusing upon 'men' at 'work', this chapter has discussed several dominant masculinities that continue to remain pervasive, persistent and privileged within a diversity of workplaces and occupations. In addition to identifying these multiple masculinities and workplaces, we have been concerned to examine the conditions, processes and consequences of their reproduction in routine organizational practices. Masculinities in contemporary workplaces are characterized by contradictory tensions. On the one hand, men often seem to collaborate, cooperate and identify with one another in ways that reinforce a shared unity between them; but on the other hand, these same masculinities can also be characterized simultaneously by conflict, competition and self-differentiation in ways that highlight and intensify the differences and divisions between men. Given these deep-seated tensions, ambiguities and contradictions, the unities that exist between men should not be overstated. They are often more precarious, shifting and highly instrumental than first appearances suggest.

Neither the multiple masculinities nor the various workplaces or occupations discussed in this chapter comprise an exhaustive account of 'men' at 'work'. Our focus has been shaped by analyses and studies conducted by ourselves and others. Further empirical work is necessary to develop the understanding of these gendered power relations, cultures and subjectivities. This is especially the case with regard to management, where analyses of gender and masculinity have been particularly neglected both by conventional and radical writers alike (Collinson and Hearn 1996).

Yet, in addition to further empirical research, more theoretical work is necessary to develop the analysis of multiple masculinities/multiple work-places. Several conceptual and theoretical problems remain unresolved within these debates (see also Collinson and Hearn 1994, and Hearn in this volume). First, the conceptualization of 'masculinity/ies' requires clarifi-cation. For example, how do the ideological/discursive and symbolic features of masculinities interrelate with economic, material and physical aspects? Second, the ways in which masculinities relate to other elements of power, culture and subjectivity in organizations needs greater consideration. For example, in what ways and with what consequences are multiple masculini-ties embedded and interwoven in other workplace practices, such as those of control, consent, compliance and resistance? Finally, while recognizing a multiplicity of possible masculinities and workplace sites, analyses also need to retain a focus upon the asymmetrical nature of gendered power relations and subjectivities.

In highlighting the diversity of mens workplace power, status and domination, this chapter is not advocating a form of enquiry that merely categorizes different 'types' of men and/or masculinity in a highly descriptive and static way. Rather, we are seeking to develop analyses that can begin to reflect and comprehend the multiple, shifting but tenacious nature of gendered power regimes as they characterize diverse workplaces. We believe that such empirically informed analytical studies have the potential to examine and understand the dynamic, shifting and often contradictory organizational relations through which men's differences and similarities are reproduced and transformed in particular practices and power asymmetries. The critical studies discussed in this chapter of both 'men'/'masculinities' and 'work' are all part of the general deconstruction of the unified, rational and transcendent subject of men. The possibility of a challenge to men's taken-for-granted dominant masculinities could facilitate the emergence of less coercive and less divisive organizational structures, cultures and practices, a fundamental rethinking of the social organization of the domestic division of labour and a transformation of 'men' at 'work'.

Notes

1 In these accounts the initial focus on 'men' was soon displaced by analysis in terms of workers, managers or bureaucrats; categories that then became interchanged in the text with 'men'. Even so, there is a mass of information in such texts that can be reformulated in terms of the construction of specific masculinities (see Morgan 1992).
2 It is crucially important that the emphasis upon men and masculinities does not become a new means of forgetting/excluding women. This exclusionary tendency is a serious difficulty with the 'men's studies' approach advocated by Bly (1990) among others. The analysis of men and masculinities is likely to be enhanced, we

contend, when the relation to women and femininity is acknowledged and addressed.

References

Acker, J. (1989) The problem with patriarchy, *Sociology*, 23(2): 235–40.

Armstrong, P. (1984) Competition between the organisational professions and the evolution of management control strategies, in K. Thompson (ed.) *Work, Employment and Unemployment*. Milton Keynes: Open University Press.

Armstrong, P. (1986) Management control strategies and inter-professional competition: the cases of accountancy and personnel management, in D. Knights and H. Willmott (eds) *Gender and the Labour Process*. Aldershot: Gower.

Barker, J. and Downing, H. (1980) Word processing and the transformation of patriarchal relations of control in the office, *Capital and Class*, 10(Spring): 64–99.

Baron, A. (1992) Technology and the crisis of masculinity: the gendering of work and skill in the US printing industry, in A. Sturdy, D. Knights and H. Willmott (eds) *Skill and Consent*. London: Routledge.

Beechey, V. (1979) On patriarchy, *Feminist Review*, 3: 66–82.

Bly, R. (1990) *Iron John: A Book About Men*. New York: Addison-Wesley.

Brittan, A. (1989) *Masculinity and Power*. Oxford: Blackwell.

Burton, C. (1991) *The Promise and the Price*. Sydney: Allen and Unwin.

Carrigan, T., Connell, R.W. and Lee, J. (1985) Hard and heavy: toward a new sociology of masculinity, *Theory and Society*, 14: 551–604.

Cockburn, C. (1983) *Brothers*. London: Pluto Press.

Cockburn, C. (1991) *In the Way of Women: Men's Resistance to Sex Equality in Organizations*. London: Macmillan.

Collinson, D.L. (1988) Engineering humour: masculinity, joking and conflict in shopfloor relations, *Organization Studies*, 9(2): 181–99.

Collinson, D.L. (1992a) *Managing the Shopfloor: Subjectivity, Masculinity and Workplace Culture*. Berlin: Walter de Gruyter.

Collinson, D.L. (1992b) Researching recruitment: qualitative methods sex discrimination, in R.G. Burgess (ed.) *Studies in Qualitative Methodology*, vol. 3. London: JAI Press.

Collinson, D.L. and Collinson, M. (1989) Sexuality in the workplace: the domination of men's sexuality, in J. Hearn *et al.* (eds) *The Sexuality of Organization*. London: Sage.

Collinson, D.L. and Collinson, M. (1992) Mismanaging sexual harassment: protecting the perpetrator and blaming the victim, *Women in Management Review*, 7(7): 11–17.

Collinson, D.L. and Hearn, J. (1994) Naming men as men – implications for work, organization and management, *Gender, Work and Organization*, 1(1): 2–22.

Collinson, D. L. and Hearn, J. (eds) (1996) *Managements and Men*. London: Sage.

Collinson, D.L., Knights, D. and Collinson, M. (1990) *Managing to Discriminate*. London: Routledge.

Connell, R.W. (1995) *Masculinities*. Cambridge: Polity Press.

Cressey, P. and Macinnes, J. (1980) Voting for Ford: industrial democracy and the control of labour, *Capital and Class*, 11: 5–33.

Dalton, M. (1959) *Men Who Manage*. New York: John Wiley and Son.

DiTomaso (1989) Sexuality in the workplace: discrimination and harassment, in J. Hearn *et al.* (eds) *The Sexuality of Organization*. London: Sage.

Farley, L. (1978) *Sexual Shakedown*, London: Melbourne House.

Friedman, A.L. (1977) *Industry and Labour*. London: Macmillan.

Hartmann, H. (1981) The unhappy marriage of Marxism and feminism, in L. Sargent (ed.) *The Unhappy Marriage of Marxism and Feminism*. London: Pluto Press.

Hearn, J. (1985) Men's sexuality at work, in A. Metcalf and M. Humphries (eds) *The Sexuality of Men*. London: Pluto Press.

Hearn, J. (1987) *The Gender of Oppression: Men, Masculinity and the Critique of Marxism*. Brighton: Wheatsheaf.

Hearn, J. (ed.) (1989) Men, masculinities and leadership: changing patterns of new initiatives. *Equal Opportunities International*, special issue, 8–10.

Hearn, J. (1992) *Men in the Public Eye: The Construction and Deconstruction of Public Men and Public Patriarchies*. London: Routledge.

Hearn, J. (1994) Research in men and masculinities: some sociological issues and possibilities, *Australian and New Zealand Journal of Sociology*, 30(1): 47–70.

Hearn, J. and Parkin, W. (1987) *'Sex' at 'Work'. The Power and Paradox of Organisation Sexuality*. Brighton: Wheatsheaf.

Hearn, J., Sheppard, D., Tancred-Sheriff P. and Burrell, G. (eds) (1989) *The Sexuality of Organisation*. London: Sage.

Henriques, J., Hollway, W., Urwin, C., Venn, C. and Walkerdine, V. (1984) *Changing the Subject*. London: Methuen.

Henwood, M., Rimmer, L. and Wicks, M. (1987) *Inside the Family: Changing Roles of Men and Women*. London: Family Policy Studies Centre.

Hyman, R. (1987) Strategy or structure? capital, labour and control, *Work, Employment and Society*, 1(1): 25–55.

Jackall, R. (1988) *Moral Mazes: The World of Corporate Managers*. New York: Oxford University Press.

Kanter, R.M. (1977) *Men and Women of the Corporation*. New York: Basic Books.

Knights, D. and Willmott, H. (1986) *Managing the Labour Process*. Aldershot: Gower.

MacKinnon, C.A. (1979) *The Sexual Harassment of Working Women*. New Haven, CT: Yale University Press.

Massey, D. (1993) Scientists, transcendence and the work/home boundary, in J. Wajcman (ed.) *Organization, Gender and Power: Papers from our IRRU Workshop*, Warwick Papers in Industrial Relations, 48: 17–25.

Morgan, D.H.J. (1992) *Discovering Men*. London: Routledge.

Oakley, A. (1985) *Sociology of Housework*. Oxford: Basil Blackwell.

Podmore, D. and Spencer, A. (eds) (1987) *In a Man's World*. London: Tavistock.

Pringle, R. (1989) *Secretaries Talk*. London: Verso.

Rogers, B. (1988) *Men Only. An Investigation into Men's Organizations*. London: Pandora.

Roper, M. (1993) *Masculinity and the British Organization Man, 1945 to the Present*. Oxford: Oxford University Press.

Rowbotham, S. (1979) The trouble with patriarchy, *New Statesman*, 98(2344/5): 970–1.

Sennett, R. and Cobb, J. (1977) *The Hidden Injuries of Class*. Cambridge: Cambridge University Press.

Walby, S. (1986) *Patriarchy at Work*. Cambridge: Polity Press.

Walby, S. (1990) *Theorizing Patriarchy*. Oxford: Basil Blackwell.

Walker, C. R. and Guest, R. H. (1952) *The Man on the Assembly Line*. Cambridge, MA: Harvard University Press.

Walter, J. A. (1979) *A Long Way from Home*. Exeter: Paternoster Press.

Watson, T. J. (1994) *In Search of Management*. London: Routledge.

Whyte, W. H. (1956) *The Organization Man*. New York: Simon and Schuster.

Willis, P. (1977) *Learning to Labour*. London: Saxon House.

Wise, S. and Stanley, L. (1987) *Georgie Porgie: Sexual Harassment in Everyday Life*. London: Pandora.

Men, masculinity and the challenge of long-term unemployment

Introduction

Traditional discourses of masculinity describe the man as the member of the household who goes out and makes a living (see, for example, Bernard 1981; Hood 1986). Paid employment, as a means both of making money and of getting out of the house, is therefore likely to be an important anchor for traditional masculine identities (Morgan 1992). Unemployment, on the other hand, decreases a man's ability to provide for himself and his family – if he has one. It typically also affects where he spends his time (Morgan 1992). Because of this, unemployment at least potentially provides a challenge to traditional masculine identities. This chapter explores the ways in which unemployed men position themselves in relation to established discourses of masculinity.

Social science approaches

To date, relatively little research has looked specifically at unemployment and masculinities. Fryer and Payne (1986) identified three main theories from mainstream psychological research on unemployment. The stage theory approach, initially proposed by Eisenberg and Lazarsfeld (1938), has seen a plethora of studies concerned with the various stages of psychological 'adjustment' that unemployed men move through over time. Kelvin and Jarrett (1985) criticize the simplistic use of stages and prefer to concentrate on the critical transition between each stage. In Fryer's opinion, however, the 'stage' literature has been largely discredited. Jahoda *et al.* (1933; 1982) championed the function and need theory (see also Warr 1983), or what Fryer prefers to call 'the deprivation hypothesis'. According to Fryer, the Jahoda model has dominated the literature. Fryer's more recent approach differs quite markedly from the first two, drawing on a conceptualization of the contextualized individual as an active agent. Despite making a significant contribution towards contemporary understandings of unemployment, all these theories have one thing in common: individual experience features as the main focus of explanation. Unemployment has usually been related to attitudes, self-image and sex-role socialization (see, for example, Bartell and Bartell 1985; Kelvin and Jarrett 1985). Even Jahoda's use of institutional economics operated from a perspective which made predictions about the ways in which unemployed individuals might be affected by degrees of poverty. This individualistic focus has tended to operate at the expense of developing accounts at the social level (Brotherton 1986).

Sociological studies of unemployment illustrate a greater awareness of the social and historical dynamics within the construction of 'roles' (see, for example, Sinfield 1981; McKee and Bell 1986). However, despite the fact that most research on the effects of unemployment has focused on male unemployment (for example Marsden and Duff 1975), there is little problematization or deconstruction of issues around masculinities and unemployment within the research literature (Morgan 1992). Moreover, there appears to be a reticence to integrate findings into a cohesive theoretical framework with reference to power relations around gender, despite a growing feminist literature in this area (Segal 1990). In summary, then, we suggest that the majority of studies about unemployed men have concerned themselves with men as the implicit norm, but not with men as gendered and relational beings, and there has often been an implicit assumption that unemployment has more profound social and psychological effects for men than for women (Henwood and Miles 1987).

The rising unemployment of the 1980s, which hit those who were working class, black and young particularly hard, posed something of a challenge for social science researchers. Many looked back to the 1930s, including some social psychologists, who reassessed the work of Marie Jahoda, Paul Lazarsfeld and others on the impact of long-term male unemployment in Marienthal (Jahoda *et al.* 1933; see Fineman 1987 and Fryer and Ullah 1987 for contemporary reviews of Jahoda's work). Whilst an uncritical focus solely on the experiences of unemployed men was beginning to be acknowledged as a problem by the mid-1980s, this was sometimes remedied by token coverage of unemployed women's lives (for example Henwood and Miles 1987), or by the occasional apologetic sentence about the lack of research about women's unemployment (Hayes and Nutman 1981). Analyses of the gendered connotations of unemployment for men have been far less common.

Some researchers have taken a more critical approach to the potential implications of rising unemployment for dominant forms of masculinity. Drawing on feminist and Marxist analyses, they have argued that changing patterns of unemployment amongst young working-class women and men might have profound effects on heterosexual and marital relationships outside the job market. In 1984, Paul Willis argued that the prolonged period of high youth unemployment in Britain was breaking down the traditional transition from school to the job market for young working-class people. In addition, the lack of a male wage and the increasing independence of some groups of young working-class women disrupted the 'normal' path into heterosexual relationships, marriage and nuclear family life, if not into parenthood. Young unemployed working-class men, both black and white, Willis argued, made less 'attractive' prospects as husbands and long-term heterosexual partners (Willis 1984). A number of feminist researchers have considered the implications of Willis's thesis for young women, and have examined the potential impact of female unemployment for young women's experiences of sexuality, leisure, family life and the move from school to the job market (for example Griffin 1985; Wallace 1987).

By the late 1980s, cuts in government funding for social science research, a powerful backlash against radical (i.e. Marxist, feminist, anti-racist) analyses and the rising influences of post-structuralism and postmodern critiques of ethnographic and other qualitative studies combined to curtail research of this kind. Long-term unemployment rates did not fall back alongside radical research, however, although debates about the relationship between unemployment and masculinity, as exemplified by Willis's work, gradually waned during the late 1980s. The early 1990s saw a resurgent interest amongst academics and publishers in studies of men and masculinity, especially by 'pro-feminist' male scholars (see Wetherell and Griffin 1991 and Griffin and Wetherell 1992 for reviews). However, relatively little of this work has considered men's experiences of unemployment (one exception is Morgan 1992; see also Connell 1991).

Theorizing unemployment and masculinities

Having sketched a brief history of the research to date around issues of unemployment and masculinity, we now turn to our own approach to this area. Using a theoretical framework which draws on feminist theory and a combination of post-structuralist and grounded analyses, we explore the process of renegotiating masculine identities for a group of adult working-class men who are long-term unemployed. We understand gender categories to be social and historical constructs, constantly renegotiated within and in relation to other systems of inequality such as 'race', sexuality, class and age. As such, masculinity cannot be presented uncritically as a monolithic and unitary entity. Rather, there are a multiplicity of masculinities in any sociohistorical context (for example, see Chapman and Rutherford 1988) and we therefore prefer to use the term 'masculinities' where this is grammatically appropriate.

Despite this discursive plurality, we also recognize that power is the central dynamic in this relational process (Segal 1990). Consequently, certain discourses of masculinity are hegemonic or culturally ascendant. They constitute the implicit yardstick by which the 'Other' is judged, and those 'Others' include women, the feminine and less powerful forms of masculinity which are subordinate by virtue of 'race', class, age, sexuality and/or disability. According to Connell (1987: 184), 'hegemony' refers to 'a social ascendency achieved in a play of social forces that extends beyond contests of brute power into the organisation of private life and cultural processes'. The term should not be employed simplistically to denote a straightforward hierarchy of 'categories' (see Morgan 1992). Rather, hegemonic definitions are constructed in a complex and constantly shifting relationship to whatever the definition excludes. For example, in the present sociohistorical context, white, middle-class, heterosexual, employed males are considered to be the 'norm'. The good news here is that there is necessarily resistance to that which is culturally ascendant; hegemonic definitions are continually contested by those they subordinate. Another piece of bad news, however, is that despite the challenge posed by these contradictions, they do not necessarily undermine existing power relations (Connell 1993).

We would argue then, that men do not simply 'choose' between rejecting or conforming to traditional masculine roles. Our argument is that certain 'available' discourses and structures constrain both the issues which are seen as important and the ways in which men position themselves in relation to those specific issues. Discourses define the issues that are constructed as relevant for a group even if certain individuals within that group reject that 'opinion'. For example, the unemployed men in our study talked about unemployment as equivalent to 'scrounging off the state'. As unemployed men, they were negatively positioned in relation to this discourse. It was hardly surprising, therefore, that every discussant was careful to reject the potential accusation that *they* were a scrounger. The individual unemployed man can thus be thought of as inhabiting a unique discursive niche (Parker 1992), positioned dynamically within a web of available discourses.

The study

In a series of unstructured group discussions with men experiencing long-term unemployment, one of the authors (SW, who is white, middle class and female) examined ways in which a marginalized group of men positioned themselves in relation to hegemonic discourses of masculinity. The discussions took place in a region of the West Midlands, England, which is geographically isolated by a system of motorways and dominated by one of the largest public housing estates in Europe. The official unemployment rate is relatively high (18.3 per cent in 1992), with associated levels of economic and social deprivation, and poor local travel, shopping and leisure facilities.

Discussion group participants were all attending a mandatory two-week course for the 'long-term unemployed' (i.e. those officially registered as unemployed for over two years). Employment Services see such courses as a means of motivating the long-term unemployed, and hence as a potential 'springboard' back into the job market. For participants the courses are compulsory, and they tend to view such schemes as more of an imposition than as an aid, and attend only with some reluctance.

Employment Services encourage course facilitators to nudge the participants on to one of the numerous Employment Training schemes, but unemployed people remain unconvinced and tend to regard this type of manoeuvre as a government strategy to massage the unemployment figures downwards (MacDonald 1994). The facilitator on this particular course created a safe space for the group to vent their feelings of anger with regard to their unemployed position. It was in this context that SW built sufficient trust with members of the group to request a recorded discussion.

Transcripts of these interviews were analysed using a method which drew on a Foucauldian type of discourse analysis (for example, Parker 1990) and constructivist grounded analysis (Henwood and Pidgeon 1992) within a feminist framework. This combination of methods provided a systematic means of exploring our data but also left us free to examine the discursive patterns that we identified from a critical perspective.

Patterns of discourse around masculinity and unemployment

We have suggested that unemployment could threaten the stability of a traditional masculine identity constructed around discourses such as bringing home a wage and freedom from the domestic sphere. We have identified such discourses as that of domestic provision and public masculinity respectively. We would expect that these kinds of discourses would be salient to men experiencing unemployment. In addition, it seems likely that unemployed men would voice a feeling of inadequacy or failure to meet the hegemonic criteria of manhood.

In the remainder of this chapter, we will discuss several recurrent patterns of discourses around unemployment and masculinities. We will do this with reference to existing literature and to our recent empirical study mentioned above. Although we discuss these discourses under separate headings, they are interwoven in complex and often contradictory ways. First of all, we explore two of the most common patterns of discourse in the construction of masculine identities, those concerned with 'public masculinity' and 'domestic provision'. We then examine how unemployed men talk about the conflict between consumption in the pub and breadwinning for the family. Finally we look at a common discursive strategy for resolving this conflict. Most of the men we interviewed were white, working-class, heterosexual adults, although the discussion groups included a few women from a similar background. We do not assume that all aspects of these men's experiences would be shared by unemployed men from other groups and social positions.

Public masculinity

Lee: *When you settle down you end up opening her purse and going out on your jack. You end up going out on your jack in the end, leaving the missus behind and the kids, and have a few.*

Lee: *With the arguments and stuff like that. I've seen a lot of blokes who take their missus out and end up giving them a hiding like, which I think is out of order, personally.*
Jan: *Especially when she's gone to the trouble to get ready.*
Lee: *And a lot of the time like, my missus chooses not to go out. My missus hardly ever goes out, but that's from her choice.*

Traditionally, employment has meant that a man will be out of the house for most of the day. It also finances activities that get him out of the house at other times; men in our study frequently bemoaned not being able to afford to spend time in the pub. Unemployment therefore not only altered what the men did, but also challenged their masculine identity. For example, in the extracts above, Lee talks about women 'choosing' to stay at home in the domestic sphere and men needing the freedom to escape to the public sphere. The home is associated with 'the missus and the kids', the sphere of arguments which could literally follow a man to the pub in the form of his wife, possibly leading him to give her 'a hiding'. The latter is to be condemned, 'especially when she's gone to the trouble to get ready', but this discursive pattern provides the justification for the man's 'escape' from the domestic sphere to the pub, that quintessential realm of *pub*lic masculinity.

This ideological separation between men and women in terms of spatial location has a long cultural history, such that the public sphere is associated with men and masculinity, and the private sphere with women and children, femininity and domesticity. However, it is a construction which remains fundamental to the definition of hegemonic masculinities in the west. Gamarnikow *et al.* (1983) describe the separation between 'male' and 'female' spheres as 'the most basic social division of patriarchy' (p. 3). This division inevitably entails an association with power relations, which is normally translated as the private being subservient to the public sphere. The political theorist Elshtain (1981) traces the historical emergence and fluctuations around the notions of public and private spheres from the birth of politics in early Greek civilization. The *polis* was set up in contrast to the necessary but subservient *oikos* (private household) with slaves and women silenced as far as public discourse issues were concerned. The persistence of the public/domestic distinction has been documented by numerous researchers (such as Rosaldo *et al.* 1974). The increasing separation between the (waged) workplace and the household during the Industrial Revolution became a vital ingredient in the development of contemporary gender relations in the west (Bland *et al.* 1978). This resulted in a parallel move from the private power of the father to a more public, state patriarchy (Hearn 1987, 1992). Unemployed men are not only less able to participate in the public sphere than their employed peers, they also talk about an invasion of the home and about feeling under surveillance by the state (McKee and Bell 1986).

The clearest examples of the discourse of public masculinity occurred when men (and in this case a woman) made comparisons between their lives on the dole and those of their male counterparts with jobs:

Neil: *Most working blokes spend at least one night every week in the pub, whereas it don't happen when you're on the dole. So you lose a lot of friends and stuff like that, from not going into the pub.*

Madge: *I'll tell you what it [waged work] does for the men. If they go out casual, it gives them that bit of independence.*
Frank: *Yeah, correct.*
Mike: *It's true.   [Madge, Nick and Frank repeat the same themes here]*
Nick: *I think a man feels better like, but he's got to pay his own way. It's worth having a few shillings in his pocket for a drink, you know.*

Unemployed men are officially denied access to the workplace environment, but the public sphere includes more than the workplace. The pub is an important cultural arena for the expression and reinforcement of traditional masculinities. Unemployed men also experience restricted access to the pub, the importance of which can be linked to the ideology of (public) consumption (Morgan 1992; Wight 1993).

Having been deprived of a place at work, feeling 'out of place' at home, and unable to afford to spend more time in the pub, unemployed men talk about occupying the urban street area. This observation may well be class specific and it certainly applied to the working-class men in our recent study. Morgan (1992) made a similar point in a review of the interwar studies of unemployment. For example, in the Marienthal study Jahoda *et al.* (1933) talk about women hurrying through the now-alien street space, which had been rendered alien by the presence of unemployed men. Willis (1984), on the other hand, notes that young working-class unemployed males located themselves in the high street. According to Willis, this group resisted the consumerist hegemony by becoming publicly motionless consumers. Bhavnani (1991) has made a similar point about young working-class women and men of diverse ethnicity and their use of public spaces such as shopping malls. This observation may well apply mainly to young unemployed people in the west who are unemployed or on the margins of the labour market.

For some unemployed men, it was their wives that appeared to propel them out of the house and into the street if they could not afford to go to the pub:

John: *After a certain time, she started 'why don't you go out?', you know. I was under her feet in the end.*
Larry: *They're happy at first.*
John: *Well yeah, at the beginning it was OK. But in the end I'd find meself going for a walk say, from here to the airport, going out for three hours, just walking, just to get out the house.*

The power to control one's own (and others') activities in the public sphere stems in part from the financial and social kudos associated with a job. If a man has no job and little money, he loses a degree of control over his own ability to 'go out' when he wants. If his partner has a job, she will be seen to have a power that he has lost, although this does not imply that women in waged work *are* accorded that 'freedom' of access to the (male-dominated) public sphere. The autonomy to move as a free and independent agent in the public sphere outside the home and the job is heavily gendered, and a focus of some contestation between women and men:

Gavin: *If she gives the word when she gets home 'I'm going out at the weekend' and you goes 'who with like?', and she turns round and says 'you can't stop me because it's my money, I'm earning it, it's my money' [repeats]. When you're sitting at home watching the telly you're thinking 'look at the time, she's still out like, where is she and that like?' It all boils round in your head like and the next thing you get on to is 'she's seeing someone else now, it's two o'clock in the morning like', you know what I mean. She buys you a four-pack.*

The fear that their wives would 'fine someone else' (with a job) was common amongst the men we interviewed. The close relationship between the discourses of public masculinity and domestic provision are illustrated particularly well by the scenario recounted by Gavin above.

Domestic provision

Alex: *I went to parents evening the other night and the teacher said 'can I bring up the subject of your daughter's PE kit?' I said 'what about it?' She said 'she hasn't got one'. I said 'it's the first I've heard about it'. [Alex repeats this] The point I'm trying to make is that a child of ten shouldn't have to worry about 'my Dad's not at work at the moment and we can't afford this and we can't afford that'.*

Traditionally, employment means that a man will earn a wage and be expected to bring this back to the home. This salary usually means that he can afford to both provide domestically and pay his way at the pub. A second recurrent discourse noted from a reading of existing literature as well as the men we interviewed, was the expectation that a 'good' family man will provide financially for 'the missus and the kids'.

Alex: *The main thing is, it's the same as everyone else, providing things for your children, a holiday really, simple things like that, which we haven't had one for three or four years. And, erm, it basically silly things like that. And school uniforms.*

Alex was typical of most of the men in our study, in that he saw male breadwinners as providing luxuries such as gifts, holidays and treats, in addition to the basics of food, clothes and shelter. Bernard (1981) has argued that there has, over the last few decades, been an escalation in what should be provided by the man as breadwinner. This escalation is closely linked to an ideology of consumption mentioned above, and to what Kelvin and Jarrett (1985) label as a 'wealth ethic'.

The source of provision does have some importance, however. The position of (male) breadwinner is associated not only with economic independence, but also social status and 'respect'. This sometimes appeared in constructions of the men's wives as pressurizing them into low paid jobs in order to gain this form of 'respect'.

Nige: *She understands in a certain way, but she keeps going on about respect. She keeps going on at me to get a low paid job. Just get a job and get the respect of the street. She knows full well that I'd be worse off.*

The implication of this pattern of discourses around domestic provision for unemployed men is a potential feeling of disempowerment and emasculation. The connection between failing to provide and feeling less of a man coincides with talk of failing to provide and losing 'your' woman:

Gavin: *If your partner goes to work, you're always, depending on what job she does, you're always thinking well, 'I'm unemployed like, I can't give her the things she wants, I can't buy her the things she wants. But there's someone out there that's got a job, got money. And all he's got to do is wave a few wads in her hand like, and she'll walk away with him.*

Although the concept of the male breadwinner has been discussed in sociological studies of unemployment (for example, see Bakke 1933; Komarovsky 1940; Bernard 1981; Sinfield 1981), there has been little deconstruction or problematization of this concept in relation to masculinities (Morgan 1992). The upper-middle-class bourgeois ideal of the man as sole economic provider emerged by the middle of the nineteenth century. Contributing to the emergence of this phenomenon was a complex interplay of factors such as Victorian individualism and a transition to market economies (see Land 1980; Bernard 1981; Hood 1986). The construct of the male economic provider (and its flipside of the woman as nurturant housewife/mother) continued into twentieth-century society, and was reflected in Keynesian fiscal policy and Beveridge's state benefit system (Wheelock 1990).

There has been a decrease in the proportion of households with men as the sole or main breadwinners since the 1960s and 70s (Bernard 1981). This has been attributed to a combination of factors such as second-wave feminism, an increasing number of women entering the labour market and an increasing number of men becoming unemployed. Bernard argues that despite these changes, a 'legitimate successor [to the position of male breadwinner] has not yet appeared on the scene' (p. 12). With the increase in adult male unemployment has come two associated conflicts or contradictions: between the continuing dominance of the male breadwinner discourse and the decrease in the proportion of men who are main or sole breadwinners; and between the discourses of the man as provider for 'the wife and kids' and the public position of men outside of the home and the workplace – in the pub. In addition, dominant discourses of masculinity have not kept pace with recent changes in women's lives (Segal 1990).

Contradictory discourses of masculinity: the good provider and the *pub*lic man

An increase in structural unemployment for men presents a growing disparity between dominant discourses such as that of the male breadwinner and actual employment patterns. Being unemployed creates a tension between domestic provision in the home and paying your way in the pub. A 'good' family man is supposed to put his missus and kids first in a situation of limited resources.

Bill: *It's not so much for yourself, you can go without yourself, but the woman and kid. If they haven't got their things, that's what causes the arguments. I went without for 12 months, I never got nothing for myself.*

Some men (such as Bill) stated that they resented 'going without', but did so to avoid arguments at home. This can be contrasted with the close association between self-sacrifice and femininity in discourses around motherhood and wifely duty for women (Gilligan 1977). An alternative to this grudgingly 'heroic' self-deprivation is the other extreme – the 'bad' family man. In the extract below, Madge describes a scenario in which the fortnightly giro cheque (social security benefit) is delivered directly to the pub so that the unemployed man can 'drink' it. This would be the ultimate escape from the domestic sphere:

Madge: *You just don't go out, you lose your respect really, not providing.*
You get the giro. I think a feller with a family, a feller could get the
giro and say 'that's mine and I'm off'.
Will: *A few people do that.*
Madge: *A few people do it, they sit in the pub and get the postman bring*
the giro to the pub, and they say, 'don't tell the wife'. They'll go
home and say 'we haven't had it', and then the wife and kids
starve. And that's true that is. Go over to [local pub] sometimes on
a Thursday, Tuesdays and Thursdays mainly, and the postman
will go in and they'll look for them, look for the fellers and give
them the giro and they're there. They'll go home and say 'hasn't
me giro come?'
John: *That's right, yeah. I know people like that.*

The 'work hard, play hard' ethos is not seen to be problematic in a situation of adequate financial resources, but it introduces almost unmanageable conflicts for an unemployed man. 'Drinking' the giro and pretending to 'the wife' that it has not arrived is represented as the behaviour of a 'bad' family man, and this possibility was raised by one of the few female participants on the scheme. The men in her discussion group did admit that such 'bad family men' might exist. Elsewhere in the discussions, participants argued that such behaviour was understandable in the circumstances. The rationale goes something like this: merely because the ability to work hard has been removed from a man, does not mean that his 'right' to go out and 'play hard' should also be totally removed. This is a 'right' that women were not assumed to have, either as waged workers outside the home or as a respite from unpaid housework and childcare.

Coping with the challenge of long-term unemployment

Given that structural unemployment magnifies a tension between the discourses of public masculinity and domestic provision, the unemployed men we interviewed drew on various strategies that appeared to resolve or at least to address this set of discursive contradictions. We argued in our introduction that individuals can be thought of as inhabiting a discursive niche (Parker 1992). We would also argue that people are constructed and are agents upon macrostructures and social policies, as well as microstructures such as interpersonal interactions. In addition, patterns of discourse used to construct gendered identities are interwoven with discourses and structures around other systems of oppression such as class. This complex and dynamic relationship between discursive and structural patterns serves as a constraint upon change. When someone is forced to reposition themselves discursively, this process is therefore both unique and constrained.

Given these structural and discursive constraints, a range of alternative positions can be taken up by unemployed working-class men. This repositioning or reconstruction of masculine identities, initiated by challenges such as unemployment, may not pose a significant threat to hegemonic forms of masculinity. For example, some of the men in our study placed themselves in women's positions when talking about the traditionally 'female' areas of housework and childcare. This discursive move could have undermined the traditional location of men in the public sphere and women in the private world of the home. Women's unpaid domestic work could then be validated as 'just as hard' (as men's waged work) if men positioned themselves as doing 'women's work':

Nige: *I know what it's like for a woman to look after kids, I do it now. But I still wanna go out to work. You work just as hard, looking after the kids, from cooking to cleaning, well I do.*

Although Nige admits that 'women's work' is as hard as men's, he still talks about housework and childcare as poor alternatives to work outside the home. There were other instances in which men in our recent study positioned themselves (or other men) as women or in roles traditionally performed by women, but with very different implications. This represented men as better women than women themselves: a common theme in films such as *Tootsie*, *Mrs Doubtfire* and *Junior*, and an important element in the patriarchal backlash against feminism:

Will: *Most blokes nowadays are more domesticated than women are. I speak to some blokes, who can handle their kids more than women can. Some women go 'argh, argh'. Serious, some women just can't handle the kids.*

Ray: *And the babee's screaming, the babee comes to you instead of the mum like, arguments like.*

However, the most common strategy used in response to the crushing effects associated with long-term unemployment is to re-establish traditional forms of masculine identity using 'powerful' patterns of discourse. For working-class unemployed men in the west, talk and action around 'fiddling' the system or 'thieving' can serve this purpose (see Wight 1993; MacDonald 1994). These individual survival strategies resist the potential damage to masculine pride posed by long-term unemployment, but they pose little challenge to traditional gender/power relations.

Frank: *I've done some casual, and it don't satisfy yer. But I'll tell you something it does do for yer, it gets you off your arse and cos you enjoy going to work it puts you . . .*

Madge: *And puts food in the table.*
Nick: *It pays the bills don't it?*
Ray: *Yeah.*
Frank: *You're not walking round the house and you're not getting around your missus and the child, you're going out and doing something. Whether you have to get up at five or six o'clock in the morning, you enjoy doing it.*

Summary

In this chapter we have begun to explore the complex relationships between long-term unemployment and masculinities. We did this with reference to both existing literature and through discussions with groups of unemployed working-class men. To some extent our study supports Paul Willis's thesis that long-term male unemployment undermines the basis of hegemonic forms of masculinity, with implications for heterosexual relationships and the domestic sphere as well as the prolonged 'leisure' time that unemployment brings (Willis 1984). Talk of masculinity, for the men in our study, tended to be anchored to ideas about getting out of the house and bringing home a sufficient amount of money to be economically independent of the state. Unemployment served to undermine hegemonic masculinities at various 'sites', especially the home and the pub. Unemployed men may therefore experience feelings of disempowerment and emasculation. However, the aggregate power of men over women should be distinguished from individually felt powerlessness (Brod and Kaufman 1994). Hegemonic masculinity is constructed in relation to subordinated masculinities (in addition to femininities). Therefore, the contradictions associated with being white and male (and therefore powerful) but also working-class and unemployed are complex and profound. Resistance to felt powerlessness, usually in the form of casual work in the informal economy, can serve to bolster a male identity constructed with reference to the hegemonic. The men in this study talked about these activities as getting a man out of the house and enabling him to earn financially.

One issue which has been discussed amongst masculinity theorists revolves around the terms 'crisis' and 'change'. Long-term unemployment could be seen to pose a challenge for dominant forms of masculinity, but our study indicates that this is not the case for this group of working-class men. One reason for this may be that discourses of masculinity and unemployment restrict the social and psychological possibilities for unemployed men. In particular, we would suggest that the subordination of working-class men (and women) under patriarchal capitalism constrains potential avenues of discursive renegotiation in situations of long-term unemployment. Pro-feminist alternatives appeared to be less available to the men we interviewed.

The latter may be more relevant for their female partners or for unemployed women – but that is another study. What *is* challenged and undermined by long-term unemployment is a particular form of hegemonic masculinity which rests on the provider (or 'breadwinner') discourse and that of public masculinity. These discourses position adult males as the sole or main breadwinner in households, regardless of whether this is the case for all or most of the men in our study.

Undermining a particular hegemonic form of masculinity does not necessarily empower women and nor does it automatically pose a profound challenge to patriarchal power, since masculinities are always located in multiple systems of domination based around class, 'race' and sexuality as well as gender. African-American feminists and radical men, for example, have considered in depth the possibility of a black masculinity which is not patriarchal but that has a role in African-American families. High levels of unemployment and the legacy of slavery have disenfranchised and marginalized African-American men both as black Americans and as men, but a simple reassertion of hegemonic forms of macho pride and heterosexual boasting has no positive implications for African-American women (Davis 1981). Long-term unemployment is unlikely to have identical implications for Anglo- and African-American men, for example, or for white and black (i.e. African-Caribbean) British men. At another level, the 'masculinity' of large groups of men in a given society can be undermined through poverty, unemployment and other means with minimal impact on the hegemonic discourses of white, upper-class, heterosexual masculine power or on the dominant position of men in those elite groups.

According to Brittan (1989), although the 'breadwinner ethic' may have collapsed among a large proportion of the North American middle classes, it is only the form of male power that has changed. This observation is supported by Segal (1990), who points out that paternal unemployment does not necessarily lead to increased sharing of household responsibilities by men (see also Messner 1993). Our research indicates that men discuss unemployment in terms that imply a degree of emasculation, but that this does not necessarily coincide with any challenge to dominant forms of masculinity, nor any shifts towards more pro-feminist alternatives.

References

Bakke, E.W. (1933) *The Unemployed Man*. London: Nisbett.

Bartell, M. and Bartell, R. (1985) An integrative perspective on the psychological response of women and men to unemployment, *Journal of Economic Psychology*, 6: 27–49.

Bernard, J. (1981) The good-provider role: its rise and fall, *American Psychologist*, 36(1): 1–12.

Bhavnani, K.-K. (1991) *Talking Politics: A Psychological Framing for Views from Youth in Britain*. Cambridge: Cambridge University Press.

Bland, L., Brunsdon, C., Hobson, D. and Winship, D. (1978) Women 'inside' and 'outside' the relations of production, in Women Studies Group (eds) *Women Take Issue: Aspects of Women's Subordination*. London: Hutchinson.

Brittan, A. (1989) *Masculinity and Power*. Oxford: Basil Blackwell.

Brod, H. and Kaufman, M. (eds) (1994) *Theorizing Masculinities*. Thousand Oaks, CA: Sage.

Brotherton, C. (1986) Book review of Kelvin and Jarrett's 'Unemployment: Its Social Psychological Effects', *Journal of Occupational Psychology*, 59: 155–60.

Chapman, R. and Rutherford, J. (eds) (1988) *Male Order: Unwrapping Masculinity*. London: Lawrence and Wishart.

Connell, R.W. (1987) *Gender and Power*. Oxford: Polity Press.

Connell, R.W. (1991) Live fast and die young: the construction of masculinity among young working-class men on the margins of the labour market, *Australian and New Zealand Journal of Sociology*, 27(2): 141–71.

Connell, R.W. (1993) The big picture: masculinities in recent world history, *Theory and Society*, 22: 597–623.

Davis, A. (1981) *Women, Race and Class*. London: Womens Press.

Eisenberg, P. and Lazarsfeld, P.F. (1938) The psychological effects of unemployment, *Psychological Bulletin*, 35: 358–90.

Elshtain, J.B. (1981) *Public Man, Private Woman: Women in Social and Political Thought*. Oxford: Princeton University Press.

Fineman, S. (1987) *Unemployment: Personal and Social Consequences*. London: Tavistock.

Fryer, D. and Payne, R. (1986) Being unemployed: a review of the literature on the psychological experience of unemployment, in C.C. Cooper and I. Robertson (eds) *International Review of Industrial and Organisational Psychology*. London: Wiley.

Fryer, D. and Ullah, P. (eds) (1987) *Unemployed People: Social and Psychological Perspectives*. Milton Keynes: Open University Press.

Gamarnikow, E., Morgan, D., Purvis, J. and Taylorson, D. (eds) (1983) *The Public and the Private*. London: Heinemann.

Gilligan, C. (1977) In a different voice: women's conceptions of self and of morality, *Harvard Educational Review*, 47(4): 481–517.

Griffin, C. (1985) Turning the tables: feminist analyses of youth unemployment, *Youth and Policy*, 14: 16–11.

Griffin, C. and Wetherell, M. (1992) Feminist psychology and the study of men and masculinity. Part 2: politics and practices, *Feminism and Psychology*, 2(2): 133–68.

Hayes, J. and Nutman, P. (1981) *Understanding the Unemployed: The Psychological Effects of Unemployment*. London: Tavistock.

Hearn, J. (1987) *The Gender of Oppression: Men, Masculinity and the Critique of Marxism*. Brighton: Wheatsheaf Books.

Hearn, J. (1992) *Men in the Public Eye*. London: Routledge.

Henwood, F. and Miles, I. (1987) The experience of unemployment and the sexual division of labour, in D. Fryer and P. Ullah (eds) *Unemployed People: Social and Psychological Perspectives*. Milton Keynes: Open University Press.

Henwood, K.L. and Pidgeon, N.F. (1992) Qualitative research and psychological theorising, *British Journal of Psychology*, 83: 97–111.

Hood, J.C. (1986) The provider role: its meaning and measurement, *Journal of Marriage and the Family*, 48: 349–59.

Jahoda, M. (1982) *Employment and Unemployment: A Social-Psychological Analysis*. Cambridge: Cambridge University Press.

Jahoda, M., Lazarsfeld, P.F. and Zeisel, H. (1933) *Marienthal: The Sociology of an Unemployed Community*. London: Tavistock.

Kelvin, P. and Jarrett, J.E. (1985) *Unemployment: Its Social Psychological Effects*. Cambridge: Cambridge University Press.

Komarovsky, M. (1940) *The Unemployed Man and his Family*. New York: Dryden Press.

Land, H. (1980) The family wage, *Feminist Review*, 6: 55–78.

MacDonald, R. (1994) Fiddly jobs, undeclared working and the something for nothing society, *Work, Employment and Society*, 8(4): 507–30.

Marsden, D. and Duff, E. (1975) *Workless: Unemployed Men and their Families*. London: Routledge.

McKee, L. and Bell, C. (1986) His unemployment, her problem: the domestic and marital consequences of male unemployment, in Allen, S., Watson, A., Purcell, K. and Wood, S. (eds) *The Experience of being Unemployed*. Basingstoke: Macmillan.

Messner, M.A. (1993) 'Changing Men' and feminist politics in the United States, *Theory and Society*, 22: 723–37.

Morgan, D.H.J. (1992) *Discovering Men*. London: Routledge.

Parker, I. (1990) Discourse: definitions and contradictions, *Philosophical Psychology*, 3(2): 189–203.

Parker, I. (1992) *Discourse Dynamics: Critical Analysis for Social and Individual Psychology*. London: Routledge.

Rosaldo, M.Z. and Lamphere, L. (eds) (1974) *Women, Culture and Society*. Stanford, CA: Stanford University Press.

Segal, L. (1990) *Slow Motion: Changing Masculinities Changing Men*. London: Virago Press.

Sinfield, A. (1981) *What Unemployment Means*. Oxford: Martin Robertson.

Wallace, C. (1987) *For Richer, For Poorer: Growing Up In and Out of Work*. London: Tavistock.

Warr, P. (1983) Work, jobs and unemployment, *Bulletin of the British Psychological Society*, 36: 305–11.

Warren, C. (1988) *Gender Issues in Field Research*, Qualitative Research Methods Series. No. 9. Newbury Park, CA: Sage.

Wetherell, M. and Griffin, C. (1991) Feminist psychology and the study of men and masculinity. Part 1: assumptions and perspectives. *Feminism and Psychology*, 1(3): 361–91.

Wheelock, J. (1990) *Husbands at Home: The Domestic Economy in a Post-Industrial Society*. London: Routledge.

Wight, D. (1993) *Workers not Wasters. Masculine Respectability, Consumption and Unemployment in Central Scotland: A Community Study*. Edinburgh: Edinburgh University Press.

Willis, P. (1984) Youth unemployment: thinking the unthinkable, *Youth and Policy*, 2(4): 17–36.

Part 2

Cultural arenas of masculinities

countries. On both sides of the Atlantic concerns had been raised about the general state of the nations' men after the traumas of the American civil war and the Crimean war. Moreover, both nations were concerned to defend their interests abroad, and so the development of a new generation of fit and healthy young men, ready, if need be, to throw down their lives in the interests of their respective countries begins to make sense as a means of calming these national anxieties.

The equation of masculinity with physical strength and endurance has also played a significant role in the power struggles between the sexes. For example, Catherine Hall (1992) notes that in response to Mary Woll-stonecraft's famous book *Vindication of the Right of Women* in 1792, which called for the equal treatment of middle-class men and women, evangelical preachers in many British churches began talking from their pulpits about the 'natural' inequalities between the sexes. Women, they said, were naturally more delicate, fragile and morally weak; a fact which, they suggested, made women less well suited to the cut and thrust of business and politics.

By the mid-nineteenth century, ideas about the 'natural' differences between men and women were also being used to justify the dichotomization of men and women's work. Middle-class women became increasingly concentrated into less physical trades such as dressmaking, schoolteaching and the retail industry, whereas in working-class society, similar concerns lead to the exclusion of women from working underground (Hall 1992). Not long after, the concept of the 'family wage' appeared, first in Britain and then in America. Here, being a *real* man meant being able to support a wife and family without her having to earn a single penny. So even if she wanted to work, for him it became a matter of honour that she didn't.

Over the course of the last 300 years, a symbolic equation of women with nature and men with culture or civilization (Ortner 1974) has also had a tremendous impact in terms of the structure of power relations between the sexes. Men, it is often assumed (even today), are more rational or reasonable than women, who for their part are ruled over by their hearts or their emotions. It is men, therefore, who are seen as most likely to contribute to the enlightenment project and to the advancement of knowledge (Seidler 1989). Women, on the other hand, became identified as the enemy. To some, they appeared to threaten, not only the pursuit of knowledge, but also civilized society itself. Three centuries ago, this belief resulted in the brutal practice of burning 'witches' at the stake. It has also led to the domination of women by more subtle means: for instance, by forcing them into silence on account of men's supposedly privileged access to 'the truth' (Seidler 1989).

Perhaps by now it is becoming clear how a cultural perspective on men and masculinity helps illuminate the issue of men's power. Men have dominated over women, by and large, because they have managed to gain a stranglehold on *meaning*. What it means to be a man, what it means to be a woman; what jobs constitute men's work and what jobs constitute women's work. It is through the ability to control the ways in which society thinks about these things that has provided men with the basis of their power. This is not to suggest for one moment that women have been entirely absent from these negotiations. Indeed, it is almost certain that they have attempted to intervene, or fight their corner, at every possible opportunity. However, the point is that because men have dominated many of the key institutions which help to produce and recycle meaning (namely, the church, schools and, more recently, the media), it is usually their 'versions' of the world which, in the words of Clarke *et al.* (1981) 'command the greatest weight and influence [and] secrete the greatest legitimacy'.

Now at first sight this argument may make the cultural approach appear to be just as tautological as some of the others we have criticized. For it would seem to be suggesting that men have achieved their privileged position in society by dominating most of its key social institutions. However, in practice the process *is* circular, in the sense of being iterative. In a crude way, it occurs like a game of football in which, whenever one side scores, they are allowed to field an additional player. This means that although the match might begin even, as soon as either team gains an advantage, its chances of going further ahead are immediately increased. For a very long time now, the state of play in the game of men versus women is that the men have so many more players on the park that they can score goals almost at will.

Yet there is a danger here, though, of overstating the level of autonomy or agency which men enjoy. Men's collective interests and their disproportionate power and influence are not maintained through active and self-conscious male conspiracies. Certainly, as far as I [NE] can recall, my father never took me aside as a young boy and whispered 'Right, I'm going to tell you how to keep your mother and your sister down.' Instead, the processes by which men maintain their dominance are much more complex, indirect and subtle.

One of the main reasons why this is the case is because patriarchy, like any culture, does not declare its own partiality. It does not offer itself as just one sense-making system amongst others. Instead it presents itself as *the* way of seeing the world; as entirely natural, normal and straightforward. Therefore, it would appear entirely understandable if each new generation of young men saw nothing particularly strange or unfair about the kinds of lives that awaited them. Men wear the trousers, men earn the money; women do the dishes and women look after the babies. 'It's just a fact of life', they say. This also helps to explain the paradoxical fact that whilst many men might accept that they live in a largely male-dominated society, a high proportion of them do not *feel* themselves to be powerful (Lips 1981; Griffin 1991; Kaufman 1994).

But while we must recognize that patriarchy naturalizes men's power and privilege (especially) in the eyes of men themselves, it is wrong to assume that they are incapable of changing the cultures that define them. After all, we have already heard how throughout history various social groups have managed to advance their own interests through the successful manipulation of the masculine ideal. The fact of the matter is, of course, that, paradoxical as it might sound, men are simultaneously the producers and the products of culture; the masters and the slaves of ideology. Furthermore, as Gramsci (1971) points out, the rule or hegemony of a dominant culture is never absolute. In other words, it never fully achieves the position of being the only available way of making sense of an event or situation. Instead, it has to be continually defended against the challenges of other subordinate cultures.

We would like to end this chapter with a brief, and in many ways quite unspectacular, illustration of what this defensive work looks like in practice. It should serve to prove the point that while women and other 'minority' groups may be in a better position to see the power of men, it is by no means impossible for men themselves. In doing this we will be drawing upon a series of interviews with a small number of 17 to 18-year-old boys from a Midlands-based single-sex independent school, conducted between October 1991 and June 1994 (Wetherell and Edley 1993).

From the very first interview it was apparent that the sixth form of the school was divided into a number of separate and somewhat antagonistic groups. At the centre of these conflicts stood two quite large collections of boys; one widely acknowledged as the 'hard lads', and another who defined themselves largely in opposition to this group. The identity of the hard boys was mainly organized around the playing of sport (particularly rugby) as well as a whole set of other loud and boisterous activities such as play fighting, drinking and small-scale vandalism. As such, they would appear to represent the articulation or inhabitation of what has variously been called 'traditional' (Christian 1994), 'retributive' (Chapman and Rutherford 1988) or 'hegemonic' (Carrigan *et al.* 1985) masculinity, with its emphasis upon certain macho values such as physical strength, courage and toughness.

At the level of discourse, the domination of the hard boys was signified by the fact that they talked about school life as being fairly unremarkable. Indeed, a phrase which kept on being repeated was that school was just a series of 'good laughs'. People got hurt during some of their break-time games, one boy even broke his arm, but basically, for them, it was 'just a bit of fun'.

In contrast, the members of the 'opposing' group had a great deal to say about these 'rough-house' games. Indeed, half of the first interview with them was spent describing the behaviour of the hard lads. For them, such macho games were experienced, not as a bit of harmless fun, but as deeply marginalizing and oppressive. The power of the hard lads was obvious to them; it confronted them almost every day of their school lives. As a consequence, it was not just easier, but positively in their interests to 'deconstruct' the hard lads' interpretations, to open out or develop a more complex discourse of power and subordination. But perhaps the most significant fact is that, as we can see from the following extract, it was by no means impossible for members of the dominant group to accomplish this same type of deconstruction for themselves.

Adrian: *Actually it's good fun having the power that we do, like when we went on camp last year, you just tell them what to do and stuff and it's much better because the year before when I went on camp I was only a cadet and I went on camp and I was an NCO and I enjoyed it more because, it meant that I wasn't the one that had to get up at half five in the morning and I was the one that could lie in bed until seven and then push in front of everybody, get up in time for breakfast in front of everybody in the queue to get to the front and stuff like that. So that's what I enjoyed but then there's like some people that I think abuse it quite a lot like erm, they had the fire engines in here one day doing a fire display and they were spraying a hose, so all that corner by the chemistry rooms was completely flooded and they got like a little drain, it's like a little dip . . .*

Philip: *And they marched people in there and made them stop.*

Adrian: *Full of water yeah, they marched people in there . . . so you had one rank and you made them go at ease and go to attention and made them stamp in it as hard as they could so all the water flying up them, and then they'd move them a rank forward and do it again like that.*

Philip: *It's a laugh though isn't it? (laughs)*

Adrian: *Yeah, well the other thing they used to do . . . when I first joined, the NCOs used to make you do press-ups in puddles and stuff like that.*

Here we have Adrian talking explicitly about the pleasures of being macho. It's fun, he says, having the power to order the younger cadets around. It's fun pushing into the queue ahead of them just because you are of a more senior rank. He even starts to talk about the 'abuse' of such power, and goes on to describe an instance of where such an abuse occurred. But then look what happens. Philip attempts to re-present the episode as benign or harmless: 'It's a laugh though isn't it?' he suggests. 'Yeah' replies Adrian, accepting his re-formulation before going on to describe yet another episode.

It was all over in an instant. Hardly anyone batted an eyelid. But in that moment both of these young men declined an opportunity to 'take the side of the other' (Billig 1987), to reinterpret their oppressive activities in terms of a different, more critical perspective. But the point is that an opportunity was there. They were presented with a chance of challenging the ideological system which both privileges and produces them. Had they taken that chance it would have been a small, but not insignificant, victory against the continuation of male domination. For ultimately, patriarchy rests upon the day-to-day maintenance of such understandings.

Acknowledgements

The authors would like to acknowledge two very different kinds of debt. The first goes to the Economic and Social Research Council (grant no. R000233129), the Open University Research Committee and the Psychology Department of the Open University for the financial support they have given this research. The second vote of thanks goes to the staff and students of the school (whose anonymity we shall, of course, respect). Needless to say, without their kindness, cooperation and openness, such work as this would never get done.

References

Archer, J. and Lloyd, B. (1985) *Sex and Gender*. Cambridge: Cambridge University Press.

Bandura, A. (1977) *Social Learning Theory*. Englewood Cliffs, NJ: Prentice Hall.

Bandura, A. and Walters, R.H. (1963) *Social Learning and Personality Development*. New York: Holt, Rinehart and Winston.

Billig, M. (1987) *Arguing and Thinking: A Rhetorical Approach to Social Psychology*. London: Cambridge University Press.

Brannon, R. (1976) The male sex role: our culture's blueprint of manhood, and what it's done for us lately, in D. David and R. Brannon (eds) *The Forty-Nine Percent Majority: The Male Sex Role*. Reading, MA: Addison-Wesley.

Brittan, A. (1989) *Masculinity and Power*. New York: Blackwell.

Brod, H. and Kaufman, M. (eds) (1994) *Theorizing Masculinities*. London: Sage.

Carrigan, T., Connell, R. and Lee, J. (1985) Towards a new sociology of masculinity, *Theory and Society*, 14: 551–604.

Chapman, R. and Rutherford, J. (eds) (1988) *Male Order: Unwrapping Masculinity*. London: Lawrence and Wishart.

Chodorow, N. (1978) *The Reproduction of Mothering: Psychoanalysis and the Sociology of Gender*. Berkeley, CA: University of California Press.

Christian, H. (1994) *The Making of Anti-Sexist Men*. London: Routledge.

Clarke, J., Hall, S., Jefferson, T. and Roberts, B. (1981) Sub-cultures, cultures and class, in T. Bennett, G. Martin, C. Mercer and J. Woollacott (eds) *Culture, Ideology and Social Process*. Milton Keynes: Open University Press.

Connell, R.W. (1987) *Gender and Power*. Cambridge: Polity Press.

Delphy, C. (1984) *Close to Home: A Materialist Analysis of Woman's Oppression*. London: Hutchinson.

Edley, N. and Wetherell, M.S. (1995) *Men in Perspective: Practice, Power and Identity*. Hemel Hempstead: Harvester Wheatsheaf.

Fagot, B.I. (1974) Sex differences in toddlers' behaviour and parental reaction, *Developmental Psychology*, 4: 554–8.

Fagot, B.I. (1977) Consequences of moderate cross-gender behaviour in pre-school children, *Child Development*, 48: 902–7.

Fasteau, M.F. (1974) *The Male Machine*. New York: McGraw-Hill.

Fling, S. and Manosevitz, M. (1972) Sex typing in nursery school children's play interests, *Developmental Psychology*, 7: 146–52.

Frosh, S. (1993) The seeds of male sexuality, in J. Ussher and C. Baker (eds) *Psychological Perspectives on Sexual Problems*. London: Routledge.

Gramsci, A. (1971) *Selections from the Prison Notebooks*, ed. and trans. by O. Hoare and G. Nowell-Smith. London: Lawrence and Wishart.

Greenson, R. (1968) Dis-identifying from mother: its special importance for the boy, *International Psychoanalytic Journal*, 49: 370–4.

Griffin, C. (1991) Experiencing power: dimensions of gender, 'race' and class, *British Psychological Society Psychology of Women Section Newsletter*, 8: 43–58.

Hall, C. (1992) *White, Male and Middle Class: Explorations in Feminism and History*. Cambridge: Polity Press.

Hargreaves, D.J. (1986) Psychological theories of sex-role stereotyping, in D.J. Hargreaves and A.M. Colley (eds) *The Psychology of Sex Roles*. London: Harper and Row.

Hartmann, H. (1979) The unhappy marriage of marxism and feminism: towards a more progressive union, *Capital and Class*, 8: 1–33.

Hearn, J. (1987) *The Gender of Oppression: Men, Masculinity and the Critique of Marxism*. Brighton: Harvester Wheatsheaf.

Hoch, P. (1979) *White Hero, Black Beast: Racism, Sexism and the Mask of Masculinity*. London: Pluto Press.

Hollway, W. (1984) Gender difference and the production of subjectivity, in J. Henriques, W. Hollway, C. Urwin, C. Venn and V. Walkerdine (eds) *Changing the Subject*. London: Methuen.

Kaufman, M. (1994) Men's contradictory experiences of power, in H. Brod and M. Kaufman (eds) *Theorizing Masculinities*. London: Sage.

Kimmel, M.S. (ed.) (1987) *Changing Men: New Directions in Research on Men and Masculinity*. Newbury Park, CA: Sage.

Lewis, M. (1975) Early sex differences in the human: studies of socio-emotional development, *Archives of Sexual Behaviour*, 4: 329–35.

Lips, H. (1981) *Women, Men and the Psychology of Power*. Englewood Cliffs, NJ: Prentice Hall.

Machung, A. (1989) Talking career, thinking job: gender differences in career and family expectations of Berkeley seniors. *Feminist Studies*, 15: 35–8.

Mischel, W. (1966) A social learning view of sex differences, in E.E. Maccoby (ed.) *The Development of Sex Differences*. Stanford, CA: Stanford University Press.

Mischel, W. (1970) Sex-typing and socialisation, in P.H. Musson (ed.) *Carmichael's Manual of Child Psychology*, 3rd edn, vol. 2. New York: John Wiley.

Olivier, C. (1989) *Jocasta's Children: The Imprint of the Mother*. London: Routledge.

Ortner, S.B. (1974) Is female to male as nature is to culture? in M.Z. Rosaldo and L. Lamphere (eds) *Woman, Culture and Society*. Stanford, CA: Stanford University Press.

Pleck, J.H. and Sawyer, J. (eds) (1974) *Men and Masculinity*. Englewood Cliffs, NJ: Prentice Hall.

Pleck, J.H. and Thompson, E.H. (1987) The structure of male norms, in M.S. Kimmel (ed.) *Changing Men: New Directions in Research on Men and Masculinity*. London: Sage.

Rotundo, E.A. (1987) Learning about manhood: gender ideals and the middle-class family in nineteenth century America, in J.A. Mangan and J. Walvin (eds)

Manliness and Morality: Middle Class Masculinity in Britain and America 1800–1940. Manchester: Manchester University Press.

Segal, L. (1990) *Slow Motion: Changing Men, Changing Masculinities*. London: Virago.

Seidler, V.J. (1989) *Rediscovering Masculinity: Reason, Language and Sexuality*. New York: Routledge.

Serbin, L.A., O'Leary, K.D., Kent, R.N. and Tonick, I.J. (1973) A comparison of teacher response to the preacademic problems and problem behaviour of boys and girls, *Child Development*, 44: 796–804.

Sidel, R. (1990) *On Her Own: Growing up in the Shadow of the American Dream*. New York: Penguin.

Snow, M.E., Jacklin, C.N. and Macoby, E.E. (1983) Sex of child differences in father-child interaction at one year of age, *Child Development*, 54: 227–32.

Terman, L. and Miles, C. (1936) *Sex and Personality*. New York: McGraw-Hill.

Tolson, A. (1977) *The Limits of Masculinity*. London: Tavistock.

Wetherell, M. and Edley, N. (1993) 'Men and masculinity: a socio-psychological analysis of discourse and gender identity'. ESRC grant no. R000233129.

Williams, J.E. and Bennett, S.M. (1975) The definition of sex stereotypes via the adjective checklist, *Sex Roles*, 1: 327–37.

'One thing leads to another': drinking, fighting and working-class masculinities

As part of my 1987/8 research on the creative activities of young people in the Wolverhampton area,[1] I conducted several interviews with groups of predominantly white, working-class young men at two youth clubs. I was somewhat surprised, initially, when the young men I spoke with from Wilton Manor[2] about their creative activities gleefully discussed how they enjoyed drinking and then fighting. I listened, with horror and fascination, as they told me that they sometimes 'glassed' other young men – that is, took empty bottles, smashed them against a rough surface, and then jabbed the bottle's jagged edge into their antagonist's face or body.

In this paper I will consider both how these young men viewed drinking and fighting as key signifiers of masculinity, which were shaped within social, economic and political contexts, and what these signifiers revealed about their subjectivities. To do so, I will briefly review how young men's masculinities were discussed in the recent literature on youth. I will then describe the research setting and the constraints that this setting placed on the young men I interviewed. The main part of the chapter will explore how these young men were located in one of two groups: those somewhat older and predominantly unemployed young men who claimed to fight less than before, and their younger and employed counterparts who claimed to fight frequently. I will conclude by suggesting how these findings contribute to current debate about young men's masculinities.

Brief literature review

It was not until the 1940s that young people began to be studied as forming a distinct, shared and meaningful culture (Parsons 1954). Whilst such a perspective acknowledged how young people actively shaped their leisure activities, it ignored power differences between the genders and assumed that youth culture was a unified entity singularly fashioned against the adult male role. This ignored both diversity within masculinity and the links between forms of masculinity and femininity.

The youth subcultures perspective replaced this mechanical and unilinear model of youth culture. Rather than assuming that social structures imposed order on individuals, the youth subcultures perspective examined how social structures and human agency were negotiated through young peoples' lived cultures. It thereby sought to capture the ways in which working-class young people were active players in a game they did not always willingly play according to superordinates' agendas. In developing such a model, re-searchers elaborated an explicitly political analysis with which they critically examined key institutions in their culture. Their analyses showed how those disadvantaged in such institutions were at least somewhat aware of, and resisted, these institutions (see, for example, Hall and Jefferson 1976; Willis 1977).

Studies of youth subcultural fighting, in particular, suggested that fighting provided working-class young men with a means of affirming their place in society. Working-class communities had developed a sense of their insularity and, concomitantly, their distinct place in society at least partly through their focus on local territory. In the postwar era, where there was a dramatic transformation of such territory, and where consumption became increas-ingly important, working-class young men were thought to turn to their territory, and to key activities in it.

Fighting in and for these territories seemed to offer a particularly important means by which these young men could heighten their experience with a pace and tension unavailable elsewhere. Some studies also suggested that gender and class shaped such fighting (see, for example, Cohen 1972; Willis 1977; Corrigan 1979).

Despite these insights, feminist, Asian and African-Caribbean researchers began criticizing the youth subcultures perspective. They suggested that its celebration of working-class young men's resistance ignored how their resistance was linked to their oppression of young women and of Asian and African-Caribbean young people (see, for example, McRobbie 1978; Amos and Parmar 1981; Carby 1982). However, as Roman and Christian-Smith (1988) argued, feminist cultural studies researchers in particular reproduced some of the youth subcultures perspective's assumptions about young women and therefore did not adequately depict it. They looked at young women in isolation from men, assumed that their oppression could be singularly accounted for by exploring their activities in one sphere, the home, and posited that activities in these spheres offered 'exemplars of autonomous female cultures of "resistance"' (p. 17).

These, and other key components of the youth subcultures framework were questioned by the mid-1980s. At this time researchers began to consider how 'plurality and heterogeneity [could] serve as the basis of a new dynamic of [young people's] empowerment, solidarity, and resistance' (McCarthy 1988: 189) and to apply such insights to the study of masculinities. Carrigan *et al.* (1987) argued that the study of *hegemonic* masculinity required an examination of how this dominant form subordinated other forms of masculinity and forms of femininity. Researchers began to explore how young men's subjectivities were shaped in wider contexts and how these subjectivities were multiple and fixed contingently in contexts where subjects sought to fashion a 'whole' self (Roman *et al.* 1988; Mac an Ghaill 1994).

Connell (1993) suggested that such examinations should be located historically. With regard to working-class men, he claimed that industrialization provided the basis for their hegemonic form of masculinity. This form emphasized physical strength, solidarity forged through struggles against managers and the patriarchal organization of the home. However, this hegemonic form of masculinity was now being threatened by post-Fordist work practices, which were resulting in a decreasing 'core' of full-time workers, and an increasing 'periphery' of casualized, usually female workers (Murray 1989). As more young men faced structural unemployment, they could respond by either trying to 'move up' to the middle class through training and education, accepting the situation or literally fighting against the dominant in school, on the streets and through crime.

Within these widening contexts, researchers began assessing how young men 'chose' forms of masculinity, particularly in and through schooling. They explored how the secondary school curriculum, which organized knowledge hierarchically and concomitantly located young people in this hierarchy by their academic success or failure, shaped these choices for young men (Connell 1989). Whilst academically successful young men were more likely to choose high status subject areas, those less successful were 'directed into low-level, practical-based vocational subject areas, whose cultures continued to reflect the masculine world of manual labour [which emphasized] chauvinism, toughness and machismo' (Mac an Ghaill 1994: 42). These forms of masculinity were unequal; those (usually middle-class young men) with higher qualifications could later wield power in large institutions. Their masculinity was thereby affirmed on a much wider scale than that of working-class young men whose power usually was affirmed in personal, embodied activities like sports, fighting, or sexual prowess (Connell 1989).

The following analysis considers how the working-class young men with whom I spoke constructed drinking and fighting in and against wider contexts; and how these constructions brought them to fashion fragile and contradictory masculinities. As I shall show, whilst some (younger) employed young men engaged in drinking and fighting, other somewhat older unemployed young men, who felt pessimistic about their futures, claimed to fight less than before. I will first discuss the research setting and how these young men perceived it.

The research setting and young men's views of it

Research took place in youth clubs in two communities of Wolverhampton. From the early days of the Industrial Revolution until recently, much British manufacturing and distribution was located in Wolverhampton. As these economic sectors have diminished in importance, the remains have moved away from cities like Wolverhampton (Willis *et al.* 1988). Given the transformation of work in the area, it is not surprising that the young men I spoke with, like those Willis (1977) interviewed, had not viewed secondary school as promising them good jobs for hard work. Few of them obtained many qualifications, and those that they had were in vocational areas affirming the physically-based and embodied forms of masculinity they had been developing since childhood (Canaan 1991). Most of these young men went on training schemes after finishing secondary school – as building workers, factory workers and painters, for example – that promised work emphasizing physically based forms of masculinity. Yet they maintained that these schemes neither trained them nor, consequently, enabled them to work afterwards.

These young men also felt pessimistic about the future. When I asked some of them where they thought they would be in ten years time, Bob who was 20 and unemployed said, 'The same place I am now . . . on the dole.' Neil also 20 and unemployed said 'I don't look into the future. I live day by day.' These young men felt trapped in their present circumstances and did not imagine that things would change in the future. They felt cheated by training schemes they had been on, spent long days isolated in their homes, and had little money to socialize with friends in the evening.

Some of them recognized that traditional working-class forms of masculinity, with their ties to labour, were being deconstructed (Connell 1993). Steve, aged 18, who worked part time in the Territorial Army, stated that 'there's loads and loads of jobs going in Britain, but they are for like a skilled person'. However, for unskilled workers like himself, the situation was different because employers 'can never get short of labourers, not with three million people on the dole'.

Recognizing that unemployment had risen significantly, particularly for those holding manual labour jobs, and that there was more competition over remaining jobs, these young men felt that government policies constrained them and intruded on their lives. Clearly these young men were not amongst the upwardly mobile few who, as Connell (1993) noted, got qualifications and sought middle-class jobs.

These young men, like those studied by Cohen (1972), also felt excluded from forms of consumption available to middle-class people. Some of them resented middle-class leisure consumption. When Neil and his friends left a nightclub one night and saw a Rolls-Royce parked across the road, they began 'diving on it and bouncing up and down'. They sought to damage a consumer item which signified the wide gulf separating their more limited consumption from that of their middle-class counterparts.

But not all young men I interviewed were so pessimistic. Some, including Dean a 16-year-old apprentice bricklayer and Keith, an 18-year-old trainee engineer were more optimistic about their working futures. Keith 'loves' his present apprenticeship as an engineer, believing that his firm paid him well and encouraged him to get more qualifications. Dean noted that his job as a bricklayer would enable him, after he completed an apprenticeship, to set up his own trade. Keith concurred, stating that 'you can do what you want, set up your own business'. As I shall show below, these optimistic employed young men fought, whilst their more pessimistic and older unemployed counterparts claimed that their prior interest in fighting had waned.

Both optimistic and pessimistic young men felt pride in their local area or 'territory'. Many had fought over it because, as Sam a 20-year-old man who was unemployed said, one's territory was 'your identity, it's what you are'. Unemployed John, 20, added that he was also proud in being unlike middle-class people who 'showed off about their wealth. So I'm proud to be from somewhere that isn't money-orientated.' John's comments, and those of others, suggest that their territory represented their place in the world, at present and into the future. Whilst they may have wanted greater consumer power, they did not, however, want to be as concerned about acquisition as middle-class people. They used their territory to distinguish themselves from both similarly located (working-class) people from other local areas (who they sometimes fought against (see below) and (middle-class) people occupying a different social and geographical location and set of values. These young men felt a strong sense of community. This differed from middle-class people who, as Connell (1993) showed, could have their sense of self and place in society affirmed in sites more powerful and further afield. Thus, local territory was particularly important for those lacking the cultural capital to move far from it both literally and figuratively.

As I shall now show,[3] this demarcation and affirmation of place was, for the younger, employed young men, located on their bodies and on multiple layers of their territory. By fighting over these layers, they displayed 'hardness'. Their somewhat older and unemployed counterparts, who could not afford to enter some key spheres that younger men acted in, lacked contexts for affirming such hardness. Some of them turned, instead, to heterosexual relationships which had contradictory results at best.

Drinking and fighting: how drinking and fighting are linked

Young men reportedly linked drinking to hardness. Drinking had this function because, as Steve acknowledged, it brought a young man to lose self-control and encounter a usually hidden part of his identity: '[W]hen you've had a drink, you're a totally different person, Jekyll and Hyde.' With this part of the self, young men took more risks than usual.

The world took on a heightened, dream-like quality when these young men drank. They performed outrageous acts with friends, in which they demonstrated bodily might or acted violently towards a subordinate. Thus individual acts of hardness took place amongst peers who drank and laughed together at individual and collective acts of strength, power and daring. Peers competed to see who had most and least self-control – that is, who could drink most and take it manfully, and who could push the bounds of self-control by performing outrageous acts in the group context. By performing such acts, young men could affirm solidarity with other individuals and/or the group generally.

Whilst young men engaged in many acts after drinking, they talked mostly about fighting. They claimed that drinking made them feel stronger which gave them more confidence to fight. As Andrew[4] an unemployed 18-year-old said, 'I've had more fights being drunk. I've found that when I'm drunk, I'm stronger.' Keith and Andrew observed that they often got into a temper before having a fight, which heightened their concentration. Just as the mild-mannered Dr Jekyll became the vicious and violent Mr Hyde, so, too, did a young man change his identity when his temper was ignited and he began to fight. He focused on pummelling his opponent, and felt only the impact but not the pain of his opponent's punches. Getting angry, then, allowed a young man to concentrate singularly on giving, but not receiving, blows. He therefore felt stronger and more in control of his body.

But even before young men became angry and then fought, they exercised another kind of control. Steve noted that when young men drank they engaged in a complex, evaluative process, 'See, when you're out, and you've had a few beers, one thing leads to another. You got to watch people, like, and see how them acting. You can always tell when them trying to act as if them hard, you can always tell the quiet ones. They just stand there . . . The quiet ones nearly always turn out to be the hardest.' When young men went out drinking, they scrutinized peers to see if any of them might, later in the evening, seek a fight. They thereby learnt which ones were only 'acting hard' – that is, displaying hardness outside but not inside the fight – and which '*were* hard' – that is, displaying hardness only in a fight (Canaan 1991). Making such an assessment early gave a young man information he might need later on. Thus, when young men went out drinking, they were ranking themselves relative to those around them to determine who they could, and could not, beat up if a fight occurred. Fighting required psychological awareness of oneself and others as well as physical control.

Young men did not just compare themselves to others; peers also put pressure on them to do so. Andrew had been forced to fight a young man who drew a picture of him and would not then tear it up. He did not want to fight this young man, 'but everyone was saying, "Hit him". If I didn't hit him, it would be like I was soft . . . I didn't want to hit him but I didn't have no choice so in the end I did.'

Andrew felt peer pressure forced him to 'prove' that he was 'hard' rather than 'soft'. Whether the pressure was externally or internally motivated, when young men experienced the heightened concentration of being in a temper and having a fight, they lost awareness of the flow of events from past to future. As Neil put it, 'I black out. I don't know what's going on.' But it was not simply one's sense of time that vanished. As Steve said, other things also faded: '[F]ighting ain't fair, there's no rules to fighting. There's no Queensbury rules outside [the boxing ring]'. Steve did not mean that rules did not precede and enable a fight; his comment above about reading other young men's gestures and words before a possible fight indicated that fighting was preceded by a subtle and ritualized system of meaning. However, at the moment when past and future faded, so did all the rules. Unlike Corrigan's (1979) point that fighting involved singularly structureless action that young men controlled, these young men separated the unstructured moment of being caught up in a fight from the structured action which preceded and followed it.

Keith and Andrew maintained that the link between his body and self was also severed in the fight. The moment of apparently greatest self-control, when one could punch one's antagonist yet feel no pain from his punches, was also when one stood outside one's body. As Andrew said, 'It's a weird sensation, scary and good. People like to be scared, like on rollercoasters . . . [It's] scary because it's different, you ain't used to it . . . But it's good too, cos you ain't feeling it. You can go back for longer.' Whilst Andrew felt strong enough to take on anyone and experienced no pain from the blows he received, this capacity to control bodily pain frightened him. As on a rollercoaster, he was taken for a ride rather than driving himself.

These young men also felt frightened because they were unaware of what they did to their antagonists when they were in the thick of a fight. As Neil said, 'Sometimes I feel scared. It's like, you kick somebody, you knocked 'em over, you don't know what you've done to them. You could kill 'em.' As this suggests, fighting, like drinking, was construed as a key activity through which young men could exercise the power and control of hardness. Yet these activities were also those where they lost control.

Masculinity was, then, fundamentally contradictory. The act which most confirmed it – fighting after drinking – also negated it because drinking, which gave one the daring to take on others and control one's body during a fight, also brought one to lose self-control and control over what one did to his antagonist. Thus it is not surprising that these young men repeatedly were called upon, and took up the challenge, to prove their hardness.

These young men also sought proof of their hardness in widening social contexts, ranging from intra-peer group relations on estates to supporters of the city's football team against supporters of another city's football team.

They looked to such contexts because they believed that just as individual male identities could be acknowledged through fighting, so could the identity of their territory be acknowledged through fighting for it. When I asked some of them why they fought, David a 16-year-old mechanic said, 'It's just areas, ain't it?' Keith then said, 'Like it's just stating their territory.' They were 'stating' the hardness of their territory, as Andrew indicated: '[Y]ou don't want other kids coming over here starting to cause trouble and thinking they can get away with things and before you know it, the area's got a name, "Oh, you can go up there and do what you want". The area gets to be hard [or soft].' Thus hardness (or softness) could extend beyond a young man's bodily bounds to those of his territory. This is not surprising since these young men perceived their territory as being as central to their identities, as indicative of where they came from, and where they could go to.

Fighting also had more immediate meaning for these young men. Neil reportedly sometimes fought with strangers after rowing with someone he was close to: 'It's like if I had an argument with a close, like someone in the family, like I'd go out at night. And you start clicking it over, and someone can knock you. And you, you'll hit 'em. Cos like, them bigger than you. And it's like, you're getting back at yourself for the fight.' After hurting people he cared about, Neil wanted 'someone to come and hurt' him. Sam concurred, noting that 'Yeah, you wanna get it out of your system, feel bad about it . . . and then you like pick a fight because then you can blow up. Maybe you might hurt them, but they'll hurt you as well. And then it's out of your system.'

As these comments suggest, fighting provided a context for retrieving the emotions and reversing the outcome of a prior psychological drama. Rather than verbally discussing differences with the person they rowed with, these young men displaced their anger on to a physical level and towards another less important person. This physical fight enabled them both to let out earlier anger, and to punish themselves, on the surface of their bodies, for hurting someone who mattered. Hardness, then, focused on demonstrating control over oneself and others, and at times allowing others to hurt one physically, as retribution for one's emotional hurting of someone significant. Thus, emotions were shifted to a physical level where they could be contained, tangibly 'balanced'. This form of masculinity kept clear of direct contact with emotions.

But these forms of masculinity began to wane for the older unemployed young men, who claimed to be less interested in demonstrating hardness through drinking and then fighting than before, as I shall now show.

Severing the tie between drinking and fighting

The older unemployed young men I interviewed said that they fought much less than before. When Bob was working he 'used to fight every week . . . I'd spend 20 quid a night and just get really stoned. And just end up fighting . . . Like when you'm on the dole, you can't get pissed so much, you don't fight so much.' Without the money that manual labour provided, he could not drink and then fight. Similarly, Neil noted that since stopping working two months previously he had 'about one or two fights. Like when, when I was working . . . I was fighting nearly every week.' The fact that these young men believed that they fought considerably less since becoming unemployed, even though many still fought monthly or every two months, suggests that what had decreased was their investment in this activity. These young men tied this lessened interest in fighting partly to their unemployment.

Steve, like Neil and Bob, maintained that fighting and employment were linked. He claimed that he knew many young men who engaged in violence at football matches. Some were 'unemployed like, but most of them . . . [have] boring jobs, like, accounts, and that'. Thus young unemployed working-class men, for whom present and future full-time employment could not be guaranteed, lacked the linchpin of their hegemonic form of masculinity – waged labour – and the prestige that went with it. They could no longer afford to drink heavily in pubs or go to football matches. If traditional forms of working-class masculinity were bolstered by both the money and prestige of a job, then these young men lost both. Perhaps their lessened interest in fighting, which occurred after they lost their jobs, signified their feeling that they no longer could view themselves in and through traditional hegemonic masculinity, as Connell suggested (1993).

Unlike their younger counterparts, who viewed females as pawns in a game through which they sought to test their partner's sexual morals and thereby assert their own power (Canaan 1991), older young men like Neil looked to a female partner as a companion. Yet some pressure remained in heterosexual relationships. Neil, for example, felt the need to 'protect my girlfriend when we're out. And . . . like if you start fighting, she might get dragged into it.'

Protection did not just involve physically insulating a partner from other young men's violence; it also enabled a young man to position his partner as his subordinate, as 20-year-old John who was unemployed suggested: 'If you're single, you ain't got no responsibility. All you gotta worry about is yourself. And if you're going out with somebody else, you gotta worry about you and her . . . A girl's gonna say, "Well, I got my own two feet, I got my own life, I can support myself." But as a male, it's just a reaction.'

Even if a young woman asserted – as John's comments suggest happened to him – that she could take care of herself and thus was her partner's equal, John refused to accept such equality. Thus his statement that a young man had to be responsible for his female partner and himself pointed to the inequality that remained in young men's heterosexual relationships. Perhaps these young men became less interested in asserting dominance over other males as they asserted dominance over female partners. Interestingly, this occurred at a time when they had lost the ability and interest to wield traditional hegemonic form of working-class masculinity through work. But if they were now more concerned with asserting dominance over female subordinate partners than over male equals, would they also assert this dominance through physical as well as psychological means? And if they had already developed strategies for shifting emotions from a psychological to a physical level, how would this impact on their relationships with young women? Only a more in-depth analysis can answer these questions.

Conclusion

Drinking and then fighting were centrally important to the constructions of masculinity of the young men I spoke with from their mid- to late teen years. When they were entering either work or a training scheme (which they believed would lead to work) after secondary school, in leisure they began to go to pubs, clubs and football matches where they drank and reportedly fought frequently. In these contexts and within their territory, they fought to show peers either that they controlled themselves and any opponent(s) – if they won a fight – or, if they lost, that they could take a beating and therefore control bodily pain. Whilst drinking and then fighting were activities that they thought would demonstrate hardness, because drinking engendered both the loss and maintenance of control, these activities were, at best, contradictory. Thus, these young men denied masculinity as they confirmed it. It is perhaps for this reason that they repeatedly competed to show their might within peer groups, between territories and in leisure contexts beyond these territories.

For these younger men, fighting enabled them to acknowledge masculine strength and power in multiple leisure contexts, just as their present work situation and its concomitant pay packet enabled them to affirm hegemonic working-class masculinity. Thus, they accepted and even celebrated their present positions largely because the deconstruction of hegemonic working-class masculinity that Connell (1993) discussed was not (yet) affecting them. Whilst the situation was different for their older, unemployed counterparts, they too accepted their positions. Many felt pessimistic about future work possibilities and lacked the money and interest in engaging in leisure drinking and fighting as fully as earlier. They accepted the erosion of key aspects of the hegemonic form of masculinity and sought to affirm that which appeared available, relationships with young women. Thus, both groups of young men neither fought against their circumstances nor sought middle-class respectability, two of the three options that Connell claimed were open to working-class men. The third option that both groups 'chose', that of accepting their circumstances, took two different forms depending on each group's age and employment status. This suggests that further research must examine more closely the multiple ways in which this option, and the others, are enacted by the young men who 'choose' them.

Notes

1 I was the ethnographer for the Gulbenkian Foundation research project on 'Youth and the Arts', directed by Paul Willis, which resulted in *Moving Culture* (Willis *et al.* 1990a) and *Common Culture* (Willis *et al.* 1990b).
2 All names of people I interviewed and the communities they lived in are pseudonyms.
3 This first section incorporates comments from older young men about their prior enthusiasm for drinking and then fighting, as well as from the younger men.
4 Whilst Andrew was unemployed, he was not pessimistic about his future because he had not yet tried very hard to get a job and was thinking about going on a training scheme. Thus his attitude towards his present and future was different from that of the older unemployed young men who had tried to get jobs and had been on very unsuccessful training schemes.

References

Amos, V. and Parmar, P. (1981) 'Resistances and responses: the experiences of black girls in Britain, in A. McRobbie and T. McCabe (eds) *Feminism for Girls: An Adventure Story*. London: Routledge and Kegan Paul.

Canaan, J.E. (1991) Is 'doing nothing' just boys' play? Integrating feminist and cultural studies perspectives on working class masculinities, in S. Franklin, C. Lury and J. Stacey (eds) *Off-Centre: Feminism and Cultural Studies*. London: Routledge.

Carby, H. (1982) Schooling in Babylon, in Centre for Contemporary Cultural Studies (eds) *The Empire Strikes Back: Race and Racism in 70s Britain*. London: Hutchinson.

Carrigan, T., Connell, B. and Lee, J. (1987) Toward a new sociology of masculinity, in H. Brod (ed.) *The Making of Masculinities: The New Men's Studies*. London: Unwin and Hyman.

Cohen, P. (1972) *Subcultural Conflict and Working Class Community*, Working Paper in Cultural Studies, no. 2. Birmingham: University of Birmingham.

Connell, R.W. (1989) Cool guys, swots and wimps: the interplay of masculinity and education, *Oxford Review of Education*, 15(3): 291–303.

Connell, R.W. (1993) The big picture: masculinities in recent world history, *Theory and Society*, 22: 597–624.

Corrigan, P. (1979) *Schooling the Smash Street Kids*. London: Macmillan.

Hall, S. and Jefferson, T. (1976) *Resistance Through Rituals: Youth Subcultures in Post-war Britain*. London: Hutchinson.

Mac an Ghaill, M. (1994) *The Making of Men: Masculinities, Sexualities and Schooling*. Buckingham: Open University Press.

McCarthy, C. (1988) Marxist theories of education and the challenge of a cultural politics of non-synchrony, in L.G. Roman and L.K. Christian-Smith with E. Ellsworth (eds) *Becoming Feminine: The Politics of Popular Culture*. London: Falmer.

McRobbie, A. (1978) Working class girls and the culture of femininity, in Women's Studies Group, CCCS (eds) *Women Take Issue: Aspects of Women's Subordination*. London: Hutchinson.

Murray, R. (1989) Fordism and post-Fordism, in S. Hall and M. Jacques (eds) *New Times*. London: Lawrence and Wishart.

Parsons, T. (1954) *Essays in Sociological Theory*. New York: Macmillan.

Roman, L.G. and Christian-Smith, L.K. (1988) Introduction, in *Becoming Feminine: The Politics of Popular Culture*. London: Falmer.

Roman, L.G. and Christian-Smith, L.K. with E. Ellsworth (eds) (1988) *Becoming Feminine: The Politics of Popular Culture*. London: Falmer.

Willis, P (1977) *Learning to Labor: How Working Class Kids Get Working Class Jobs*. New York: Columbia University Press.

Willis, P., Bekenn, A., Ellis, T. and Whitt, D. (1988) *The Youth Review: Social Conditions of Young People in Wolverhampton*. Aldershot: Avebury.

Willis, P., Jones, S., Canaan, J. and Hurd, G. (1990a) *Moving Culture: An Enquiry into the Cultural Activities of Young People*. London: Calouste Gulbenkian Foundation.

Willis, P. with Jones, S., Canaan, J. and Hurd, G. (1990b) *Common Culture*. Buckingham: Open University Press.

8 Andrew Parker

Sporting masculinities: gender relations and the body

Introduction

Sport means different things to different people. For some it represents the routines of daily work; for others it serves a more cathartic, stress-reducing purpose; for others still, it constitutes little more than fun, games and play. In this chapter I will discuss sport in a very general sense, as something which envelops all of these things. In particular, I will be concerned with the way in which sport might mean different things to different people depending on their biological sex, their gender identity and their ethnicity.

Central here are questions surrounding the way in which male and female bodies are diversely presented within the penetrative channels of consumer culture, and what the role of the sport and leisure industry is within this process. Moreover, I will consider how men in particular are depicted in relation to sporting practice, and how this might influence popular perceptions of the male 'self'.

Whilst raising these issues, this chapter will draw on the work of key theorists within the sociology of sport (and sociology in general) in order to map out the major concepts and debates surrounding both historical and present-day research into sport. It is hoped that an analysis of this kind may, in some way, allow us to develop a more accurate understanding of the social construction of sporting masculinities.

The development of modern sport

Many of the common assumptions attached to modern-day sport appear to have originated within the English public schools of the nineteenth century. Here, traditional folk games were transformed by the upper-class codes imposed upon them into more orderly and standardized forms of 'play'. Over time, these activities came to constitute a central element within the public school educational ethos, in that not only were they valued for their competitive and repressive qualities, but in addition, they were seen as a kind of nurturing ground for the attitudes and values imperative to the maintenance of British imperialism (Mangan 1981; Holt 1989).

These male-dominated ideals gained much recognition during the latter part of the nineteenth century, and eventually made the transition into the wider sporting sphere. Graduates of the public schools, for example, spread the games-playing ethos through a variety of societal institutions, thereby enhancing a wider rationalization of sport. In addition, Pierre de Coubertin, the founder of the modern Olympics, also adopted and reinforced the chauvinistic spirit of the English games-playing tradition, and in doing so, publicly promoted sport as a predominantly male concern (Hargreaves 1984).

From these early beginnings, dominant masculine images of sport persisted. The Victorian era witnessed the emergence of commonsense cultural assumptions equating manliness with sporting prowess. Where sport was concerned, women came to be viewed as weak and frail, passive and emotional. They were seen more in terms of their reproductive capacity than in relation to their athletic potential. Rendered ill-suited to vigorous exercise, women became the victims of an unfounded 'scientific' logic which located them as 'biologically' inferior to men. In this way cultural values and attitudes came to determine the limits of female activity, and male superiority within sport became 'the natural order of things'. Men, it seemed, were physically and psychologically 'built' for such pastimes, whereas women were not (Hargreaves 1994).

Of course, vestiges of these beliefs are still evident within society today. Certainly, it is possible that, even within our own lives, we have come across sex and gender differentiation in sport. Research has shown, for instance, that the practices of physical education in schools may well carry spurious gendered inferences towards 'sex-appropriate' sports participation (Scraton 1993). Worse still, these norms may then be reinforced by the blatant processes of female exclusion operational within elite sporting arenas.

Experiences of schooling also tend to show that if children cross over taken-for-granted 'biological sporting boundaries', they may well find themselves the subjects of intense peer group ridicule, particularly in relation to notions of sexuality (Parker 1992). Granted, there are issues of immaturity to consider here. But, at the same time, we must also question how and where such values and ideas originate, and the extent to which they might go on to shape the contours of adult life.

Theorizing sport

Given the pervasive influence of popular belief surrounding the 'biological' and/or 'cultural' differences of men and women, how, we might ask, has sport been theorized?

For many years sport evaded much critical analysis. It was seen as something which was relatively neutral: an area of culture which provided entertainment and enjoyment, whilst remaining separate from wider societal 'contamination'. During the 1960s when analyses of sport became more popular, issues of sex/gender identity and difference failed to be addressed. Instead, an apolitical standpoint was adopted. This constituted part of a broader functionalist approach whereby sport was celebrated as a facilitator of physical well-being and all-round personal development, and as a positive reproductive site for the attitudes, norms and values beneficial to the functioning of society (Loy and Kenyon 1969).

During the 1970s and 80s, however, such perceptions changed. Within this period, sport was recognized as a much more complex cultural sphere, involving entrepreneurial exploitation and profit, nationalistic fervour and ideological bias. In turn, theorists adopted a more critical approach within their writings.

Neo-Marxist critiques emerged, for example, which cited sport as an appendage of bourgeois domination within the context of wider capitalist relations (Vinnai 1973; Brohm 1978; Beamish 1982). According to these accounts, sporting practice mirrored the productive labour demands of industrial capitalism, and therefore served to reinforce the power relations of the workplace. Dismissing the potential of human agency, such analyses cast individuals as the docile recipients of culture, caged by the constraints of sport, and unable to escape its repressive influence.

There were variations along this theme. Similar conclusions, however, were reached in terms of the overall significance of sport and its role within the processes of social reproduction. What is more, although within some aspects of this work issues of sexuality were raised, discussion gravitated towards the sublimation of male desire, and in general the power relations of gender difference were negated.

The advent of the 1980s witnessed the adoption of a more humanistic approach within this area, and one which refuted previously deterministic notions of personal constraint (Gruneau 1983; Hargreaves 1987). Drawing its inspiration from the work of Antonio Gramsci (1971), this body of 'cultural Marxist' thought directed its attention to the way in which those involved in sport might challenge and contest issues of financial exploitation, commercialization and political bias, by means of their own actions.

The focus of this debate was Gramsci's notion of hegemony, which allowed a more intricate exploration of class relations in sport, particularly in terms of the power struggles between dominant and subordinate groups. Yet, although this modified Marxist stance did pave the way for a detailed critique of male domination and gender inequality, such issues again escaped the rigorous scrutiny they deserved.

This is not to say that cultural Marxist contributions have not had a significant impact on more recent analyses of sport. On the contrary, of late, the concept of hegemony has been widely used within an emerging 'sports feminist' tradition in order to create a backdrop against which male domination in sport might be theorized (Hargreaves 1986; Hall 1988). Furthermore, and again in accordance with the broader feminist resurgence, a predominantly male critique of sport has been established around similar theoretical concerns, the specific aim of which has been to evaluate critically the role men might play in their domination of women within sports settings (Sabo and Runfola 1980; Messner and Sabo 1990).

Collectively this critique has used the concept of hegemony in two main ways. First, theorists have indicated that although men dominate within sporting circles (as well as within society at large), this dominance is not total. It is at all times contested and challenged and should therefore be referred to as a position of 'male hegemony'. Second, commentators have also come to recognize that a particular brand of masculinity has emerged as historically dominant in and around sport – the ideals in play here being those associated with white, middle-class, heterosexual males. Individuals who do not meet these criteria (be they male or female) are necessarily marginalized and must, therefore, occupy a subordinate hierarchical position in terms of sex/gender identity.

Sport, health and consumer culture

Although an analysis of the historical development of modern sport provides some clues as to how it has become a male-dominated concern, such evidence scarcely shows how this position of male hegemony is maintained. How does sport perpetuate notions of male superiority amidst the challenge of contemporary contestation? How does it promote images of sex/gender identity? A good starting point, perhaps, is the relationship between sport and the media, and in particular the contemporary marketing techniques of consumer culture.

Consumer culture, Hargreaves (1987: 132) states, is 'that way of life in the modern era, which is organized around the consumption of goods and services for the mass market'. Advertising, of course, has been largely responsible for the ubiquitous development of consumer culture: a culture which has transformed traditional values of thrift and industry into a new spontaneous, life-course outlook celebrating impulsive, credit-fuelled consumption, self-expression and paganism (Featherstone 1991).

The body has been ever-present within the marketing orbits of mass consumption, and has come to represent the central focus of consumer culture today. Its worth rests not in its autonomous development, but in its ability to match popular ideals of youth, health, fitness, and beauty (Shilling 1993).

This physical and bodily emphasis has marked the arrival of sport and leisure into the consumption debate. Indeed, as Hargreaves (1987) has pointed out, sports culture connects so intimately with consumer culture because both employ the body as a central means of expression:

> a good deal of the strength of consumer culture resides in its ability to harness and channel bodily needs and desires – for health, longevity, sexual fulfilment and so on . . . Sports culture's stress on play, contest, strength, energy, movement, speed and skill etc., allows such themes to be given a particularly vivid, dramatic, aesthetically pleasing and emotionally gratifying expression. To be sportive, is almost by definition to be desirable, fit, young and healthy.
>
> (p. 134)

Although, as Shilling (1993) has correctly inferred, specific periods in history have witnessed governmental promotions in the direction of health and fitness education, recent unprecedented expansion within this area has been on a more individual and voluntary basis. Because such a vast number of people have become preoccupied with issues of health and physical appearance, once-trivialized notions of 'keep fit' now constitute the cornerstone of a multimillion dollar fitness industry.

Masculinity and the body

But how does the relationship between sport and consumer culture directly affect popular perceptions of masculinity and the body? The extensive use of visual images seems crucial here. As Featherstone (1991: 178) states,

> The perception of the body within consumer culture is dominated by the existence of a vast array of visual images. Indeed, the inner logic of consumer culture depends upon the cultivation of an insatiable appetite to consume images.

Through its widespread employment of body imagery, the media makes individuals more conscious and more aware of their bodily state. Satisfaction with outward appearance often appears to dominate inner feeling. The degree to which we measure up to 'the look' has come to represent the currency of social relations, our value within society and our potential for social acceptability (Shilling 1993).

Sport and exercise play a key role within this body/media nexus. To 'look good' we are told, is to 'feel good'. To maintain one's body is to express a desire to lead a healthy lifestyle, to 'enjoy the good things in life', and to appeal to others. Physical fitness and participation in sports and leisure activities represent a sense of pride in oneself, a sense of cleanliness and purification against the evils of alcohol, tobacco, and the bodily abuse of daily life.

To be healthy and diet conscious is to have some kind of sexual attraction over and above those who are not. The enhancement of sexual prowess is paramount. Indeed, as Featherstone (1991) accurately points out, consumer culture explicitly condones such beliefs in so far as within the confines of its discourse exercise and sex are often 'blurred together through neologisms such as "sexercise" and "exersex"' (p. 182).

The development of the sport/media relationship has had a dramatic impact on the way in which both male and female bodies have been presented and perceived. Men, as well as women, are expected to respond to the influential and pervasive forces of consumer culture. Masculinity is clearly defined within this realm, particularly within the context of sport. Emanating from film, television, videos, books, and magazines, notions of muscularity, strength and power emerge, wrapped up with generous helpings of fearless domination, to produce images of the ideal man (Dyer 1982; Mishkind *et al.* 1986).

Where might these images originate? Take prime-time British television, for example, and the masculine standards it portrays. On a twice-daily basis, popular Australian soap operas clearly equate notions of maleness with muscularity and manliness. ITV's *Gladiators* reputedly attracts 14 million viewers weekly, who watch male (and female) contestants negotiate situations of direct physical combat with muscular bodybuilders, the majority of whom are, to all intents and purposes, professional sportsmen (and women). Just children's entertainment? Perhaps. But in the unlikely event that such masculine (and feminine) norms are entirely discarded by the adult male population, we must remember that children do grow up, ultimately becoming active agents in the social construction of masculinity within any given period.

Besides the more explicit messages which media portrayals of health and fitness promote, other less visible codes and values are also evident in and through the routines of popular sporting activity. Analysed closely, these can be seen to represent commonsense assumptions regarding, for instance, questions of sexuality and ethnicity. Indeed, in highlighting the way in which sport mediates and reinforces particular attitudes towards such issues, I will now attempt to identify more precisely the complexities of male hegemony within contemporary sports practice.

Heterosexuality, homophobia and sporting ritual

Sport offers complex and contradictory portrayals of masculine construction in relation to sexuality. Physical bonding in the name of team spirit, homophobic taboos, blatant misogyny and the objectification of women are all evident within popular forms of male sporting conquest or related social settings. Acceptable too are the practices of intimate celebration, back slapping, bath sharing and 'pseudo-erotic' ritual (Dunning 1986; Kidd 1987). Meaningful, emotional relations with other males, however, are out of the question.

Enter Stonewall FC, Britain's only gay men's football team. Experiencing a modest amount of recent success in London's Wandsworth and District Sunday Football League, this group of amateur players, Troughton (1994: 18) declares, constitutes 'the biggest challenge to the male ego since the vibrator'. Place this isolated example of homosexual acceptance against a media obsession with the macho social exploits of Britain's footballing élite, and what do we have? A sporting tradition, which via the annals of popular media coverage, takes heterosexuality for granted and dismisses as deviant any alternative form of masculine representation.

Association football, of course, is not alone in its adoption of such views and assumptions. On the contrary, various commentators have cited the way in which attitudes throughout sport collectively contribute to the reification of heterosexuality within the sporting world in general (see Pronger 1990; Hargreaves 1994).

As regards women, the pervasivenes of dominant heterosexual norms often calls into question the 'femininity' and sexuality of sports participants, particularly in relation to those activities which contain a more physical and competitive element (Messner 1988). Just as men are often labelled 'wimps' when they fail to measure up to popular images of strength, power and physical prowess, so women who pursue their sporting/leisure goals within competitive spheres are frequently termed 'butch', 'lesboes' or 'lezzies' because they do not fit the 'natural' feminine norms ascribed to them (Gilroy 1989; Hargreaves 1994).

Translating this masculine logic into the complex world of professional sport, Hargreaves (1994) has outlined the way in which some women appear to attract more attention than men in relation to questions surrounding their sex/gender identities. Of particular interest is the case of the women's tennis player Martina Navratilova.

A sporting legend within her own right, the openly gay Navratilova responded critically in late 1991 to the way in which the world's media framed the enforced retirement of the black American basketball star Earvin 'Magic' Johnson. An equally eminent star within US sporting circles, Johnson shocked the athletic fraternity earlier that year by announcing that he had tested HIV positive, and, as a result, would have to leave the game.

At the time of his announcement, Johnson had received a wave of sympathy and support from both the US media and public, even though it was clear that his heterosexual exploits had been far from conservative. Reminiscing over her own media treatment, and the way in which she had been discriminated against on account of her sexuality during the course of her career, such sympathy, Navratilova claimed, would not have come her way under similar circumstances:

> If I had the AIDS virus, would people be understanding? No, because they would say I'm gay – I had it coming. That's why they're accepting it with him, because supposedly he'd got it through heterosexual contact. If it had happened to a heterosexual woman who had been with a hundred or two hundred men, they would call her a whore and a slut, the corporations would drop her like a lead balloon and she would never get another job in her life.
>
> (in James 1991: 38)

In retrospect it may be worth considering here the discrepancy between the overall public appeal of the two sports concerned. Having said that, two main issues remain. First, this statement spells out the massive double standards of the media, in its treatment of sportsmen in comparison to sportswomen over matters of sexuality. Second, and more importantly, in terms of a wider media and public response, it illustrates the extent to which heterosexuality is not only condoned, but implicitly glamorized within popular culture and through certain sections of the sporting press.

Hence the implicit message is that not only is it more acceptable to become HIV positive via heterosexual endeavour, it is also more acceptable to lead a sexually promiscuous lifestyle if you are a male élite athlete. If you're famous and you're a man, and you have AIDS, that's just unlucky. But if you're a woman, and/or you're gay, that's different.

Sport, ethnicity and masculine construction

The Navratilova/Johnson case offers a clear example of media discrimination based around issues of biological sex and sexuality. But moreover, it serves to raise poignant issues concerning the hierarchical position occupied by marginalized and subordinated sex/gender identities within our society. How, for example, would the media have reacted if Johnson had been gay or bisexual? What would have been the implicit message if an equally famous white heterosexual male, or a white gay male elite athlete had suffered a similar fate? The permutations multiply in relation to women. Indeed, as well as issues of sexuality, sex and gender, what this scenario also brings to the fore are notions of race and ethnicity, and pinpoints them as imperative within any theoretical discussion surrounding masculine construction.

By and large, the hegemonic masculine norms and values espoused within consumer culture have a tendency to negate issues of ethnicity. In this arena, masculinity is something which is narrowly structured around images of white males. Such practices reflect the severely racist assumptions which continue to permeate our society, via the institutional and personal relations of everyday life.

In terms of the body, the historic development of racism has been littered with images of physicality, sexuality and violence. As Shilling (1993) has pointed out, aside from women in general, traditionally black men have been made to suffer the consequences of white male fears regarding the 'uncontrollable' desires of their own bodies. Viewed as 'dangerous Others', black peoples, it seems, have conventionally represented some kind of uncivilized, animalistic force posing a sexual threat to the white moral order (Westwood 1990; Shilling 1993). In this respect the negative construction of black bodies has located black people as central within a variety of moral panics, particularly those concerning issues of violent crime, sexual deviance, rape, health and disease (Staples 1982; Shilling 1993).

As regards masculine construction, sport is just one part of that society where such prejudicial assumptions have been evident (Westwood 1990). In recent years, for example, the use of racist chants by supporters and the throwing of banana skins have become all-too-familiar features of English professional football matches (Williams 1991).

In the case of adolescent sport in Britain, concerns have also been aired for some time as to the way in which black males have been excessively encouraged to follow a sporting lifecourse by those within educational circles. Prominent here are racist undertones regarding physiological difference, and academic shortfall (Lashley 1980; Cashmore 1982; Mac an Ghaill 1994). Moreover, there is evidence to suggest that Asian children may also be subjected to the uninformed views and attitudes of teachers in school about the physical and sporting preferences of their respective cultures (Flemming 1988).

Such occurrences reflect something of a more typical pattern when set against the historic prevalence of racism within the wider sporting sphere. Indeed, in addition to the contribution sport made to the naturalization of men's superiority over women, its modern-day development, Majors (1990) declares, also carried with it the ideological implication that 'working-class men as well as men of color could not possibly compete successfully with "gentlemen"' (p. 109).

Representing one of the few analyses of the development of black masculinity in relation to sport, the work of Majors (1990) draws attention to the way in which male athletic roles within the US have come to be dominated by blacks during the period since the Second World War. Witnessing a significant shift away from white, middle-class supremacy, sport, Majors claims, has, allowed blacks to create and display a unique masculine identity by way of their expressive lifestyle behaviours – which collectively constitute what he calls 'cool pose'.

Reiterating some of the earlier observations made by Staples (1982), Majors describes how although many blacks within American society have accepted the norms and values surrounding social definitions of masculinity, they have been unable to put these into practice on account of the racist restrictions which have denied them access to such areas as education, employment and institutional power. Causing widespread status frustration, this situation, it appears, has led many black males to develop strategies of masculine construction within other 'interpersonal spheres':

> black men often cope with their frustration, embitterment, alienation and social impotence by channelling their creative energies into the construction of unique, expressive, and conspicuous styles of demeanor, speech, gesture, clothing, hairstyle, walk, stance, and handshake. For the black male, these expressive behaviors . . . offset an externally imposed invisibility, and provide a means to show the dominant culture (and the black male's peers), that the black male is strong and proud and can survive, regardless of what may have been done to harm or limit him.
>
> (Majors 1990: 111)

Citing how a variety of black male elite athletes have adopted such methods of creativity over time, Majors goes on to initiate an analysis of the historic and political development of 'cool pose' in and through sport. What is more, whilst highlighting the individual habits of popular black sporting figures, Majors is also quick to point out that this phenomenon has more recently come to involve college, high school and playground athletes who, by way of their involvement, represent crucial reproductive agents of such fashionable expressive trends.

Although this work implies that as a result of the development of interpersonal strategies, sport has become something which might play a positive role in the lives of black males, we must be careful not to assume that the development of self-expression, and/or the more recent emergence of black male prominence within particular sports, necessarily means that racism is no longer problematic within this cultural sphere. There is ample evidence to suggest, for instance, that even within our own society various sports are still redolent with the politics of 'race' (Westwood 1990; Jarvie 1991). However, as Majors (1990) concludes, what we can be sure of is that these developments do serve a specific purpose in terms of agency. For in facilitating the articulation of black masculine construction, such reactionary measures constitute a form of popular cultural resistance which, in contesting the white male domination of sport, necessarily represent a challenge to the hegemonic ideals in place.

Conclusions

My aim within this chapter has been to map out some aspects of the relationship between masculinity and sport by drawing specific attention to the influential powers of consumer culture and the bodily images which it mediates.

Whilst notions of biological sex, sexuality and ethnicity have been highlighted in relation to sporting practice, it is important that we consider these issues as part of a more collective societal order in and around which the formation of gender identity takes place. That is to say, that masculine construction is not limited to such spheres. Rather, it surrounds and interweaves these and many other lifestyle areas.

Having said that, an acknowledgement of differing masculine identities is crucial. As Carrigan *et al.* (1985) have accurately stated, we cannot discuss masculinity as a fixed entity in terms of an all-encompassing male societal role. Instead, we must recognize the existence of a multiplicity of masculinities according to the diverse cultural values in place at any given time. Moreover, what Carrigan *et al.* go on to argue, and what I have put forward here, is that these divergent masculine forms are arranged in terms of hierarchical position, above which specific hegemonic ideals set the masculine agenda. In this sense, what this work has endeavoured to show is that ultimately, sport, via its links with consumer culture, does have a role to play in the promotion and maintenance of such ideals.

Acknowledgements

I would like to thank Professor R.G. Burgess, Professor G. Jarvie and Dr M. Mac an Ghaill for their constructive comments on earlier drafts of this chapter.

References

Beamish, R. (1982) Sport and the logic of capitalism, in R. Gruneau and H. Cantelon (eds) *Sport, Culture and the Modern State*. Toronto: University of Toronto Press.

Brohm, J.-M. (1978) *Sport: A Prison of Measured Time*. London: Pluto Press.

Carrigan, T., Connell, R. and Lee, J. (1985) Towards a new sociology of masculinity, *Theory and Society*, 5(14): 551–602.

Cashmore, E. (1982) *Black Sportsmen*. London: Routledge and Kegan Paul.

Dunning, E. (1986) Sport as a male preserve: notes on the social sources of masculine identity and its transformations, *Theory, Culture and Society*, 3(1): 79–91.

Dyer, R. (1982) Don't look now, *Screen*, 23(3/4): 61–73.

Featherstone, M. (1991) The body in consumer culture, in M. Featherstone, M. Hepworth and B.S. Turner (eds) *The Body: Social Processes and Cultural Theory*. London: Sage.

Flemming, S. (1988) Asian lifestyles and sports participation, in A. Tomlinson (ed.) *Youth Cultures and the Domain of Leisure*. Brighton: Leisure Studies Association Conference Papers no. 35.

Gilroy, S. (1989) The emBody-ment of power: gender and physical activity, *Leisure Studies*, 8: 163–71.

Gramsci, A. (1971) *Selections from the Prison Notebooks*. London: Lawrence and Wishart.

Gruneau, R. (1983) *Class, Sport and Social Development*. Amherst, MA: University of Massachusetts Press.

Hall, M.A. (1988) The discourse on gender and sport: from femininity to feminism, *Sociology of Sport Journal*, 5: 330–40.

Hargreaves, J. (1987) *Sport, Power and Culture*. Cambridge: Polity.

Hargreaves, J.A. (1984) Taking men on at their games, *Marxism Today*, August: 17–21.

Hargreaves, J.A. (1986) Where's the virtue, where's the grace? A discussion of the social production of gender relations in and through sport, *Theory, Culture and Society*, 3(1): 109–21.

Hargreaves, J.A. (1994) *Sporting Females*. London: Routledge.

Holt, R. (1989) *Sport and the British*. London: Clarendon.

James, M. (1991) Martina in Aids protest, *Guardian*, 21 November, 38.

Jarvie, G. (1991) There ain't no problem here, *Sport and Leisure*, Nov/Dec: 20–1.

Kidd, B. (1987) Sports and masculinity, in M. Kaufman (ed.) *Beyond Patriarchy*. New York: Oxford University Press.

Lashley, H. (1980) The new black magic, *British Journal of Physical Education*, 11(1): 5–6.

Loy, J. and Kenyon, G. (eds) (1969) *Sport, Culture and Society*. New York: Macmillan.

Mac an Ghaill, M. (1994) *The Making of Men*. Buckingham: Open University Press.

Majors, R. (1990) Cool pose: black masculinity and sports, in M.A. Messner and D.F. Sabo (eds) *Sport, Men and the Gender Order*. Champaign, IL: Human Kinetics.

Mangan, A.J. (1981) *Athleticism in the Victorian and Edwardian Public Schools*. Cambridge: Cambridge University Press.

Messner, M.A. (1988) Sports and male domination: the female athlete as contested ideological terrain, *Sociology of Sport Journal*, 5: 197–211.

Messner, M.A. and Sabo, D.F. (eds) (1990) *Sport, Men and the Gender Order*. Champaign, IL: Human Kinetics.

Mishkind, M.E., Rodin, J., Siberstein, L.R. and Striegel-Moore, R.H. (1986) The embodiment of masculinity, *American Behavioural Scientist*, 29(5): 545–62.

Parker, A. (1992) 'One of the boys? Images of masculinity within boys' physical education', unpublished MA dissertation. University of Warwick.

Pronger, B. (1990) Gay jocks: a phenomenology of gay men, in M.A. Messner and D.F. Sabo (eds) *Sport, Men and the Gender Order*. Champaign, IL: Human Kinetics.

Sabo, D.F. and Runfola, R. (eds) (1980) *Jock: Sports and Male Identity*. Englewood Cliffs, NJ: Prentice Hall.

Scraton, S. (1993) *Shaping up to Womanhood: Gender and Girls' Physical Education*. Buckingham: Open University Press.

Shilling, C. (1993) *The Body and Social Theory*. London: Sage.

Staples, R. (1982) *Black Masculinity*. San Francisco: Black Scholar Press.

Troughton, T. (1994) Seems like a nice team, *Mail On Sunday Review (Night and Day)*, 10 April, 18–19.

Vinnai, G. (1973) *Football Mania*. London: Ocean Books.

Westwood, S. (1990) Racism, black masculinity and the politics of space, in J. Hearn and D.H.J. Morgan (eds) *Men, Masculinities and Social Theory*. London: Unwin Hyman.

Williams, J. (1991) Having an away day: English football spectators and the hooligan debate, in J. Williams and S. Wagg (eds) *British Football and Social Change*. Leicester: Leicester University Press.

Are you sitting comfortably? Men's storytelling, masculinities, prison culture and violence

Prisons as cultural arenas for the construction of masculinities

In the face of overwhelming evidence against, powerful men in public positions have continued to insist throughout the 1990s that 'prisons work'. An ironic response is that prisons do in fact work because they reproduce the social order that values hegemonic masculinity and reproduces 'normal' men (Sim 1994a: 107). Indeed, of all the alternatives of being manly available to men, in prison the preferred versions do appear to be the tough, aggressive forms of masculinity which Jimmy Boyle (1977) so accurately portrays in his autobiography. Prisons are indeed renowned as centres of excellence (along perhaps with the armed services and Eton school's 'hallowed turf') for the manufacture of such violent versions of masculinity; not least by the men employed or confined in prison themselves (Scraton 1991; and Sim 1994a).

Notably, the popularity of the 'prisons works' discourse continues to be supported by a collusive absence of gendered critique relating to custodial policies and practices in political and academic debate and research. Yet, such a critique can in fact provide a challenge to traditional patriarchal approaches to evaluating prisons through understanding how masculinities are situated within this particular cultural arena. Indeed, my intention in this chapter is to explore the use of sociological methodology to understand how men produce and reproduce masculinities and violence in prison by focusing on the highly gendered practice of storytelling. Through my application of this, I set out to provide a challenge and an alternative to collusive, masculinist, and often violent, practices employed by men in prison as inmates, prison officers, managers, policy makers, and researchers. It is highly relevant to note at the outset, how men's storytelling in and about prison contributes to the production and reproduction of particular versions or discourses of doing or accomplishing masculinity in this cultural arena. The reference in the title to 'sitting comfortably' therefore applies as much to those men in prison who are researched, as well as those who usually escape being researched, as it does to those doing the researching; clearly, I include myself in this.

Analyses of prisons as universities of crime are familiar within academic, political and popular media discussions of crime and punishment. Yet, such evaluations continually fail to acknowledge issues relating to men and masculinities. For example, the emphasis is often restricted to an individualized 'rotten egg' analysis, or a focus on 'inmate culture', rather than on the wider relations between all men in and outside prisons; or on 'men as prisoners rather than prisoners as men' (Sim 1994a: 101 – original emphasis). However, from a reading of recent debates linking gender, power and identity in the study of masculinities, there is clearly far more to be said about the characteristics of prison as a cultural arena.

There have been some good examples of applying recent developments in theorizing gender to the sociology of prisons. Caroline Newton (1994) describes, for example, how the concept of solidarity and informal codes between prison inmates is similar to the social relations of male bonding in other forms of 'fratriarchies' (p. 193). She analyses this in terms of the power relations of hegemonic masculinity, acknowledging that 'the roles and hierarchies within prisons are directly related to masculinities' (p. 197). Joe Sim (1994a) takes this analysis a stage further by incorporating the gendered practices of all men involved in the day-to-day routines of prison culture, its management, policy and operations. All men in this cultural arena are united by the fact they all have more or less access to masculine positions of power. Where this cultural unity between men exists across cultural arenas, it is also possible to talk of broader discursive contexts which help to shape the management and social relations of prison life. This type of analysis of prisons and masculinities is of course extremely complex. However, these points suffice as a starting point for talk about the intricacies of relations between men in prison.

Men's storytelling, cultural arenas and violence

This chapter has emerged from the coming together of three broader projects to explore qualitative issues in men's lives relating to masculinities and violence.[1] Men's life histories were collected in prison and with men on probation in the community. These stories were analysed in relation to the experiences, meanings and investments some men had in a range of violent activities (see Thurston and Beynon 1995).

The meanings of violence, taken from a reading of these stories, relate very powerfully to the various cultural arenas or 'lifespheres' within which the violence occurred and the stories told. Clearly, such 'lifespheres' are not readily separated. Within and across a range of cultural arenas, selves and stories transcend groups and boundaries. Thus, within the complex interplay of selves within contexts, the study of life stories men tell facilitates purchase upon gendered violence as simultaneously a personal act and a vehicle for cultural expression and group identity.

Most discussions of men changing their politics and identities have recently been the territory of more privileged men in the academy, and I again include myself here. However, as Bob Connell (1991) points out, men are changing in different ways and cultural circumstances to the perhaps more noticeable class- and race-specific activities of anti-sexist men's politics. Rather, as Connell notes, 'Changes are produced in dire conditions as well as comfortable ones, and may be far from benign' (p. 141).

The possibility of social change is also the concern of Ken Plummer's project to map out a 'sociology of stories' (Plummer 1983, 1995). He highlights the social role which stories and storytelling perform, and asks: 'how might stories perform functions of maintaining dominant orders and how might they be used to resist or transform lives and cultures?' (Plummer 1995: 25).

A number of key theoretical and political issues emerge relating to a sociology of stories, not least of which is locating storytelling – its production and consumption – within specific communities, social contexts and cultural arenas. This has, of course, been a concern for a variety of sociological investigations.[2] As a guide to starting to talk within sociology about the specific focus of such a method and its politics, Ken Plummer (pp. 29–30) draws attention to the social nature of stories; the making and consuming of stories, the strategies of storytelling; and the relationship of stories to wider frameworks of power.

These concerns have guided my research practices and subsequent analyses because of their relevance to a critique of masculinities, power and violence within prisons. For example, in this chapter I will focus particularly on how storytelling functions between men as an integral part of the institutional power relations of prison culture. Here, the recent theoretical developments emerging from feminist and pro-feminist scholarship provide the themes which an empirical and theoretical sociology of stories – as well as the more focused use of 'life history' methodology – can develop.[3] Connell (1991) sums this up succinctly as follows: 'For the analysis of masculinity, life-history method is particularly relevant because of its capacity to reveal social structures, collectivities, and institutional changes at the same time as personal life' (p. 143).

The stories I have selected from the research are told within my own narrative of being a male researcher in a prison for men. I will, therefore, focus on some of the characteristics of prison culture which emerged as part of my own 'story' of getting access to do research in one prison.[4] Following this, I will discuss some stories which provide a particular focus on the construction of gendered heterosexuality in prison. In the light of these arguments, I will go on to consider some of the possibilities, boundaries and practicalities of bringing about transformative practices.

'Getting sussed out': doing research in a prison for men

My first visit to the prison was with another white, male colleague[5] to meet the prison governor and his assistant in order to arrange access to do research. They were both white men in their early fifties. In this meeting they scrutinized the proposed research project in relation to formal and informal procedures and criteria. The project proposals were screened as to any potential problems they might present *vis-à-vis* the smooth running, security, and anonymity of the prison and its personnel. Once my colleague and I had sufficiently assured them of the project's validity and our authenticity, the dynamics of the meeting shifted. The two officials quickly moved into a dialogue of joking and banter, explaining that they had 'some really violent men who'd be just what you're looking for!' This left me feeling uneasy and anxious, with the implicit requirement to 'play the game', to join in and be 'one of the boys'.[6]

It is important to note that prison culture was not so unusual or unworldly as I had been led to expect from popular and academic representations of the institution. As white middle-class men, the proposal to do life history interviews with institutionally and, for the most part, structurally disempowered men was not seen as problematic. It is, of course, quite 'normal' for men with access to cultural power to be interested in other men's lives. This is especially true within criminal justice contexts, where some men routinely enter into relations of surveillance and judgement over other men who have been positioned as less powerful within the social relations of power/ knowledge. Indeed, central to my telling of this story is the two prison officials' engagement in an activity of distancing themselves from 'criminally dangerous men', and alignment with me and my colleague as 'respectable' and 'authoritative'.[7] The way in which the two officials articulated this – discursively and interactionally – offered my colleague and myself positions of agreement and collusion to take up. That we were invited to take part in this activity is significant in relation to the politics of men doing research on issues of masculinities. We had to be seen to be more than presentable, authentic, convincing – we also had to fit into their definition of legitimate masculinity.

Other incidents similarly involved being groomed by other powerful men in the prison. On my second visit, I had to be interviewed by a senior prison officer (SPO) in the security division. This took the form of a briefing, which I recorded after the interaction.

SPO: Now, have you been in prison before?
RT: No, this is my first time.
SPO: And, you haven't got any objections or worries about coming in to one?
RT: No, not really.

SPO: *Cos there's some who haven't the y'know for it . . . Now, if you're talking to the cons, you should know a thing or two. Right, first, those bastards will try to pull the wool over your eyes for certain. They'll try it on, they always do. Don't whatever you do offer to do something for them. Do you see?*

RT: *Yes, I understand. Yes, it's very clear.*

SPO: *One thing that you'll know about, is not to get involved with them. They're bastards some of them, they'll draw you in.*

Through this process of being 'sussed out' by a variety of men in authority in the prison, the message seemed to be quite clear: prison officers and officials were OK, inmates were not. For powerful men in the prison, inmates were not to be trusted, they were deceitful, underhanded, and above all dangerous individuals. They were somehow 'different'. Furthermore, to establish relationships with these men might 'blow the game', for to do this would involve making a connection between them and other men in the prison. For men at the top of the prison hierarchy, power and control seemed to rest on this symbolic difference – their gendered, professional identities were created through the social activities which routinely sustained such differences. Indeed, these stories seem to function to legitimize the incarceration of less powerful men. Plummer characterizes this relationship between stories and power in the following way:

> The story telling process flows through social acts of domination, hierarchy, marginalisation and inequality. Some voices – who claim to dominate, who top the hierarchy, who claim the centre, who possess resources – are not only heard much more readily than others . . . These social acts become habitual networks of domination congealing around gender, race, age, economic opportunity and sexuality: certain stories hence are silenced from a saying.
>
> (Plummer 1995: 30)

'The lads call them the "nancy boys"': the construction of gendered heterosexuality in men's stories in prison

My experiences of entering this arena gave an insight then into the way the prison culture was perceived and communicated by those men with both formal and informal investments in sustaining particular identities and relations of power/knowledge from the top of the prison hierarchy. This involved the normalization of certain masculinities and, through this, the regulation and control of others.[8] This routine process became increasingly apparent during my subsequent and regular visits (two or three times a week) to one area of the prison – the Vulnerable Prisoner Unit. Subsequently, I was to observe a range of differences being constructed in a range of men's stories.

These related most to gender and sexuality, which will be my focus here, but also to race, disability, economic status and age.

The Vulnerable Prisoner Unit (VPU) in the prison was positioned institutionally (through Rule 43 of prison rules) both physically and symbolically through its location at the bottom of the main building; and culturally, through the construction and sustaining of relations of difference. The hierarchy of the unit itself was at once striking in terms of human proximity to the day-to-day workings of power and status: 'They're the lowest of the low', as one prison officer on the main landings commented. I recorded the following in my fieldnotes during my early visits to the unit:

> The VPU is apparently at the bottom of the hierarchy of prison overall. But, I've also noticed that this is extended in the unit. The prison officers have their office at one end of the landing nearest to the main exit to the main landings. From this point a continuum is visible which runs the whole length of the landing. Those inmates who have work responsibilities on the landing and in the prison workshops are next. These men get the meagre perks to be got: extra food (left-overs), and more attention (conversation) from the prison officers. These men routinely express their heterosexuality (through stories relating to their wives and girlfriends, violence against 'Others', and through the private/public display of pornography on their cell walls). Their privacy is honoured – they are more valued – their stories are listened to. Next, and notably more on one side of the landing, are the older, and then the younger men with convictions of sex offences farther away. It is no coincidence that this side is closest to the 'recreation' yard where men from the main landings often urinate into the VPU cells. Farthest away from the symbolic centre of the prison and at bottom of the unit, a cell is shared by a black man awaiting a court hearing, and a man from a psychiatric unit whose crime was being 'caught' having sex with another man.

In most cultural arenas women are positioned as the Other in relation to which powerful men construct their power and identities. This is no different in the prison I visited. Women were routinely objectified (through legitimized pornography),[9] portrayed as the 'cause of all evil', and regularly blamed for violence in the stories men told about their own violence. However, in the (physical) absence of women in prison, sex offenders were more accessible as the location of 'Otherness'.[10]

In order for (some) men to define themselves as 'normal', sex offenders are named and constructed routinely in relation to versions or aspects of 'femininity', homosexuality, or as non- or sub-human. Newton (1994: 198) extends this point, quoting Connell and Segal:

> At a structural level, hegemonic masculinities rely on these distinctions:
> '"The justifying" ideology for the patriarchal core complex and the

overall subordination of women requires the creation of a gender-based hierarchy among men' (Connell 1987: 215) . . . 'It is a way of keeping men separated off from women and keeping women subordinate to men' (Segal 1990: 16).[11]

The categorization and construction of inmates in the VPU as 'different' represents a process of objectification which works to sustain an idea of violence against these men – and women – as acceptable. With the association of femininity, and labelling of the VPU as the place for sex offenders, the unit was routinely the target of abuse and violence. This is illustrated discursively in the following story told by a man on the 'main' landing:

> They're all fucking beasts down there. Fucking nonces. There was this tall skinny cunt. He was down for messin' about with his little sister, the monster. My mate, right, gave him hell. He punched him once. It's like if you chucked a nonce in with the boys, he'd be fucking killed.

For men (in prison), the experience of identity is tied up with their experiences of power and powerlessness in and outside prison. The knowledge constructed about sex offenders is perceived as a threat to the exercise of gendered power, and the reconstruction and valuing of powerful identities of gendered heterosexuality may be about resisting other forms of powerlessness.[12]

Clearly, it was legitimate to produce and consume stories about some men's violence (i.e. heterosexual violence) and not others (i.e. the violence done by men convicted of sexual violence against women, children and other men). Because of this tenuous distinction, my proposal to talk with men on the VPU, to encourage different stories to be told and heard about *their* violence, was also met with hostility by some prison officers. I recorded the following in my fieldnotes:

> In the prison gym today being shown around the prison by one of the officers from the VPU. He introduced me to the prison officer with responsibility for the gym. I explained my interest in men's violence, and talked a little bit about 'what it means to be a man', that 'It's mostly men who commit violent offences, and I'm interested in their stories.' Then the VPU officer explained that I was doing research in the VPU. The PO from the gym responded in a 'joking' manner: 'I thought you said you were talking about male violence. They're a load of nancies down there, a load of wimps. [Laughter] You want to be talking to some of the men on the main landing. They're *really* violent! [Laughter] I would have thought they'd have better tales to tell!'

My proposal to talk to men in the VPU about their stories of violence seemed to threaten to disrupt the dominant relations between men in prison. There was clearly a price to pay – in terms of respect and status – for some men with perceived power to interact meaningfully with (i.e. listen to/take seriously) 'sex offenders'.

Joking clearly emerged during the research as a strategy for negotiating status and policing gender relations within the dominant hierarchies of the prison for both prison officers and inmates.[13] One of the ways I picked up on this was through the felt effect of these interactions as deterring me from pursuing the research in the VPU.

For the prison officers who had volunteered to work on the VPU there was a constant reminder of their own status within the subculture of the prison officers. One of the prison officers on the 'main' landings told me the following story after I explained I was working on the VPU: 'The officers on the VP unit – you know they work with nonces, well the lads [other prison officers] call them the "nancy boys"' [laughter].

While I was visiting the prison, this group of 'named' prison officers, whilst subjected to this type of 'joking', were also engaged in a process of attempting to transform the VPU into a less oppressive environment. To some extent changes had occurred. Inmates in the unit told stories illustrating some degree of positive regard with these officers in comparison with others they had known, whilst the officers reported a significant reduction of suicide attempts on the landing and 'breaches' resulting in solitary confinement. This core group of colleagues sustained a committed interest in creating a more positive environment. Their motivation for doing this, however, is significant and not as selfless as first perceived. During the research this emerged as an attempt by them to create for themselves a context which was simultaneously 'safer', and more aligned to constructing less aggressive and oppressive identities.[14] It was no coincidence that these men were older than the average landing prison officers. The following story was told to me by 'John' – one of the officers on the VPU – while we were walking around the prison site on the way to the unit:

> All the older, sloppy officers spend most their lives patrolling the prison grounds, that sort of thing. It's a cop-out really. I think they lose it, their bottle like. All of a sudden, they lose confidence in knowing whether they can handle situations . . . Now, I've been in the service for nearly 20 years. You get used to it over the years. Mind you, it affects some people differently. It's like I don't feel I have to prove myself any more, now I'm older. It's different when you're younger. I was always rolling around then . . . That all stopped when I started wearing glasses, thank God.

John's story reveals some of the contradictions and tensions around being an older prison officer, maintaining a purchase on still being able to 'handle himself', an investment in a particular version of masculinity, whilst acknowledging his reluctance and fear of having to do this. There seems to be some degree of negotiation here for John, between memories of an older self and the rewriting of his present self. Drawing on Kaplan (1986), Beverley Skeggs (1991: 136) characterizes such 'change' as 'an oscillation between moments of relative incoherence, the breaking up of old political languages and positions and moments when new formulations, often tentative and transitory, are being realised'.

One of the effects, however, of the prison officers' subculture of joking and abuse towards those working on the VPU was perceived very clearly by the group of five or six officers who managed the unit. One of the officers talked about giving up their project and returning to a respected position as an officer on the 'main' landings. This was exacerbated by the prison governor not endorsing these changes.

Apparently, for both the prison officer subculture and the man with most power in the prison, listening to these 'different' or changing stories might mean losing purchase on positions of power through being seen to 'lose face'.[15] This relates to Joe Sim's (1994a) discussion of the possibilities and boundaries to changing the culture of prisons so that they might challenge dominant relations between men. In a conference report of his work (1994b), Sim questions the reluctance of the prison system to change, despite there being a number of good examples of such transformations. The suggestion is that powerful men at all levels of the criminal justice system have a personal and political investment – albeit an asymmetrical one – in reproducing hegemonic masculinity.[16] The Home Secretary's sustained position that 'prisons work', paradoxically flying in the face of available research, is a thoroughly worrying illustration of this.

Reconstructing stories and telling new ones: possibilities for challenging research on men, violence and masculinities

The process of doing this research has encouraged me to consider the value of doing critical life story work as a possible basis for pragmatic intervention. After all, doing nothing with the research, leaving it as a publication or conference paper, may well be an act of collusion with those in society (and in the academy!) who do not want to raise questions around masculinities and men's power; such people may, instead, prefer to continue to take hegemonic forms of masculinity as the norm in both social research and social policy. Christine Griffin (1991) challenges the idea and practice of 'doing nothing' in research methodologies. She suggests that to challenge sexism in practice (or praxis) is to recognize both commitment and responsibility to gender politics in research. The possible outcomes, uses and politics of research, of course, do not end after the fieldwork or report writing stage. A whole range of sometimes disappointing, sometimes dangerous, and sometimes constructive things happen to research once it has passed out of the hands of the researcher. But does this have to be such a haphazard process?

In her research of the practices and experiences of black women in secure psychiatric hospitals, Sallie Westwood (1992) has suggested that life history work might provide a focus for challenging and transformative research. She argues that such 'research methods and skills can be appropriated for counter-hegemonic work' (Westwood 1992: 197). Whilst it must be acknowledged that counter-hegemonic work with men who use violence may need to be markedly different, critical life story work might usefully feature in interventions with some violent men in ways that actively challenge their power/knowledge.

From the research, it is emerging that this might best be done at critical incidents or transition points in their lives. The narratives that some of the men produced in this cultural arena illustrate that their sense of self has undergone, or is in the process of undergoing, a potential transformation – or 'oscillation between moments' (Skeggs 1991: 136) – as a result of their experience and self-evaluation of self in the context of prison. Furthermore, movement between these different gendered/sexual positions is constrained within prisons (and other cultural arenas) by the power located in discourse/ knowledge, and circumscribed by categories of cultural difference.

Afterword

An extension to the wider project has now emerged, necessarily focusing on how a cultural critique of masculinities and violence can effectively engage men in a process of change that results in the reduction of their violence. The site for this project is Mid Glamorgan Probation Service, where pilot programmes for men convicted of violence are currently being developed.[17] This work incorporates a sensitivity to policy, as well as theoretically informed research that evaluates the effectiveness and politics of such intervention. The life history method is proving to be an accessible and relevant practice method for practitioners working with men.[18] I have been involved with colleagues in introducing the method to practitioners through training in order for them to first, gain a more in-depth understanding of the links between masculinities and violence; second, develop practice methods and exercises for re-education programmes; and third, develop the material as part of the evaluation of interventions. This can be done, for example, through a reading of the way stories change as a result of participation on a groupwork programme.[19]

Enabling new stories to be told is the aim of this further stage of the research. As a form of intervention it is about making a space for the process of shifting patterns of identity formulation within groups of men. Encouraging men to tell new stories is simultaneously about asking them to rewrite their identities and their violence *as men* within particular cultural arenas. How motivated men will be to do this depends on how they see the pay-offs of such change in relation to their purchase upon power in their lives. Similarly, questions emerge as to how such interventions will be taken up and 'owned' by other more powerful men who run individual units in prisons, govern prisons, or manage policy in the criminal justice system.[20] Thus the possibilities of men changing in order to stop or reduce their violence and control, on either side of the law, must clearly be located within an understanding of the positions adopted by certain groups of men in terms of historical and structural relations of power within and across cultural arenas.

Acknowledgements

I would like to thank a number of people across a number of cultural arenas for their continuing support throughout the project, and for their openness for listening to new stories. Thanks go to: John Beynon at the University of Glamorgan, Ann Gray at the University of Birmingham, my colleagues at the Research, Resource and Development Unit in Mid Glamorgan Probation Service, and Beverley Skeggs for giving valuable feedback on earlier versions of the chapter. I would also like to acknowledge my thanks to the following agencies for their involvement and interest: The Leverhulme Trust, Mid Glamorgan Probation Service, the Prison Service, the University of Glamorgan, Gwent Probation Service, and South Glamorgan Probation Service.

Notes

1 The project was originally set up as part of a student research course on qualitative methods. From here, it was developed into a project attracting funding from the Leverhulme Trust on 'Men, masculinities and violence'. Currently it is continuing through my PhD at the Cultural Studies Department, University of Birmingham, and as part of the research and development of community interventions run by Mid Glamorgan Probation Service.

2 See Plummer (1983) for a detailed survey and discussion of the politics and practices involved in the study of 'life documents'.

3 Some recent arguments for and uses of life history methodology for studying men and masculinities include: Jackson (1990); Connell (1991); Liddle (1993); Christian (1994); Jefferson (1994).

4 The prison I visited to do the research was a 'local prison' where most inmates were either on remand, awaiting a court hearing or already convicted and awaiting sentence or transfer to other more long-term prisons.

5 My companion on this occasion was John Beynon from the University of Glamorgan, the Leverhulme project supervisor.

6 My reading of this interaction is informed by Christine Griffin's (1991) account of her experiences of doing research.

7 This reminded me of the importance of the links Foucault makes in his analyses of the relations of knowledge/power within the cultural arena of prison (see Foucault 1991).

8 This analysis is informed by Beverley Skegg's analysis of sexuality, masculinity and power (Skeggs 1991).

9 One of the stories told to me during the research recounted how prison officers had shown a pornographic film to inmates as a 'Christmas treat'. This display of pornography on cell walls was also informally allowed to be as a 'perk'.

10 This must be unpicked further by recognizing the links between the cultural construction of sex offenders and young men and black men both in and outside prison.

11 Newton (1994: 200) also notes that this analysis requires further contextualization *vis-à-vis* race and class in terms of the divisions between women.

12 My reading of this was informed greatly by Henrietta Moore's far more in-depth discussion (1994) of the relationship between identities, culture, power and violence.

13 This reminds me of John Beynon's analysis (1989) of joking in 'a school for men'.

14 This reading is informed by Stanko's analysis of men's experiences of victimization (Stanko 1990).

15 Henrietta Moore (1994: 151), drawing on Wendy Hollway (1984), refers to this as a 'thwarting of investment', which she defines as: 'the inability to sustain or properly take up a gendered subject position, resulting in a crisis, real or imagined, of self-representation and/or social evaluation.'

16 I have drawn on Hollway (1984, 1989) for her development of the concept of 'investment' in relation to the construction of gendered identities.

17 There is a growing recognition of the importance of addressing issues relating to the theoretical development of understanding masculinities and crime within the field of probation work. Recent discussions and reports on such work, include: Burnham *et al.* (1990); Senior and Woodhill (1992); Stanko (1993); Benstead, Wall and Forbes (1994); and Benstead *et al.* (1994).

18 Shaw (1966) and Becker *et al.* (1966) provide the bases for such an integration of empirical research through the life history or 'boy's own' method, and possibilities for practice intervention.

19 The possibility for integrating empirically informed research in the context of probation practice has been partly due to recent discussions of probation policy and practice. This can be characterized as a shift from a view that 'nothing works' to 'something works'. See MacDonald (1994) and Raynor and Vanstone (1994).

20 At the time of writing, the Home Office seem to be intent on imposing a particular version of macho management in the probation service. A perceived feminization of the service is being used as a scapegoat to scrap social work training for probation officers, and to encourage the militarization of the service by employing ex-military and police men.

References

Becker, H. (1966) Introduction, in C.R. Shaw *The Jack-Roller*, 1966 edn. London: University of Chicago Press.

Benstead, J., Brown, A., Forbes, C. and Wall, R. (1994) Men working with men in groups: masculinity and crime, *Groupwork*, 7(1): 37–49.

Benstead, J., Wall, R. and Forbes, C. (1994) Cyberpunks, Ronnie Biggs and the culture of masculinity: getting men thinking, *Probation Journal*, March: 18–22.

Beynon, J. (1989) 'A school for men': an ethnographic case study of routine violence in schooling, in S. Walker and L. Barton (eds) *Politics and the Processes of Schooling*. Milton Keynes: Open University Press.

Boyle, J. (1977) *A Sense of Freedom*. London: Pan Books.

Burnham, D., Boyle, J., Copsey, M., Cordery, J., Dominelli, L., Lambert, J., Smallridge, M., Whitehead, V. and Willis, S. (1990) Offending and masculinity: working with males, *Probation Journal*, September: 106–11.

Christian, H. (1994) *The Making of Anti-Sexist Men*. London: Routledge.

Connell, R.W. (1987) *Gender and Power*. Cambridge: Polity Press.

Connell, R.W. (1991) Live fast and die young: the construction of masculinity among young working-class men on the margin of the labour market, *Australian and New Zealand Journal of Sociology*, 27(2): 141–71.

Foucault, M. (1988) The dangerous individual, in L.D. Kritzman (ed.) *Michel Foucault: Politics, Philosophy, Culture: Interviews and Other Writings 1977–1984*. London: Routledge.

Foucault, M. (1991) *Discipline and Punish*. London: Penguin.

Griffin, C. (1991) The researcher talks back, in W.B. Shaffer and R.A. Stebbins (eds) *Experiencing Fieldwork: An Inside View of Qualitative Research*. Newbury Park, CA: Sage.

Hollway, W. (1984) Gender difference and the production of subjectivity, in J. Henriques, W. Urwin, C. Venn and V. Walkerdine *Changing the Subject: Psychology, Social Regulation and Subjectivity*. London: Sage.

Hollway, W. (1989) Subjectivity and method in psychology: *Gender, Meaning and Science*. London: Sage.

Jackson, D. (1990) *Unmasking Masculinity: A Critical Autobiography*. London: Unwin Hyman.

Jefferson, T. (1994) Theorising masculine subjectivity, in T. Newburn and E. Stanko (eds) *Just Boys Doing Business: Men, Masculinities and Crime*. London: Routledge.

Kaplan, C. (1986) *Sea Changes: Culture and Feminism*. London: Verso.

Liddle, M. (1993) Masculinity, 'male behaviour' and crime: a theoretical investigation of sex-differences in delinquency and deviant behaviour, in E. Stanko (ed.) *Masculinity and Crime: Issues of Theory and Practice: Conference Report*. Uxbridge: Centre for Criminal Justice Research, Brunel University.

MacDonald, G. (1994) Developing empirically-based practice in probation, *British Journal of Social Work*, 24: 405–27.

Moore, H. (1994) The problem of explaining violence in the social sciences, in P. Harvey and P. Gow (eds) *Sex and Violence: Issues in Representation and Experience*. London: Routledge.

Newton, C. (1994) Gender theory and prison sociology: using theories of masculinities to interpret the sociology of prisons for men, *The Howard Journal*, 33(3): 193–202.

Plummer, K. (1983) *Documents of Life*. London: Unwin Hyman.

Plummer, K. (1995) *Telling Sexual Stories: Power, Change and Social Worlds*. London: Routledge.

Raynor, P. and Vanstone, M. (1994) Probation practice, effectiveness and the non-treatment paradigm, *British Journal of Social Work*, 24: 387–404.

Scraton, P., Sim, J. and Skidmore, P. (1991) *Prisons under Protest*. Milton Keynes: Open University Press.

Segal, L. (1990) *Slow Motion: Changing Masculinities, Changing Men*. London: Virago Press.

Senior, P. and Woodhill, D. (eds) (1992) *Gender, Crime and Probation Practice*. Sheffield: PAVIC Publications and Sheffield Polytechnic.

Shaw, C.R. (1966) *The Jack-Roller*, first published 1930. London: University of Chicago Press.

Sim, J. (1994a) Tougher than the rest: men in prison, in T. Newburn and E. Stanko (eds) *Just Boys Doing Business? Men, Masculinities and Crime*. London: Routledge.

Sim, J. (1994b) *Men in Prison*. Paper to 'Who do you think you are talking to: a conference examining the links between masculinities and violence', Newcastle under Lyme, October 1994.

Skeggs, B. (1991) Challenging masculinity and using sexuality, *British Journal of Sociology of Education*, 12(2): 127–39.

Stanko, E. (1990) *Everyday Violence: How Women and Men Experience Sexual and Physical Danger*. London: Pandora.

Stanko, E. (1993) *Masculinity and Crime: Issues of Theory and Practice: Conference Report*. Uxbridge: Centre for Criminal Justice Research, Brunel University.

Thurston, R. and Beynon, J. (1995) Men's own stories, lives and violence: research as practice, in R.E. Dobash, R.P. Dobash and L. Noakes *Gender and Crime*. Cardiff: University of Wales Press.

Westwood, S. (1992) Power/knowledge: the politics of transformative research, *Studies in the Education of Adults*, 24(2): 191–8.

From 'little fairy boy' to 'the compleat destroyer': subjectivity and transformation in the biography of Mike Tyson

Introduction: the social and the psychic

My aim in what follows is to offer an interpretation of how Tyson transformed himself first from a pudgy, passive, lisping schoolboy – the butt of local bullies – to a feared neighbourhood bully and thief, and then to a boxing prodigy who went on to become the youngest-ever world heavyweight champion. To do this involves a particular understanding of subjectivity and its transformations which I have detailed at length elsewhere (Jefferson 1994a). Rather than attempt to summarize or simply assert that argument here, I will introduce the key concepts *in situ*, thereby hopefully demonstrating their usefulness in practice. I will also, occasionally, compare and contrast Tyson's transformations with similar changes in the lives of either Malcolm X or Muhammad Ali. This emphasis on the shared social underpinnings of psychic processes will focus particularly on the question of the scarring psychological impact of racism.

Mike Tyson was born on 30 June 1966, the same year that Ali politicized the world heavyweight boxing championship by refusing to go to Vietnam, and one year after Malcolm was shot for pursuing 'freedom by any means necessary'. If Malcolm and Ali represented the apotheosis of America's black revolution, the first black superheroes of the modern era, it is tempting to see Tyson as its satanic nemesis. And if Malcolm and Ali epitomized the hope and optimism of the expansionary 1960s, it is tempting to regard Tyson as emblematic of the despair and pessimism of the recessionary 1980s, the manifestation of a terrible nihilistic rage, the return of the repressed.

It is tempting, but too simple, for a number of reasons. In the first place it offers too deterministic a reading, regarding people as a simple product of the social forces of their time. Second, and relatedly, its determinism precludes raising seriously the question of agency, the notion that 'social forces' are themselves the outcome, ultimately, of a multitude of actions taken (or overlooked) by human subjects. The question of the subjectivities underpinning human actions brings us to the final problem with the above reading, namely, the unitary and fixed nature of the assumed subjectivities of Malcolm, Ali and Tyson – heroes or anti-hero – thus precluding the possibility of contradictions in their personalities and, most importantly, the enormous transformations observable in all their biographies.

However, on the positive side, our initial reading does alert us to the importance of social factors, even as it downplays the significance of the psyche (despite the Freudian reference to 'the repressed'). The point is that both the social and the psychic are important, *and their interpenetration*. One person who has attended to the importance of both levels and the complexity of their interpenetration is the Marxist psychoanalyst Eugene Wolfenstein. His monumental biography of Malcolm X moves skilfully back and forth between a (Marxist) historical analysis of North America's black revolution and a (Freudian) interpretation of the life history of Malcolm. Given the problems of space, I am going to focus on the psychic level, though without neglecting the level of the social. In so doing, I hope to demonstrate how attention to this level illuminates the complex contradictoriness of human behaviour, an understanding of which is essential to any hope of understanding the activities of groups that collectively create the structures that constitute 'society'. Whilst such an analysis helps illuminate the differences between Tyson, Ali and Malcolm, it can also show up similarities. This serves to make two important political points: that the line between hero and anti-hero is less clear than rhetorical journalese would have us believe; and that psychic processes are not unique to each individual, but are shared and therefore socially underpinned.

A caveat, finally. Some would argue that psychoanalysis and secondary sources do not mix, that you can only psychoanalyse patients, based on what they say in a therapeutic situation. My first response to this echoes Wolfenstein's, namely, that 'plausibility', not 'truth', is the aim:

> our own psychoanalytic interpretations of Malcolm's activity, just because they are formed outside the context of the therapeutic interaction, cannot be considered true, but only more or less plausible. At best, we may hope to provide a coherent, internally consistent, and empirically inclusive view of his character and emotional development.
> (Wolfenstein 1989: 38)

Through a series of studies of Tyson which address different questions, my intention is progressively to broaden and deepen the picture and in that way move towards a more definitive biographical account (see Jefferson 1993, 1994a, 1994b). But a stronger response to those who think that psychoanalysis and secondary sources do not mix is to remind readers that though psychoanalysis works on 'primary' materials (e.g. dreams, memories, etc.)

produced by the client, such materials are 'texts'. These 'texts' must be interpreted, *just like the 'texts' constituting secondary sources*. Much secondary source material consists of what was (allegedly) said, i.e. primary 'texts'. If it does not, that only adds an extra level of interpretation. But, however you look at it, on the analyst's couch or in the library, there is no escaping the need to interpret 'texts' (see Freeman 1993).

From fairy boy to bully boy: confusion, anxiety, delinquency and race

For brevity's sake, I wish to focus on the period of Tyson's life only up until he acquired the world heavyweight championship crown. Let me start with a quotation from Tyson, speaking from his Indiana prison cell. Like all quotations, it should not be taken at face value and will need interpreting, but it offers both a start and a theme:

> I spent so much time to get on top and when I got there, it was not what I thought it would be. It was all in my mind. It was not reality, but what was in my mind was reality to me. This is why I became confused, why so many bad things happened. But my life is in some kind of place now.
> (*Daily Express* 20 November 1993: 3)

The tricky relation between 'mind' and 'reality' will be implicit throughout; but I wish explicitly to pick up on Tyson's 'confusion', not least because it echoes Illingworth's judgement, in the best biography to date of Tyson, that 'feelings of confusion about his life' are central to an understanding of the young Tyson (Illingworth 1992: 6). These confusions had multiple sources: chronic poverty; an absent father; a mother who could not cope, who drank and who fought with her boyfriend; constant moves into poorer and poorer neighbourhoods; and a genetic endowment that gave him a body and a head too big and bulky for either his years or his soft, lisping voice, the kind of combination that made him a constant target of bullying. Poor, abandoned, neglected, unsettled, odd and bullied; small wonder that he chose passivity. But withdrawal into some less threatening inner world gave him no respite in the outer one, but only 'earned more beatings' (p. 4). This confusion, stemming from a chronically chaotic family life and a relentlessly hostile environment, was, according to Illingworth, what lay behind the rage that was to transform Tyson from 'little fairy boy' to local bully boy, once an older boy had grossly overstepped the mark in ripping the head off one of Tyson's beloved pigeons. I shall return below to the question of rage and transformation; but for the moment I wish to explore further the notion of confusion, especially its relationship to goodness and badness, to whiteness and blackness, and to anxiety.

Once of the things that probably added to the young Tyson's confusions was that when he was no good at anything, in the passive days before he got into thieving and bullying, for example, he was deemed 'good' though he felt 'bad' (unhappy, insecure, afraid, etc.). Yet when he became 'good' at something (gained a reputation as a bully and a thief) he was dubbed 'bad' even though he felt 'good' (more confident, less afraid, etc.). Learning to box (as we shall see later) offered one form of resolution of this confusion: in the ring it was 'good' to be 'bad'; he was positively rewarded for being bad (aggressive), he was good at it, and never felt better than when 'doing bad' in the ring. Yet, he achieved the (good) transition from delinquent to boxer only via the (bad) exchange of the freedom of ghetto streets for the punishment of the reformatory. The man who taught him was a white ex-boxer called Stewart. He was also instrumental in getting Tyson out of the reformatory and into Cus D'Amato's famous Catskill training camp for aspiring young boxers. There, in an all-white training camp, the elderly D'Amato, who was to guide Tyson to boxing immortality, became manager, mentor, sage and father figure, and his partner Camille a surrogate mother. So, the 'reformation' of Tyson and his subsequent (good) success as a boxer was achieved only once he had been plucked from his (bad) black family and neighbourhood and transplanted, via the reformatory, into a (good) white surrogate family.

Though Malcolm X's family background was initially very different, principally in having a coping mother and a big, powerful, politically militant, religious father who was probably murdered by the Black Legion (a local variant of the Ku Klux Klan) when Malcolm was only six years old, there are points of similarity around the issue of 'confusion'. For, once Malcolm's father died, the family became dependent on welfare, a development which destroyed their mother's self-respect and eventually her sanity, led Malcolm into delinquency, and split up the family. Malcolm's feelings about this were complexly ambivalent, according to Wolfenstein's orthodoxly Freudian interpretation: guilt and shame for contributing to his mother's pain coupled with anger at her inability to love him well enough to cope; pride at being 'bad' (uppity) like his Garveyite father coupled with a displacement of Christian guilt (the other side of his 'moral patrimony') on to his father's destructive successors, namely, the welfare people. Boxing then as now (Joe Louis had just won the heavyweight crown) would have been one way to resolve this confusing clash of good and bad; and he did indeed attempt it – unsuccessfully. Losing twice to a white boy, 'his one possibility of breaking the vicious circle of self-destructive aggressive action no longer existed' (Wolfenstein 1989: 138). The result was a further descent into defiance, expulsion from school, followed by sentencing to a detention home, run by a good white couple. He was 13 years old. There they were able to break the 'vicious circle of Malcolm's self-destructive action' by being accepting, loving, non-punitive parental substitutes, thus enabling Malcolm to feel good and proud – but only by repressing his bad, aggressive, defiant, black self; in other words by becoming the 'house nigger' who identifies with the oppressor by attempting to be white.

In both cases then, though with different psychic origins, feeling good was associated (if more ambivalently than I have time to explore here) with 'doing bad', which was also the only means available of positively identifying with their blackness, given that the option of 'being good' was only available on white terms. In short, in addition to the particular confusions each felt as a result of their unique family traumas, both were precluded from feeling good by being good (and thus resolving the confusion), given the omnipresence of racism in their lives. In the event, Tyson's (partial) resolution of this confusion was achieved in the boxing ring (and possibly only here, given the evidence of his continuing problems outside), whereas Malcolm eventually resolved his confusion (after his hustling years of 'doing bad' as drug-addicted dope dealer, thief, and pimp, and a lengthy prison sentence) when he was able to reclaim positively his black, Garveyite heritage, first by joining the Nation of Islam, and later through his own unique, revolutionary philosophy of Afro-American internationalism.

Though 'confusion' is a useful descriptive term, it has no theoretical status within psychoanalysis. Moreover, it offers no clues as to why the transformations of Tyson, via boxing, and Malcolm, via a religious conversion, take these particular paths. It is true, as we have seen, that Malcolm had no talent for boxing (and Tyson none for preaching, as it happens), but that only re-poses the question of how to account for the motivations behind the choices made. Which brings us to a core concept within psychoanalysis that does have the necessary theoretical scope, namely, anxiety.[1] It will, however, first need some reconstruction if it is to be freed of its biological heritage and thus able to aid a non-reductively social understanding of the psyche.

Broadly, we can talk of two types of psychoanalytic theorizing about anxiety, though both have to do with conflict. The first, classically Freudian, sees anxiety as the outward manifestation of the conflict between libido and the (desexualized) demands of society 'handled' by the self-preserving instincts of the ego. In other words, 'damned-up libido . . . [is] converted into manifestly felt anxiety' (Hinshelwood 1991: 221). The characteristic defence against such neurotic anxiety is repression. The second follows on from Freud's later adoption of a dualistic theory of instincts – the life (libido) and death (aggressive) instincts. This enabled Klein to relocate 'the conflict . . . as an internal conflict between the instincts', and to argue that 'such a conflict develops two forms: depressive anxiety and persecutory anxiety' (p. 221). This Kleinian shift, precipitated by her interest specifically in the fears, anxieties and sadistic phantasies of very young children, involved a series of important revisions. One was an emphasis on the 'phantasy *content* of anxiety rather than the energy from which it is derived' (p. 221). This revision 'led directly to a radical change in the view of the nature of anxiety – from a physiological transformation to a psychological content' (p. 113). Relocating the conflict 'as an internal conflict between the instincts' elevated aggression (death instinct), not libido, to the central role in human development:

> If anxiety is an interaction between sadism and libido and thus libido
> and aggression are on an equal footing, then this demotes libido as the
> crucial element of instinctual life; and if excessive anxiety inhibits or
> distorts development through the interference with the natural progress
> of the libido, then aggression is the real motor of development.
>
> (p. 119)

Finally, this elevation of the importance of aggression was accompanied by
a concern with 'the primitive (or psychotic) defence mechanisms [that] are
ranged against anxieties that derive from the activity of the death instinct'
(p. 122), as opposed to the neurotic defences.

These revisions never break with an instinctual basis for anxiety. However,
when Klein focused on the primitive, pre-Oedipal defence mechanisms *which
are essentially relational* ('denial, splitting, excessive forms of projection and
introjection, related identifications, and idealization' (p. 122), she provided a
way for a further reconceptualization of anxiety: one which sees it as socially
produced, but unique in its manifestations in particular individuals. Here I
draw on the work of Hollway and her colleagues (Henriques *et al.* 1984;
Hollway 1989). In a sophisticated reworking of concepts derived from
Foucault, Lacan and Klein, they manage the very difficult task of showing
how subjectivity can be both a product of various social discourses, and of a
unique personal biography. Foucault-derived social discourses provide the
possible subject positions, and a reworked Lacanian notion of desire enables
the actual choices made by particular individuals to be understood. Klein,
divested of her biological assumptions, provides the crucial key. The result, as
I summarized in an earlier paper, is to make 'the inter-subjective management
of anxiety' central to a theory of subjectivity:

> The shift towards a more social reading of Klein is achieved first by
> suggesting how anxiety can be conceptualised as a product of human
> relations, not nature, without losing its ubiquitous character; then by
> showing how the defence mechanisms of splitting and projection are
> constantly implicated in the inter-subjective management of anxiety;
> and finally by illustrating how 'the continuous attempt to manage
> anxiety, to protect oneself . . . provides a continuous, more or less
> driven, motive for the negotiation of power in relations' (Hollway
> 1989: 85). This continuous attempt to defend against a feeling of
> powerlessness within a person's actual relationships thus gives sub-
> stance to what is 'unsatisfiable and contentless' (*ibid.*: 58) in Lacan's
> notion of desire, rescues Klein's notion of anxiety from its biological
> moorings, and links both with a Foucauldian-derived notion of power.
>
> (Jefferson 1994a: 26)

In other words, the key to unlocking the discursive choices made – choices
that collectively constitute a person's identity – is to be found in the defensive

attempts people make to ward off anxiety, to avoid feelings of powerlessness. If this is so, power, not desire, becomes 'the motor for positioning in discourses and the explanation of what is suppressed in signification' (Hollway 1989: 60). Let us go back to Tyson and see how this assists in making sense of his transformation from 'passive little boy' to aggressive gang member and thief.

As I mentioned earlier, the incident widely regarded as critical in this transformation was the infamous pigeon incident. To the sadistic bully involved, Tyson was undoubtedly a 'safe' target, given his reputation for passivity. But on this occasion, an enraged Tyson turned and fought back. In terms of anxiety, we might say that Tyson's feelings of vulnerability and powerlessness became overwhelming, insupportable; and that these became assuaged in the fight back. Moreover, the fact that he was successful in defeating the older boy was undoubtedly an important moment of empowerment for the young Tyson, not just in the immediate sense, but in showing the rewards of another 'active' way of being-in-the-world.

However, to dwell too long on an incident which has acquired a quasi-mythical status, and which has probably too definite a place as a transformative event, would be a mistake. The important point is how to understand the change of identity that Tyson underwent, somehow, in the movement out of passivity. Even here there is an evidential problem; for despite the stories of violence, bullying, robbing and thieving, and his revolving-door relationship with local reformatories, it is not clear just how 'bad' Tyson actually was. Bobbie Stewart, the man who was to teach Tyson to box in the Tryon detention centre, was apparently puzzled by this: 'Tyson became a puzzle to Stewart. If he was such a bad kid, why had he been put in Tryon, a less-than-minimum-security [sic] facility? Stewart checked Tyson's file: all the crimes were petty, the worst being the theft of fruit from a grocery store' (Illingworth 1992: 8).

One might have two responses to this: it demonstrates the appalling racism of US criminal justice in constantly incarcerating a hungry black kid for stealing fruit; or, Tyson was fortunate in only getting caught for his minor offences. For our purposes, however, the more significant point is the fact that Tyson-the-champ remembered himself as the 'bad boy'. In other words, whatever the 'reality' at the time, Tyson later chose to identify with the 'bad boy' image, rather than with the position of innocent victim of a racist system of criminal justice. This needs unravelling.

Illingworth says that Tyson 'played along' with the account of the pigeon incident because 'it fit ever so conveniently into his public persona as some primal force of destruction' (p. 5). Perhaps. Though, it should be remembered that his bad-boy image was a very mixed blessing for his management team: it made for welcome publicity but it also frightened off certain would-be sponsors. Moreover, it suggests a degree of self-consciousness about his media image that is not supported by other aspects of his behaviour with journalists, which seemed marked as much by boredom, impatience and a wish to avoid them (sleeping through press conferences, for example) than any desire to promote a particular image. But Illingworth's other comment about the 'empowerment' Tyson felt 'when the urges were tempered into systematic violence' (p. 5) seems more revealing since it suggests the importance of social rewards ('empowerment') attaching to the bad-boy image.

In choosing to identify with a bad-boy image, regardless of how badly the youthful member of the Jolly Stompers Brooklyn gang actually behaved, Tyson is embracing what I call the 'tough guy' discourse (Jefferson 1993: 7), wherein 'toughness' connotes 'one's ability to survive on the streets' as well as 'the ability to meet and resist physical challenges' (p. 8). Given the class and race relations of the contemporary North American ghetto, and the social powerlessness of its inhabitants, the 'tough guy' discourse undoubtedly offers ghetto males an attractive subject position or identity, albeit one based on a pathetic caricature of patriarchal power (captured who knows how self-consciously in the name of Tyson's gang). In making men subjects not objects of discourse, the 'tough guy' discourse allows an agency that other discourses for comprehending the ghetto do not. The 'good/evil' discourse, which comprehends the ghetto in terms of its overshare of 'evil' people, and the 'deprivation/reformation' discourse, with its recasting of 'evil people' in terms of 'deprived victims' to be reformed, both offer only object status to the young men who are their primary concern (pp. 6–8).

So, Tyson embracing the 'tough guy' discourse is perhaps only to be expected. But it seems to go deeper with him. Whereas many a successful man with a delinquent past might play down the latter, putting it down to youthful immaturity, or to 'survival tactics' long outgrown, Tyson seemed to relish being 'raw material to feed cultural curiosity about the nature and origins of sociopathic viciousness' (Illingworth 1992: 5). He seemed to want 'the world to believe that he was a nine-year-old man-child wreaking havoc without a care for the feelings of his victims' (p. 5). Illingworth talks of this side of Tyson as a 'persona', with its connotations of something to be donned or discarded at will. This still begs the question of why he identified with this 'sociopathic' persona, and not the more socially acceptable one of 'deprived victim'. I suggest that the feelings of powerlessness felt by the young multiply deprived and multiply victimized Tyson so painful that they needed to be constantly suppressed. Hence the overidentification with the empowering 'tough guy' discourse, even in memory. But, as we shall see in the next section, suppressed feelings never entirely disappear.

From bully boy to the compleat destroyer: boxing and the 'resolution' of anxiety

In taking up the subject position in the 'tough guy' discourse and becoming the delinquent gang member, Tyson had taken the first transforming step away from his passive, withdrawn identity. But respect from the wider world, to say nothing of mother love, was still lacking.[2] He may have felt better, but certainly very far from 'good'.[3] The second crucial step was his take-up of boxing at the age of 13. One version of how this came about says that a visit by Ali to the detention centre then holding the young Tyson so impressed him that he decided to learn to box. As Illingworth puts it, 'the allure of Ali promised the acquisition of money and power without compromise. For the boy who had learned to be alone, the idea of Ali . . . promised that, if he so chose, he would never need anyone else again' (p. 7). Whether or not this specific event formed the initial desire is less important, once again, than the fact that boxing became central to Tyson's identity. However, in so far as it provides a first stab at the meaning of boxing, and one which squares with commonsense understanding of boxing's undoubted 'pull' with young, disadvantaged ghetto males, it is a useful starting point, especially since it also embraces an emotionally based motivation ('never need anyone else again'). As before, my task is to reread it in relation to both (social) discourse and (psychic) desire.

In a brilliant portrayal of the boxer's world 'from the native's point of view', the French sociologist Loic Wacquant raises the possibility that the ultimate meaning of boxing can only be experienced 'organismically', in the body, 'beneath (or is it *beyond*?) the level of discourse' (Wacquant 1993: 5). Be that as it may, he does, thankfully, make the attempt to convey this '*carnal knowledge*' (p. 6) using words. Whilst remaining agnostic on this question, I do take the view that things only acquire a social meaning in a discourse – a series of statements displaying a certain regularity (Jefferson 1994a: 16). In this connection 'carnal knowledge' remains a prediscursive 'thing' until it is rendered meaningful within discourse. Second, Wacquant contrasts 'how boxers think and feel about their trade' with 'top-down' or 'outsider' accounts. This is a valuable corrective, grippingly executed. But from my point of view, these insider accounts collectively constitute another discourse on boxing which is *less* significant for the would-be fighter than the better-known (because more public) outsider accounts. It is these dominant discourses on boxing with which the novitiate must identify if he is to be sucked in, since insider knowledge is necessarily denied him at first. Later, the insider discourse will undoubtedly provide at least some of the motivations for remaining a prizefighter. For this reason, then, I need to concentrate on some of boxing's dominant discursive meanings, before addressing some aspects of the insider discourse, in so far as these became meaningful to Tyson.

According to Wacquant, 'If there is a single set of recurrent images and narrative strategies . . . that dominates the public representation of boxing, it is no doubt that of violence: the unmediated, unbridled fistic onslaught of man upon man' (Wacquant 1993: 6–7). Within any dominant discourse of boxing, it is certainly true that 'violence' is in some way part of the definition of the activity. But this is not the cowardly violence of the wife-beater or of the robber preying on the weak and vulnerable, but a specific form of courageous violence, underpinned by a 'hypermasculine ethos':

> Boxing is a true 'blood sport' in ways that few if any other athletic activities are, as reflected in the hypermasculine ethos that underpins it. The fistic trade puts a high premium on physical toughness and the ability to withstand – as well as dish out – pain and bodily arm [sic]. The *specific honor* of the pugilist, like that of the ancient gladiator, consists in refusing to concede and kneel down. One of the visible outward signs of that much-revered quality called 'heart' said to epitomize the authentic boxer is the capacity to not bow under pressure, to 'suck it up' and keep on fighting, no matter what the physical toll.
>
> (p. 8)

It was such a conception of boxing that led me in an earlier paper to call it the extreme example within sport of the highly masculine 'will to win' discourse, and contrasted this with both the more gender-neutral 'fitness and fun' discourse, and with the more feminine 'poetry in motion' discourse (Jefferson 1993). When this conception of the nature of the sport is combined with the promise of the fabulous rewards that boxing holds out to the gifted few, the 'money and power without compromise' that Ali represented to the pubescent Tyson, its appeal to poor young men with highly restricted avenues of escape from the ghetto is not difficult to comprehend.[4] But to rest there tells only half the story: it ignores why, despite its wide appeal, it comes to matter enormously to only the few who become sufficiently motivated to endure the discipline, fear and pain involved in becoming a trained boxer.

In talking of what boxing would have meant to Malcolm X, Wolfenstein says:

> Malcolm . . . had everything to gain by becoming a boxer himself: an escape from poverty and anonymity, an appropriate outlet for aggression, an affirmative racial identity, an earned claim to his father's throne, a victory over one brother [who was a keen amateur boxer] and the admiration of another.
>
> (Wolfenstein 1989: 138)

In other words, it would have provided both social and psychic rewards: a route to fame and fortune *and* a way of 'breaking the vicious circle of self-destructive aggressive action' (p. 138); or, as I expressed it earlier, a way of resolving the complex contradictions around 'good/bad' and black/white by enabling him to be both good and bad simultaneously. Though Tyson's family circumstances alter some of the specifics (in his case earning his mother's love rather than his father's throne, for example), the advantages boxing held out to him over the delinquent route were identical – social rewards and psychic release: the legitimate expression of 'bad intentions' (Oates 1987: 66).

Without some notion of 'psychic release' it is hard to understand the intensity of the commitment of some working-class males to becoming a boxer, given that the appeal is all but universal. As Stewart allegedly put it, in reply to Tyson's 'I want to be a fighter' plea: 'So do the rest of these scumbags' (quoted in Illingworth 1992: 8). But Tyson proved to be different, as Stewart found out when he finally agreed to take him on: 'I didn't care if he could box – I was amazed with his mind . . . It almost scared me. None of the other kids were like that' (p. 8).[5] This extraordinary determination had him 'working on slipping punches' (p. 10) in the small hours in his cell, and was later harnessed by an impatient management team who put him through 27 fights in his meteoric 20-month journey to the title, partly as 'a way of maintaining control over Tyson', and partly in order to sustain 'his burning intensity' (Illingworth 1992: 75–6).

In order to explore further this 'burning intensity', it is necessary first to say something about the sort of fighter Tyson was. In becoming at 20 the youngest-ever heavyweight champion of the world in the shortest-ever time span of 20 months, Tyson displayed a rare combination of speed, 'defensive excellence' and an incredible knockout punch, a punch which gave him 15 *first-round* knockouts in his 27-fight journey to the title (p. 74). Such power made him as feared inside the ring as he had once been outside it in his Brownsville gang days when, according to his sister Denise, 'everyone was afraid of him' (p. 5). Four of the six other entrants in the heavyweight division of the 1983 US National Championships apparently dropped out when Tyson arrived. He went on to win – with two first-round knockouts (p. 58). Tyson appeared to relish the image of brutality developing around him. He spent hours poring over old boxing films, from which he assembled the stylistic elements of his chosen ring persona: spartan, warrior-like, and fearsome. From Dempsey, the 'Manassa mauler', he borrowed the spartan haircut; from the first-ever black heavyweight champion, Jack Johnson, the warrior-like black shorts and boots, with no socks nor robe, that were to become his hallmark.[6] The almost pathological brutality of his after-fight comments, whether by accident or design, completed the picture ('I always try to catch them on the tip of the nose because I try to push the bone into the brain', quoted in Berger 1990: 125).

This, then, was one side of the picture: Tyson the bully boy on his way to becoming 'Iron Mike', the 'compleat destroyer'. But what is happening to the 'little fairy boy' during these transformations; for, as Pontalis reminds us about childhood beliefs, these may have 'vanished in their original shape', but 'one never gives up anything' (1993: 30). This requires us to look at the other side of 'Tyson, the compleat destroyer', at Tyson's occasional passivity in the ring, a passivity which was a further reason why his management team kept him fighting so constantly as a journeyman pro, petrified as they were that his 'burning intensity' might become a fatal passivity were he to be allowed any longer layoffs (Illingworth 1992: 76).

Illingworth cites several examples of Tyson's passivity between 1981–3, when Tyson was in his mid-teens and still an amateur. On the first occasion, in an undercard bout in Scranton, Pennsylvania, Tyson 'won on points', but only after he twice attempted to quit and, in the final round, 'stopped punching' (p. 45). In the 1982 Junior Olympics final, Tyson 'broke down in tears' before the fight, apparently 'drained of all wiillingness to fight', and had to be taken to the ring. There he recovered sufficiently to win 'by a technical knockout' (p. 48). However, in the US National Championships of 1982 and the National Golden Gloves tournament of 1983 'the flaw, the overwhelming passivity, struck again', and he lost on both occasions (p. 56). This dangerous passivity seemed to strike when Tyson's early flurries failed to produce the hoped-for knockout. Then, frustration would affect his technique, making him 'look like a fighter out of control'; or, his 'will to fight . . . drained away' and 'he tended to hug his opponent and lock arms – to "clinch"' (p. 57).

According to Illingworth, Scranton was only symptomatic. The clue to 'the *cause* of Tyson's passivity' could be found in what Tyson supposedly said when he broke down in tears before the Junior Olympics, namely, 'I'm "Mike Tyson", everyone likes me now' (p. 48). As Illingworth goes on to explain, using the Scranton example:

> In Scranton, it was not just the prospect of losing the fight that had paralyzed Tyson. It was that in defeat the emotional attachments with D'Amato, Ewald [D'Amato's partner], the other boys in the house, and Atlas [Tyson's trainer] would be severed. Fighting, and winning fights, made these bonds possible. Losing confirmed the fear he had lived with since childhood: that he was alone, unloved, and quite possibly unlovable.
>
> (p. 48)

So, the 'burning intensity', the strength of Tyson's identification with boxing, is not just about winning, becoming the champ, about 'money and power without compromise'; it is also about a set of desires or needs, usually suppressed, that occasionally burst through the conscious motivations. Earlier, I talked of these desires or needs in terms of anxiety or powerlessness. It does not seem difficult, or far-fetched, to reinterpret Tyson's tearful remarks about 'everyone' liking him now in terms of a deep anxiety that this was not true, of an immobilizing powerlessness that must at all costs be denied. Tyson desperately wanted it to be true that 'everyone', but especially those close to him, liked him as a person; but the response of 'everyone' close to him, in teaching him to control and surmount this fear in the ring, only convinced him that the 'truth' of his identity lay only in the boxing ring, as the 'compleat destroyer'. Then, and possibly only then, in the act of destroying another man, the psychic anxiety underpinning the feared passivity could be (if temporarily) assuaged, and the delight of all those close to him, and his fans, could be a 'good enough' testimony of love. In this sense, then,

Illingworth is surely right to see Tyson's passivity as 'the opposite side of that which also made him so devastating' (p. 49). Theoretically, it would seem to conjoin fear and rage in a gendered dialectic that merits further investigation, the hypothesis being that deep-rooted anxiety gets transformed into more socially acceptable (since heavily masculine) rage. This gives an additional psychic dimension to Wacquant's description of 'prizefighting' as 'this extravagant spectacle of disciplined lower-class male fury' (1993: 45).

Given this dialectical relationship between fear and rage, it is interesting that controlling fear was the psychological cornerstone of D'Amato's philosophy of boxing. He constantly drummed into the young Tyson that all boxers are afraid; what mattered was to learn to control one's own fear, and to remember opponents were afraid too. We would not be totally distorting this philosophy to say that Tyson was being actively taught to suppress (control) his own fear, partly by projecting it on to his opponent. This teaching, in combination with Tyson's unique fears, may have added to the intensity of the 'psychic energy' behind Tyson's devastating ring performances: 'It was as if he entered the ring so emotionally coiled that a psychic energy built up that was desperate for release, and the only place it could go, the only relief for Tyson, was to destroy the other man' (Illingworth 1992: 50). Whether or not D'Amato really understood the psychic roots of Tyson's fear, he seemed instinctively to know that controlling it was the key to unleashing his extraordinary destructiveness.

Conclusion: the return of the suppressed

This 'extraordinary destructiveness' was, of course, the key to the heavyweight crown, though D'Amato did not live to see this realization of his reason for living. Behind this destructiveness lay an astute management team, growing belief, frightening reputation, sheer ability and awesome power, as well as Tyson's 'burning intensity'. The combination not only lifted the title, but promised something rarer – a place amongst the 'greats': a champion fit to be compared with the likes of Ali, Louis, Dempsey and Johnson. But, in the event, all this was not enough. In the ring, at his destructive best, the moment of victory could be sweet indeed: opponent and inner doubts simultaneously vanquished; the contradictions of identity (good/bad, black/white) temporarily resolved.[7] Outside the ring, however, things were always far less straightforward – hardly surprising in the light of my argument about the role of boxing in resolving contradictions for Tyson.

But Tyson was particularly ill-equipped to deal with the fame and fortune that accompanies the heavyweight championships. Lacking social skills and denied emotional ones, his transition from multiple privations to celebrity status and riches beyond imagining was constantly trouble-strewn. Allegations of sexual assault by angry women, a stormy, short-lived marriage, brawling, the deaths of those closest to him – D'Amato, Jim Jacobs and Lorna his mother, management difficulties, the list goes on and on. Then, after he had already lost his crown and amidst constant media stories of a man careering out of control, came his downfall event: the sensational rape trial, which led to his conviction and a six-year gaol sentence.

I cannot rehearse here the transformations of subjectivity involved in all this. But they are of a piece with the dual-sided nature of Tyson's identity – little fairy boy/bully boy; passive quitter/compleat destroyer; gentle/vicious; needy/needing no one, and so on. In looking closely at these apparent contradictions, at two significant transitional moments in Tyson's life (becoming a bully and then a boxer), I have tried to show their inextricable connectedness: the psychic roots of social 'rage'. Inevitably, in a short chapter, this has involved omissions and simplifications. The real Tyson is undoubtedly more complex than I have words and concepts to 'capture' him; he is indeed much more than a discursive construction. But, if this has made readers think more deeply about the problems of conceptualizing subjectivity and its transformations, and has offered a plausibly interpreted case study which is reasonably sensitive to the available evidence by way of example, it will have served its purpose.

Notes

1 Melanie Klein, for example, explicitly made anxiety the centre-point of her work: 'From the beginning of my psychoanalytic work my interest was focused on anxiety and its causation' (Klein 1948:41).

2 During his nine-month incarceration in the Tryon detention centre where he learned to box, 'Not once . . . did Lorna [his mother] visit the facility, send any Christmas presents, or write a letter' (Illingworth 1992: 9).

3 According to Illingworth, when he arrived at the Tryon detention centre, 'Tyson didn't just have self-esteem problems. They were more fundamental. He had no sense of self-worth at all. It was the affliction of the abandoned personality, the unloved. "He felt bad about his body, being so big, and the kids taunted him for it", Stewart [his boxing teacher] said. "I'd never seen anyone that bad. He was scared of his own shadow. He barely talked, never looked you in the eye. He was a baby" ' (Illingworth 1992: 8).

4 For a more nuanced account of the 'glamorous' appeal of boxing in 'low-income neighbourhoods', see Wacquant (1993: 21).

5 According to Joe Martin, who taught Muhammad Ali to box, it was Ali's determination too, rather than his ability, that stood out at first: 'when he first began coming around, [he] looked no better or worse than the majority . . . About a year later . . . he stood out because . . . he had more determination than most boys . . . He was easily the hardest worker of any kid I ever taught' (quoted in Hauser 1992: 19). Quite why Ali was this determined is an open question. Certainly his family background was altogether more secure, settled, religious and 'respectable' than Tyson's (Hauser 1992: 15).

6 See Roberts (1979) for a biography of Dempsey and Gilmore (1975) for a biography of Johnson.

7 It is worth emphasizing the point that the 'contradictions of identity' could only ever be 'temporarily resolved'. Even after one of Ali's greatest triumphs, when he had recaptured the heavyweight title from George Foreman in Zaire, he confessed that he could never escape thinking of the relationship between fighting and slavery: 'Then there was this nightmarish image I always had of two slaves in the ring. Like in the old slave days on the plantations, with two of us big, black slaves fighting, almost on the verge of annihilating each other while the masters are smoking bit cigars, screaming and urging us on, looking for the blood' (Ali and Durham 1975: 247).

References

Ali, M. and Durham, R. (1975) *The Greatest: My Own Story*. New York: Random House.

Berger, P. (1990) *Blood Season*. London: Queen Anne Press.

Freeman, M. (1993) *Rewriting the Self*. London: Routledge.

Gilmore, A.T. (1975) *Bad Nigger! The National Impact of Jack Johnson*. Port Washington, NY: National University Publications, Kennikat Press.

Illingworth, M. (1992) *Mike Tyson: Money, Myth and Betrayal*. London: Grafton.

Jefferson, T. (1993) Tougher than the rest: Mike Tyson and the destructive desires of masculinity', unpublished paper first presented to 'Women, Feminism and the Law' day school on 'Discourse, Identity and Power', University of Sheffield, 12 June 1992.

Jefferson, T. (1994a) Theorising masculine subjectivity, in T. Newburn and E. Stanko (eds) *Just Boys Doing Business? Men, Masculinities and Crime*. London: Routledge.

Jefferson, T. (1994b) 'The Tyson rape trial: a case study in the problems of biographical writing', unpublished paper first presented to 'Auto/Biography Christmas Conference', University of Warwick, 17–19 December 1993.

Hauser, T. (1992) *Muhammad Ali: His Life and Times*. New York: Touchstone.

Henriques, J., Hollway, W., Urwin, C., Venn, C. and Walkerdine, V. (1984) *Changing the Subject: Psychology, Social Regulation and Subjectivity*. London: Methuen.

Hinshelwood, R.D. (1991) *A Dictionary of Kleinian Thought*, 2nd edition. London: Free Association Books.

Hollway, W. (1989) *Subjectivity and Method in Psychology: Gender, Meaning and Science*. London: Sage.

Klein, M. (1948) On the theory of anxiety and guilt, *The Writings of Melanie Klein*, vol. 3. London: Hogarth.

Oates, J.C. (1987) Kid dynamite, *Life*, March: 64–74.

Pontalis, J.-B. (1993) *Love of Beginnings*. London: Free Association Books.

Roberts, R. (1979) *Jack Dempsey: The Manassa Mauler*. Baton Rouge, LA: Louisiana State University Press.

Wacquant, L.J.D. (1993) *From the Native's Point of View: How Boxers Think and Feel about their Trade, working paper*. New York: Russell Sage Foundation.

Wolfenstein, E.V. (1989) *The Victims of Democracy*. London: Free Association Books.

'Empowering men to disempower themselves': heterosexual masculinities, HIV and the contradictions of anti-oppressive education[1]

Introduction

This chapter is about anti-oppressive education. In particular, it is an attempt to unravel some of the complexities and contradictions that are involved in developing anti-sexist, anti-heterosexist and anti-homophobic[2] strategies aimed at heterosexual men and boys. The chapter begins from the fundamental premiss that anti-oppressive education needs to be directly concerned with challenging the power of hegemonic forms of heterosexual masculinity,[3] particularly in relation to women, gay men, and those forms of masculinity subordinated within existing social relations. However, the chapter argues that this can only be achieved by addressing the investments – both conscious and unconscious – that heterosexual men and boys have in the forms of masculinity that they occupy. To this end, the chapter explores the limitations of some of the approaches currently available in this area, and suggests that the basis for an alternative model is to be found within recent debates in cultural studies, lesbian and gay studies, and in critical feminist social psychology.

HIV and the struggle over hegemonic heterosexual masculinities

One among several good reasons for addressing the issue of anti-oppressive education for heterosexual men and boys lies in the history of popular responses to the HIV epidemic. As AIDS activists and gay and lesbian within wider social relations of age, class, dis/ability, gender and 'race' at particular times and in particular locations. The risk is that popular discussion of masculinities as problematic and dysfunctional very quickly translates into a desire to restrict and police especially working-class young men (both white and black) with little regard for their subordinate social positions or the 'survivalist' strategies that potentially underlie apparently self-confident and sometimes belligerent forms of masculinity. Sex educators and others interested in developing anti-oppressive work with heterosexual men and boys are left with an uncomfortable tension between the need to address the oppressive consequences of heterosexual masculinities and the need to respect the lives of those with whom they are working.

A number of approaches are available which seek to address these contradictions and I propose to focus on four – namely, disciplinarianism, participatory rationalism, skills training, and attempts to find the 'real man within' – with the intention of sketching some of their main strengths and weaknesses. All of these approaches have produced interesting and valuable work, and it is far from my intention to rubbish them. However, I aim to explore some of their limitations as a basis for suggesting a possible alternative agenda for anti-oppressive work with heterosexual men and boys.

Disciplinary responses, such as anti-discrimination policies that rigorously police overt expressions of sexism or homophobia, are perhaps the most obvious form of anti-oppressive educational practice. As Phil Cohen (1988) has argued in the context of anti-racism, disciplinary approaches have the advantage of protecting vulnerable groups from harassment and are therefore of the utmost importance. However, as he goes on to argue, they are unlikely to shift boys' fundamental investments in forms of discriminatory behaviour. In effect, boys learn not to be sexist, racist or homophobic in front of teachers and youth workers but easily revert to such behaviour once out of sight of a disciplinary gaze. Indeed, as Cohen suggests, discriminatory attitudes or behaviours may even reappear in more entrenched or violent forms since they can now be used to defy authority (pp. 92–3).

In recognition of such problems, a number of alternative educational strategies seek to provide heterosexual men and boys with positive incentives for change rather than enforcing conformity through negative sanctions. For example, much of the work done in personal and social education pro-grammes in schools can be defined as a form of 'participatory rationalism' (for a widely used example, see TACADE 1986). Rob Pattman (unpublished) has documented such an approach used in relationships education lessons at a north of England secondary school.

Pattman argues that the lessons aim to use participatory strategies (for example, small group discussions, case histories and role play) to allow pupils the space to think through their beliefs and values and come to more rational and objective conclusions. For example, it is assumed that boys' sexual objectification of girls will be punctured by rational investigation and abandoned. In practice, Pattman found little evidence that this was the case.

On the contrary, he argues that the 'rational' values promoted in the lessons simply conflicted with the values held in the boys' peer group. This is apparent in the following exchange. Pattman has asked the group, 'How do you talk about girls with your mates?':

Tony: I suppose one-sided really. When you're with your mates you don't really see them as other people, you see them as machines . . .
Me: Do you express these views in sex education classes?
Tony: No, not really.
Me: How are you supposed to talk about sex and girls in sex education classes?
John: You have to keep your mouth shut, don't you. You have to watch what you say.
Tony: You can't be that open. In certain matters you can. But when it comes to what you feel and what your mates feel you don't say anything.

(Pattman, unpublished)

Pattman's findings suggest that the 'rational values' promoted in the lesson do not necessarily shift the boys' *feelings* or their investments in their own peer group values. It appears that Tony's peer group values 'feel right' or make 'imaginative sense' in a way that the 'rational' values promoted by the lesson simply do not.

In contrast to this approach, skills training tends to focus on masculinities as forms of learned behaviour that can be supplanted by new and alternative skills. Based in social learning theory's influential accounts of gender acquisition (see, for example, Bandura 1965), skills training has been more usually associated with assertiveness courses for women than with anti-oppressive work with men. However, in the context of HIV prevention there has been a growing emphasis on equipping both men and women with the appropriate skills to negotiate sexual activity (see, for example, Massey 1988; Aggleton *et al.* 1990). The assumption here is that men have underdeveloped skills or have learned inappropriate ways of relating to women sexually. Role play and positive feedback from training facilitators aims to allow boys and men to learn new skills more appropriate to negotiating safer sex. Useful though this might be, skills training seems to share participatory rationalism's optimism about the possibility of shifting boys' and men's investments in particular ways of behaving. Not only is it unclear why men should give up positions of power, like participatory rationalism, skills training tends to ignore the possibility that existing forms of heterosexual masculinity 'feel right' or 'make imaginative sense' to the men and boys who inhabit them.

The final broad approach to anti-oppressive work with heterosexual men and boys can be loosely defined in terms of attempts to 'find the real man within' (for examples that draw on this approach, see the journals *Achilles' Heel*, and *Working With Men*). Work of this kind tends to view heterosexual masculinities as highly defensive and potentially dysfunctional forms of identity, and aims to 'get behind' these defences to the 'real' men inside by encouraging men to talk among themselves and connect with their true feelings. For instance, Neil Davidson's influential book, *Boys Will Be . . . : Sex Education and Young Men*, begins with the statement 'The main aim of this book . . . is to inspire confidence in *men* to start talking with young men and with each other, about what they really feel, think, and believe sex to be about' (Davidson 1990: ix).

Similarly, he describes a difficult moment in a session with a group of young heterosexual men when he has to remind himself

> It's times like this when I need to be quite clear that there is a difference between their true selves and how they have been conditioned to feel and behave. This is not always easy. I have come up against some of men's most deep-rooted assumptions.
>
> (p. 99)

Given its allegiances to feminism, it is unsurprising that work of this kind is often characterized by an explicit anti-sexist and anti-homophobic agenda that is not necessarily so apparent in the last two approaches. Equally, its connections to American ego therapy give it a purchase on the ways in which boys and men have active investments in heterosexual power relations that are not necessarily open to rational argument nor easily redirected through skills training. However, it is arguable that the notion of a 'real man' hidden behind the distorting layers of 'male conditioning' oversimplifies the complex ways different forms of heterosexual masculinity are produced and lived out under concrete local conditions; it offers little real insight into the ways in which these forms of masculinity interact with and are part of wider social relations, and provides an underdeveloped account of investments boys and men make in the forms of masculinity they occupy.

Towards a new model of heterosexual masculinities: making 'imaginative sense'

The recent explosion of debate on masculinities has thrown up a number of critical positions which begin to sketch an alternative approach to the issues raised by heterosexual masculinities and power relations. The first of these is to be found in some of the insights afforded by lesbian and gay studies (see, for example, Sedgwick 1985, 1991; Butler 1990, 1993; Dollimore 1991). Of particular relevance are arguments that gender routinely 'speaks' heterosexuality, and that contemporary forms of hegemonic heterosexual masculinity are formed in opposition to and are thereby intimately connected with homosexual masculinities. For example, Judith Butler argues that gender is systematically (though not inevitably) spoken through a 'heterosexual matrix' in which heterosexuality is presupposed in the expression of 'real' forms of masculinity and femininity. She writes:

Although forms of sexuality do not unilaterally determine gender, a non-causal and non-reductive connection between sexuality and gender is nevertheless crucial to maintain. Precisely because homophobia often operates through the attribution of a damaged, failed or otherwise abject gender to homosexuals, that is, calling gay men 'feminine' or calling lesbians 'masculine', and because the homophobic terror over performing homosexual acts, where it exists, is often also a terror over losing proper gender ('no longer being a real or proper man' or 'no longer being a real or proper woman'), it seems crucial to retain a theoretical apparatus that will account for how sexuality is regulated through the policing and the shaming of gender.

(Butler 1993: 238)

Such arguments suggest that, as historically specific cultural constructions, contemporary heterosexual masculinities presuppose an opposition to homosexuality, and that, at least in part, they derive their coherence as identities from this opposition. Similarly, Eve Kosofsky Sedgwick (1985) has drawn attention to the highly relational character of hegemonic forms of heterosexual masculinity, arguing that both men's heterosexual relations with women and their opposition to homosexuality act as ways of regulating relations between men, and policing subordinated heterosexual masculinities as well as gay men themselves. Such arguments are clearly important for anti-oppressive education. In particular, they suggest that shifting boys' and men's investments in hegemonic male identities is likely to be highly problematic. This is because challenging the homophobic, heterosexist and sexist relations through which heterosexual masculinities are constructed is likely to question the boundaries of those identities, in the process threatening men's fundamental sense of themselves.

A notion of investment – that hegemonic heterosexual masculinities 'feel right' or 'make imaginative sense' – has also been central to debates within two other broad approaches: contemporary subcultural accounts and critical feminist social psychology. Subcultural accounts of heterosexual masculinities have focused on the ways in which they act as 'attempted collective solutions' to social contradictions (see, for example, Willis 1977; Cohen 1986; Mac an Ghaill 1994). For instance, in his recent study of masculinities and schooling, Máirtín Mac an Ghaill argues that differentiated heterosexual masculinities are produced and inhabited through the collective actions of boys as they 'handle' or 'negotiate' their concrete social environment, and through relations of similarity with and opposition to other groups within that social environment. Characteristic of this approach is its description of heterosexual masculinities as actively produced, highly relational, and local. Mac an Ghaill argues that heterosexual masculinities cannot be understood as unitary wholes or things in themselves, but only as they are produced and reproduced in relations of subordination and resistance that are organized round age, class, disability, gender, 'race', and sexuality. Thus he is particularly careful to explore the ways in which, within particular social contexts, heterosexual masculinities exist at the intersection of a range of social relations and come to 'speak' these in often unpredictable ways. In consequence, he suggests that heterosexual masculinities cannot be seen as static or unchangeable since they are always in the process of production and reproduction. Similarly, he argues that, although they draw on more widely available forms and social relations, heterosexual masculinities have to be understood as deeply embedded in the specificities of local conditions and historical moments. This analysis suggests that we will be unable to understand or effectively address issues raised by heterosexual masculinities unless we grasp the ways in which they are active responses to this social and historical environment. This does not mean 'reading off' particular forms of heterosexual masculinity from a particular age, class or ethnic position. Rather, it means understanding the complex ways in which relations of age, class, disability, ethnicity, gender and sexuality are refracted within particular social sites (for example, particular schools, particular segments of the labour market, particular types of family); it means paying close attention to the ways in which those social sites make available heterosexual masculinities through their own discursive practices, and grasping the ways in which heterosexual masculinities are inhabited and reworked as boys and men actively negotiate the wider social environment and the local environment of these individual social sites.

However, as Mac an Ghaill acknowledges (and as is pursued by Cohen 1986), a purely subcultural focus on heterosexual masculinities as attempted, collective resolutions to real contradictions leaves unexplored a crucial aspect of gender and sexual identification: namely, the unconscious. Recent debates in critical feminist social psychology have been particularly concerned to explore the relationships between unconscious processes and social relations (see, in particular, Hollway 1984, 1989; Walkerdine 1990) and these provide a potentially fruitful way into thinking about the unconscious investments that heterosexual men and boys may have in the forms of heterosexual masculinity that they inhabit. For example, in 'Gender difference and the production of subjectivity' (Hollway 1984), Wendy Hollway explores the ways in which unconscious processes shape a group of heterosexual men's emotional relationships with women, and, in the process, reproduce gendered relations of power. Hollway's key argument is that specific men inhabit specific forms of heterosexual masculinity because these provide apparent (although always partial) resolutions to unconscious contradictions. For example, Hollway explores the ways in which several of her respondents' accounts reveal fears of emotional intimacy, and argues that these can be understood in terms of unconscious anxieties established in early childhood: particularly the process through which boys separate themselves from their mothers and establish a cultural identity as male. Although

Hollway's argument is based largely in a Lacanian framework, this analysis has strong resonances of feminist object-relations theory which theorizes heterosexual masculinities in terms of boys' experiences of separation from the mother. For example, Jessica Benjamin has argued that

> Male children achieve their distinct identity by denying their identification or oneness with their mothers. Initially all infants not only love their mothers but also identify with them and wish to emulate them. But boys discover that they cannot be or become her . . . A male child's independence is bought at the price of saying: 'I am nothing like she who strives and cares for me'. Thus male identity emphasises difference from the nurturer over sameness, separation over connectedness, boundaries over continuity.
>
> (Benjamin 1983: 604–5)

From this perspective, emotional closeness and vulnerability are inherently problematic for heterosexual masculinities. Emotional intimacy recapitulates early childhood feelings of being merged with the mother and brings with it anxiety over loss of boundaries and, ultimately, identity. Thus Hollway argues that one of her respondents, Jim, unconsciously attempts to resolve such anxieties by inhabiting the social identity of 'romantic hero'. As a romantic hero, Jim is able to 'speak' himself as strong and rational, and can experience his partner as emotional and vulnerable. This allows him to misidentify his own feelings of need as hers and maintain a strong sense of separateness from her. The importance of this analysis lies in the potential purchase it gives us on boys' and men's investments in the forms of heterosexual masculinity that they occupy and the power relations embedded in these. Psychoanalytic perspectives offer an account of the unconscious and irrational dynamics that suffuse relations of gender and sexuality and without which it is virtually impossible to make sense of the range of anxieties, fantasy identifications and overheated emotions that seem to surround boys' and men's investments in the forms of heterosexual masculinity which they occupy.

Implications for anti-oppressive education

Individually, these three approaches (lesbian and gay theory, contemporary subcultural analysis and critical feminist social psychology) offer a rich array of concepts and methodologies through which to approach the study of heterosexual masculinities. The difficulty lies in reconciling their differences. Subcultural accounts risk being overly voluntaristic and rationalist: boys and men can appear to 'choose' their own masculinity. Psychoanalytic accounts risk being overly reductive and determinist, reducing the complex processes through which different heterosexual masculinities are produced, reproduced and lived out to, for example, a supposedly universal early childhood relationship between 'the boy' and 'the mother'. Equally, the subcultural approach's emphasis on the relational, contingent and specific character of heterosexual masculinities risks losing some of the conceptual and political clarity of lesbian and gay, and feminist theories in which there is a clear-eyed focus on the subordination of gay men and women by heterosexual men.

The contradictions between lesbian and gay theory, contemporary subcultural accounts and critical feminist social psychology mean that there is no easily available alternative model through which to develop anti-oppressive work with heterosexual men and boys. However, these approaches do point to some ways forward. There is a clear need for a much richer empirical understanding of the ways in which varying forms of heterosexual masculinity are produced and lived in different social sites: for example, schools, 'the family', the labour market, and popular culture. This will necessarily entail producing a much richer empirical understanding of heterosexual masculinities as localized relations of power, suggesting specific sites and concrete forms of intervention. Equally, this specifically local focus should provide a much more complex account of the ways in which heterosexual masculinities exist at the intersection of wider social relations. It is clearly of crucial importance to understand the connections between relations of age, class, disability, gender, 'race' and sexuality, and to be able to grasp the ways in which heterosexual masculinities 'speak' and are 'spoken through', for example, class and ethnic divisions.

However, this alternative agenda also suggests that new forms of anti-oppressive practice will have to be centrally concerned with the investments that men and boys have in the forms of heterosexual masculinity they inhabit. However partially or irrationally, heterosexual masculinities actively address and resolve at a subjective level real psychic and social contradictions, and anti-oppressive education will need to find ways of shifting these investments if it is to be successful. As Pattman's research makes clear, existing forms of heterosexual masculinity and existing power relations are likely to 'feel right', or 'make imaginative sense' to the boys and men who inhabit them. If boys and men are to disinvest from existing forms of heterosexual masculinity, then they will need alternative ways of making imaginative sense of the social and psychic contradictions that their existing identities address. Phil Cohen has made a similar point in relation to anti-racism. He writes

> Our conclusion . . . is that popular racism cannot be tackled by simply giving students access to alternative sources of experience, or new means of intellectual understanding; rather it is a question of articulating their lived cultures to *new practices of representation*, which make

it possible to sustain an imaginative sense of social identity and difference without recourse to racist constructions.

(Cohen 1987: 2)

I do not pretend to know what such a strategy might look like in practice, since the groundwork that would make it possible is only now beginning (although Cohen's work on drama and photography in education gives some useful leads on this matter – see Cohen 1987, 1989 – as may other theatre-in-education work). However, we clearly need to generate a more complex understanding of the ways in which heterosexual masculinities are collectively produced and reproduced, and of the psychic and social contradictions addressed in this process. On this basis, it seems to me neither naive nor educationally redundant to hope to give heterosexual boys and men some critical purchase on these processes, and (paraphrasing Cohen) to find ways of articulating their lived cultures to new practices of representation which make it possible to sustain an imaginative sense of sexual and gender identities without recourse to constructions that subordinate gay men, women, and other forms of heterosexual masculinity.

Notes

1 An earlier version of this paper was given at the sixth Social Aspects of AIDS Conference, South Bank Polytechnic, 9 May 1992 as part of East Birmingham Health Authority's Young People, Sexual Health and HIV Research Programme.
2 Heterosexism is used here to refer to the presumption that heterosexuality is normal, natural and universal. Homophobia is used to refer to active and explicit opposition to gay men and lesbian women whether or not this is fuelled by unconscious fears and desires.
3 The use of the term 'masculinities' indicates the availability of competing forms of masculinity; the term 'hegemonic' indicates that these competing masculinities exist in relations of subordination and resistance.

References

Aggleton, P., Horsley, C., Warwick, I. and Wilton, T. (1990) *AIDS: Working with Young People*. Horsham: AVERT.
Bandura, A. (1965) Influence of model's reinforcement contingencies on the acquisition of imitative responses, *Journal of Personality and Social Psychology*, 1: 589–95.
Benjamin, J. (1983) Master and slave: the fantasy of erotic domination, in A. Snitow, C. Stanell and S. Thompson (eds) *Desire: The Politics of Sexuality*. London: Virago.
Boffin, T. and Gupta, S. (eds) (1990) *Ecstatic Antibodies: Resisting the AIDS Mythology*. London: Rivers Oram.
Butler, J. (1990) *Gender Trouble: Feminism and the Subversion of Identity*. London: Routledge.
Butler, J. (1993) *Bodies That Matter*. London: Routledge.

Carter, E. and Watney, S. (eds) (1989) *Taking Liberties: AIDS and Cultural Politics*. London: Serpent's Tail.

Cohen, P. (1986) *Rethinking the Youth Question*, working paper 3. London: Post-16 Education Centre, Institute of Education, University of London.

Cohen, P. (1987) *Racism and Popular Culture: A Cultural Studies Approach*, working paper 9. London: Centre for Multicultural Education, Institute of Education, University of London.

Cohen, P. (1988) The perversions of inheritance: studies in the making of multi-racist Britain, in P. Cohen and H.S. Bains (eds) *Multi-Racist Britain*. Houndmills: Macmillan.

Cohen, P. (1989) *Really Useful Knowledge: Photography and Cultural Studies in the Transition from School*. Stoke-on-Trent: Trentham Books.

Davidson, N. (1990) *Boys Will Be . . . : Sex Education and Young Men*. London: Bedford Square Press.

Dollimore, J. (1991) *Sexual Dissidence: Augustine to Wilde, Freud to Foucault*. Oxford: Oxford University Press.

Holland, J., Ramazanoglu, C. and Scott, S. (1990a) *Sex, Risk and Danger: AIDS Education Policy and Young Women's Sexuality*. London: Tufnell Press.

Holland, J., Ramazanoglu, C., Scott, S., Sharpe, S. and Thomson, R. (1990b) *Don't Die of Ignorance – I Nearly Died of Embarrassment: Condoms in Context*. London: Tufnell Press.

Holland, J., Ramazanoglu, C., Scott, S., Sharpe, S. and Thomson, R. (1991) *Pressure, Resistance, Empowerment: Young Women and the Negotiation of Safer-sex*. London: Tufnell Press.

Holland, J., Ramazanoglu, C. and Sharpe, S. (1993) *Wimp or Gladiator: Contradictions in Acquiring Masculine Sexuality*. London: Tufnell Press.

Hollway, W. (1984) Gender difference and the production of subjectivity, in J. Henriques, W. Hollway, C. Urwin, C. Venn and V. Walkerdine (eds) *Changing the Subject: Psychology, Social Regulation and Subjectivity*. London: Methuen.

Hollway, W. (1989) *Subjectivity and Method in Psychology: Gender, Meaning and Science*. London: Sage.

Mac an Ghaill, M. (1994) *The Making of Men: Masculinities, Sexualities and Schooling*. Buckingham: Open University Press.

Massey, D. (1988) *Teaching About HIV and AIDS*. London: HEA.

Pattman, R. (unpublished) 'Sex education and the liberal paradigm', unpublished PhD research. University of Birmingham.

Sedgwick, E.K. (1985) *Between Men: English Literature and Male Homosocial Desire*. New York: Columbia University Press.

Sedgwick, E.K. (1991) *Epistemology of the Closet*. Harvester Wheatsheaf: Hemel Hempstead.

TACADE (1986) *Curriculum Guide C: Programme Ages 11–14, Fostering Skills in Responsibility, Decision Making, Communication, Self-confidence and Goal Setting*. Salford: TACADE/Quest/Lyons International.

Walkerdine, V. (1990) *School Girl Fictions*. London: Verso.

Watney, S. (1993) *Practices of Freedom: Writings on HIV Disease*. London: Rivers Oram.

Willis, P. (1977) *Learning to Labour: How Working Class Kids Get Working Class Jobs*. Aldershot: Saxon House.

Part 3

Critical evaluations of masculinities

White fright

Richard Johnson

(Answers, of a kind, to Rozena's and Claudette's questions)

No, I'm not afraid
Of your
Black self
Sharp laugh
To cut or heal
Your vehemence
Righteousness

I should fear
A nation's anger though
You could be extermination
With justice
For the reasonable
Justified unconsidered
Havoc of my kind

And I do fear
Redundancy
In what I was before
Entering this New World
So vast and shrinking small
Unable this time
To turn it

Your denial
Of change
Is strange
Your expectation of carelessness
Would fix me also
In unending
No

Yet anticipate

Fresh confusion
On my boundaries
If you subvert
These annexations
You would take unwanted
Security away

My whitest continent
Prepares again
Its walls and camps and gangs
Can other forces
Gather from
The hard exchange
Of friends?

(February to May 1993)

Reading black masculinities

What does a man want?
What does the black man want?
(Frantz Fanon 1967: 8)

Introduction

One of the key questions in black masculinity studies – 'what does the black man want?' – has been at the centre of recent attempts to theorize the complexity of black experience. Over the last two decades, studies in black masculinity have radically altered critical understandings of black men. Earlier sociology of race relations theories of black masculinity, in which black kinship structures were shown to be based on socially dysfunctional gender relations, tended to view black male sexual cultures as the pathological reflection of white hegemonic masculinities (Moynihan 1965; Frazier 1966; Hare and Hare 1984). Many of these studies analysed black male identification with racist stereotypes of sexual superiority as an hyperbolic inversion of white masculinity, and saw – in this projection of a sexist phallocentrism which is yet a form of cultural resistance – a form of mourning for white paternity as the lost object of desire which requires a compensatory cultural narrative. No doubt such an analysis could itself be accommodated into a phallocentric narrative, which ascribes the possession of the 'phallus' to white men and its lack to the social inferiority complex of black men.

From the mid-1970s, debates within black cultural studies on the ambivalent and contradictory sites of black identity and ethnicity, and their complex interaction with state institutions and racial ideologies, have challenged these functionalist race relations theories (Mercer and Julien 1988; hooks 1991; Gilroy 1993b). For example, Mercer and Julien (1988) have sought to theorize the nature of black sexuality, black gender politics and ethnic identity in terms of a number of key questions which avoid the heterosexist and phallocentric assumptions of race relations theories: these include the place of phallocentrism and misogyny in the sexual cultures of black men; essentialist and anti-essentialist ideas of racial and gendered identity; the place of black men in black familial and kinship structures; notions of racial community and interracial sexual relations.

These questions themselves generate concerns, such as the racial and cultural basis of male subjectification. For instance, is there a 'crisis' in black masculinity, whose origin lies in the 'emasculation' and social death of black men under colonialism and slavery, and which may be mapped on to black matrilineal family structures in which the absent name and law of the father has been replaced by matriarchal kinship patterns and fratilineal bonding between young black men? From a black feminist position, bell hooks (1991) and Hortense Spillers (1987) have questioned the race relations assumption that there is an absence of black fatherhood in the 'symbolic order'[1] of postcolonial cultures (the Caribbean, US and UK), which can be linked to the fratricidal and tribal culture of black male kinship – as demonstrated by territorial rivalries over the 'hood' and the 'street' – without regard to wider cultures of masculinity. The prevalence of fratricidal culture amongst young black men – crudely, the use of homicidal violence as a demonstration of machismo attitudes – remains a key issue for an analysis of the patriarchal underpinning of black cultural politics of 'home' and the family as argued by Paul Gilroy (1993b: 192–207) and Mark Costello and David Wallace (1990).

Another set of questions concerns the bewildering diversity of subject positions, social experiences and cultural identities which constitute 'blackness' as a social category – the shifting discursive political and cultural constructions of black identity which cannot be grounded in a fixed set of racial categories, nor biological morphologies, but which are articulated in terms of relations of representation and their politics. This politics of representation, Stuart Hall argues, means the end of the innocent notion of the black essential subject (Hall 1992: 254).

Further questions concern the ideologies and discourses of black masculinity through which black men both represent themselves and exclude others. In whose name, under whose hegemony[2] (or cultural fiction) do black men undertake to express their respective identities and identifications? Psychoanalytically inclined theorists such as Homi Bhabha, following the Frantz Fanon of *Black Skin, White Masks*, refer to the psychic splitting and ambivalence of black and white male subjectivities (Bhabha 1986). For instance, how do the unconscious fears, fantasies and desires of white men concerning black men relate, through the psychoanalytic process of identification, to black male gender and racial identification, white male narcissism, or to the wider processes of cultural 'translation' and 'hybridity'?[3] These questions are crucial to an understanding of the place of black male sexual cultures in black communities, the place of fictions of racial authenticity in black gay and black straight cultures, and the profound ambivalence of interracial desire and sexuality. In order to address these questions, this chapter will explore some of the key resources of black masculinity studies: cultural studies, discourse analysis, psychoanalysis, queer theory, and feminist critiques of patriarchy. On the other hand, I will examine a range of complex debates within black masculinity studies as it tries to address the political, sociocultural ideologies of race and gender and ethnic identities – an attempt which has passed through deconstruction, psychoanalysis, and hegemonic analyses of social formations.

Black youth and criminal sexualities: law, hegemony, and discourse

Recent studies of black men have sought, in particular, to question dominant representations of black masculinity, and to show how moral panics created by official discourses on race-related crime issue in a paranoid policing of the state's internal and external frontiers, a strategy which descends in advance on the 'problem' category of black youth. In so far as black youths are represented as a generalized threat to civic society and its sexual morality, a reading in which Gilroy (1987) and Hall et al. (1978) detect a racist misrecognition of the diversity of black experience, recent studies have argued that the racialization of crime which views young black men as criminal elements within society requires a dissensual model of the inter-relations between race, hegemony, and power rather than a consensual model. Consensual theories of the state (as in pluralist accounts of parliamentary democracy) view the state as a static equation between private interests and communal consensus, a view which downplays the conflictual components or dialectical processes which simultaneously determine social subjects as either legitimate or illegitimate and set up the drive to legislate against those subjects deemed 'foreign' or 'alien' to state legitimacy. It follows that hegemonic domination at the level of politics and the juridical process may manifest itself in a dissensual and epistemic violence[4] against racial Others, or that the restraining forces of coercion within the state can be used to police both the civic and ideological spheres against any perceived threat to its own 'racial' frontiers. The dominant representations of black youth as deviant and criminal thus clearly raises questions concerning the relations between black youth and governmentality, state legislation and racial persecution, white law and black men, which a straightforwardly consensual model of politics fails to address. If the juridical value of justice in a parliamentary democracy can be shown to be determined by a racial prescription of universally sanctioned rights before the law, it may also be shown to be dependent on a repressive hypothesis concerning racial difference, that is, the state itself may be aberrant regarding race and black masculinity, an aberration which is legitimated through a demonization of the bodies and psyches of black men. Here the assumed absence of paternity and parental legitimation in the social relations of young black men acquires the status of a state ideology which serves to reinforce negative stereotypes of black masculinity as in need of constant state surveillance and policing. The demonization of the sexual cultures of black men not only marks a failure of European cultures to account for their own 'racial imaginary' (Mercer 1992), but also underlies the impossibility of any distinction between justice, power, public unconscious, and so on, which fails to include the necessarily ambivalent and racialized nature of the state and civic society within such distinctions.

In *Policing the Crisis*, Stuart Hall *et al.* (1978) interrogate how the complex genealogies of state racism, in ideas of civic society, cultural continuity and national identity, involve a paternalistic scene of legislation in which the disruptive alterity of black men within the social – thematized around a metaphor of crisis and moral panics over 'mugging' – is seen as both an *excess* and *defect* within society that defies legitimacy. Here the management of coercion and consent in the public unconscious demands an 'enemy within' on which all the fears and aberrant desires of the community can be projected, and through which the social bond, cultural ties and narrative knowledge of the community may come into expression. Readers of Hall *et al.* (1978) will notice how an aberrant and pathological account of black masculinity becomes normative in the 1970s, and gives rise to the same anxieties and prescriptions over racial authenticity and degradation, multiculturalism and immigration that the New Racism of the 1970s exploited for its own political and hegemonic purposes.

Adopting the term 'hegemony' from the writings of the Italian Marxist Gramsci, Hall uses the term to address the way in which a class achieves dominance or total social authority in a particular sociopolitical situation, not so much by either coercion or consent but by a combination of the two, so that it gains acceptance for its way of looking at the world over the whole social formation at the level of the economic, the political and the ideological. To that extent the impact of Thatcherism, Hall implies, on British social relations was implicit to the rise of a new racism in the 1970s which 'othered' black peoples as *not quite the same* to 'us' at *both* the superstructural level of the state and civil society and at the microstructural level of individual psychology and sexual and physical practices. The class interrelations between concrete institutions such as the criminal justice system and state apparatuses such as the police and the media thus became racialized in their representations of black men, and especially black 'youth'. Enoch Powell's infamous 'rivers of blood' speech in April 1968, for example, in which he argued that blacks could never be fully integrated into the public or cultural spheres of British life because they represent an internal threat to British legal and civic institutions requiring constant state surveillance, crudely reinforced a distinction between blackness and Englishness as incompatible ethnic identities (Gilroy 1987). However the way the speech was reported in the media, the moral panic Powell's highly emotive rhetoric induced, had a major and negative impact on black–white social relations for some time afterwards. Powell's racist rhetoric of crisis drew on the languages of race, ethnicity and sexuality in order to mark out a perceived threat from black men whom he classified as potential muggers and rapists. His drive to proclaim what English cultural identity is – a drive based on an idealization of English culture and on an aggressivity to those deemed to be outside it – was indissociable from a fantasmatic desire for English cultural identity as such. Such racism marks out the danger from the 'enemy within' in an attempt to reconstitute a hegemonic and exclusive sense of English ethnicity defined in terms of a commonsensual and imaginary appeal to national belonging and national identity. Powell's message of fear, violation and sexual threat is thus symptomatic of a racism grounding itself in cultural xenophobia.

The use of the French philosopher, Michel Foucault, and his theorizing of power, discourse and sexuality to address how technologies of the self and racial articulation interact have become focal points of these studies in cultural difference and conflict: see Rutherford (1990) and Spivak (1988). The discursive rules and categories that constitute discourse and therefore knowledge, according to Foucault, determine the way a society reasons and comprehends itself. Rejecting a notion of the state as a coherent site in which political power and civic society meet, Foucault argues that the state is an ensemble of discursive practices, knowledges, technologies and institutions, which together amount to the outcome of power as comprised in government (Foucault 1979). Discursive practices of a particular social formation are therefore linked to the exercise of power in processes of governing. 'In every society,' Foucault writes, 'the production of discourse is controlled, organised, redistributed, by a certain number of procedures whose role is to ward off its powers and dangers, to gain mastery over its chance events, to evade its materiality' (cited in Young 1981: 48–9). Racist discourses, such as the New Racism of the 1970s, reproduce social procedures of exclusion and prohibition in an attempt to police the borders of English cultural identity and governmental institutions from 'immigrant' and alien cultures and their supposed lawlessness (Hall *et al.* 1978; Gilroy 1982). Racist discursive appeals to Englishness may represent blacks as the alien Other, as undesirable residents in the green fields and shires of imaginary community. On the other hand, these discourses are themselves discontinuous practices invested, as they are, in an 'imaginary' discourse of cultural continuity. According to Foucault, it is in 'discourse' rather than in ideology that the play of power and resistance takes place. This idea has been taken up in black anti-racist cultural politics. If racism is a conceptual reproduction of an idea, an idea of Otherness, then this discursive idea can also be contested, subverted, and challenged. In other words, blacks who experience the negative interpellation of blackness in racist discourse can appropriate and change these interpell-ations by transforming them into a site of contestation or political struggle, a focal point for what Foucault terms 'reverse discourse' – the contestation of dominant regimes of truth by marginal and deviant collectivities.

The politicization of black ethnic consciousness, and especially the adoption of a masculinist rhetoric of cultural and social resistance to the law and the juridical apparatus, constitutes a reverse discourse combating the *racial* working through of hegemonic crisis. Juridical and civic genres of discourse which legislate racial and cultural difference in terms of a series of 'black panics', drawing above all on a racial dissensus between equality before the law and a demonized representation of black masculinity, has produced a militant black political oppositionalism that contests the formal diremption of law and racial inequality, racial and sexual division, fears, and anxieties. A reverse political discourse is, however, not the same as an oppositional racial politics based on a competing demand to legislate or control the discourse of governmentality. The radical forms of black masculinity that emerged in the 1960s included forms of romantic national-ism and repressive gender politics that required an internal policing and coercive consensus for black women and black gay men every bit as authoritarian as the white patriarchial structures they sought to contest. This dialectical contradiction pursues a complex and heterogeneous course; at times, for example, reverse discoursing can amount to a shared politics of kinship, as in the supportive patterning of social relations between South African migrant workers, women, and village life under apartheid; at other times, a racial politics of representation seems to engender tensions between black women and men, over issues such as paternity, domestic violence, and interracial desire and sex; and at others, racial and cultural politics come to signify in ways which marginalize or oppose gender relations, such as the Clarence Thomas–Anita Hill, Mike Tyson and O.J. Simpson, high profile sexual harassment, rape and murder cases (Morrison 1992).

Politically speaking, the social and cultural reproduction of heroic and transcendent versions of black 'manliness' has a racial specificity which has governed and authorized black political action, and that in turn has implications for how an anti-vanguardist black politics of representation based around gender and sexuality and cultural resistance may begin to thematize itself. The development of a hegemonic analysis of nation, race, gender, and law has received a variety of theorizations in black masculinity studies which has allowed it to address with greater precision than hitherto the place of black men in kinship and family structures, cultural forms of cohesion and resistance. It should therefore come as no surprise that one of the most insistent sociological discourses on black masculinities – race relations theory – in its attribution of a psychosexual pathology to black men has come under severe scrutiny by black cultural theorists. For these critics and writers – Fanon (1967), Gates (1988) and Lott (1992) – there is a racial imaginary which haunts the cultural transmission of what being a black man is, a racial imaginary which actively misreads and misnames relations of kinship, motherhood and fatherhood in black communities – a cultural misrecognition at the heart of race relations theory which will now be addressed.

The sociology of race relations and dysfunctional models of black masculinity

To resume. In a body of work collectively known as the sociology of race relations the alienation or social dysfunction of black men in relation to the public sphere is explained as the result of a symbolic castration and emasculation. Theorizing the lack of fathers in black familial structures (and the consequent dominance of matrilineal relations) as an emasculation of black men, race relations focuses on the structuring absence of black fathers in the psyche of young black men, whose violent aggressivity towards and alienation from white patriarchal authority and white hegemonic masculinity, instanced in black criminal counterculture and avoidance of paternity, provides an illustration of the negative effect of black ethnicity on the social integration of black men, and a telling psychosocial narrative for the underachievement of the black underclass in the private and public spheres. Race relations's cultural narrative of black family and social life as a crisis in black masculinity can be seen to serve a double function; not only does it inscribe the black family as a site of cultural reproduction for matriarchal or 'feminized' black men, but the narrative can also be read as one of sociocultural blame – black mothers are responsible for reproducing the social dysfunction of the race as a whole (Lawrence 1982; Staples 1982; Gilroy 1993b).

The advantages of race relations theory lies in its holistic explanation of race, individual psychology and civic society; an explanation which accounts for the reproduction of black masculinities within racist societies, in addition to offering solutions based on social policies such as reverse or positive discrimination, positive role models and images in schools, or, in certain instances, the empowering of black communities through cooperation, black financial infrastructures, and integration through higher education and open access politics. But the theory's view of black kinship structures as incompatible with a positive black masculinity and ethnic identity; its static, and integrationist model of the state and civic society based on a normative white consensus of what 'good' masculinity is or could be; its unproblematizing of masculinity as a category or concept and consequent misreading of black femininity; its privileging of the phallus as the key signifier of masculinity; its failure to take into account discontinuities, contradictions and fractures within and between men in their relations to patriarchy; and its failure to theorize the relationship between capitalism and racism in anything more than a perfunctory way seriously undermines its relevance as a theory.

In other words, race relations theory produces a set of racial codes in which black masculinity is read in terms of a behavioural social pathology structured on the symbolic substitution of female for male authority. This theory points to the erasure of white racism as the real which founds that conceptualization of black men as both passive victim and phobogenic object to be feared, but it is a theory incapable of deconstructing its own relation to the cultural fictions and racial imaginary which incorporate representations of black men. Taking up the idea of black masculinity as socially anomic, as the phallocentric absence of hegemonic masculinity, recent black feminist and cultural studies focus on the fantasmatic constructions of masculinity in the cultural symbolic, the way it colonizes racial and sexual difference, a reduction founded on its own narcissistic projection of absence and lack on to 'others' who are neither white nor male (hooks 1991). Discussing the coexistence of race and psychical identification, these studies argue for the irreducibility of race, gender and class to a single dominant–deviant paradigm. Accordingly, the need to rethink the sexual cultures of black men apart from dominant racial and stereotypical representations becomes an important element of black masculinity studies. To avoid the subsumption of these cultures into an ontology of drug-related sex, death and violence, or symbolic metaphors of black male pathology, these studies present a contrasting theory of black male identification to material and cultural ties, reflecting differences between images of black men in sociology, film and media and emergent psychoanalytical and materialist discourses on black masculinity and psychic identification over the last decade.

Race, gender and psychic identification

Deconstructing the ideology and ethnocentrism of 'normal' psychosexual development, these black masculinity studies (Fanon 1967; Bhabha 1986) argue that there is no one dominant paradigm that can account for the shifting and multiple subject-positions and identifications involved in being both black and a man. This involves scrutiny of the ways in which racial ideologies and colonial discourse explicitly feature sexual stereotypes; it considers how, for example, phylogenetic and biological codes inform stereotypical representations of black men's genital sexuality, and how the conflation of sexual fears with racial phobias in racist representations of black men by white men not only inscribes power relations, but is also symptomatic of a deeper ambivalence between desire and demand in the way race intersects with dominant cultural modes of male authority. The mapping of the racial dynamics of sexuality is thus another aspect of ideological exploration through which to disentangle this complex web of male pathology.

In *Black Skin, White Masks*, first published in French in 1952, translated into English in 1967, the Martiniquan psychiatrist, Frantz Fanon, introduces a psychoanalytical dynamic into the analysis of black masculinity which clearly focuses on the relation of the symbolization of race and gender to colonial and imperialist economic and social hegemony, the diverse historical specificities of their mutual implication, and in particular the ways in which such relation is constantly reidentified as a *symptom* within the sexual morality of European culture. If racism is a form of cultural troping, both a making sense of and a disavowal of the failure to acknowledge that sameness exists within difference, then the gendering of racial formation calls forth a particular form of double subjugation or oppression of black subjectivization which is crucial to how certain cultures narrate themselves. Fanon's reading of culture as pathological symptom is mirrored in his reading of the symbolic experience of racism as a stain or haemorrhage placed upon the black body which interrupts the subjectivization of the black self. In his reading of the trauma occasioned by this non-subjectivization, the consequence of a split between one's identity and how one is represented in racist discourse, Fanon introduces the notion of the 'epidermal schema' – the compulsive and scopic identification of black skin as a phobic and genitally deformed object – and to that extent he believes that there is a dialectical, or mutual implication, of projection and internalization in white racial fantasies of black sexuality. For a number of reasons, this is no surprise, not least because the schema, which reproduces black masculinity as a phobic object without intentionality, is subtended through a sexual logic of threat, violation and racial fear. Mary Ann Doane has aptly described this sexual phobia as 'a phobia of sexual anxiety and fear revolving around the imago of the "genital nigger" or the oversexed black male who is envisaged as having an enormous penis' (Doane 1991: 220). The 'consciousness of the body as a solely negating activity' (Fanon 1967: 110) is crucial in understanding how black and white men have differential positionalities both in relation to hegemonic masculinity and the sexual demands and racial imaginary that mediate their bodies and psyches. In Fanon's psychoanalytical restructuration of the experience of the black male psyche in racist social formations, the fundamental point emerges that this psyche, in its melancholic trajectory of loss, mourning and narcissistic injury, involves *both* a dissociation of affectivity and phobic positionality.

Fanon's restructuration helps to explain how dissociation of affectivity emerges from the racial epidermal schema and why the black body can actually impede what he terms the 'postural schema of the white man' (p. 160) through castration anxiety. To the extent that the black man 'impedes the closing of the postural schema of the white man,' he embodies the threat of castration, a threat 'posited as that of an *overpresence*, a monstrous penis' (Doane 1991: 225). In other words, in this reverse scenario the white fantasy of the monstrous black penis returns as an *excess* of symbolization, an excess or disfiguring surplus in the subjectivization of white men, an excess which troubles white male sexual identity secured through 'having' a penis and the masculinist privileges associated with its possession. In as much as hegemonic forms of masculinity in contemporary sexual cultures are constituted by their privileged ownership of the 'phallus' as signifier, the literal embodiment of the black man as penis – endowed as he is with the object which white men sacrificed in order to become 'civilized' – both recalls and displaces such privileged symbolization, becoming the occasion of white masculine mourning (for the loss or lack of primordial masculinism) and envy and fear. The psychic alienation and paranoia that results from this narcissistic wounding has violently played itself out time and time again through the lynching of black men for real or imagined transgressions of rigid racial codes, an expressive violence which terminated ritualistically with the real castration of the black man's genitals. There is an intense sexualization of racial politics in colonial and post-colonial societies. In one sense, that intensity derives from the fragility of white hegemonic masculinities, a fragility internal to the fact that nobody can actually 'own' the phallus, and that attempts to symbolize ownership of the phallus are always fantasmatic. In this sense, again, interracial sexual conflicts carry the traces of the failure of the white man's hegemonic symbolization of the ownership of the phallus. But, in another sense, the experience of psychic and subjective self-alienation which results from the racist misrecognition of the black body also constitutes a narcissistic wound in the psyche of black men.

To sum up, if the black unconscious is the discourse of the Other, i.e. structured by the phobic desire of others, then the above analysis of why black men both demand and fail to achieve hegemonic masculinity has a particular urgency, given the continued dereliction of black male public and private spheres. In both instances of failure it is the genital sexuality of black men which represents the impossibility or limit-term of hegemonic masculinity; black men represent the impasse through which the dark side of the cultural symbolic speaks itself. Whereas such failure of symbolization needs to be accompanied by a greater attention to the ways in which the whole masquerade of masculinity may be destabilized by the diversity of sexual roles and identities men inhabit, such destabilization has tended to be overlooked by critics whose heterosexist assumptions remain intent upon grounding black male sexual ambivalence in fantasies of phallic unity or the culturalist narrative of the black family romance (Hare and Hare 1984). In the next section this sexual ambivalence will be addressed.

Black queer
representa...

In order to
gender id
sexual id
opposit
interra
often
conc
pat
de
ac
actu
masc
cultu
1988).
differen
is of cou
experienc

The soci
matter, and
the self situate
spheres of the workpla
In these instances, there is no
black masculinity for it simply is – a...

David Marriott

ay in which images of black men in gay
rtypes of colonial fantasy – black men in
tal – they interrogate transcultural desi
unt representations of blackness and
subject into a space that mirrors
1992: 44). Although these representa
black readers reading against the gra
signs of identity' (p. 44) – this
fundamental ambivalence betw
black gays, when confronte
alternatively included as gay
theme in these studies of a
what they see. This a
representations of bla
readings of white ga
occurs in their ess
and Julien 1988
Mercer and
pe's Black
framing o
racial e
in a st
fetis
pe

porn remain complicit with
aged either as stud, savage, or
res and fantasies which continue
which 'fix the position of the black
object of white desires' (Mercer
ions are resisted and appropriated by
n – 'over-turning signs of otherness into
reverse discoursing is founded upon a
en demand and desire. The ways in which
with a racist homoerotic imaginary, feel
spectators and repelled as blacks is a recurring
nbivalence. Black gays want to look but do not like
nbivalence between black gay desire and phobic
ckness is obviously relevant to Mercer's and Julien's
sexual politics and gay art. An example of both readings
ays on the photography of Robert Mapplethorpe (Mercer
, Mercer 1992).

Julien describe the photographic codes at work in Mapplethor-
ales as a fetishized and objectified 'way of looking', where the
black nude males as sexualized and racialized objects in white
otic fantasies masks a racial fetishism which *fixes* black masculinity
reotypical regime of representation. To the extent, therefore, that this
nism and objectification depends upon a scopic fixation on the black
his and skin, the one monstrous, and the other acting as a signifier of racial
otherness, then the photographs of *Black Males* become readily comprehensible as a racist form of othering. The connections between objectification
and racial fetishism in this analysis derives from feminist theories of cinematic
spectatorship. Mercer and Julien acknowledge their debt to Laura Mulvey's
influential 'Visual pleasure and narrative cinema', first published in 1975, in
which Mulvey uses Lacanian psychoanalytic theory to suggest the classic
sexing of the look in cinema: the man looks, the woman is looked at. But as
Lebeau (1995) has pointed out, Mulvey, and so much feminist film theory
that follows, assumes a distinction between identification and recognition

narcissistic or identificatory look at the 'image seen' is an adequate psychoanalytical reading of identification, 'which disturbs the very notion of an identity in place and, with it, the distinction between subject and other' (p. 42). If there is no simple exterior relation of resistant black identity to white mastery or power but an excess or surplus which is both irreducible to either subject position and inscribed within both processes of identification, then it is precisely there that a reading against the grain or a contestation of racial discourse must begin.

In a later essay Mercer (1992) partially revises the earlier account so as to include the question of enunciation: who is speaking to whom. That is, what impact, if any, does Mapplethorpe's own homosexuality have on the ways in which his photography may be read? In moving from looking to a concern with the enunciatory contexts of racial and sexual identities, though not exclusively so, the homoerotic dimension of *Black Males* is allowed to 'thicken' Mercer's description of race, culture and marginality. Foremost amongst this shift is the representation of gay desire retheorized as a question of spectatorship involving a variety of discursive regimes, social meanings and value. For Mercer, the ways in which different subject-positions are ideologically recuperated *vis-à-vis* homoerotic images is an important differential in this context, i.e. a black gay man confronted by these images may feel implicated in ways of looking which are not in accordance with how a heterosexual white woman, or a heterosexual black man, for example, may feel implicated. Accordingly, the internal conflicts around gender and sexuality in black masculinity itself become just as important an aspect of black gay ambivalence and spectatorship as do the 'dialectics of white fear and fascination' (Mercer and Julien 1988: 134) which underpin representations of colonial fantasy.

This ambivalence between identification and representation undermines a simple reading of the photographs as racist. The value of Mapplethorpe's photographs, for Mercer, lies in the way they make visible white ethnicity as a process of identification. Such 'a process of identification' abuts on to questions of reading and interpretive contexts rather than on an either-or distinction between racial fetishism and sexuality. However, if there is a basic indetermination between racist ideology and reverse discourse in *Black Males*, such undecidability cannot be grounded in contexts of reading. The idea that there is an indeterminate relation between spectatorship and image cannot then be grounded in a social identification which upholds a narcissistic recognition of the self and forgets that representation prevents the subject from ever coinciding with itself. In addition, from an awareness of this undecidability of representation the possibility that black cultural productions may then themselves be grounded in racist knowledges, discourses and social meanings must ensue. As Stuart Hall (1992) forcefully argues, the awareness of the disarticulation of 'race' and ethnicity in recent black masculinity studies entails a rejection of the language of racial essentialism.

The scenarios of representation – subjectivity, identity, politics – which cannot escape the heterogeneity of interests and identities also deconstruct fixed racial categories as well as transcendental notions of black 'manliness' or authenticity. The emergence of a black gender politics predicated on difference and equivocity is thus ample testimony to the consequences of this shift in black masculinity studies, which may be summarized as follows.

Conclusion

The emergence of a new theoretical paradigm in black cultural studies, which takes as its fundamental orientation the endogenous or inner discontinuities of race and sexuality, in addition to the exogenous or external impact on race relations of institutions, state apparatuses and governmental powers, has resulted in a major contribution to black masculinity studies, and, in particular, to a theorizing of blackness, sexuality and gender as representations articulated in discourse which forestall, if not deconstruct, any notion of identification as a simple process, 'structured around fixed "selves"' (Hall 1992: 255). Both 'whiteness' and 'blackness' are socially constructed categories or referents in wider discourses of culture, politics, sexuality and ethnicity. Black political and cultural attempts to stabilize 'blackness' in a masculinist referent of oppositional resistance, or trope of kinship, or phallic hyperbole as in gangsta-funk and hip-hop, constitute a symbolic reading of race as the 'truth' of self. Far from accepting a view, like that of Frantz Fanon (1967: 231), that 'the Negro is not. Any more than the white man' – a double negation which places a horizon of dissensus between race and ontology, prediscursive self and social being – this essentialist cultural ethnocentrism, on the contrary, is a determined attempt to retain the position and influence of racial authenticity over ethnicity, gender and class.

Combining both intercultural as well as psychoanalytic concepts, recent studies on black cultural politics explore the ways in which 'race' functions as an arbitrary signifier or process of signification which bars other contexts in order for its own meaning to take place. In fact the intellectual and institutional contexts of black cultural studies over the last decade – encompassing several major paradigm shifts in both theory and practice concerning such issues as the interrelationship between race and sexuality, cultural difference and national identity, the formation of black masculinities in settler communities and families, the relationship of black men to their bodies, unconscious desires and fantasies, and interracial relations – has also resulted in a disarticulation of 'race' as a foundational concept. Focusing on such key areas as racism, nation, psychology, class and culture, the assertion that there is no essential, underlying black identity apart from the discursive effects of power, sexuality and class is implicit to the view taken by many black cultural theorists in the 1980s, who have sought to answer the question 'what does the black man want?', a question originally formulated in the writings of Frantz Fanon. Theses studies, or investigations, as I have tried to show, have made significant inroads into our understanding of black men and their changing roles within black communities. If 'gender is the modality in which race is lived' (Gilroy 1993a: 85), then clearly theories which can interrogate race, gender and sexuality in terms of representation and identification, and which question phallic and heterosexist notions of sexuality whilst avoiding reductive accounts of patriarchal hegemony, constitute a significant advance on race relations and masculinity studies of the 1970s. And, as we have seen, over the last decade these theories, which have contested essentialist accounts of race as prediscursive and which have examined the fantasmatic underpinning of masculinist spectatorship and identification, have become central to discussions of black masculinities. This body of criticism, drawing on discourse analysis and psychosocial accounts of gender formation, has brought to critical attention the ambivalence, fantasy and desire at the heart of patriarchal and phallocentric notions of white and black masculinities and, in so doing, has fundamentally shifted the ways in which we understand what precisely it means to be both black and a man.

Notes

1 The symbolic is a term introduced by the French psychoanalyst Jacques Lacan to refer to the domain of social meanings, values, and differentiation through which a person can both represent his/her desire and is thus constituted as a 'subject'.
2 'Hegemony' is the term elaborated by the Italian Marxist Gramsci to address the way a class achieves total authority in a social formation by gaining acceptance of its way of representing the world. See also Chantal Mouffe (1981).
3 For a definition of the terms 'cultural translation' and 'cultural hybridity' see the interview between Rutherford and Bhabha in Rutherford (1990).
4 'Epistemic violence' refers to the ways in which western legal traditions constitute an institutionalized form of violence against black Others produced by the dominant systems of knowledge which inform their legalistic understanding of blacks as criminal, illegal immigrants, etc.

References

Bhabha, H. (1986) Introduction to F. Fanon *Black Skin, White Masks*. London: Pluto Press.
Costello, M. and Wallace, D. (1990) *Signifying Rappers: Rap and Race in the Urban Present*. New York: Ecco.
Doane, M. (1991) *Femmes Fatales. Feminism, Film Theory, Psychoanalysis*. London: Routledge.

Fanon, F. (1967) *Black Skin, White Masks*, translated by C.L. Markmann. New York: Grove Press.

Foucault, M. (1979) On governmentality, *Ideology and Consciousness*, 6: 5–22.

Frazier, E.F. (1966) *The Negro Family in the United States*. Chicago: The University of Chicago Press.

Gates, H.L., Jr. (1988) *The Signifying Monkey. A Theory of African-American Literary Criticism*. New York: Oxford University Press.

Gilroy, P. (1982) *The Empire Strikes Back. Race and Racism in 70s Britain*. London: Routledge.

Gilroy, P. (1987) *There Ain't no Black in the Union Jack: the Cultural Politics of Race and Nation*. London: Hutchinson.

Gilroy, P. (1993a) *The Black Atlantic. Modernity and Double Consciousness*. London: Verso.

Gilroy, P. (1993b) *Small Acts. Thoughts on the Politics of Black Cultures*. London: Serpent's Tail.

Hall, S., Critcher, C., Jefferson, J., Clarke, J. and Roberts, B. (eds) (1978) *Policing the Crisis: Mugging, the State and Law and Order*. London: Macmillan.

Hall, S. (1992) New ethnicities, in J. Donald and A. Rattansi (eds) *'Race', Culture and Difference*. London: Sage Publications and Open University.

Hare, N. and Hare, J. (1984) *The Endangered Black Family: Coping with the Unisexualization and Coming Extinction of the Black Race*. San Francisco: Black Think Tank.

hooks, b. (1991) *Yearning: Race, Gender and Cultural Politics*. London: Turn-around.

Lawrence, E. (1982) In the abundance of water the fool is thirsty: sociology and black 'pathology', in *The Empire Strikes Back. Race and Racism in 70s Britain*. London: Routledge.

Lebeau, V. (1995) *Lost Angels: Psychoanalysis and Cinema*. London: Routledge.

Lott, E. (1992) Love and theft: the racial unconscious of blackface minstrelsy, *Representations*, 39: 23–50.

Mercer, K. and Julien, I. (1988) Race, sexual politics and black masculinity: a dossier, in R. Chapman and J. Rutherford (eds) *Male Order: Unwrapping Masculinity*. London: Lawrence and Wishart.

Mercer, K. (1992) Skin head sex thing. Racial difference and the homoerotic imaginary, *New Formations*, 16: 1–23.

Morrison, T. (ed.) (1992) *Race-ing Justice, En-gendering Power: Essays on Anita Hill, Clarence Thomas and the Construction of Social Reality*. New York: Pantheon.

Mouffe, C. (1981) Hegemony and ideology in Gramsci, in T. Bennett (ed.) *Culture, Ideology and Social Process*. London: Batsford and Open University.

Moynihan, D.P. (1965) *The Negro Family: The Case for National Action*. Washington, DC: US Department of Labor.

Rutherford, J. (ed.) (1990) *Identity: Community, Culture, Difference*. London: Lawrence and Wishart.

Spillers, H. (1987) Mama's baby, papa's maybe: an American grammar book, *Diacritics*, 17(2), summer: 65–81.

Spivak, G. (1988) Can the subaltern speak?, in C. Nelson and L. Grossberg (eds) *Marxism and the Interpretation of Culture*. Basingstoke: Macmillan Education.

Staples, R. (1982) *Black Masculinity: The Black Man's Role in American Society.* San Francisco, CA: Black Scholar Press.

Wilson, W.J. (1978) *The Declining Significance of Race: Blacks and Changing American Institutions.* Chicago: University of Chicago Press.

Young, R. (1981) *Untying the Text: A Poststructuralist Reader.* London: Routledge.

Is masculinity dead? A critique of the concept of masculinity/ masculinities

Researching and writing about men and masculinities is not new and not particularly unusual. Mainstream social science is full of relevant studies. What is new is the relatively rapid growth of interest within the social sciences in men and masculinities as an explicit and gendered topic for inquiry. This shift certainly dates from the late 1970s and, indeed, there has been a marked acceleration of concern and curiosity since 1987 – a year that brought the publication of a whole clutch of books on the subject (see Hearn 1989). The forces that have prompted this are several, and not altogether consistent (see Edwards 1994). They include most obviously the variety of feminist work but also gay politics and writing, and the full range of men's responses to feminism. Some of these have developed under the banner of 'Men's Studies'; others have located themselves within 'Critical Studies on Men'.

Masculinity in focus

In much of this broad development of interest, the concept of masculinity has been specially favoured. The concept of masculinity, or now masculinities, has served as a symbolic icon for the more general increase in interest in the study of men, critical or otherwise. It is as if this concept exemplifies the field of concern and even, possibly, distills the aggregation of activity of men in the social world into one neat word.

However, and perhaps because of its iconic significance, the concept of masculinity has often been used rather loosely in these elaborated discourses. Yet despite the variety of uses of 'masculinity', the concept has usually retained its roots in social psychological research on sex role and identity. Masculinity and now masculinities are concepts that are used in a variety of ways, and with a variety of frameworks. These include psychological characteristics, gendered experiences, gender identity, sex-role socialization, gendered behaviours, psychoanalysis, power analysis and institutional practices. In many of these uses and formulations, the idea of masculinity acts as a reference point against which behaviours and identities can be evaluated. Masculinity effectively acts as a normative and indeed culturally specific standard (Eichler 1980).

Often though not always, the concept of masculinity is linked to a cultural constructionist position, which posits that all people, and in this context men especially, are subject to the control of gender. In this view, masculinity can be a shorthand for social limitations on men. Accordingly, such an underlying 'logic' can be developed in association with a liberationist perspective.

For a number of years, at least since 1978, I have been studying and writing about men and indeed using and developing the concept of masculinity/ masculinities. In the last few years, I have, for a variety of reasons, become increasingly unsure of the usefulness of the concept of masculinity/masculinities in critically studying men. There are a number of problems with the concept of masculinity or, more accurately, with the way the concept is used. They include:

- the wide variety of uses of the concept
- the imprecision of its use in many cases
- its use as a shorthand for a very wide range of social phenomena, and in particular those that are connected with men and males but which appear to be located in the individual
- the use of the concept as a primary and underlying cause of other social effects.

Furthermore, with some usages of the concept, the focus on men might be developed to divert attention away from women, rendering them invisible and excluding them as participants in discourse. While masculinity might be a focus of attention, it is necessary to retain in any analysis an understanding of the relation of men to women. The exclusionary tendency is a particular problem with some approaches within Men's Studies. Worse still, an overemphasis on masculinity and a neglect of social relations between women and men can lead on to a redefinition of men as victims of historical, cultural and gendered processes, to which men are bound. Similarly, in this view, women may easily become blamed for men's problems.

These and other critiques will be examined in the course of this chapter.

The meanings of masculinity

Masculinity has become a very popular concept in pro-feminist, anti-feminist and indeed, some feminist literature; it is used within a variety of disciplinary frameworks, including psychology, social psychology, sociology, anthropology and history. In many ways, the simplest formulations of masculinity have been developed in association with psychological and individualist approaches. These include, most significantly, the Bem Sex Role Inventory (Bem 1974, 1977) which purports to measure individuals' (women's or men's) sense of themselves on masculinity and femininity scales. Individuals' self-ranking is scored in accordance with traits that are previously judged to be desirable for a woman or a man, in society. Accordingly, 'aggressive' indicates masculinity and 'cheerful' indicates femininity. The concept has thus been used as an umbrella term summarizing 20 measures of individuals' beliefs of the appropriateness of certain specific personality characteristics for a man (masculinity) and a woman (femininity). In this view, masculinity is individually possessed. It is a 'something' that is held differentially by different people. This methodological individualism links with other approaches to gender that emphasize sex differences and sex-role socialization. Such measures are fraught with conceptual and political problems, most obviously because of their reification of the social and their cultural specificity (Eichler 1980).

Another set of approaches derives from psychoanalysis. Psychoanalytic approaches are, of course, various. Whereas, orthodox Freudianism emphasized 'castration anxiety' and 'penis envy', subsequent feminist work has turned this on its head (Segal 1993: 628). Paternal absence has been seen as a crucial element in the formation of masculinity with the work of Nancy Chodorow (1978) figuring in an especially influential way. In such feminist accounts, 'the fragility of masculinity, and its need to repress the type of attachments and dependencies of infancy, are presented as the cornerstone of patriarchy, of male dominance' (Segal 1993: 628, citing Chodorow 1980). The impact of this feminist literature on men's writing on masculinity has been considerable, and has been recently expertly reviewed and critiqued by Antony McMahon (1993). Briefly, he argues that this taking up of Chodorow's ideas, often in a much simplified form, often by men, leaves aside a materialistic analysis of men's practices. Such a latter approach is indeed suggested by materialist feminist and related literatures.

Masculinity has also been represented as a 'deep centre', an essence of men. Rather than conceptualizing masculinity as the cultural expression of gender, in this formulation masculinity is that which is assumed to lie behind mere culture. The most well-known exploration of this view is to be found in Bly's (1990) mythopoetic work on the obscuring of male essence through the loss of appropriate initiation in the modern world. Identifying the attempt to find an essential masculinity appears in very different frameworks that are supposedly social constructions. For example, Brannon (1976) has characterized masculinity as: ' "No sissy stuff"; "be a big wheel"; "be a sturdy oak"; "give 'em hell" '. (Also see Kimmel 1990.)

Such essentially psychological approaches to masculinity generally present a more particular and specific version of masculinity than more sociological literatures. In the latter, the concept of masculinity is generally used to refer to

the cultural construction of men, the construction of men as ge,
example, Tolson (1977: 12) refers to Oakley's (1972) distinction b.
'sex ' and 'gender', with the latter a psychological and cultural term. To
continues:

> This definition of gender allows us to appreciate the highly particular
> ways in which 'masculinity' is commonly understood . . . 'masculinity'
> is not simply the opposite of 'femininity' but there are many different
> types of gender identity . . . and different expressions of masculinity
> within and between different cultures.
>
> (Tolson 1977: 12)

In this view, masculinity is an example of gender, it is a gendered form; and
furthermore, that gendered form is given different expressions in different
cultures. Thus this formulation suggests two levels or aspects of culture: first,
a generalized form of culture that is transcultural; and second, a specific form
of culture that is distinct within and between cultures. To put this slightly
differently, there are many masculinities that are expressions of masculinity,
singular. Thus, in this view, masculinity is both a generalizable, cultural
phenomenon and a variety of culturally specific expressions of gender and
possible gender identities. In other words, the generalizable cultural form of
masculinity may be assumed to pre-exist the culturally specific. A rather
similar argument is to be found in a more recent text – Clyde Franklin (1984),
The Changing Definition of Masculinity. Here again, as the title suggests,
masculinity as gender is subject to changing definitions. This time the
emphasis is on the changing historical construction of gender as Franklin
considers the different meanings of masculinity in the history of the United
States. In particular, he provides us with a modernist reading of masculinity
that is changed from rural to urban, from communal to associative, from
traditional to modern.

However, even such historical reviews of masculinity are relatively
unusual. More commonly psychological or social psychological models have
in turn fed into more sociological and situational sex-role studies of
masculinity. The growth of these perspectives in the 1950s and 60s,
particularly in the United States, has been expertly summarized by Carrigan,
Connell and Lee (1985) in their landmark article 'Towards a new sociology of
masculinity'. For example, they cite a number of studies which illustrate this
turn to situationally based analyses. These include that by Helen Hacker
(1957), which argued that male homosexuality may be one possible form of
flight from the 'new burdens of masculinity' that are characterized by
challenge and conflict. On the other hand, it could be argued that male
homosexuality might well bring more challenge and conflict to those men's
lives, not least from some heterosexual men. Another example is Ruth
Hartley's (1959) study of sex-role pressures on the socialization of the male
child. This identified the importance of anxieties around sexuality, especially

for the mother, in bringing up boys in the relative absence of the father. This is argued to lead to overstraining to be masculine and hostility towards anything that is classified as feminine. Again there are conceptual problems in this framework. For example, the relative absence of the father could be used to argue that boys are likely to grow up in more feminine ways. The understanding of these dynamics only comes from placing these relative sex roles in the context of broader structures of power, in this case, particularly power around male heterosexuality. Sex-role theory may be helpful in describing some elements of the situation, but is not very instructive in analysing power, contradiction and change.

The limitations of sex-role theory approaches are discussed in some detail by Carrigan, Connell and Lee (1985), particularly in terms of their tendency, either contingently or inherently, to neglect power (also see Connell 1985, 1987). This movement to the centrality of *power* in the analysis of masculinity has now been taken up enthusiastically. Connell and his colleagues have highlighted the interplay of power and social positions, the contribution of gay scholarship and psychoanalysis, the importance of contradiction, transformation and resistance. 'Masculinity' has itself been transformed as a concept to that plural 'masculinities', which may be 'hegemonic' or 'subordinated' or presumably contradictory. Above all, masculinities are no larger individual possessions, but are institutional practices located in structures of power.

Since this work in the 1980s, Connell and his colleagues have extended their theoretical analyses into biographical and life story work (for example, Connell 1989), macrohistorical and global accounts (for example, Connell 1993a) and most recently, an extended study of *Masculinities* that brings these elements together (Connell 1995). In the last few years, there has been increasing interest in the links between masculinity and power (Brittan 1989), masculinity and violence (Miedzian 1992), masculinity and crime (Messerschmidt 1993), masculinity and child abuse (Hearn 1990) and masculinity and the law (Collier 1995).

Many of these themes figure strongly in the special issue of the journal *Theory and Society* on masculinities (Connell 1993b). Several of the articles included make a clear reference to the provisional and historically and culturally specific status of the concept of masculinity. Segal (1993) refers to the concept in inverted commas throughout her paper and as already noted, McMahon (1993) delivers a major critique of men's psychologization of certain feminist literature in their analyses of masculinity. McMahon writes:

> The term 'masculinity' is in constant employment in the broader literature about men. 'Masculinity' is abstract, fragile, insecure, unemotional, independent, non-nurturant and so on. All the attributes of men discussed in the literature are spoken of as aspects of masculinity. It is remarkable how seldom writers on masculinity

explicitly indicate what kind of concept they take masculinity to be. Michael Kimmel defines masculinity as 'what it means to be a man' but this still leaves the matter rather open. Connell has noted that the concept of masculinity is thoroughly bound up with modern notions of individual identity and the self, which are clearly difficult to think beyond. The usefulness of the concept is generally taken for granted, and what is offered is a description, frequently a list of traits.

The idealism and reification in the literature on male personality haunt the uses to which the idea of masculinity is put. Men's practices are the result of, or the expression of, masculinity. While men's practices are criticized, it is masculinity that is seen to be the problem. Calls for masculinity to be 'redefined', 'reconstructed', 'dismantled' or 'transformed' become common. Instead of wondering whether they should change their behaviour, men 'wrestle with the meaning of masculinity'. Domination is an aspect of masculinity rather than something men simply do. Even practice-based analyses of masculinity find it hard to avoid construing masculinity as some kind of thing-in-itself. Though Arthur Brittan defines masculinity in usually concrete and explicit terms, as the dominant form of male behaviour in any particular milieu, he also speaks of the way men 'have a multitude of ways of expressing their masculinity' and summarizes his work as being concerned with the way men 'live their masculinity'.

Like the accounts of male personality, many descriptions of masculinity are really descriptions of popular ideologies about the actual or ideal characteristics of men. In the literature on masculinity, the ideological nature of the term is most clearly theorized by the term 'hegemonic masculinity', defined as the 'culturally exalted form of masculinity'. In popular usage, notions of masculinity (and femininity) are inextricably embedded in naturalizing and policing discourses, which construct appropriate models of gendered practice, and which can be used to bring the appropriateness of an individual's gender identity into question. Thus, men may well experience themselves as 'expressing their masculinity' or experience doubts about the status of their masculinity.

Masculinity seems to hold sway over men, just as sex roles did in earlier formulations. Barbara Ehrenreich noted how the 'male role' became an explanatory cliché in academic and popular accounts of men. It is possible that 'masculinity' is suffering the same fate.

(McMahon 1993: 690–1)

Most recently, there have been attempts to develop concepts of masculinity and masculine subjectivity that draw together post-structuralist thinking with psychoanalytic (for example, Jefferson 1994). These present more complex and generally more contextualized accounts, though there remains a danger that even such complexity can be used as causal explanation of men's actions, rather than vice versa.

I should perhaps add at this point a comment on my own use of the concept. It will come as no surprise to recognize that I have used the term in a number of ways in previous work. In *The Gender of Oppression* (Hearn 1987), I examined both the structural relations of the *gender class* men and the differing agentic positions of *particular* men, both as individuals and groups. Within this framework, masculinity was seen as appearance, as a set of signs that someone is a man and not a woman. Elsewhere I have used the concept of masculinity or masculinities more loosely, whether within a social constructionist or post-structuralist framework.

Having considered some of the different meanings of the concepts, I now want to move on to some more fundamental critiques.

The material basis of masculinity

A first fundamental critique has already been hinted at, in referring to McMahon's (1993) commentary on masculinity. This concerns the anti-materialist assumptions of many, probably most, versions of the concept of masculinity. Whatever the possible meanings, definitions or theoretical perspectives of masculinity, the question remains: how does this 'quality' relate to what men do, to men's material practices? Not only do most versions of masculinity fail to address that question, but more fundamentally, they tend to divert attention away from material practices, whether in work, sexuality, violence or elsewhere, and away from a materialist or materially based analysis of gendered power relations.

Historical and cultural differences

A second set of fundamental problems with the concept of masculinity arises from the issues of difference and variety. These exist both in time and in space, and both societally and personally. This perspective follows very much from Liz Stanley's (1984) analysis of gender and sex and the variation that can be recognized between cultures, within one culture over time, and within one culture at one point in time. Let us then consider a number of types of difference and variety.

First, there is difference and variation historically and societally over time. This is especially important in the study of historical societies and situations when masculinity is not present as a concept. For example, in nineteenth-century Britain, the concept of 'manliness' was used rather than, and in distinction from 'masculinity'. 'Manliness' itself had changing meanings. It was also very much a middle-class-based concept, referring to the 'transition from Christian immaturity to maturity, demonstrated by earnestness, selflessness and integrity' (in the early Victorian period) changing to 'neo-Spartan virility, as exemplified by stoicism, hardness and endurance' (in the late Victorian period) (Mangan and Walvin 1987: 1). The fundamental point here is not that masculinity varies historically, rather it is that in some historical structures the contexts of masculinity may be irrelevant or misleading (see Hearn 1992, 1994).

A second example comes from geographical, spatial and crosscultural variation. There are, of course, innumerable examples of the inapplicability of 'masculinity' to cultural situations. A particularly interesting example is that described by Anna Meigs (1990) in her study of the Hua of New Guinea. Rather than there being a simply dichotomous gender system, instead there are 'multiple gender ideologies'. A major distinction amongst the Hua is between *figapa* (uninitiated/like women) and *kakora*. *Figapa* is to be found with children of both sexes, premenopausal women, postmenopausal women who have borne two children or less, and – significantly – old men. These groupings all contain what are assumed to be called female substances. On the other hand, *kakora* is to be found with initiated males (this initiation involves vomiting and nose bleeding) and women who have borne three or more children. Thus *figapa* and *kakora* are not strict opposites. There is more of a continuum: males become more *figapa* as they get older – through sexual activity, food prepared by women, casual contact and the gaining of female substances, and females lose *figapa* through childbirth and the loss of female substances.

Again, to repeat the point in this cultural scheme, masculinity does not figure. Indeed, I begin to wonder to what extent masculinity is an ethnocentric or even Eurocentric notion. Interestingly, David Gilmore concludes his crosscultural review of manhood in the following way:

> When I started researching this book, I was prepared to rediscover the old saw that conventional femininity is nurturing and passive and that masculinity is self-serving, egotistical and uncaring. I did not find this. One of my findings here is that manhood ideologies always include a criterion of selfless generosity, even to the point of sacrifice. Again and again we find that 'real' men are those who give more than they take; they love others. Real men are generous, even to a fault, like the Me-hinaku fisherman, the Samburu cattle-herder, or the Sambia or Dodoth Big Man. Non-men are often those stigmatized as stingy and unpro-ductive. Manhood therefore is also a nurturing concept, if we define that term as giving, subverting, or other-directed. It is true that this male giving is different from, and less demonstrative and more obscure than, the female. It is less direct, less immediate, more involved with exter-nals; the 'other' involved may be society in general, rather than specific persons.
>
> (Gilmore 1993: 229)

In other words it is sensible not to make too many assumptions about what masculinity might be or even whether masculinity is relevant or meaningful in a particular society. This is especially important when examining men historically and/or crossculturally.

Masculinity and the individual

Comparable difficulties in time and space exist for the relationship of supposed masculinity to the individual. In terms of aging and movement through the life-course – what is thought of as personal time – it is not at all clear how masculinity might be thought to figure. How might masculinity begin and when does it begin? I am not referring here to the charting of the socialization of boys into masculinity. Rather there is a more fundamental question of how masculinity could be said to relate to the male sex/gender at all. Is masculinity relevant from day one of the male infant, or before birth, or increasingly as the child ages? There are clearly major problems with these kinds of questions, because they tend to force into perception a relatively simple notion of masculinity, one that can be talked of as a 'something' at all. At the very least, masculinity in this life-course perspective means quite different things at the ages of 2 and 20. More dramatically, masculinity is a somewhat meaningless concept, as it shifts between the worlds of the infant, of growing up, of adult life and old age and dying.

Masculinity can also be evaluated against a further source of diversity and variation – that through the life of the body, personal existence – what might be thought of as personal space and ontology, paralleling societal space and culture. Again, it is far from clear how masculinity might relate to the embodied social selves of men (Mishkind *et al.* 1987) or indeed the embodied social selves of men as experienced by women, other men, girls and boys. As in the previous example, it could be hypothesized that there are multiple selves beyond the physical body that may be experienced by the individual or others: for example, the body might be perceived through the leaving of traces following previous events (such as an accident) or the body might be perceived through the inscription of the social on the physical in some other way.

The key issue that arises, albeit in different ways, from these various forms of variation is that masculinity may not be the most appropriate or relevant concept to describe and analyse, particular social situations. Masculinity applied inappropriately can be a misleading and confusing concept, as that *what is* is not seen.

Unities, differences and the interrelation of oppressions

The emphasis on variety and difference outlined in the previous section does, however, bring with it some dangers. The most significant of these is the possible retreat to relativism; that there are simply varieties of social arrangements that may be constructed as 'masculinities' or 'manliness' or 'manhood'. Such relativism presents a very partial picture of men. First, it removes attention from the interrelations of the unities of men, and the differences between men (Collinson and Hearn 1994; Hearn and Collinson 1994). Not only are there differences between men but men are also bound together as a gender class in power relations with women. Ironically, part of the way in which men's gender class power is maintained is through the promotion of a false monolith of the way men are supposed to be – heterosexual, able-bodied, independent.

Second, relativistic approaches to masculinity do not adequately deal with the relationship of unities and differences between men to other social divisions and oppressions, such as class, race, disability (Collinson and Hearn 1994; Hearn and Collinson 1994). Thus one might consider combinations of social divisions and oppressions such as the situation of young black men or older gay men.

Engaging with this multiplicity of unities, differences and various social divisions and oppressions is, in some ways, an elaboration of the plural approach to 'masculinities' mentioned above (Carrigan *et al.* 1985; Kimmel and Messner 1988). However, in another sense, engaging with this multiplicity or multiplicities subverts the whole enterprise of a particular sociology of masculinity.

The realization of such multiplicities brings, however, a wide range of further questions. These include the limitations of a 'types' approach to men, the numerical size and complexity of all the possible types that there might be, the possible discontinuity between experience and social location, and the deconstruction of each particular social categorization. Furthermore, multiple differentiation of men raises all the debates that there are about the nature of difference/differance/deferrals. In particular, increasingly complex differentiations of men lead the reader towards epistemological questions, including the case for anti-foundationalism. For by increasing the complexities of the categories of men, the possibility is raised that all foundations of knowledge are flawed. This possibility should, however, not be taken to suggest any diminution of power, domination and oppression (see Hearn and Parkin 1993).

Heterosexual dichotomies

A related perspective which also raises a fundamental critique of masculinity is the critique of dichotomizing and dichotomized theory and practice in sexual politics. This perspective has been very important in certain strands of both feminist and gay politics and scholarship (see, for example, Grosz 1987). In such a view, it is not taken for granted that gendered power relations are in any primary sense between males/men and females/women. Indeed, it is the crosscutting categories and relations of gay men and straight men, lesbian women and straight women, lesbians and gay men, and straight people that need to be engaged with – in other words, simple dichotomies fall.

For example, Simon Watney (1991) in the early 1980s, and following the election of the new Conservative government in 1979, explicitly attacked liberationist theories of sexual politics that appeared, perhaps unwittingly, to propose such dichotomous views. In a response to David Fernbach (1990), Watney argued against both 'the arbitrary and vitiating categories of masculinity and femininity as if they themselves were unproblematical and reinforcing the most fundamental aspect of the overall ideology of sexuality as we experience it' (Watney 1991: 295) and the 'straightforward attempt to read off a specifically gay politics from a crude patriarchal analysis of sexual relations in capitalist societies which was not necessarily socialist at all' (p. 297). He continued that the attempt at

> a temporary resolution of the masculinity/femininity dichotomy as the answer to *all* our present difficulties was flawed: 'not only does it avoid the question of how the class/sexuality matrix constructs individuals and self-conscious social groupings *across* the boundaries of sex, class, race and gender, it also posits an "equality in difference" solution about the history of British feminism shows [*sic*] to be inadequate to deal with the basic inequalities within and between the sexes'.
>
> (p. 301, citing Wilson 1979)

However, these debates do not stop there. They also raise the more fundamental question of the limitations of the categorization of 'men' in the first place. Men, like women, are also subject to the social dialectics which produce women and men as categories. These are not innocent categories. In saying this, I am thinking of that which produces the categories 'men' and 'women', not necessarily that which produces 'gender', for gender does not necessarily include conceptions of 'men' and 'women', and may, indeed, almost certainly, include other gendered categories.

To assume *a priori* that masculinity/masculinities exist is to reify the social construction of sex and gender, so that the typical dimorphism is assumed to be natural. Qualities (of masculinity/femininity) are assumed to complement other dimorphic structures of men/women, male/female or the masculine/the feminine. This in itself reproduces a heterosexualizing of social arrangements (Wittig 1992).

Instead of this assumed heterosexual dimorphism – which the concept of masculinity certainly suggests – it is more accurate to describe, analyse and intervene in social situations, depending on the differential construction of gender. The presence of 'multiple gender ideologies' (Meigs 1990), 'the third sex' and 'the third gender' (Herdt 1994), and the deconstructive movement beyond the 'heterosexual matrix' (Butler 1990) are all examples of attempts to be specific about different gendered arrangements rather than to assume the pre-existence of any masculinity.

Representation

Finally, other difficulties arise in making sense of masculinity in particular arenas and media. For example, it is far from clear how a concept of masculinity helps the analysis of representation and imaging men. It is hard to know what the term 'images of masculinity' might mean – imaging is a process such that masculinities do not pre-exist their imaging. So a picture, a photograph, an advertisement showing a man is not made more comprehensible by bringing in a notion of masculinity. Whether these are Marlboro ads, pictures of men drinking beer, men holding each other, or men asleep, their sense is made by particular references used by the reader, and not through some generalized notion of masculinity (see Mercer and Julien 1988; Hearn and Melechi 1992; Rogoff and Van Leer 1993; Silverman 1993; Hearn 1995).

Needless to say, questions of representation are of recurring importance in social analysis more generally. Social reality is always mediated (Game 1991).

Conclusions

This chapter has presented a critique of the concept of masculinity. The recent move to the plural concept of masculinities represents an advance, but does not fully resolve these difficulties. Thus in conclusion I will first reiterate some of the limitations of masculinity/masculinities, and then outline some possible ways forward.

The concept may divert attention from women and gendered power relations. The use of the concepts is often imprecise. Meanings stretch from essential self to deep centre, gender identity, sex stereotype, attitudes, institutional practices and so on. What is exactly meant by masculinity is often unclear. Masculinity is often a gloss on complex social processes. The concept is sometimes attributed a causal power – for example, that masculinity is said to cause a social problem, such as violence – when masculinity is rather the result of other social processes. As McMahon concludes,

> it is true that the term 'masculinity' is a term in discourses about identity, which have powerful social effects, but this is no reason to attribute explanatory power to masculinity – unless one believes all practices are effects of discourse. And to say that the problem with gender relations is the way in which masculinity is constructed, with the

solution a 'reconstruction of masculinity' is to displace theoretical attention from men's political practices.

(McMahon 1993: 692)

Certainly to *begin* the analysis of men with masculinity/masculinities, or to search for the existence of masculinity/masculinities is likely to miss the point. It cannot be assumed *a priori* that masculinity/masculinities exist. To do so is to reproduce a heterosexualizing of social arrangements.

So what are the possible ways forward from this? What are we to do with this strange concept, this icon of interest in men, this potential fetish that may easily obscure men and the power of men's material practices? I would like to finish off by putting forward four proposals for developing work in this area:

First, when masculinity/masculinities are referred to, they should be used more precisely and particularly.

Second, it is often much more appropriate to base analysis on the concept of 'men' and what men do or think or feel. It is generally preferable to move from 'masculinities' back to 'men'. Accordingly, it is generally more accurate to refer to 'men's practices' or 'men's social relations' or 'men's assumptions' or 'beliefs about men' and so on.

Third, it is clear that 'masculinities' are much talked of and about, and for this reason alone, it is very useful to explore the multiplicity of 'discourses of masculinity' and 'multiple masculinities'.

Finally, and more tentatively, it may be appropriate to develop concepts that more accurately reflect women's and men's differential experiences of men and that provide the means for critical analysis. Such concepts might include those that embody both the material and the discursive at the same time, like 'material practice' and 'discursive practice'. More to the point, it would probably be helpful to conceptualize the material discursive practices of and about men in terms of the extent to which and the ways in which they are 'masculinized' rather than to speak of some independent substance of masculinity itself.

The materialist deconstruction of masculinity is necessary as one part of the materialist deconstruction of the category of sex (see Hearn 1992; Wittig 1992). To date, 'masculinity' has certainly served a purpose in developing a focus of attention on men; the question is whether it has served its purpose.

Note

This chapter is a revised version of a presentation at the Social Science Research Unit, the Institute of Education, University of London, May 1993. I am grateful to the seminar participants there for their critical comments, to David Collinson for ongoing debate on these issues and to Valerie Bentley for typing the text.

References

Bem, S. (1974) The measurement of psychological androgyny, *Journal of Clinical Psychology*, 42(2): 155–62.
Bem, S. (1977) On the utility of alternative procedures for assessing psychological androgyny, *Journal of Consulting and Clinical Psychology*, 45(2): 166–205.
Bly, R. (1990) *Iron John: A Book about Men*. New York: Addison-Wesley.
Brannon, R. (1976) The male sex role: our culture's blueprint of manhood and what it's done for us lately, in R. Brannon and D. David (eds) *The Forty Nine Percent Majority*. Reading, MA: Addison-Wesley.
Brannon, R. and David, D. (1976) *The Forty Nine Percent Majority*, Reading, MA: Addison-Wesley.
Brittan, A. (1989) *Masculinity and Power*. Oxford: Blackwell.
Butler, J. (1990) *Gender Trouble, Feminism and the Subversion of Identity*. New York: Routledge.
Carrigan, T., Connell, R.W. and Lee, J. (1985) Towards a new sociology of masculinity, *Theory and Society*, 14(5): 551–604.
Chodorow, N. (1978) *The Reproduction of Mothering*. Berkeley, CA: University of California Press.
Collier, R. (1995) *Masculinity, Law and the Family*. London: Routledge.
Collinson, D.L. and Hearn, J. (1994) Naming men as men: implications for work, organization and management, *Gender, Work and Organization*, 1(1): 2–22.
Connell, R.W. (1985) Theorizing gender, *Sociology*, 19(2): 260–72.
Connell, R.W. (1987) *Gender and Power*. Cambridge: Polity Press.
Connell, R.W. (1989) Cool guys, swots and wimps: the interplay of masculinity and education, *Oxford Review of Education*, 15: 291–303.
Connell, R.W. (1993a) The big picture: masculinities in recent world history, *Theory and Society*, 22(5): 597–624.
Connell, R.W. (ed.) (1993b) Special issue: Masculinities. *Theory and Society*, 22(5).
Connell, R.W. (1995) *Masculinities*. Cambridge: Polity Press.
Edwards, T. (1994) *Erotics and Politics*. London: Routledge.
Eichler, M. (1980) *The Double Standard. A Feminist Critique of Feminist Social Science*. London: Croom Helm.
Fernbach, D. (1990) Ten years of gay liberation, in *Politics and Power Two*. London: Routledge and Kegan Paul.
Franklin, C.W. (1984) *The Changing Definition of Masculinity*. New York: Plenum.
Game, A. (1991) *Undoing the Social*, Milton Keynes: Open University Press.
Gilmore, D. (1993) *Manhood in the Making. Cultural Concepts of Masculinity*. New Haven, CT: Yale University Press.
Grosz, E. (1987) Feminist theory and the challenge to knowledges, *Women's Studies International Forum*, 10(5): 475–80.
Hacker, H.M. (1957) The new burdens of masculinity, *Marriage and Family Living*, 19: 227–33.
Hartley, R. (1959) Sex-role pressures and the socialisation of the male child, *Psychological Reports*, 5: 457–68.
Hearn, J. (1987) *The Gender of Oppression. Men, Masculinity and the Critique of Marxism*. Brighton: Harvester Wheatsheaf.

Hearn, J. (1989) Reviewing men and masculinities – or mostly boys' own papers, *Theory, Culture and Society*, 6: 665–89.

Hearn, J. (1990) Men's violence and 'child abuse', in Violence Against Children Study Group *Taking Child Abuse Seriously*. London: Unwin Hyman.

Hearn, J. (1992) *Men in the Public Eye. The Construction and Deconstruction of Public Men and Public Patriarchies*. London: Routledge.

Hearn, J. (1994) Research in men and masculinities: some sociological issues and possibilities, *The Australian and New Zealand Journal of Sociology*, 30(1): 47–70.

Hearn, J. (1995) Imaging the aging of men, in M. Featherstone and A. Wernick (eds) *Born Dying: Images of Aging*. London: Routledge.

Hearn, J. and Collinson, D.L. (1994) Theorizing unities and differences between men and between masculinities, in H. Brod and M. Kaufman (eds) *Theorizing Masculinities*. Thousand Oaks, CA: Sage.

Hearn, J. and Melechi, A. (1992) The Transatlantic gaze: masculinities, youth and the American imaginary, in S. Craig (ed.) *Men, Masculinity and the Media*. Newbury Park, CA: Sage.

Hearn, J. and Parkin, W. (1993) Organisations, multiple oppressions and post-modernism, in J. Hassard and M. Parker (eds) *Postmodernism and Organisations*. London: Sage.

Herdt, G. (ed.) (1994) *Third Sex, Third Gender, Beyond Sexual Dimorphism in Culture and History*. New York: Zone.

Jefferson, T. (1994) Theorising masculine subjectivity, in T. Newburn and E. Stanko (eds) *Just Busy Doing Business. Men, Masculinities and Crime*. London: Routledge.

Kimmel, M. (1990) After fifteen years: the impact of the sociology of masculinity on the masculinity of sociology, in J. Hearn and D.H.J. Morgan (eds) *Men, Masculinities and Social Theory*. London: Unwin Hyman.

Kimmel, M. and Messner, M. (eds) (1988) *Men's Lives*. New York: Macmillan.

McMahon, A. (1993) Male readings of feminist theory: the psychologisation of sexual politics in the masculinity literature, *Theory and Society*, 22(5): 675–96.

Mangan, J. and Walvin, J. (eds) (1987) *Manliness and Morality: Middle-class Masculinity in Britain and America 1800–1940*. Manchester: Manchester University Press.

Meigs, A. (1990) Multiple gender ideologies and statuses, in P. Reeves Sanday and R. Gallaher Goodenough (eds) *Beyond the Second Sex*. Philadelphia, PA: University of Pennsylvania Press.

Mercer, K. and Julien, I. (1988) Race, sexual politics and black masculinity: a dossier, in R. Chapman and J. Rutherford (eds) *Male Order: Unwrapping Masculinity*. London: Lawrence and Wishart.

Messerschmidt, J.W. (1993) *Masculinities and Crime*. Lanham, MD: Rowman and Littlefield.

Miedzian, M. (1992) *Boys will be Boys*. London: Virago.

Mishkind, M., Rodin, J., Silberstein, L.R. and Striegel-Moore, R.H. (1987) Embodiment of masculinity: cultural, psychological and behavioural dimensions, in M.S. Kimmel (ed.) *Changing Men*. Newbury Park, CA: Sage.

Oakley, A. (1972) *Sex, Gender and Society*. London: Temple Smith.

Rogoff, I. and Van Leer, D. (1993) Afterthoughts . . . a dossier on masculinities, *Theory and Society*, 22(5): 739–62.

Segal, L. (1993) Changing men: masculinities in context, *Theory and Society*, 22(5): 625–42.

Silverman, K. (1993) *Male Subjectivity at the Margins*. New York: Routledge.

Stanley, L. (1984) Should 'sex' really be 'gender' or 'gender' really be 'sex'? in R.J. Anderson and W.W. Sharrock (eds) *Applied Sociological Perspectives*. London: Allen and Unwin.

Tolson, A. (1977) *The Limits of Masculinity*. London: Tavistock.

Watney, S. (1991) On gay liberation: a response to D. Fernbach, in *Politics and Power Four*. London: Routledge and Kegan Paul.

Wilson, E. (1979) Beyond the ghetto, *Feminist Review*, 4: 28–44.

Wittig, M. (1992) *The Straight Mind and Other Essays*. New York: Harvester Wheatsheaf.

Author index

Acker, J., 63
Aggleton, P., 172
Althusser, L., 24
Amos, V., 115
Anthias, F., 2
Archer, J., 101
Armstrong, P., 71

Bailey, P., 41
Bakke, E. W., 85
Balibar, E., 21
Bandura, A., 101, 172
Barker, J., 40, 69
Baron, A., 38, 65
Bartell, M., 78
Bartell, R., 78
Bauman, Z., 2, 11, 21
Beamish, R., 128
Becke, U., 25, 43
Beechey, V., 36, 63
Bell, C., 46, 49, 78, 83
Bem, S., 204
Benjamin, J., 176
Bennett, S.M., 101
Berger, P., 163
Bernard, J., 45, 51, 77, 85, 86
Beveridge Report, 12, 21
Beynon, J., 54, 140
Bhabha, H., 186, 192
Bhavnani, K.K., 1, 49, 83
Billig, M., 110
Bland, L., 49, 83

Bly, R., 73, 204
Boffin, T., 169
Bowles, S., 33, 57
Boyle, J., 139
Brah, A., 1, 2
Brannen, J., 27, 47
Brannon, R., 101, 204
Brittan, A., 2, 3, 24, 27, 50, 54, 55, 65,
    90, 97, 102, 104, 206
Brod, H., 3, 89, 97
Brohm, J.M., 128
Brotherton, C., 46, 78
Burnham, D., 150
Burton, C., 36, 62
Butler, J., 3, 50, 173, 174, 212

Canaan, J.E., 7, 117, 119, 122
Carby, H., 115
Carrigan, T., 24, 66, 109, 116, 136,
    205, 206, 211
Carter, E., 2, 169
Cashmore, E., 134
Chapman, R., 24, 79, 97, 109
Chodorow, N., 35, 97, 99, 204
Christian, M., 109
Christian-Smith, L.K., 115
Clarke, J., 108
Clatterbaugh, K., 2
Cobb, J., 66
Cockburn, C., 62, 65, 67, 70
Cohen, P., 115, 117, 171, 174, 177, 178
Collier, R., 206

Collinson, D.L., 4, 6, 61, 64, 65, 66, 67, 68, 69, 71, 72, 73, 211
Connell, R.W., 4, 5, 6, 24, 35, 39, 50, 52, 56, 66, 79, 80, 97, 102, 116, 117, 118, 122, 123, 141, 144, 145, 205, 206
Corrigan, P., 115, 120
Costello, M., 186
Coulson, M., 1
Craig, S., 3
Cressey, P., 70

Dalton, M., 61, 71
Davidson, W., 173
Davies, B., 3, 58
Davis, A., 90
Deem, R., 50
Delphy, C., 104
Deutsch, H., 99
Di Tomaso, 64
Dinnerstein, D., 35
Doane, M., 193, 194
Dollimore, J., 2, 173
Downing, H., 69
Duff, E., 78
Dunning, E., 132
Dyer, R., 3, 131

Edley, N., 97, 109
Edwards, T., 3, 7, 202
Eichler, M., 203, 204
Eisenberg, P., 77
Elshtain, J. B., 82

Fagot, B., 101
Fanon, F., 4, 191, 192, 193, 198
Farley, L., 64
Fasteau, M.F., 101
Featherstone, M., 129, 130, 131
Fernbach, D., 212
Fineman, J., 46, 78
Flemming, S., 134
Fling, S., 101
Foucault, M., 21, 56, 189
Franklin, C.W., 205
Frazier, F.F., 185
Freeman, M., 155
Friedman, A.L., 41, 71

Frosh, S., 100
Fryer, D., 45, 46, 77, 78

Gamarnikow, E., 48, 82
Gates, H.L., 191
Giddens, A., 1, 2, 13, 25, 26, 43
Gilbert, P., 1
Gilligan, C., 52, 86
Gilmore, A.T., 209
Gilroy, P., 185, 186, 187, 188, 191
Gilroy, S., 132
Gintis, H., 33, 34, 57
Gramsci, A., 21, 109
Greenson, R., 99
Griffin, C., 6, 79, 108, 147
Grosz, E., 211
Gruneau, R., 128
Guest, R.H., 35, 61
Gupta, S., 169

Hacker, H.M., 205
Hall, C., 107
Hall, M.A., 129
Hall, S., 115, 186, 187, 188, 189, 197, 198
Hare, J., 185, 194
Hare, N., 185, 194
Hargreaves, D., 100
Hargreaves, J., 128, 129, 130
Hargreaves, J.A., 127, 132
Hartley, R., 205
Hartmann, H., 63, 104
Harvey, D., 2
Hayes, J., 78
Haywood, C., 6, 55
Hearn, J., 1, 4, 6, 10, 44, 61, 62, 63, 64, 65, 72, 73, 83, 97, 202, 206, 208, 209, 211, 213, 214
Hemphill, E., 4
Henriques, J., 4, 65, 158
Henwood, F., 78
Henwood, K.L., 81
Henwood, M., 67
Herdt, G., 212
Heward, C., 5, 38, 43
Hinshelwood, R.D., 157
Hite, S., 47
Hoch, P., 106

Holland, J., 169
Hollway, W., 3, 159, 175, 176
Holt, R., 127
Hood, J.C., 22, 45, 51, 77, 86
hooks, b., 185, 186, 192
Humphries, M., 2, 3
Hunt, R., 2, 3, 34, 58
Hyman, R., 41, 71, 84, 93

Illingworth, M., 159, 160, 163, 165

Jackall, R., 71
Jahoda, M., 77, 78, 83
James, M., 137
James, S., 33, 133
Jarrett, J.E., 77, 78, 85
Jarvie, G., 135
Jefferson, T., 9, 153, 154, 160, 161, 162, 207
Jephcott, P., 26
Johnson, R., 5
Jordan, B., 33
Julien, I., 185, 195, 196, 197, 213

Kanter, R.M., 65, 71
Kaplan, M., 147
Kaufman, M., 3, 89, 97, 108
Kelvin, P., 77, 78, 85
Kenyon, G., 128
Kessler, S., 4
Kidd, B., 132
Kimmel, M.S., 97, 102, 204, 211
Knights, D., 70
Komarovsky, M., 85

Land, H., 86
Lashley, H., 134
Lawrence, E., 191
Lazarsfeld, P.F., 77
Lebeau, V., 196
Lee, J., 24, 205, 206
Lees, S., 55
Lewis, M., 101
Lips, H., 108
Lloyd, B., 101
Lott, E., 191
Loy, J., 128

Mac an Ghaill, M., 3–4, 6, 50, 53, 58, 116, 134, 174–5

McCarthy, C., 116
MacDonald, R., 81, 88
Machung, A., 92
Macinnes, J., 70
McKee, L., 78, 83
MacKinnon, C.A., 64
McMahon, A., 204, 206, 207, 208, 213, 214
McRobbie, A., 57, 115
Majors, R., 134, 135
Managan, A.J., 127, 209
Manosevitz, M., 101
Marriott, D., 10
Marsden, D., 78
Massey, D., 67, 70, 172
Meigs, A., 209, 212
Melechi, A., 213
Mercer, K., 185, 188, 195, 196, 197, 213
Messerschmidt, J.W., 206
Messner, M.A., 90, 129, 132, 211
Metcalf, A., 3
Middleton, P., 3
Miedzian, M., 206
Miles, I., 78, 100
Mischel, W., 101
Mishkind, M.E., 131, 210
Moraes, D., 40, 41
Morgan, D.H.J., 27, 44, 61, 73, 77, 78, 79, 80, 83, 85
Morrison, T., 190
Moynihan, D.P., 185
Murray, R., 116

Newton, C., 140, 144
Nutman, P., 78

Oakley, A., 67, 205
Oates, J.C., 162
Olivier, C., 99
Ortner, S.B., 107

Parker, A., 8, 192
Parker, I., 81, 87
Parkin, W., 211
Parmar, P., 115
Parsons, T., 114
Pattman, R., 171, 172, 177
Payne, R., 77

Phizacklea, A., 53
Pidgeon, N.F., 81
Pleck, J.H., 101
Plummer, K., 2, 5, 141, 143
Podmore, D., 70
Pontalis, J.B., 163
Pringle, R., 62, 69
Pronger, B., 132

Redley, M., 33
Redman, P., 9
Richards, B., 35
Roberts, R., 36
Robinson, K.H., 54
Rogers, B., 70
Rogoff, I., 213
Roman, L.G., 115, 116
Roper, M., 61, 70
Rosaldo, M.Z., 49, 83
Rotundo, E.A., 198
Rowbotham, S., 63
Runfola, R., 129
Rutherford, J., 3, 11, 79, 97, 109, 189

Sabo, D.F., 129
Sawyer, J., 101
Scraton, C., 127, 139
Sedgwick, E.K., 2, 169, 173, 174
Segal, L., 3, 43, 78, 80, 86, 90, 97, 144,
    145, 204, 206
Seidler, V.J., 103, 107
Sennett, R., 66
Serbin, L.A., 101
Shilling, C., 130, 134
Sianne, G., 25
Sidel, R., 97
Silverman, K., 213
Sim, J., 139, 140, 147
Sinfield, A., 2, 78, 85
Skeggs, B., 147, 148
Snow, M.E., 101
Spencer, A., 70
Spillers, H., 186
Spivak, G., 189
Stanley, L., 64, 208
Staples, R., 134, 191

TACADE, 171
Taylor, S., 1

Terman, L., 100
Thompson, E.H., 101
Thorne, B., 50
Thurston, R., 8, 140
Tolson, A., 36, 103, 205
Troughton, T., 132

Ullah, P., 78
Utting, R., 32

Van Leer, D., 213
Vinnai, G., 128

Wacquant, L.J.D., 161, 165
Walby, S., 4, 22, 63
Walker, C.R., 61
Walkerdine, V., 4, 175
Wallace, C., 79, 186
Wallerstein, I., 21
Walter, J.A., 65
Walters, A.H.,
Walvin, J., 209
Warr, P., 77
Watney, S., 2, 169, 122
Watson, T.J., 71
Weber, M., 21
Weeks, J., 3
Westwood, S., 5, 25, 134, 135, 148
Wetherell, M.S., 47, 79, 97, 109
Wheelock, J., 86
Whyte, W.H., 61
Wight, D., 83, 88
Wilkinson, H., 25
Williams, J.E., 101, 134
Willis, P., 55, 57, 65, 68, 79, 83, 89,
    115, 117, 154
Willmott, H., 70
Willott, S., 5, 6
Wilson, E., 212
Wilson, W.J., 195
Wise, S., 64
Wittig, M., 212, 214
Wolfenstein, E.V., 154, 156, 162
Wolpe, A.M., 54
Wood, J., 4, 55

Young, R., 189
Yuval Davis, N., 2

Subject index

African-Caribbean, 24, 26, 43, 90, 115
AIDS, 2, 5, 9, 133, 168–9, 178
  See also HIV
androgyny, 47
anthropology, 2
anti-racist, 53, 177
anti-sexist, 9, 53, 141, 168, 173
Asian, 24, 26, 43, 51, 115, 134

black men, 10, 97, 134, 135, 149, 185,
  186–202
bodies, 22, 57, 118, 121, 126, 129, 134,
  193, 195, 198

capitalism, 63, 70, 89, 103, 128, 192
case study, 33, 45–7, 166
Child Support Agency, 23–4, 27–9, 31,
  33, 43
colonialism, 2, 166
Conservative Party, 25–6, 33, 43, 212
consumption, 6, 24, 36, 81, 83, 115,
  117–18, 129–30, 141
contraception, 42
crime, 116, 134, 140, 144, 150, 159,
  189, 206
criminology, 2
crisis, 22–3, 89, 150, 186, 188, 191
cultural studies, 2, 8, 115, 149, 168,
  185, 187, 192, 198

deskilling, 53
diet, 131

disability, 80, 144, 175, 211
division of labour, 1, 5, 35, 38–9, 44–5,
  73
domestic labour, 3, 62
drug, 157, 192

economics, 23, 32, 46, 78, 86
emotions, 44, 71, 99, 107, 121, 123
empowerment, 52, 85, 116, 159, 160
enlightenment, 107
equality, 50, 53–4, 122, 190
essentialism, 197
ethnography, 54–5, 57
  see also methodology
Europe, 23, 44, 80, 169, 188, 193

fantasy, 10, 32, 176, 194, 197, 199
fatherhood, 25–9, 33, 186, 191
feminism, 1, 3, 50, 59, 65, 86, 88, 173,
  202, 212
films, 88, 106, 163, 195
football, 3, 7, 21, 108, 120, 122–3, 132,
  134

gay politics, 202, 211–12
gay theory, 64, 176–7
generation, 5, 23, 104–5, 107–8, 195
guilt, 156

health, 8, 23–4, 26, 37, 47, 99, 107,
  129–31, 134, 169, 178
HIV, 9, 132–3, 168–72, 178

homophobia, 5, 171, 174, 178, 195
humour, 69, 106

interviews, 7, 81, 108, 114, 142

legal profession, 30
libido, 157
life histories, 8, 39, 140
London, 43, 132

male sex role, 24, 101–2, 104–5
managerialism, 70
market place, 69
medical, 169
mens's studies, 8, 73, 185, 203
methodology, 139, 141, 149
military, 21–2, 150
motherhood, 26, 86, 191

naturalization, 134
'new man', 3, 24, 27
New Right, 50
nuclear family, 24, 26, 32, 79, 169

oedipal, 44, 99, 158
Oedipus, 35
oppression, 1, 4, 6, 52, 57, 87, 115, 193,
    208, 210–11

performance, 38, 54, 69, 100
phallus, 185, 191, 194

pornography, 64, 144, 149
post-structuralism, 79
poverty, 33, 78, 90, 155, 162
professions, 38, 42, 70–1

queer theory, 5, 195

rape, 134, 166, 190
rationality, 71
religion, 36, 40–1, 72
repression, 98, 157

safer sex, 169
science, 44, 65, 70, 77–9, 97, 202, 214
sex education, 10, 172
sexism, 10, 147, 171
social justice, 50
socialization, 38, 78, 102, 105, 204–5,
    210
suicide, 31, 146

technology, 30, 58, 65, 67
Thatcherism, 21, 188
trade unions, 22, 70

wages, 27, 62, 70
war, 38–40, 42, 107, 134
workplace, 5–7, 54, 61–7, 69–70, 72–3,
    83, 86, 128, 195

young people, 6, 47, 114–16

THE MAKING OF MEN
MASCULINITIES, SEXUALITIES AND SCHOOLING

Máirtín Mac an Ghaill

Wayne: 'You can't trust girls because of what they expect from you . . . And you can't be honest with your mates because they'll probably tell other people.'

Rajinder: 'There's a lot of sexuality . . . African Caribbeans are seen as better at football . . . and dancing . . . the white kids and Asians are jealous because they think the girls will really prefer the black kids.'

Richard: 'Okay sharing the housework and things like that are fair. But it's all the stuff not making girls sex objects. It's ridiculous. What are you supposed to do. Become gay?'

William: 'We wanked each other one night when we were really drunk. Then later on when I saw him, he said he had a girlfriend. I knew he hadn't. We just had to move apart because we got too close.'

Gilroy: 'It's the girls who have all the power. Like they have the choice and can make you look a prat in front of your mates.'

Joanne: 'You lot are obsessed with your knobs . . . all your talk is crap. It's just to prove you're better than your mates. Why don't you all get together and measure your little plonkers?'

Frank: 'My dad spends all his time in the pub with his mates. Why doesn't he want to be with me? Why doesn't he say he loves me? . . . It does my head in.'

Máirtín Mac an Ghaill explores how boys learn to be men in schools whilst policing their own and others' sexualities. He focuses upon the students' confusions and contradictions in their gendered experiences; and upon how schools actively produce, through the official and hidden curriculum, a range of masculinities which young men come to inhabit. He does full justice to the complex phenomenon of male heterosexual subjectivities and to the role of schooling in forming sexual identities.

Contents
Introduction: schooling as a masculinizing agency – Teacher ideologies, representations and practices – Local student cultures of masculinity and sexuality – Sexuality: learning to become a heterosexual man at school – Young women's experiences of teacher and student masculinities – Schooling, sexuality and male power: towards an emancipatory curriculum – Conclusion: sociology of schooling, equal opportunities and anti-oppression education – Notes – References – Index.

224pp   0 335 15781 5 (Paperback)   0 335 15782 3 (Hardback)

POWER IN STRUGGLE
FEMINISM, SEXUALITY AND THE STATE

Davina Cooper

What is power? And how are social change strategies shaped by the ways in which we conceptualize it? Drawing on feminist, poststructuralist, and marxist theory, Davina Cooper develops an innovative framework for understanding power relations within fields as diverse as queer activism, municipal politics, and the regulation of lesbian reproduction. *Power in Struggle* explores the relationship between power, sexuality, and the state and, in the process, provides a radical rethinking of these concepts and their interactions. The book concludes with an important and original discussion of how an ethics of empowerment can inform political strategy.

Special features
- brings together central aspects of current radical, political theory in an innovative way
- offers a new way of conceptualizing the state, power and sexuality.

Contents
Introduction – Beyond domination?: productive and relational power – The politics of sex: metaphorical strategies and the (re)construction of desire – Multiple identities: sexuality and the state in struggle – Penetration on the defensive: regulating lesbian reproduction – Access without power: gay activism and the boundaries of governance – Beyond resistance: political strategy and counter-hegemony – Afterword – Bibliography – Index.

192pp   0 335 19211 4 (Paperback)   0 335 19212 2 (Hardback)

GENDERED WORK
SEXUALITY, FAMILY AND THE LABOUR MARKET

Lisa Adkins

Gendered Work contributes to current debates on the labour market via an exploration of the significance of sexual and family relations in structuring employment. Through detailed studies of conditions of work in the British tourist industry, it shows how men and women are constituted as different kinds of 'workers' in the labour market not only when segregated in different occupations but also even when they are nominally located in the same jobs.

This differentiation is shown to be connected to two key processes: the sexualization of women workers which locates women as sexual as well as 'economic' workers, and the operation of family work relations within the sphere of employment when women work as wives rather than waged-labourers in the context of the contemporary labour market. These two processes are then drawn together to show the ways in which labour market production is gendered. This book therefore makes an important contribution to the growing feminist literature which is exposing the deep embeddedness of gender within labour market processes and practices.

Special features
- New empirical material on the terms and conditions of typical contemporary jobs for women.
- New ways of understanding the gendered structure of the labour market.
- Reviews a range of analyses (feminist and sociological) in a constructively critical way to throw light on change and continuity in employment in the consumer society.

Contents
Introduction — Sexuality and the labour market — Family production in the labour market — Sexual servicing and women's employment — The condition of women's work — References — Index.

192pp   0 335 19296 3 (Paperback)   0 335 19297 1 (Hardback)

UNIVERSITY OF WOLVERHAMPTON
LIBRARY